Monitoring and Modelling of Geological Disasters Based on InSAR Observations II

Monitoring and Modelling of Geological Disasters Based on InSAR Observations II

Guest Editors

Chisheng Wang
Bochen Zhang
Chuanhua Zhu
Biao Lu

MDPI

Basel • Beijing • Wuhan • Barcelona • Belgrade • Novi Sad • Cluj • Manchester

Guest Editors
Chisheng Wang
School of Architecture & Urban Planning
Shenzhen University
Shenzhen
China

Bochen Zhang
College of Civil and Transportation Engineering
Shenzhen University
Shenzhen
China

Chuanhua Zhu
School of Architecture & Urban Planning
Shenzhen University
Shenzhen
China

Biao Lu
Department of Civil and Environmental Engineering
Politecnico di Milano
Milan
Italy

Editorial Office
MDPI AG
Grosspeteranlage 5
4052 Basel, Switzerland

This is a reprint of the Special Issue, published open access by the journal *Remote Sensing* (ISSN 2072-4292), freely accessible at: https://www.mdpi.com/journal/remotesensing/special_issues/ES569JPZ29.

For citation purposes, cite each article independently as indicated on the article page online and as indicated below:

Lastname, A.A.; Lastname, B.B. Article Title. *Journal Name* **Year**, *Volume Number*, Page Range.

ISBN 978-3-7258-5363-2 (Hbk)
ISBN 978-3-7258-5364-9 (PDF)
https://doi.org/10.3390/books978-3-7258-5364-9

Cover image courtesy of Chisheng Wang

Contents

remote sensing

MDPI

Article

A Bayesian Source Model for the 2022 Mw6.6 Luding Earthquake, Sichuan Province, China, Constrained by GPS and InSAR Observations

Guangyu Xu [1,2], Xiwei Xu [3,*], Yaning Yi [1], Yangmao Wen [4], Longxiang Sun [4], Qixin Wang [1] and Xiaoqiong Lei [1]

1 National Institute of Natural Hazards, Ministry of Emergency Management of China, Beijing 100085, China; gyxu@ecut.edu.cn (G.X.); yaningyi@ninhm.ac.cn (Y.Y.); qixinwang@ninhm.ac.cn (Q.W.); xiaoqionglei@ninhm.ac.cn (X.L.)
2 School of Surveying and Geoinformation Engineering, East China University of Technology, Nanchang 330013, China
3 School of Earth Sciences and Resources, China University of Geosciences (Beijing), Beijing 100083, China
4 School of Geodesy and Geomatics, Wuhan University, Wuhan 430079, China; ymwen@sgg.whu.edu.cn (Y.W.); lxsundays@whu.edu.cn (L.S.)
* Correspondence: xiweixu@ninhm.ac.cn

Abstract: Until the Mw 6.6 Luding earthquake ruptured the Moxi section of the Xianshuihe fault (XSHF) on 5 September 2022, the region had not experienced an Mw >6 earthquake since instrumental records began. We used Global Positioning System (GPS) and Sentinel-1 interferometric synthetic aperture radar (InSAR) observations to image the coseismic deformation and constrain the location and geometry of the seismogenic fault using a Bayesian method We then present a distributed slip model of the 2022 Mw6.6 Luding earthquake, a left-lateral strike-slip earthquake that occurred on the Moxi section of the Xianshuihe fault in the southwest Sichuan basin, China. Two tracks (T26 and T135) of the InSAR data captured a part of the coseismic surface deformation with the line-of-sight displacements range from ~−0.16 m to ~0.14 m in the ascending track and from ~−0.12 m to ~0.10 m in the descending track. The inverted best-fitting fault model shows a pure sinistral strike-slip motion on a west-dipping fault plane with a strike of 164.3°. We adopt a variational Bayesian approach and account for the uncertainties in the fault geometry to retrieve the distributed slip model. The inverted result shows that the maximum slip of ~1.82 m occurred at a depth of 5.3 km, with the major slip concentrated within depths ranging from 0.9–11 km. The InSAR-determined moment is 1.3×10^{19} Nm, with a shear modulus of 30 GPa, equivalent to Mw 6.7. The published coseismic slip models of the 2022 Luding earthquake show apparent differences despite the use of similar geodetic or seismic observations. These variations underscore the uncertainty associated with routinely performed source inversions and their interpretations for the underlying fault model.

Keywords: Luding earthquake; InSAR; Bayesian inversion; strike-slip fault; coseismic slip distribution

1. Introduction

On 5 September 2022, an Mw 6.6 earthquake struck Luding County, Sichuan province, China. As of 17:00 on September 11, the Luding earthquake in Sichuan has killed 93 people, including 55 in Ganzi prefecture and 38 in Ya'an City. Another 25 people are missing, including 9 in Luding County and 16 in Shimian County. Focal mechanism solutions from United States Geological Survey (USGS) indicate that this earthquake is associated with a north–northwest striking left-lateral or west–southwest striking right-lateral fault. The location and sense of motion are consistent with movement on or near the Moxi section of the Xianshuihe fault zone (Figure 1). Almost 22 aftershocks occurred in the period from 5 September 2022 to 5 October 2022, recorded by the China Earthquake Networks Center (CENC). The largest aftershock was the Mw 4.5 earthquake on 7 September 2022.

The Luding earthquake occurred at the east–south margin of the Xianshuihe fault, which is a part of the "eastern Tibet seismic belt" or "N-S tectonic zone" that has experienced a staggering number of M > 7 earthquakes [1]. Since 1700, the XSHF has experienced as many as 17 M > 7 and 29 M > 6.5 earthquakes throughout nearly its entire length along the NW-striking [2,3]. For example, the 1792 M6.75, 1904 M7, and 1981 M6.9 earthquakes on the 45 km long Daofu segment, the 1816 M7.5 and 1973 M7.6 earthquakes on the 90 km long Luhuo segment, and the 1793 M6.7 and 1893 M7.3 earthquakes on the ~62 km long Qianning segment (e.g., [4]). The nearest previous earthquake sequence is the 2014 Kangding Mw5.9 earthquake and its aftershocks, which occurred ~88 km to the northwest of the 2022 Luding earthquake at depths ranging from 5 to 13 km [5].

The 2022 Luding earthquake is the largest earthquake to have occurred near the Moxi section of the Xianshuihe fault, and gives us valuable insight into the poorly understood tectonics of this area. Studying the fault geometry and slip distribution of the Luding earthquake is essential to evaluate regional earthquake hazards, especially because it was near a major city (Kangding). Although several studies have investigated the coseismic slip model of the Luding earthquake using geodetic or seismic data (e.g., [6–8]), the fault slip shows obvious variations both in the shape and coverage area. Meanwhile, some questions about the Luding earthquake remain unresolved, such as how to understand the three aftershocks with normal mechanisms in a strike-slip earthquake sequence, and whether there is any post-seismic deformations accompanied by the intensive aftershocks. Both GPS and InSAR observations recorded the coseismic deformation of the Luding earthquake, but the current research is somewhat limited in the process of combining these two dataset to study the Luding earthquake.

In this study, we use both GPS and Sentinel-1 InSAR data to image the coseismic deformation and present an analysis of the fault location, geometry, and slip distribution of the 2022 Luding earthquake in the framework of Bayesian theory. We then compare our models with the published coseismic slip models to evaluate the impact of model assumptions and employed data sets on the estimated pattern of the coseismic slip. Addtionally, we provide insights on the 2022 Luding earthquake and explore the relationship between coseismic deformation and landslides triggered by the earthquake. Finally, we use the inverted coseismic slip distribution to calculate the Coulomb stress change on the nearby XSH fault.

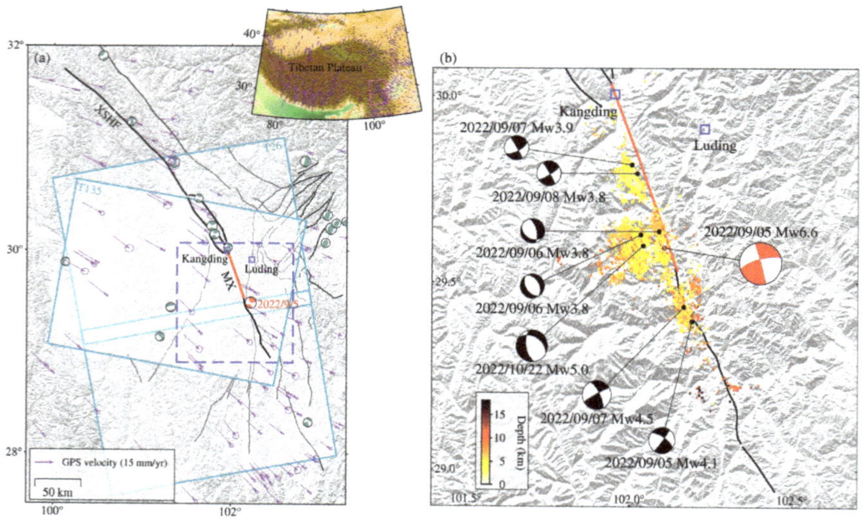

Figure 1. Tectonic setting of the 2022 Luding earthquake. (**a**) Cyan-white beach balls represent focal mechanisms of the historical earthquake since 1990 from GCMT [9]. The red beach ball denotes the

focal mechanism of the 2022 Luding earthquake from GCMT. The dashed blue rectangle shows the area plotted in (**b**). The purple arrows represent GPS velocities [10]. The thin black lines show the active faults. The bold black line denotes the Xianshuihe fault and the red line represents the Moxi section of XSH fault [11]. The light blue polygons are the outlines of areas covered by ascending and descending Sentinel-1 InSAR observations. (**b**) The black beach balls denote focal mechanisms of Mw $\geq$ 3.8 earthquakes in Luding earthquake sequence [12]. The red beach ball denotes the focal mechanism of the 2022 Luding earthquake from USGS. The colored dots represent relocated aftershocks [13].

2. Observations and Coseismic Surface Deformation Field

2.1. InSAR Data

We generated coseismic interferograms from ascending track 26 (26 August 2022 to 19 September 2022) and descending track 135 (2 September 2022 to 14 September 2022) using Sentinel-1 C-band data in the terrain observations with progressive scans in azimuth (TOS) mode (Table 1). We processed the SAR data and generated interferograms with the GAMMA-processing software (version 2023) [14]. All interferograms were generated from the Single Look Complex (SLC) products. The multi-look ratio between the range and azimuth direction was set at 10:2 for Sentinel-1 data. Image co-registration for TOPS mode SAR data is very important and requires extremely high accuracy. To ensure very high co-registration accuracy, a method considering the effects of the scene topography and a spectral diversity method [15] considering the interferometric phase of the burst overlap region were used. After the high-quality co-registration between the TOPS SLC data, the effects of the topography were removed from the interferograms using the 90 m Shuttle Radar Topography Mission (SRTM) digital elevation model (DEM) [16]. The interferograms were then filtered using a power spectrum filter [17] to reduce the effects of phase noise and unwrapped using a minimum-cost flow algorithm [18]. The interferograms were finally geocoded to the WGS84 geographic coordinates with 90 m resolution.

Table 1. Sentinel-1 images used in this study.

Satellite	Reference	Secondary	Direction	Track	Perpendicular Baseline (m)	Incident	Azimuth
Sentinel-1	26 August 2022	19 September 2022	Ascending	26	34	42	−10
Sentinel-1	2 September 2022	14 September 2022	Descending	135	50	35	−169

A troposphere delay may also cause phase errors in InSAR measurements. To account for the potential tropospheric delays and residual orbital errors, a linear function among location (x, y), elevation (h) and error phase were estimated with observations away from the deformed areas (e.g., [19,20]). After the correction, the standard deviations of the ascending and descending line-of-sight (LOS) displacements slightly decreased, respectively.

Both interferograms show obvious coseismic deformation, although the near-fault area exhibits interferometric phase-coherence loss, probably due to vegetational cover or large areas of landslides triggered by earthquakes (Figure 2). The ascending interferogram shows two lobes of deformation with a steep E–W fringe gradient towards the western edge of the interferogram, suggesting that this part of the interferogram is close to the causative fault of the earthquake, and a peak-to-trough LOS deformation of ~15 cm (5 fringes). In the descending interferogram, only one lobe of deformation is visible and the peak-to-trough LOS deformation is ~12 cm (4 fringes). In addition, another three concentric fringes can also be identified in the descending interferogram, which covers an area further to the east of the mapped fault. The InSAR observations all show the largest amplitudes west of the Moxi section of XSHF, suggesting that the fault is slightly dipping westward, as confirmed by the relocated aftershocks [13]. We also performed pixel-offset tracking analysis on both ascending and descending tracks of Sentinel-1 images using the offset tracking method integrated into InSAR Scientific Computing Environment (ISCE) software (version 2022) [21]. The resulting surface displacements have lower precision and higher noise than LOS observations, but provide useful information near the fault, where LOS observations are mainly decorrelated. (Figure S1). The results of pixel-offset tracking do not show significant surface deformation near the Moxi fault trace (Figure S1), suggesting that the fault slip may not reach the surface.

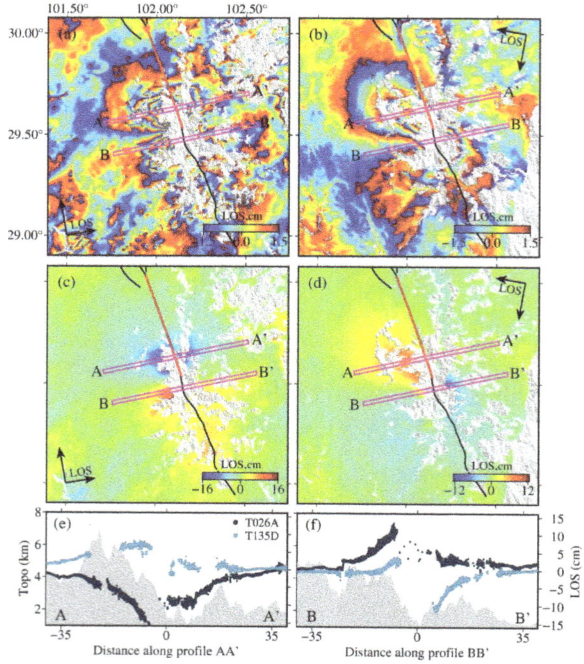

Figure 2. Coseismic InSAR data of the 2022 Luding earthquake. (**a**,**b**) Interferogram of ascending 26 and descending 135, unwrapped and then re-wrapped such that adjacent fringes differ by 3 cm LOS displacement.; (**c**,**d**) LOS displacement of ascending 26 and descending 135; (**e**,**f**) LOS displacements along the two profiles (AA′ and BB′) shown in (**c**,**d**).

2.2. The Coseismic Displacement of GPS and Strong Motion Data

Coseismic offsets for the Luding earthquake derived from 71 continuous GPS data and 3 strong motion data have been already described in [6] (Figure S2). Henceforth, we refer to these three strong motion sites as GPS sites, as we also utilize the static coseismic deformation obtained from these stations. The complex coseismic deformation pattern highlights a general NNW–SSE-oriented strike-slip mechanism, which is consistent with the deformation field depicted by the InSAR observations. Generally, the GPS coseismic displacements exhibit a typical left-lateral deformation pattern. Sites located east of the fault move towards the north, while sites located west of the fault move towards the south. Sites to the northwest and southeast move toward the fault, while sites to the northeast and southwest move away from the fault (Figure S2). The site closest to the Moxi fault is the strong motion station (51LDJ), about 11 km east of the fault, which measured the largest horizontal displacements (10.8 ± 0.4 cm). The site ls22, located about 42 km west of the Moxi fault, measured 1.5 ± 0.1 cm horizontal displacement, which is the largest among the sites west of the fault. [6] did not provide the vertical component given that most of the stations have a low signal-to-noise ratio. Large areas in the near field of the fault lack any GPS data, especially SW of the fault, which weakens the ability to constrain the fault geometry and slip distribution.

2.3. The Comparison between Coseismic InSAR and GPS Offsets

We compared the InSAR coseismic LOS displacement with independent GPS observations to validate the agreement between the two independent observations for the ground deformation of the 2022 Luding earthquake. We only used the GPS sites that have sufficient InSAR observations nearby. The horizontal GPS coseismic offsets were projected to LOS. We compared the GPS-derived LOS displacements with InSAR LOS displacements using the mean of all pixels within 500 m of each GPS station (Figure 3). We confirmed that a good agreement exists between the ascending and descending InSAR and GPS offsets with a large number of sites near the red dashed line (Figure 3). There are some sites for which the InSAR LOS displacements differ by more than 2 mm from the GPS LOS displacements (sites 47, 28 and 72 in Figure 3a and sites 13 and 10 in Figure 3b). Although these sites are all located very close to the black dashed lines, suggesting that the differences between the InSAR LOS and GPS-derived LOS displacements are within acceptable limits, we should still pay attention to the InSAR observations at these locations.

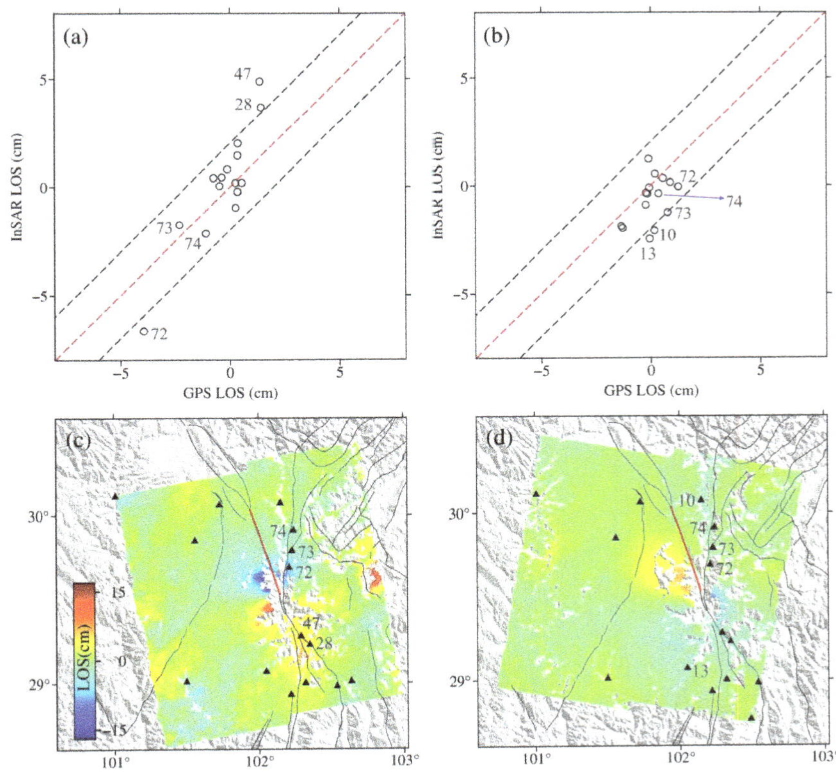

Figure 3. Comparison between InSAR LOS data at the locations of the GPS sites and GPS data projected to LOS from horizontal components. (**a**) Ascending track InSAR LOS versus GPS LOS. (**b**) Descending track InSAR LOS versus GPS LOS. The red dashed line represents perfect agreement and the black dashed lines show a deviation of 2 mm. (**c**) Ascending InSAR LOS map. (**d**) Descending InSAR LOS map. The black triangles denote GPS sites.

2.4. The Three-Dimension Coseismic Deformation of the 2022 Luding Earthquake

To investigate the pattern of coseismic deformation and strain release along the fault, we inverted the three-dimension coseismic deformation of the 2022 Luding earthquake combined with the InSAR and GPS observations. The vertical components of the GPS offsets are not available; therefore, the decomposed vertical component from the InSAR data is crucial information. For each pixel where information from both ascending and descending tracks is available, Equation (1) is utilized to estimate the east–west and vertical components of the three-dimension coseismic deformation [22].

$$[U_n \sin\Phi - U_e \cos\Phi]\sin\lambda + U_u \cos\lambda + \delta_{los} = d_{los} \quad (1)$$

where ϕ is the azimuth of the satellite heading vector, λ is the radar incidence angle at the reflection point, and δ_{los} is the measurement error. U_e, U_n and U_u denote the east, north, and vertical components of surface displacement field, respectively.

Equation (1) contains three unknowns (U_e, U_n and U_u), but we only have two input InSAR LOS displacements (ascending and descending track InSAR data). In this case, we notice that both the ascending and descending tracks are insensitive to motion in the north–south direction. We therefore use the Kriging interpolation method to obtain a smooth interpolated north–south component (U_n) of the GPS offset in the inversion and solve for the U_e and U_u using the InSAR LOS displacements. The results show that the west side of the Moxi fault mainly moves eastward, with a maximum displacement of ~18 cm (Figure 4a). Since the north–south component of the surface displacement field is interpolated from the north–south component of the GPS offset, the accuracy of the surface displacement in locations without GPS sites cannot be well constrained. Therefore, it is evident that the northward movement of large sections of the western part of the Moxi fault is unreliable, as it contradicts the measurements from two GPS sites located northwest of the fault. Considering the relatively small magnitude (~2 cm) of the northward movement in this area (Figure 4b) and the small proportion (~10%) of the north–south component when projected to the LOS direction, it is unlikely to significantly impact the inversion results of the east–west and vertical components. The east side of the Moxi fault mainly moves northward, which is well constrained by enough GPS sites located northeast of the fault (Figure 4b). At the western side of the southeast end of the Moxi fault, there is a clearly noticeable uplift area with a maximum vertical displacement of ~10 cm. Located approximately 10 km north of the uplift area and west of the Moxi fault, there is a subsidence zone that correlates with the occurrence of numerous relocated aftershocks (Figures 1 and 4).

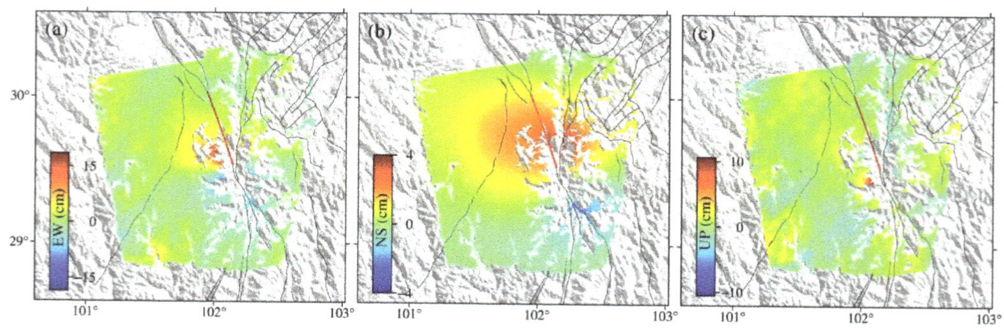

Figure 4. Three-dimension coseismic surface deformation. (**a–c**) East, north, and vertical components of the surface displacement field, respectively.

2.5. Aftershock Seismicity

The precisely relocated aftershock distribution shows that aftershocks occur in four major regions [13]: (1) along major XSHF within the ruptured area (area A in Figure 5a); (2) along XSHF but outside the ruptured segment, one to the north (area B in Figure 5a) and another to the south (area D in Figure 5a) of the mainshock rupture area; and (3) to the west of the mainshock rupture area (area C in Figure 5a), which is outside of XSHF. Considering that the aftershock distribution can offer insights into fault geometry, we attempted to determine the strike and dip angles of fault planes based on the aftershock locations in the four areas, which can serve as a reference. Firstly, we used an L2 norm to fit all located events by a straight line to determine the fault trace of the four areas, respectively. Then, we determined the fault dips by fitting the aftershock locations in profiles perpendicular to the derived fault traces (Figure 5b–m). Due to the approximate circle shape of the aftershock distribution in area C, we made profiles that were perpendicular to and parallel to the derived fault trace (Figure 5d). The results indicate a notable consistency in the derived fault strike orientations of aftershocks in areas A, B and D, all of which align with the XSHF (Figure 5a). The distribution of aftershocks in Region A is most consistent with the southeastward trend of the Moxi Fault. The best-fit line of the aftershock distribution in area A has a strike of 162°. The derived fault trace of aftershocks in area C is nearly perpendicular to the XSHF (Figure 5a). The fault dips derived from the aftershock profiles do not show any regularity due to their relatively discrete distribution in depth (Figure 5f–m). Given the relatively discrete distribution of aftershocks along the depth direction, different perspectives may yield varying results. Among them, the aftershock distribution along the depth direction in profile HH′ shows an obvious linear distribution, which suggests that the fault may dip to the east in this area (Figure 5m).

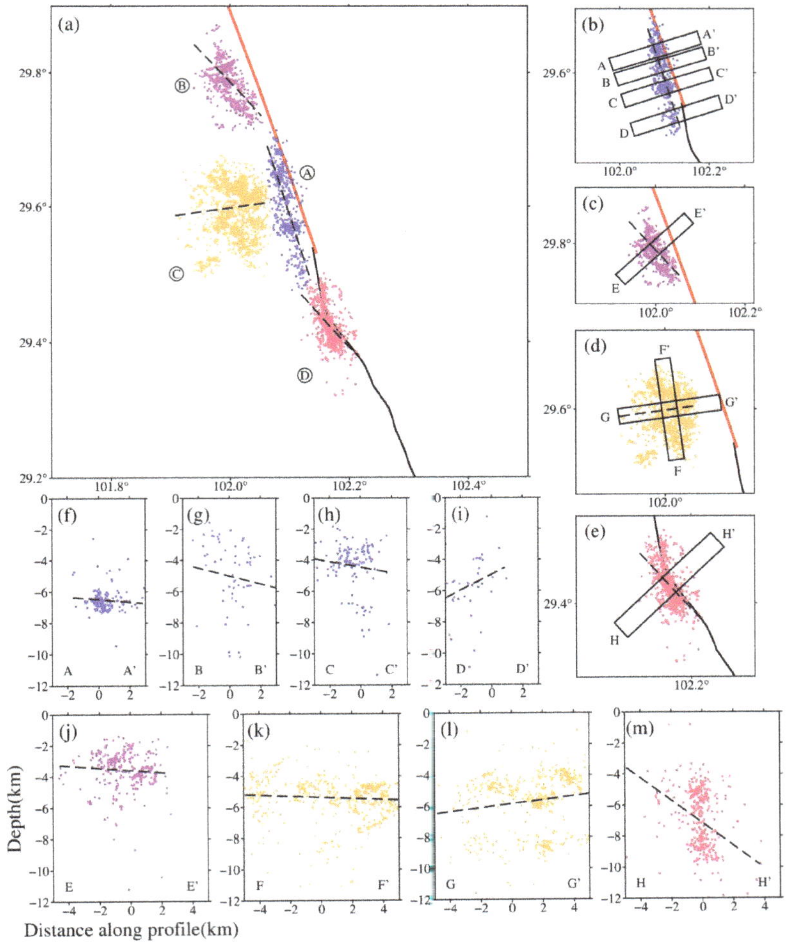

Figure 5. The precisely relocated aftershock distribution. The four different colors of scatter points correspond to the aftershocks in the four mentioned regions A, B, C, and D representing the distribution

of aftershocks. (**a**) Aftershocks in four major regions A, B, C and D. The black dotted lines represent derived fault trace using least squares method. (**b–e**) Separate aftershock distribution in four areas. The black rectangles denote profiles (AA′, BB′, CC′, DD′, EE′, FF′, GG′ and HH′). (**f–m**) Aftershock profiles in depth. The black dotted lines represent fault cross-section derived using least squares method.

3. Modelling

To constrain the location and geometry of the seismogenic fault of the 2022 Luding earthquake, we inverted the InSAR and GPS observation using a two-stage process based on the Bayesian theory: (1) determining the fault parameters with a uniform slip model; (2) estimating the detailed coseismic slip distribution (e.g., [23,24]). To gain a clearer understanding of the role of the GPS and InSAR observations in constraining fault parameters, we conducted separate inversions using GPS alone, InSAR alone and a combination of GPS and InSAR observations.

3.1. The Nonlinear Inversion for Model Parameters

To reduce the computational burden in the inversion, we down-sampled the coseismic InSAR measurements using a resolution-based quadtree method [25]. These down-sampled InSAR data and coseismic GPS offsets are then inverted using a Markov chain Monte Carlo algorithm, which was equipped with Geodetic Bayesian Inversion Software (GBIS) (version 2018) [26] to find the posterior probability distribution of the fault location, size, orientation and slip on a rectangular fault in an elastic half-space [27]. Due to the atmospheric changes between satellite acquisitions that are correlated in space, we calculated a variance–covariance matrix for each InSAR track using the semivariogram method (et al., [28]).

3.2. The Linear Inversion for Slip Distribution

Under the determined location and geometry of the seismogenic fault inverted from the nonlinear inversion, we further extended the fault length and width along the strike and dip directions, respectively. Then, the extended fault plane was subdivided into small fault patches with fixed sizes. Finally, we used a variational Bayesian approach [29] to determine the posteriori probability density function (hereafter PDF) of the slip distribution, data weight ratio and regularization parameters. The variational Bayesian slip distribution inversion method uses an optimization strategy to approximate the posterior PDF of the target, which is detailed in [29]. According to Bayes' theorem, we write the posterior PDF as:

$$p(\mathrm{m}|\,\mathrm{d_{obs}}) \propto p(\mathrm{m})\exp\left[-\frac{1}{2}(\mathrm{d_{obs}}-\mathrm{Gm})^{\mathrm{T}}\mathrm{C}_{\chi}^{-1}(\mathrm{d_{obs}}-\mathrm{Gm})\right] \quad (2)$$

where m is the model vector, $p(\mathrm{m})$ is the prior distribution, $\mathrm{d_{obs}}$ is the data vector, G is the green functions matrix and C_{χ} is the misfit covariance, describing both data and forward prediction uncertainties. We computed Green's functions assuming a homogeneous elastic half-space medium [27].

To weaken the excessive gradient between the slips of the sub-fault patch, we used the Laplacian operator for a priori smoothing. We did not impose any restrictions on the amplitude and direction of the slip to follow the characteristics of the fault rupture reflected in the data itself. Our final solution consists of an ensemble of models that are statistically distributed according to the posterior PDF.

3.3. Accounting for Epistemic Uncertainties

When imaging a slip distribution on a fault, the physics of the forward model is usually assumed to be of minimum complexity to simplify the computation. The uncertainties in fault dip, strike or position, which are the first-order parameters controlling the fault geometry, are assumed to have the largest contribution on the uncertainties of the fault geometry. Accounting for the uncertainties of fault geometry in our forward predictions is crucial, as it corresponds to one of the largest sources of epistemic errors. We thus account for epistemic uncertainties following the approach developed by the authors of [30] for the fault geometry. The epistemic uncertainties are described by the matrix C_p, which is added to the observation uncertainties matrix C_d to obtain the misfit covariance:

$$C_\chi = C_d + C_p \tag{3}$$

The covariance matrix C_p of epistemic uncertainties is calculated from the sensitivity of Green's functions. Some studies show that fault dip parameters obtained from the nonlinear inversion of the InSAR data are not very accurate. Therefore, it is a common process in linear inversions to determine the fault dip parameters by using a grid search method. In this study, we account for the epistemic uncertainties caused by our poor knowledge of the fault dip and fault position, and integrate them into the Bayesian inversion framework. We assume a 1 km uncertainty in the location of the surface projection of the fault, and a 5° uncertainty in the fault dip (Figure S3), the fault rotating as a whole around its assumed dip.

4. Results

We compared the fault geometry inferred from the separate GPS and InSAR dataset and joint inversions. We found that the optimal uniform slip model determined in all the inversions roughly followed the fault trace of the Moxi fault. These results were not only consistent with each other but also with the independent seismological results (Table 2, Figures 6 and 7, Figures S4–S11). The GPS data supports a steeper dip angle (71.9°) than that inferred from the InSAR data (57.3°). The InSAR data supports a shallower depth (2 km) than that inferred from the GPS data (3 km). The joint inversion of the GPS and InSAR data yields a model with some parameters (fault location, strike, length) lying in between those found from the separate inversions (Table 2). The joint inversion results reveal that the fault is shallower approaching the surface (~0.09 km). The fault width (13.9 km) obtained by the joint inversion is more reasonable than those obtained by GPS inversion alone (2.2 km). The joint inversion further improves the fitness of the InSAR data (RMS = 9.4 mm, Figure 7) compared to the separate InSAR data inversion (RMS = 10.0 mm, Figure S9), while somewhat increasing the misfit of GPS data (RMS = 2.0 mm, Figure 6) compared to the separate GPS data inversion (RMS = 1.3 mm), especially at the 51LDJ site (Figure S6). The convergence of parameters and distribution of joint inversion are more steady and reasonable compared to the separate data inversions (Figures S4, S5, S7, S8, S10 and S11). Most importantly, the joint inversion improves the stability of the inversion parameter results compared to individual data inversion (Table 2). The optimal uniform fault model, determined from the joint inversion of the GPS and InSAR data, reveals a strike of 164° and a dip of 74° to the west. The rupture is estimated to be 19 km long and 14 km wide, with a depth ranging from 0.09 km to 13.45 km, and a left-lateral slip of 1.09 m. The geodetic moment magnitude of the 2022 Luding earthquake model is Mw 6.6, assuming a shear modulus of 30 GPa.

Table 2. Source parameters of 2022 Luding earthquake.

Source	Lon (°)	Lat (°)	Depth (km)	Strike (°)	Dip (°)	Rake (°)	Length (km)	Width (km)	Slip (m)	M0 (10^{19})	Mw	Data
USGS	102.236	29.679	12	254/345	73/88	178/17	-	-	-	1.158	6.6	seismic data
GCMT	102.24	29.50	18.0	164/73	78/83	7/167	-	-	-	1.2	6.7	seismic data
[7]	102.104	29.533	6.10	167.37	73.66	3.3	21.78	10.98	-		6.56	InSAR(Ascending + Descending)
[6]	-	-	-	162,-	80,79	-	70,-	20,-	-	-	6.67, 6.30	GPS + InSAR(Descending)
[8]	102.086	29.589	9.5	163	80	-	50	25	1.5	1.12	6.63	GPS + InSAR(Descending) + seismic data
[13]	102.086	29.589	9.3	166	86	-	39	21	-	-	-	seismic data
[31]	-	-	6.0	161	86	-	-	-	-	-	6.5	GPS
Uniform slip model 1	102.133 [−0.68/0.75km]	29.548 [−0.39/0.48km]	2.89 [−2.47/1.48]	163.22 [−2.16/1.95]	71.87 [−13.10/16.59]	7.00	27.88 [−7.17/3.43]	2.21 [−0.96/5.44]	4.59	0.85	6.59	GPS
Uniform slip model 2	102.153 [−1.04/0.43km]	29.510 [−0.52/0.79km]	1.97 [−1.90/1.47]	173.94 [−5.40/2.49]	57.27 [−8.11/3.55]	14.83	17.01 [−0.88/0.89]	6.55 [−4.06/2.90]	1.97	0.66	6.51	InSAR (Ascending + Descending)
Uniform slip model 3	102.147 [−1.05/0.43km]	29.53 [−0.52/0.79]	0.09 [−0.08/0.38]	164.33 [−0.72/0.76]	73.62 [−2.53/2.61]	−0.13	18.74 [−0.84/1.42]	13.92 [−1.80/0.95]	1.09	0.85	6.59	GPS + InSAR (Ascending + Descending)

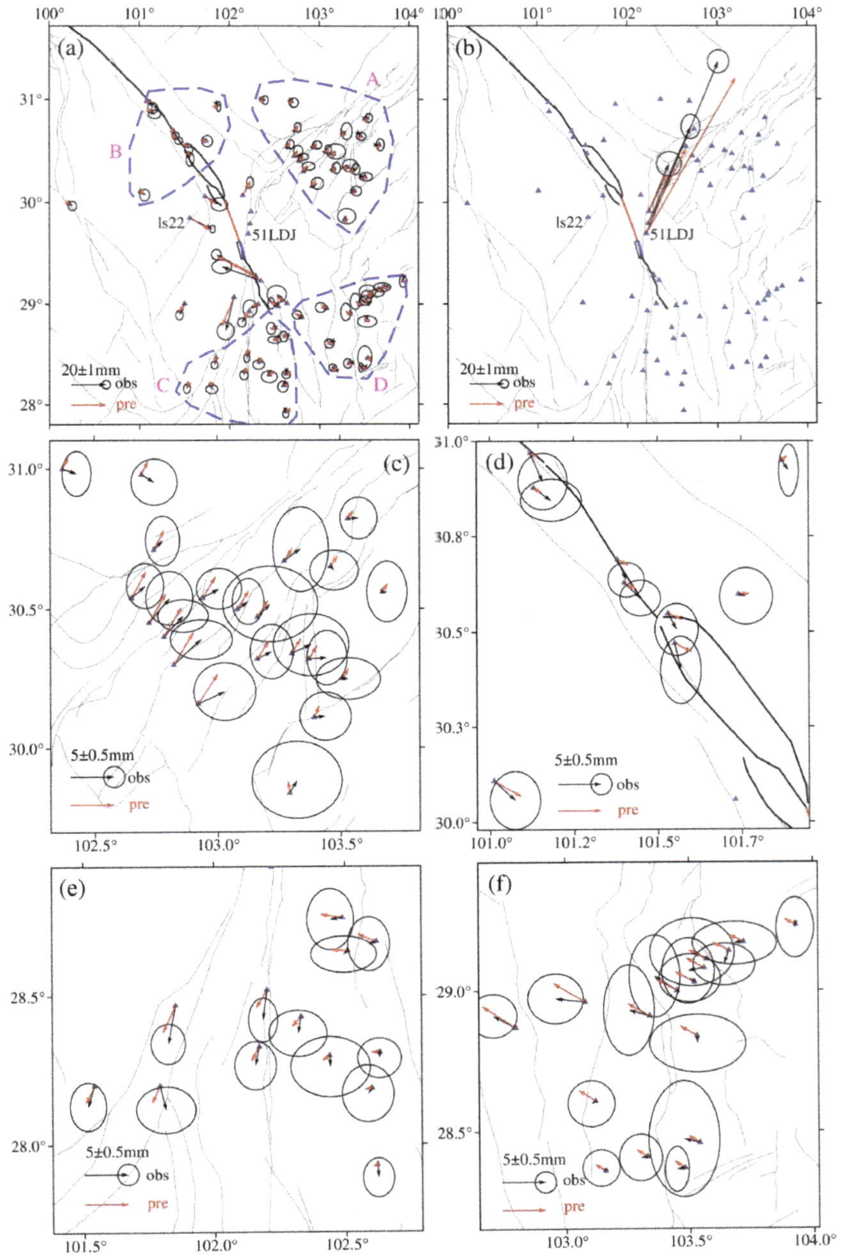

Figure 6. GPS-fitting results of uniform slip model inverted with joint GPS and InSAR data. (**a**) The black arrows show horizontal displacements. (**b**) The black arrows show static horizontal displacements of three strong motion sites. The red arrows denote model predictions. The blue line represents surface projection of uniform slip model. The thin black lines show the active faults. The bold black line denotes the Xianshuihe fault and the red line represents the Moxi section of XSHF [11]. The dashed blue lines outline the areas zoomed in (**c**–**f**).

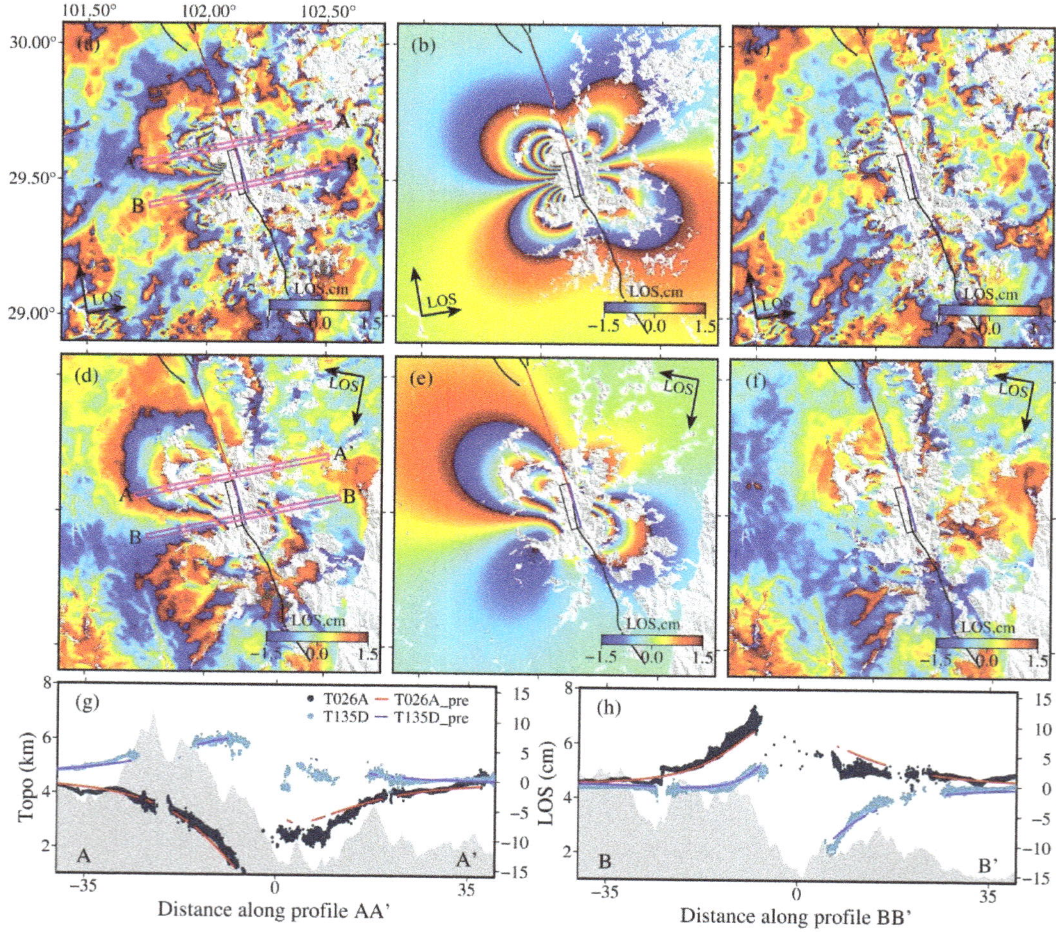

Figure 7. Inversion result of uniform slip model with joint GPS and InSAR data. (**a**,**d**) InSAR observations of ascending track 026 and descending track 135. (**b**,**e**) Model prediction for ascending track 026 and descending track 135. (**c**,**f**) Residuals for ascending track 026 and descending track 135. The black line in (**a**–**f**) represents surface projection of uniform slip model. (**g**,**h**) Fitting result of profile AA′ and BB′.

Figures 8 and 9 show the simulated GPS offsets, interferograms and residuals from our best distributed slip model. The optimal distributed slip model shows an elliptical-shape slip distribution with a maximum slip of 1.82 m at a depth of ~5.3 km (Figure 10). The rupture fault is dominated by sinistral strike-slip motion. The total released geodetic moment magnitude is approximately 6.7, which is in agreement with GCMT and USGS results. The main slip area is distributed at a depth of 0.9–11 km (Figure 10). We found that the coseismic deformation of GPS and ascending and descending InSAR data can fit quite well using a single-segment fault, which gives an RMS of about 1.5 mm and 9 mm for InSAR data, respectively.

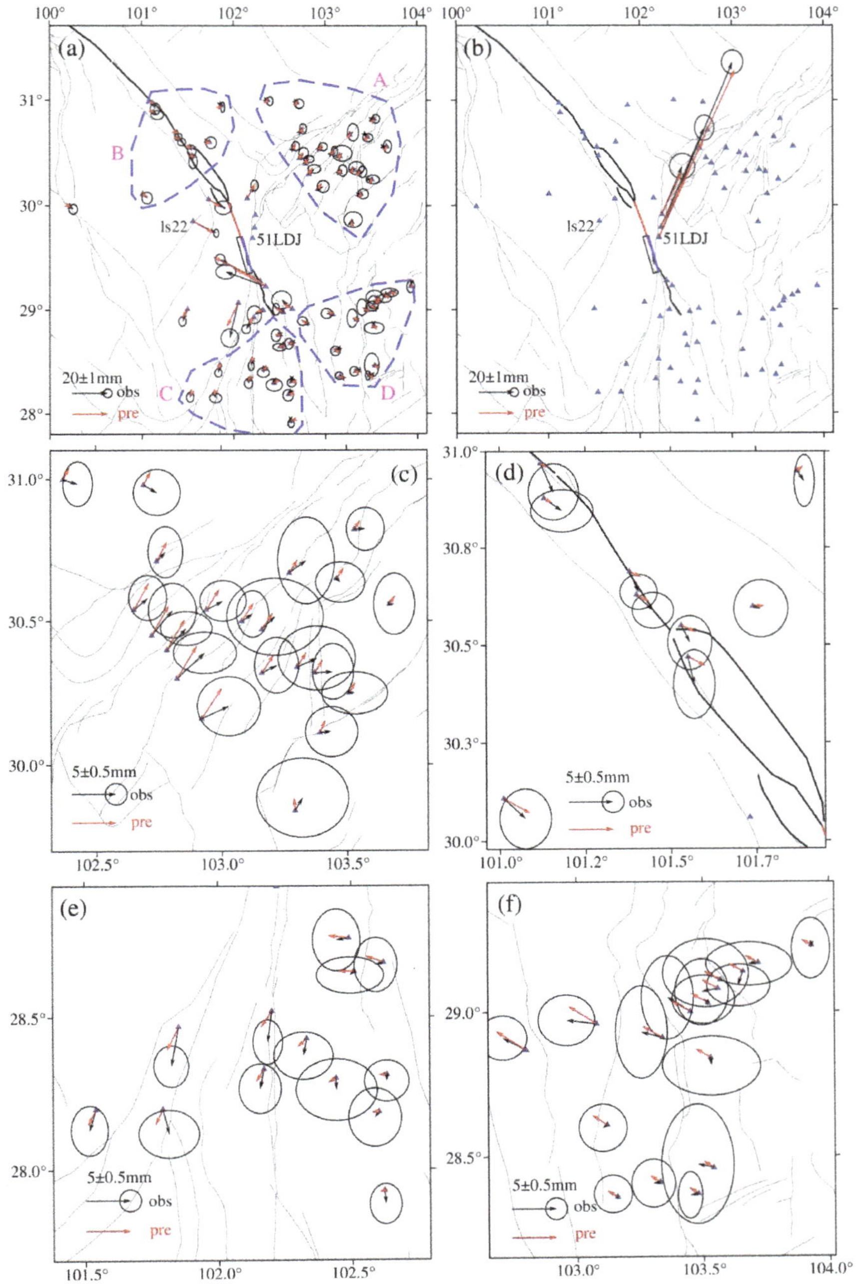

Figure 8. GPS fitting results of optimal distributed slip model inverted with joint GPS and InSAR data. (**a**) The black arrows show horizontal displacements. (**b**) The black arrows show static horizontal displacements of three strong motion sites. The red arrows denote model predictions. The blue line represents surface projection of uniform slip model. The thin black lines show the active faults. The bold black line denotes the Xianshuihe fault and the red line represents the Moxi section of XSHF [11]. The dashed blue lines outline the areas zoomed in (**c**–**f**).

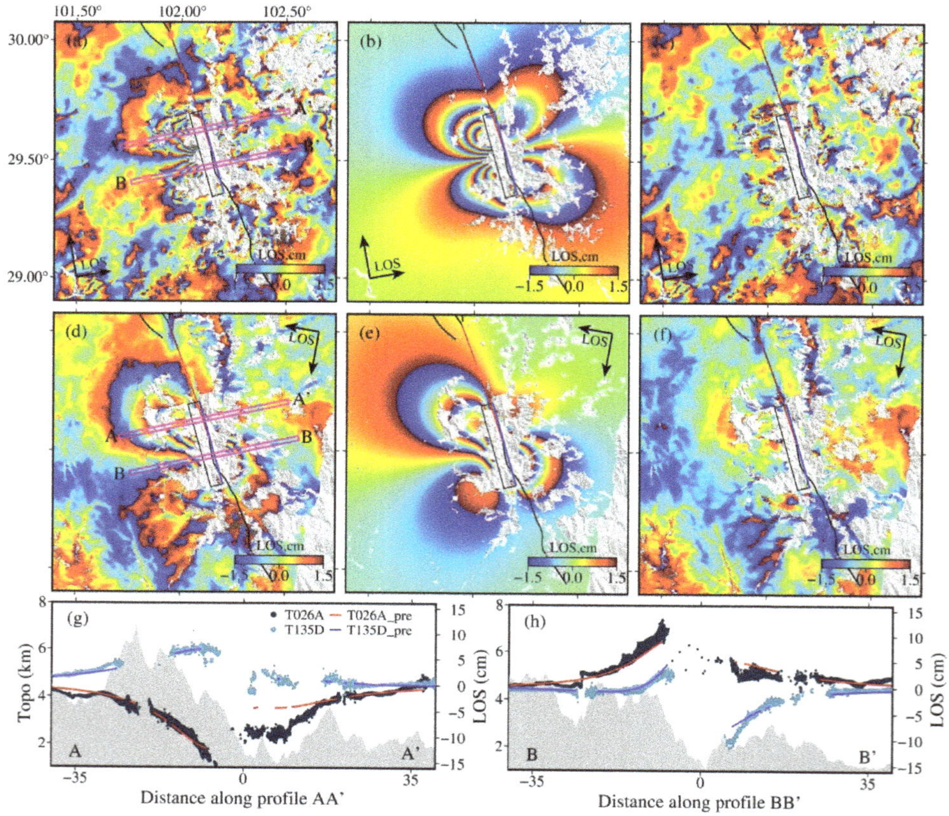

Figure 9. Inversion result of optimal distributed slip model with joint GPS and InSAR data. (**a**,**d**) InSAR observations of ascending track 026 and descending track 135. (**b**,**e**) Model prediction for ascending track 026 and descending track 135. (**c**,**f**) Residuals for ascending track 026 and descending track 135. The black line in (**a**–**f**) represents surface projection of distributed slip model. (**g**,**h**) Fitting result of profile AA′ and BB′.

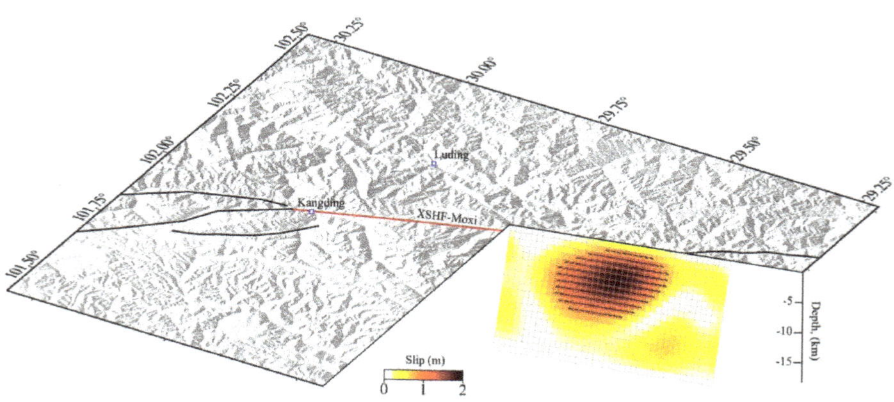

Figure 10. Perspective view on the fault-rupture plane with coseismic slip distribution. Active faults are shown in black and the red line represents the Moxi section of XSHF [11]. The black arrows on the fault plane represent slip vectors with a value larger than 0.8 m.

5. Discussion

5.1. The Comparison of Published Coseismic Slip Models

The coseismic slip model of the 2022 Luding earthquake has already been extensively studied using both geodetic and seismic observations. Several slip models have been published in the literature (e.g., [6–8,13,31–34]). Remarkably, there are substantial differences in terms of both magnitude and slip distributions among many of these models (Figure S12). For example, the maximum slip in the model of [33] was 0.26 m, whereas a peak slip of 2.5 m was obtained in the model of [34]. Moreover, there are notable differences in the spatial distribution of slips among these models. The model of [6] is characterized by a highly heterogeneous slip with three ruptured asperities and a secondary fault perpendicular to the main fault. The models of [13,34] show that the mainshock is mainly featured by two large asperities. The models of [7,8,31–33] show relatively smooth slip variations with only one large asperity. Different models provide different answers regarding whether surface rupture occurred in this earthquake. The models of [6,31,33,34] indicate that the slip reached the surface and extended over a considerable distance, while other models show that the rupture did not reach the surface. The maximum slip reaching the surface is ~1 m in the model of [6], ~1.2 m in [31], ~0.3 m in [33] and ~1 m in [34], and the total length of the slip reaching the surface is ~14 km in the model of [6], ~10 km in [31], ~40 km in [33] and ~10 km in [34] (Figure S12). Here, we should note that the actual situation is that field investigation reports indicate that no significant surface rupture was observed as a result of this earthquake, although they also claim that the surface rupture may be buried by the landslides [35]. Except for the model of [6], the models derived from only geodetic data (i.e., [7,31–33] and the coseismic slip model of this study) generally featured one large asperity.

It is crucial to acknowledge that the resultant slip model is influenced by various factors, including fault geometry, model parameterization, data selection, regularization, and the calculations of Green's functions in the inversion. Therefore, it should be note that this comparison is not intended to determine which model is superior to others [36]. Instead, it is offered to record the fluctuations in these kinds of inversions and offer an understanding of the uncertainty in slip inversions. Nevertheless, we hope that this comparison is informative for assessing how well we can currently resolve the fault structure and coseismic slip model of the Luding earthquake with currently available data.

5.2. Some Thoughts on the 2022 Luding Coseismic Rupture

From the currently published study of the 2022 Luding earthquake, we have discovered that there are still some unresolved issues, such as how many asperities ruptured during this earthquake (one or two asperities); whether there is any post-seismic deformation; and how to understand three aftershocks with normal mechanisms in a strike-slip earthquake sequence. In response to these above questions, we have provided some of our thoughts.

The currently published models of coseismic slip distributions can be mainly classified into two categories: a single asperity [7,8,31–33] and two asperities [13,34]. We should notice that the model of [6] has three asperities, which we will discuss later. The results of two asperities in coseismic slip models are mainly derived from teleseismic data [13,34]. Although the authors of [8] also used the teleseismic data, they inferred only one large slip path in the coseismic slip model. The authors of [13] argued that the authors of [8] may have used a large smoothing factor in their model which resulted in only one asperity. The results of one asperity in coseismic slip models are mainly derived from geodetic data. The coseismic slip model of this study derived from the joint inversion of GPS and InSAR data is also featured with one asperity. Our smoothing factor and coseismic slip distribution were obtained simultaneously using a variational Bayesian method without subjective choice. Therefore, we suggest that if we used geodetic data to constrain the coseismic slip model of the Luding earthquake, one asperity should be a reasonable result. The coseismic slip model with one asperity can fit well with the observation data. The authors of [8] also used geodetic data in their inversion, and this may be the reason why they only obtained a slip patch even though they used seismic data. Looking back to the model of [6], the authors also used the geodetic data for the inversion and obtained a coseismic slip model with three asperities, which is inconsistent with other models obtained using geodetic data.

The findings of Ref. [13] indicate that some post-seismic processes may have occurred after the Luding earthquake, derived from the relocated aftershock results. To explore whether the aftershock activity was accompanied by the post-seismic deformation, we tried to use InSAR data to image the post-seismic deformation of the Luding earthquake. The post-seismic InSAR observations were generated using the same method as the coseismic results in Section 2. The ascending InSAR of the post-seismic period was from 7 September 2022 to 13 October 2022, and the descending InSAR was from 14 September 2022 to 20 October 2022 (Figure S13). The results showed a large involvement of the post-seismic InSAR observations are decoherence, which also appeared in coseismic interferograms. There are virtually no available post-seismic InSAR observations in the areas corresponding to the two aftershock distribution areas (A and D). The most likely location of post-seismic deformation is near region A, because the location of aftershocks in this region is in most coincidence with the location of the seismogenic fault of the mainshock. The post-seismic InSAR observations in region A are decoherence, and we can not identify post-seismic deformation with some available observations in region A. Although there are enough available post-seismic InSAR observations in regions B and C, no obvious post-seismic deformation signal was observed. We suggest that from the available geodetic observations, there was no surface post-seismic deformation accompanied by the aftershock activity.

The findings of Ref. [12] indicate that there may be a series of SSE/NNW-trending normal faults in the west side of the middle part of the aftershock distribution (between the Gongga Mountain and the Xianshuihe fault zone) that have not been recognized before, which corresponds to three Mw > 3.5 aftershocks with normal mechanisms. Two Mw 3.8 aftershocks occurred one day after the mainshock, which is included in the observation period of the coseismic InSAR. From Figure S14, we can see that the two Mw 3.8 earthquakes with normal focal mechanisms occurred near the northwest side of the seismogenic fault of the mainshock. In this area, the part of the coseismic InSAR observation is incoherent. The ascending and descending track InSAR observations show an opposite deformation, which suggests that the horizontal deformation is dominant here (Figure S14). We did not see clear subsidence signals from normal fault earthquakes in InSAR observations, and we suspect that the small magnitude of these two normal fault earthquakes may not have caused enough surface deformation. Therefore, our geodetic observations can not constrain the fault model of these normal fault earthquakes. Moreover, the aftershock distribution in this region does not show an obvious linear distribution, so it is difficult to constrain the earthquakes of these normal fault mechanisms. The occurrence of normal fault mechanism earthquakes in strike-slip earthquake sequences also exists in some strike-slip events, such as the 1999 Mw 7.1 Hector Mine earthquake [37] and the 2001 Skyros earthquake [38]. Due to the dislocation of strike-slip faults, the positions near one end of the strike-slip faults received the effect of a spreading extension. Therefore, we can see that the normal fault earthquakes mainly occurred on the northwest side of seismogenic fault of the Luding earthquake.

5.3. The Relationship between Coseismic Deformation and Landslides Triggered by the Earthquake

One of the notable aspects associated with the Luding earthquake is the occurrence of extensive landslides across a wide area. Slope stability is related to many factors, such as topography, geology, rainfall, earthquake, etc. Some studies have focused on the analysis of the factors that cause landslides due to the Luding earthquake. Here, we tried to explore the relationship between the coseismic deformation and the landslide areas. The earthquake-triggered landslides were detected and mapped by using on-screen visual interpretation and change-detection methods. Pre-earthquake, Planet images (captured on 7 July and 29 July 2022) and post-earthquake Gaofen-6 images (captured on 10 September 2022) were therefore collected. The Planet satellite's multispectral band offers a spatial resolution of 3 m, while the Gaofen-6 satellite provides an 8 m spatial resolution for its multispectral band and a 2 m resolution for its panchromatic band. We then carried out image pre-processing operations on the acquired satellite images, including geometric correction, radiometric correction, ortho-rectification, co-registration, image fusion and color enhancement, etc. Finally, a total landslide area of 18.6 km^2 was identified and mapped with the assistance of GIS and ENVI tools.

From Figures 11 and S15, we can see that the landslides triggered by the Luding earthquake are mainly concentrated in the middle of the fault model derived from geodetic observations, which is consistent with the location of the maximum coseismic deformation. Meanwhile, the landslide area is also the main incoherent area of InSAR observations. All detected landslides were located within ~15 km of the earthquake epicenters, with ~50% of the landslide area coinciding with the surface projection of the fault model. A large part of the landslides is located in the main coseismic deformation area, which seems to indicate the influence of coseismic surface deformation on slope stability. We suggest that it is the interaction between the surface deformation and the terrain that causes a large number of landslides triggered by Luding earthquake.

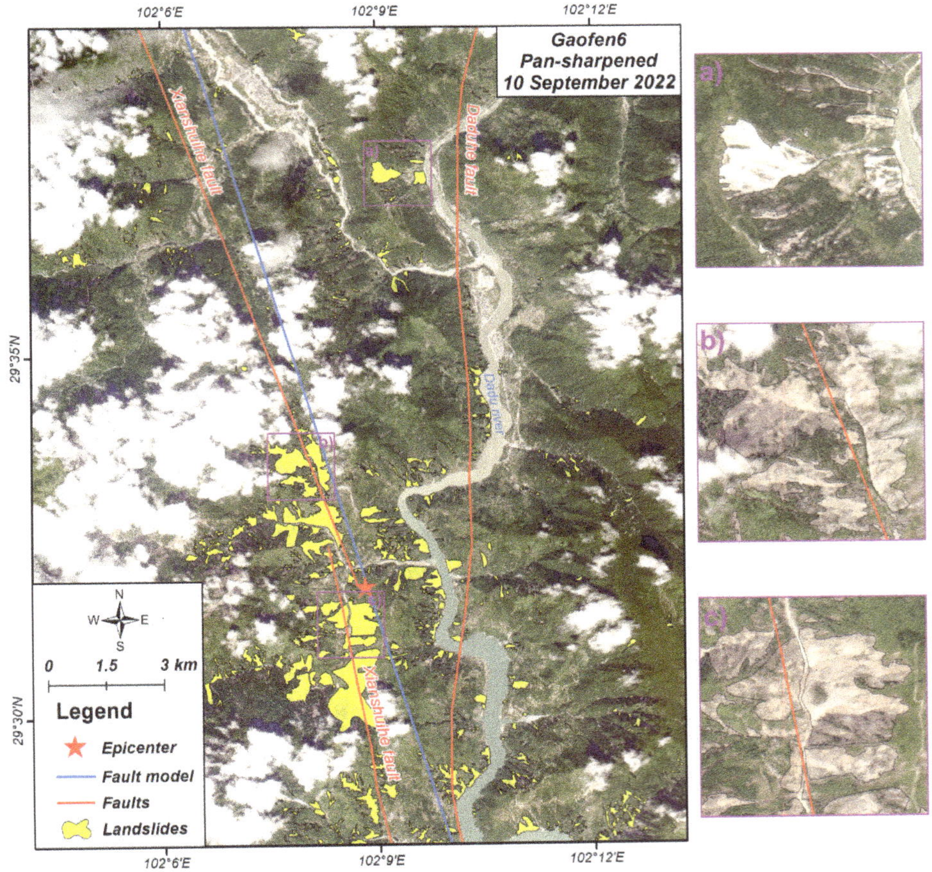

Figure 11. Landslides triggered by 2022 Luding earthquake from Gaofen-6 true color image of the epicentral region. The yellow polygons denote landslide area. The blue line represents surface projection of distributed slip model. The red lines represent active faults [11]. (**a**–**c**) Selected area in purple rectangle boxes in the main figure.

5.4. Coulomb Stress Change

Coulomb stress change calculations strongly depend on the parameterization of the causative coseismic slip model [39]. We used the coseismic slip model of the Luding earthquake derived in our study as the input for calculating the Coulomb stress changes. We estimated both the fault geometry and slip distribution of the earthquake using InSAR, based on data from ascending and descending tracks, as well as coseismic displacements inferred at GPS stations. The effective friction coefficient used in the calculation was 0.4, and the receiving fault strike was consistent with the direction of the mainshock. We calculated the Coulomb stress change at depths of 2, 4, 6 and 8 km using Coulomb 3.3 software [40]. The results show that the regions with positive Coulomb stress change are mainly located at the north and south extremities of the rupture of the Luding earthquake, and in the lobes east and west of the rupture (Figure 12). The relocated aftershocks at different depths are mainly concentrated in areas with positive Coulomb stress changes, which imply that these aftershocks may triggered by stress modifications due to coseismic rupture. The unruptured section and the southeast end of the Moxi fault deserve special attention for their future seismic risk.

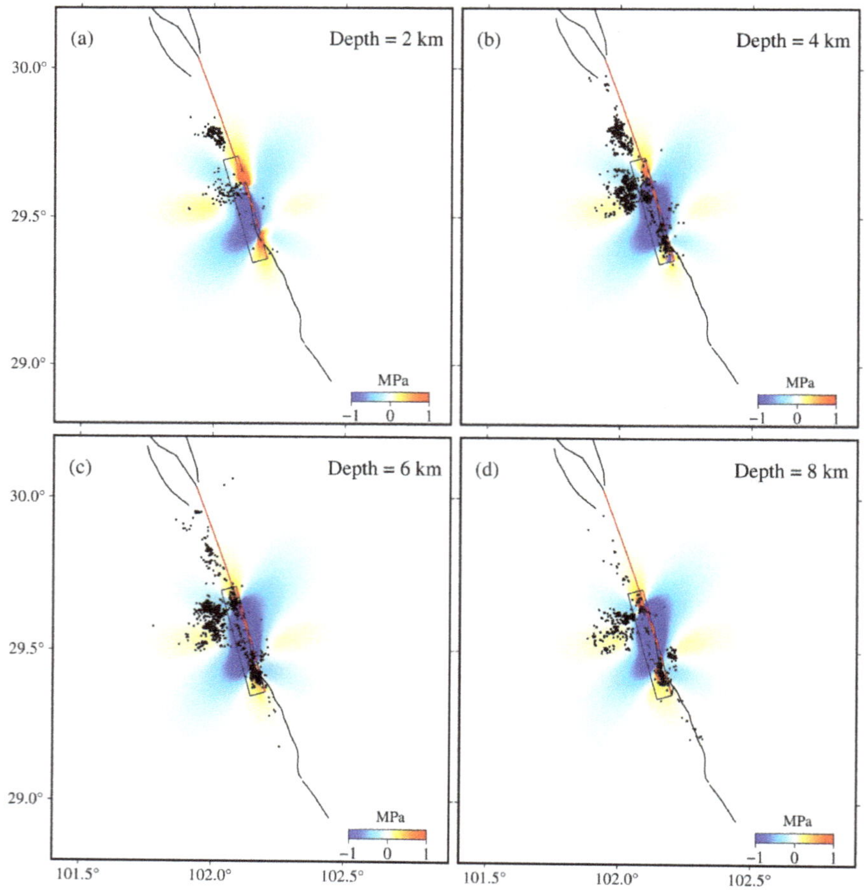

Figure 12. Coseismic Coulomb stress changes induced by the 2022 Luding earthquake at different depth levels. The black dots denote relocated aftershocks between 1 and 3 km depth in (**a**), between 3 and 5 km depth in (**b**), between 5 and 7 km depth in (**c**), and between 7 and 9 km depth in (**d**). The black line in (**a–d**) represents surface projection of distributed slip model.

6. Conclusions

Located on the Moxi section of the Xianshuihe fault, the 2022 Luding earthquake is the largest to date ever recorded by instruments. It ruptured a west-dipping fault plane with a strike of 164.3° with a primary sinistral strike-slip motion. Dense aftershocks were distributed in four areas in the west of XSHF, which implies that several faults may have been reactivated during this earthquake sequence, but relocated aftershocks could not constrain the fault geometry of the complex fault system well. Notably, the coulomb stress increased the north and south extremities of the rupture of the Luding earthquake, which is consistent with the location of the aftershocks. The maximum slip of the Luding earthquake was ~1.82 m, at a depth of ~5.3 km. Compared with two major slip patches in fault models obtained from seismic data, the geodetic data support one large slip patch. The post-seismic InSAR data does not capture obvious surface deformation around the aftershock distribution area. Despite the similar data used, the published coseismic slip models of the Luding earthquake show obvious variations, which are likely due to different processing strategies. A Bayesian source model derived from this study will be useful for understanding the real characteristics of the seismogenic fault of the Luding earthquake.

Supplementary Materials: The following supporting information can be downloaded at: https://www.mdpi.com/article/10.3390/rs16010103/s1, Figure S1: Range (a, c) and azimuth (b, d) offset of the ascending track 26 and descending track 135; Figure S2: Static coseismic offsets of 2022 Luding earthquake from GPS and strong motion data [6]; Figure S3: Assumed forward model and associated uncertainties; Figure S4: Parameters convergence of uniform slip model inverted with only GPS data; Figure S5: Distribution of model parameters in the inversion of uniform slip model with only GPS data; Figure S6: Uniform slip model inverted with only GPS data; Figure S7: Parameters convergence of uniform slip model inverted with only InSAR data; Figure S8: Distribution of model parameters in the inversion of uniform slip model with only InSAR data; Figure S9: Inversion result of uniform slip model with only InSAR data; Figure S10: Parameters convergence of uniform slip model inverted with joint GPS and InSAR data; Figure S11: Distribution of model parameters in the inversion of uniform slip mode with joint GPS and InSAR data; Figure S12: Comparison of coseismic slip models for the 2023 Luding earthquake; Figure S13: Wrapped InSAR LOS observations after the earthquake; Figure S14: Wrapped InSAR LOS displacement and focal mechanism result; Figure S15: Wrapped InSAR LOS displacement and landslides area.

Author Contributions: Conceptualization, G.X. and X.X.; methodology, G.X. and Y.Y.; software, G.X.; validation, G.X. and Q.W.; formal analysis, G.X. and Y.W.; investigation, X.L.; resources, Y.W.; data curation, G.X.; writing—original draft preparation, G.X. and L.S.; writing—review and editing, Q.W.; visualization, Y.W.; supervision, X.X.; project administration, X.X.; funding acquisition, X.L. All authors have read and agreed to the published version of the manuscript.

Funding: This research was funded by the National Natural Science Foundation of China (Nos. 41941016, U2139201, 41902217, 41572193, 42104008, 41974004) and the Jiangxi Provincial Natural Science Foundation (20232BAB213075).

Data Availability Statement: The Sentinel-1 data are distributed through ESA data hub.

Acknowledgments: We thank Yijian Zhou for sharing their relocated earthquake catalogs and helpful discussion. The Sentinel-1 data are distributed through ESA data hub. All figures presented in this study are prepared by using the Genetic Mapping Tools (GMT; [41,42]).

Conflicts of Interest: The authors declare no conflict of interest.

References

1. Deng, Q.; Zhang, P.; Ran, Y.; Yang, X.; Min, W.; Chu, Q. Basic characteristics of active tectonics of China. *Sci. China Ser. D Earth Sci.* **2023**, *46*, 356–372. [CrossRef]
2. Allen, C.R.; Zhuoli, L.; Hong, Q.; Xueze, W.; Huawei, Z.; Weishi, H. Field study of a highly active fault zone: The Xianshuihe fault of southwestern China. *Geol. Soc. Am. Bull.* **1991**, *103*, 1178–1199. [CrossRef]
3. Bai, M.; Chevalier, M.; Leloup, P.H.; Li, H.; Pan, J.; Replumaz, A.; Wang, S.; Li, K.; Wu, Q.; Liu, F.; et al. Spatial slip rate distribution along the SE Xianshuihe fault, eastern Tibet, and earthquake hazard assessment. *Tectonics* **2021**, *40*, e2021TC006985. [CrossRef]

4. Wang, H.; Wright, T.J.; Biggs, J. Interseismic slip rate of the northwestern Xianshuihe fault from InSAR data. *Geophys. Res. Lett.* **2009**, *36*, L03302. [CrossRef]
5. Jiang, G.; Wen, Y.; Liu, Y.; Xu, X.; Fang, L.; Chen, G.; Gong, M.; Xu, C. Joint analysis of the 2014 Kangding, southwest China, earthquake sequence with seismicity relocation and InSAR inversion. *Geophys. Res. Lett.* **2015**, *42*, 3273–3281. [CrossRef]
6. Li, Y.; Zhao, D.; Shan, X.; Gao, Z.; Huang, X.; Gong, W. Coseismic Slip Model of the 2022 Mw 6.7 Luding (Tibet) Earthquake: Pre-and Post-Earthquake Interactions with Surrounding Major Faults. *Geophys. Res. Lett.* **2022**, *49*, e2022GL102043. [CrossRef]
7. Han, B.; Liu, Z.; Chen, B.; Li, Z.; Yu, C.; Zhang, Y.; Peng, J. Coseismic deformation and slip distribution of the 2022 Luding Mw 6.6 earthquake revealed by InSAR observations. *Geomat. Inf. Sci. Wuhan Univ.* **2023**, *48*, 36–46, (In Chinese with English abstract).
8. Guo, R.; Li, L.; Zhang, W.; Zhang, Y.; Tang, X.; Dai, K.; Li, Y.; Zhang, L.; Wang, J. Kinematic slip evolution during the 2022 Ms 6.8 Luding, China, earthquake: Compatible with the preseismic locked patch. *Geophys. Res. Lett.* **2023**, *50*, e2023GL103164. [CrossRef]
9. Dziewonski, A.M.; Chou, T.; Woodhouse, J.H. Determination of earthquake source parameters from waveform data for studies of global and regional seismicity. *J. Geophys. Res. Solid Earth* **1981**, *86*, 2825–2852. [CrossRef]
10. Wang, M.; Shen, Z.-K. Present-day crustal deformation of continental China derived from GPS and its tectonic implications. *J. Geophys. Res. Solid Earth* **2020**, *125*, e2019JB018774. [CrossRef]
11. Xu, X.W.; Han, Z.J.; Yang, X.P.; Zhang, S.; Yu, G.; Zhou, B.; Li, F.; Ma, B.; Chen, G.; Ran, Y. *Seismotectonic Map in China and its Adjacent Regions*; Seismological Press: Beijing, China, 2016. (In Chinese)
12. Yi, G.; Long, F.; Liang, M.; Zhao, M.; Zhang, H.; Zhou, R.; Li, Y.; Liu, H.; Wu, P.; Wang, S.; et al. Seismogenic structure of the 5 September 2022 Sichuan Luding MS6.8 earthquake sequence. *Chin. J. Geophys.* **2023**, *66*, 1363–1384, (In Chinese with English abstract).
13. Zhang, L.; Zhou, Y.; Zhang, X.; Zhu, A.; Li, B.; Wang, S.; Liang, S.; Jiang, C.; Wu, J.; Li, Y.; et al. 2022 Mw 6.6 Luding, China, Earthquake: A Strong Continental Event Illuminating the Moxi Seismic Gap. *Seismol. Res. Lett.* **2023**, *94*, 2129–2142. [CrossRef]
14. Wegnüller, U.; Werner, C.; Strozzi, T.; Wiesmann, A.; Frey, O.; Santoro, M. Sentinel-1 Support in the GAMMA Software. *Procedia Comput. Sci.* **2016**, *100*, 1305–1312. [CrossRef]
15. Scheiber, R.; Moreira, A. Coregistration of interferometric SAR images using spectral diversity. *IEEE Trans. Geosci. Remote Sens.* **2000**, *38*, 2179–2191. [CrossRef]
16. Farr, T.G.; Rosen, P.A.; Caro, E.; Crippen, R.; Duren, R.; Hensley, S.; Kobrick, M.; Paller, M.; Rodriguez, E.; Roth, L.; et al. The shuttle radar topography mission. *Rev. Geophys.* **2007**, *45*, RG2004. [CrossRef]
17. Goldstein, R.M.; Werner, C.L. Radar interferogram filtering for geophysical applications. *Geophys. Res. Lett.* **1998**, *25*, 4035–4038. [CrossRef]
18. Chen, C.W.; Zebker, H.A. Network approaches to two-dimensional phase unwrapping: Intractability and two new algorithms. *J. Opt. Soc. Am. A* **2000**, *17*, 401–414. [CrossRef] [PubMed]
19. Wen, Y.; Xu, C.; Liu, Y.; Jiang, G. Deformation and source parameters of the 2015 Mw 6.5 earthquake in Pishan, western China, from Sentinel-1A and ALOS-2 data. *Remote Sens.* **2016**, *8*, 134. [CrossRef]
20. Feng, W.; Samsonov, S.; Almeida, R.; Yassaghi, A.; Li, J.; Qiu, Q.; Li, P.; Zheng, W. Geodetic Constraints of the 2017 Mw7.3 Sarpol Zahab, Iran Earthquake, and Its Implications on the Structure and Mechanics of the Northwest Zagros Thrust-Fold Belt. *Geophys. Res. Lett.* **2018**, *45*, 6853–6861. [CrossRef]
21. Rosen, P.A.; Gurrola, E.; Sacco, G.F.; Zebker, H. The InSAR scientific computing environment. In Proceedings of the EUSAR 2012, 9th European Conference on Synthetic Aperture Radar, Nuremberg, Germany, 23–26 April 2012; pp. 730–733.
22. Fialko, Y.; Simons, M.; Agnew, D. The complete (3-D) surface displacement field in the epicentral area of the 1999MW7.1 Hector Mine Earthquake, California, from space geodetic observations. *Geophys. Res. Lett.* **2001**, *28*, 3063–3066. [CrossRef]
23. Wright, T.J.; Lu, Z.; Wicks, C. Source model for the Mw 6.7, 23 October 2002, Nenana mountain earthquake (Alaska) from InSAR. *Geophys. Res. Lett.* **2003**, *30*, 1974. [CrossRef]
24. Atzori, S.; Hunstad, I.; Chini, M.; Salvi, S.; Tolomei, C.; Bignami, C.; Stramondo, S.; Trasatti, E.; Antonioli, A.; Boschi, E. Finite fault inversion of DInSAR coseismic displacement of the 2009 L'Aquila earthquake (central Italy). *Geophys. Res. Lett.* **2009**, *36*, L15305. [CrossRef]
25. Lohman, R.B.; Simons, M. Some thoughts on the use of InSAR data to constrain models of surface deformation: Noise structure and data downsampling. *Geochem. Geophys. Geosystems* **2005**, *6*, Q01007. [CrossRef]
26. Bagnardi, M.; Hooper, A. Inversion of surface deformation data for rapid estimates of source parameters and uncertainties: A Bayesian approach. *Geochem. Geophys. Geosystems* **2018**, *19*, 2194–2211. [CrossRef]
27. Okada, Y. Surface deformation due to shear and tensile faults in a half-space. *Bull. Seismol. Soc. Am.* **1985**, *75*, 1135–1154. [CrossRef]
28. Parsons, B.; Wright, T.; Rowe, P.; Andrews, J.; Jackson, J.; Walker, R.; Khatib, M.; Talebian, M.; Bergman, E.; Engdahl, E.R. The 1994 Sefidabeh (eastern Iran) earthquakes revisited: New evidence from satellite radar interferometry and carbonate dating about the growth of an active fold above a blind thrust fault. *Geophys. J. Int.* **2006**, *164*, 202–217. [CrossRef]
29. Sun, L.; Wang, L.; Xu, G.; Wu, Q. A new method of variational Bayesian slip distribution inversion. *J. Geod.* **2023**, *97*, 10. [CrossRef]
30. Ragon, T.; Sladen, A.; Simons, M. Accounting for uncertain fault geometry in earthquake source inversions–I: Theory and simplified application. *Geophys. J. Int.* **2018**, *214*, 1174–1190. [CrossRef]
31. Liang, H.; Wu, Y.; Shao, Z.; Li, J.; Li, Y.; Yi, S.; Yang, F.; Zhuang, W.; Wang, H.; Zhan, W.; et al. Coseismic slip and deformation mode of the 2022 Mw 6.5 Luding earthquake determined by GPS observation. *Tectonophysics* **2023**, *865*, 230042. [CrossRef]

32. Peng, W.; Huang, X.; Wang, Z. Focal Mechanism and Regional Fault Activity Analysis of 2022 Luding Strong Earthquake Constraint by InSAR and Its Inversion. *Remote Sens.* **2023**, *15*, 3753. [CrossRef]
33. Wu, W.; Meng, G.; Liu, T.; Wei, C.; Wei, W. Coseismic displacement field and slip distribution of the 2022 Luding M6. 8 earthquake derived from GNSS observations. *Chin. J. Geophys.* **2023**, *66*, 2306–2321, (In Chinese with English abstract).
34. Zhao, X.; Xiao, Z.; Wang, W.; Li, J.; Zhao, M.; Chen, S.; Tang, L. Fine seismogenic fault structures and complex rupture characteristics of the 2022 M6.8 Luding, Sichuan earthquake sequence revealed by deep learning and waveform modeling. *Geophys. Res. Lett.* **2023**, *50*, e2023GL102976. [CrossRef]
35. Shan, X.; Li, Y.; Gao, Z.; Hua, J.; Huang, X.; Gong, W.; Qu, C.; Zhao, D.; Chen, J.; Huang, C.; et al. Coseismic deformation of the 2022 Luding MS6.8 earthquake and seismic potential along adjacent major faults. *Chin. Sci. Bull.* **2022**, *68*, 944–953, (In Chinese with English abstract). [CrossRef]
36. Wang, K.; Dreger, D.S.; Tinti, E.; Bürgmann, R.; Taira, T. Rupture process of the 2019 Ridgecrest, California Mw6.4 foreshock and Mw7.1 earthquake constrained by seismic and geodetic data. *Bull. Seismol. Soc. Am.* **2020**, *110*, 1603–1626. [CrossRef]
37. Hauksson, E.; Jones, L.M.; Hutton, K. The 1999 M w 7.1 Hector Mine, California, earthquake sequence: Complex conjugate strike-slip faulting. *Bull. Seismol. Soc. Am.* **2002**, *92*, 1154–1170. [CrossRef]
38. Karakostas, V.G.; Papadimitriou, E.E.; Karakaisis, G.F.; Papazachos, C.B.; Scordilis, E.M.; Vargemezis, G.; Aidona, E. The 2001 Skyros, Northern Aegean, Greece, earthquake sequence: Off-fault aftershocks, tectonic implications, and seismicity triggering. *Geophys. Res. Lett.* **2003**, *30*, 1012. [CrossRef]
39. Woessner, J.; Jónsson, S.; Sudhaus, H.; Baumann, C. Reliability of Coulomb stress changes inferred from correlated uncertainties of finite-fault source models. *J. Geophys. Res. Solid Earth* **2012**, *117*, B07303. [CrossRef]
40. Toda, S.; Stein, R.S.; Sevilgen, V.; Lin, J. Coulomb 3.3 Graphic-rich deformation and stress-change software for earthquake, tectonic, and volcano research and teaching—User guide. *US Geol. Surv. Open-File Rep.* **2011**, *1060*, 63.
41. Wessel, P.; Smith, W.H. New, improved version of Generic Mapping Tools released. *Eos Trans. Am. Geophys. Union* **1998**, *79*, 579. [CrossRef]
42. Wessel, P.; Luis, J.F.; Uieda, L.; Scharroo, R.; Wobbe, F.; Smith, W.H.; Tian, D. The generic mapping tools version 6. *Geochemistry* **2019**, *20*, 5556–5564. [CrossRef]

remote sensing

MDPI

Article

A Simulation Framework of Unmanned Aerial Vehicles Route Planning Design and Validation for Landslide Monitoring

Dongmei Xie [1], Ruifeng Hu [1], Chisheng Wang [1,*], Chuanhua Zhu [1], Hui Xu [2,3] and Qipei Li [1]

1 Ministry of Natural Resources (MNR) Key Laboratory for Geo-Environmental Monitoring of Great Bay Area & Guangdong Key Laboratory of Urban Informatics, School of Architecture & Urban Planning, Shenzhen University, Shenzhen 518060, China; xiedongmei2020@email.szu.edu.cn (D.X.); huruifeng2020@email.szu.edu.cn (R.H.); czhu@szu.edu.cn (C.Z.); 2020104005@email.szu.edu.cn (Q.L.)
2 School of Fine Arts and Design, Shenzhen University, Shenzhen 518060, China; xuhui@szu.edu.cn
3 State Key Laboratory of Subtropical Building and Urban Science, Shenzhen 510640, China
* Correspondence: wangchisheng@szu.edu.cn

Abstract: Unmanned aerial vehicles (UAVs) have emerged as a highly efficient means of monitoring landslide-prone regions, given the growing concern for urban safety and the increasing occurrence of landslides. Designing optimal UAV flight routes is crucial for effective landslide monitoring. However, in real-world scenarios, the testing and validating of flight path planning algorithms incur high cost and safety concerns, making overall flight operations challenging. Therefore, this paper proposes the use of the Unreal Engine simulation framework to design UAV flight path planning specifically for landslide monitoring. It aims to validate the authenticity of the simulated flight paths and the correctness of the algorithms. Under the proposed simulation framework, we then test a novel flight path planning algorithm. The simulation results demonstrate that the model reconstruction obtained using the novel flight path algorithm exhibits more detailed textures, with a 3D model simulation accuracy ranging from 10 to 14 cm. Among them, the RMSE value of the novel flight route algorithm falls within the range of 10 to 11 cm, exhibiting a 2 to 3 cm improvement in accuracy compared to the traditional flight path algorithm. Additionally, it effectively reduces the flight duration by 9.3% under the same flight path compared to conventional methods. The results confirm that the simulation framework developed in this paper meets the requirements for landslide damage monitoring and validates the feasibility and correctness of the UAV flight path planning algorithm.

Keywords: unmanned aerial vehicle; unreal engine; AirSim; landslide monitoring; flight path planning; simulation validation

1. Introduction

Landslides are one of the most prevalent geological hazards, involving the downward movement of large volumes of rocks, debris, or soil along slopes due to the force of gravity, heavy rainfall, earthquakes, changes in water levels, human activities, and so on [1,2]. Landslides of different slope gradients exhibit varying frequencies and velocities. They can manifest as various types, including flows, slides, topples, falls, or spreads, often exhibiting a combination of different movement patterns over time or during their lifecycle. In recent years, the occurrence frequency and scale of landslides have been increasing globally; this has been attributed to climate change and other contributing factors [3,4]. Landslides frequently result in extreme and destructive consequences, negatively impacting human safety, hindering urban planning, and causing significant economic losses [5–7]. The suddenness, complexity, and high uncertainty of landslides can present challenges in emergency monitoring, leading to delayed response, imprecise control, and inefficient disaster management. Consequently, monitoring and implementing emergency responses to landslide incidents have become focal points in the field of geological disaster prevention and relief [8]. Therefore, the utilization of landslide monitoring technologies to gain insights into landslide behavior and reduce landslide risks is of paramount importance.

Traditional landslide monitoring relies on inclinometers to obtain precise measurements of slope magnitude and direction, while global navigation satellite systems (GNSSs) are utilized to monitor surface movement on the terrain. These instruments are capable of real-time monitoring and providing accurate data regarding landslide behavior, but they are limited in that each device can only generate measurement results for a single location [9]. In contrast, unmanned aerial vehicle (UAV) monitoring technology offers several advantages, such as real-time capabilities, high maneuverability, high-resolution imagery, and cost effectiveness [10], thus making UAVs more suitable for large-scale landslide monitoring. One crucial task that needs to be accomplished before conducting UAV monitoring is UAV flight path planning.

Efficient UAV flight path planning is useful for optimizing data acquisition and ensuring comprehensive coverage of the landslide area. UAVs can effectively capture high-resolution images of terrain if their flight paths are strategically designed, thus enabling precise monitoring and analysis of landslide behavior. There have been numerous comprehensive studies internationally on UAV flight path planning [11–14]. During the research process, extensive experimentation is essential, as unverified flight path algorithms can lead to errors. Therefore, testing and debugging are critical stages in UAV flight operations. Since algorithms are designed to operate on physical systems, real UAV testing is the most effective way to debug them [15]. Nevertheless, errors or incorrect parameter adjustments during testing can have severe consequences, such as triggering hazardous behaviors or even causing crashes. In the best-case scenario, this may only require repairing or rebuilding the UAV frame, but in the worst cases it could result in injuries to personnel. Furthermore, the challenging terrain in landslide areas presents significant obstacles for UAV flight operations, making on-site testing complicated, with a risk of UAV crashes and damage. Moreover, conducting UAV flights in urban areas may encounter legal restrictions, making algorithm validation in real scenarios both time consuming and costly [16]. These challenges emphasize the importance of developing a reliable and efficient UAV flight path planning method that can be tested and validated in a safe and controlled environment before actual implementation in real-life monitoring scenarios.

In response to the challenges and risks associated with conducting real-world UAV flight tests, many scholars have proposed using UAV simulators for flight simulations. Hentati et al. [17] introduced mainstream UAV simulation frameworks, such as XPlane [18], Flightgear [19], Gazebo [20], and JMavSim. However, these simulators have limitations in terms of assets and textures and lack support for motion capture (MOCAP). In contrast, simulators like AirSim and UE4 offer MOCAP support and enable the creation of UAV motion planning. Overall, JMavSim is relatively simple in terms of both configuration and functionality. XPlane and FlightGear are primarily designed for aircraft simulation and may not be well suited to the research of multirotor and fixed-wing unmanned aerial vehicles, limiting their available scenarios and applications. On the other hand, AirSim excels in these aspects. It provides dedicated interfaces that support the development and testing of deep learning and computer vision algorithms. Furthermore, it offers a wide variety of environments and scenarios, accommodating diverse research and testing requirements. Additionally, AirSim exhibits a high degree of scalability, allowing for the integration of various sensors and hardware devices. Table 1 gives the comparison between the proposed simulators. Matlekovic et al. [21] designed a microservices application for UAV infrastructure inspection, which involved high-level path planning, monitoring, and testing of autonomous UAV missions. They used Gazebo to simulate UAVs following waypoints provided by a cloud system to verify the correctness of the inspection path. While addressing communication and perception uncertainty, Ling et al. [22] proposed a scalable and maintainable distributed UAV swarm cooperative planning and perception–simulation framework. They used Bayesian reasoning-based estimation and distributed collaborative planning evaluation under incomplete perception to validate the framework's working principle and practicality through simulation examples. Fernando et al. [23] utilized MATLAB®Simulink to simulate the model control algorithm and compared the quadrotor state model with the MATLAB®6DOF dynamic model in Aerospace Blockset, validating the model's effectiveness. However, this method could not run in real time after adding 3D visualization. Park et al. [24] proposed an improved real-time flight simulation method to predict the transient response of multi-rotor UAVs under gust influence. They combined unsteady rotor aerodynamics suitable for flight simulation with nonlinear flight dynamics to accurately predict UAV responses under gusts and verified the necessity of the simulation. While most of these simulation frameworks allow the creation of 3D worlds using different physics engines and sensor models, they still face challenges in creating large-scale complex scenes. Some frameworks, like Hector [25], lack support for popular hardware frameworks like Pixhawk and protocols like MavLink, limiting their usability. Moreover, the development and refinement of UAV flight path planning algorithms in the real world can be costly and involve significant risks. The use of UAV simulators offers a safer and more cost-effective alternative for testing and validating UAV flight path planning methods before actual implementation in real-world scenarios.

Table 1. Summary of the comparison between different simulators.

	FlightGear	**XPlane**	**JMavSim**	**Gazebo**	**AirSim**	**UE4Sim**
Commercial Free	Free	Commercial	Free	Free	Free	Free
Vehicles	Airplanes	AIrplanes	Multirotor	Multirotor and robots	Multirotor	Multirotor, cars
Scene Fidelity	High	Medium	Low	Low	Low	Low
Interface ROS	No	No	Yes	Yes	No	No
Sensors	Diversity of sensors	Easy incorporation of sensors	No incorporation of sensors	Easy modification of sensors	Monocular depth cameras	Easy modification of sensors
Obstacles	Yes	Yes	No	Yes	Yes	Yes
SITL-HITL	Yes	Yes	Yes	Yes	Yes	No
MAVLink	Yes	Yes	Yes	Yes	Yes	No
Ease of Development	Medium	Medium	High	High	Medium	Medium

Therefore, this paper proposes a method for UAV flight path planning and simulation, specifically dedicated to landslide monitoring. The approach involves constructing a virtual landslide scenario in the Unreal Engine 4 (UE4) and integrating AirSim to simulate UAV flights and reconstruct the landslide area from a 2D to a highly realistic 3D scene. The effectiveness, authenticity, and applicability of the simulation are assessed and the correctness of its flight path planning algorithm is validated by evaluating the quality of the reconstructed model. The main advantage of this method is its ability to significantly reduce the testing costs and risks associated with conducting actual UAV flights in landslide-prone areas. Instead, the proposed simulation framework offers a safe and cost-effective alternative for verifying the accuracy and reliability of the flight path planning algorithm. By providing a realistic representation of landslide scenarios, this approach offers valuable insights for effective disaster prevention and mitigation strategies in areas susceptible to landslides.

The main contributions of this study are as follows:

1. An UAV flight simulation approach that amalgamates UE4 and AirSim is proposed, which address challenges encountered in other simulation frameworks, including texture fidelity, asset constraints, and protocol compatibility and so on;
2. Utilizing the simulation framework to optimize the flight path algorithms, substantiating the practical utility of the proposed framework, and validating the correction of the algorithms;

3. Simulation technology is used in advance to simulate the actual flight, which effectively reduces the input of manpower and material costs, avoids risks, and improves the execution efficiency of actual flight tasks.

2. Methods

2.1. Landslide Terrain Modeling

2.1.1. Landslide Terrain Modeling

In the simulation environment, the initial step is to build a high-accuracy scene model of the terrain. Advanced UAV technology is employed to capture images of the landslide scene from multiple angles. These images are subsequently utilized for automated matching and solving of aerial triangulation [26], leading to the generation of sparse point clouds based on real images. Further, dense point clouds are reconstructed, and texture mapping is applied to assign high-resolution textures to the 3D model. As a result of this intricate process, a highly realistic 3D scene model is obtained [27].

Aerial triangulation plays a pivotal role in the process of oblique photogrammetry. Its principle is to compute the connection points obtained from the feature matching of images. Subsequently, the coordinates of ground control points measured in reality are employed to incorporate all image areas into the ground coordinate system, yielding the exterior orientation elements for each image. The accuracy of aerial triangulation directly determines the quality of the final results. The fundamental formula for the collinearity condition equation is as follows:

$$x = -f\frac{a_1(X - X_s) + b_1(Y - Y_s) + c_1(Z - Z_s)}{a_3(X - X_s) + b_3(Y - Y_s) + c_3(Z - Z_s)} \tag{1}$$

$$y = -f\frac{a_2(X - X_s) + b_2(Y - Y_s) + c_2(Z - Z_s)}{a_3(X - X_s) + b_3(Y - Y_s) + c_3(Z - Z_s)} \tag{2}$$

Here, x and y represent the image plane coordinates of the image points and f represents camera's focal length. X_S, Y_S and Z_S are the object space coordinates of the shooting station. X, Y and Z are object space coordinates of object square points. The notations a_i, b_i, c_i (= 1, 2, 3) comprise the nine directional cosines composed of the three external azimuth elements of the image.

After acquiring the position and orientation of each photo, a sparse point cloud model is generated. To reference the sparse point cloud to the local coordinate system, a height field calculation method based on pairwise depth maps is employed, facilitating the creation of a dense point cloud and mesh. Subsequently, the constructed mesh is overlaid with texture mapping, resulting in the production of a comprehensive 3D model.

2.1.2. Levels of Detail

The rendering capability of modern computer hardware still faces challenges when handling massive terrain datasets, impeding the attainment of real-time performance and higher resolutions [28]. To address this issue, the levels of detail (LOD) technique presents an effective solution. This approach represents terrain with varying levels of detail, utilizing higher detailed models for areas close to the viewpoint and employing coarser terrain models for distant areas, resulting in a visual representation aligning with the capabilities of the human visual system.

The terrain data is stored in the computer as digital elevation model (DEM) data, and it is managed and organized using a pyramid model as shown in Figure 1. The entire area of the landslide terrain is initially structured as a quadtree, with each terrain data block representing a quadtree node [29]. Starting from the root node of the quadtree, each node is recursively subdivided to generate four children nodes at the next level, continuing until the highest resolution of the raw landslide terrain data is reached.

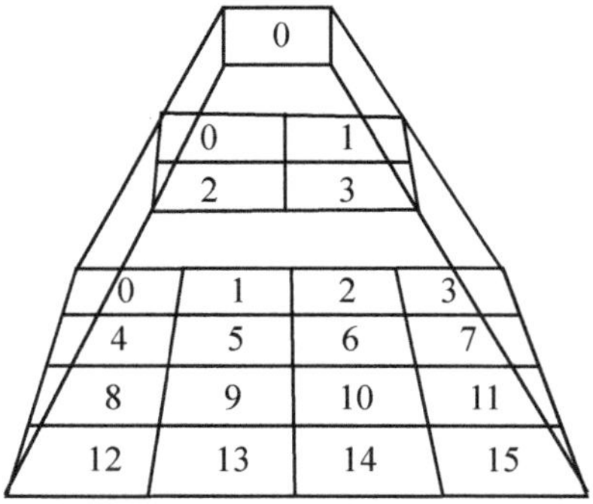

Figure 1. Multiscale terrain pyramid.

To simplify the terrain representation and effectively manage large-scale landslide terrain data, the method proposed in this paper adopts a quadtree-based LOD algorithm [30]. This approach organizes and manages the terrain data using the quadtree structure, enabling the selective loading and combination of different resolution levels of landslide terrain data into memory before rendering the scene. The quadtree-based LOD algorithm involves traversing the terrain nodes and determining whether they require subdivision based on certain conditions. Through selective loading and rendering of only the essential portions of the terrain data, the algorithm optimizes memory usage and achieves efficient rendering.

A roughness factor is utilized to account for the required rendering resolution. This roughness factor R represents the steepness of the terrain, with higher values indicating steeper terrain regions that require higher resolution rendering. The mathematical expression for roughness R is as follows:

$$R = \frac{max(\Delta h_1, \Delta h_2, \cdots, \Delta h_6)}{D} \tag{3}$$

Here, Δh_1 to Δh_6 denote the differences between the average elevation values at the midpoints of each terrain node's edges and the elevation values at the boundary endpoints, while D represents the edge length of the terrain node. The corresponding terrain representation is illustrated in Figure 2. By calculating the roughness for different terrain regions, the algorithm intelligently selects the appropriate level of detail for rendering, thereby facilitating efficient and realistic visualization of the landslide terrain data.

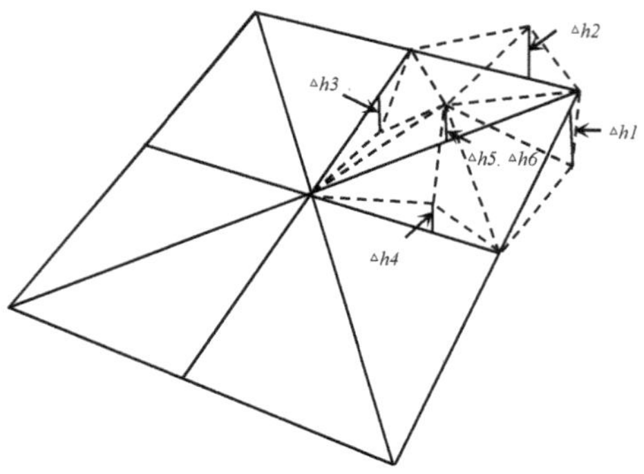

Figure 2. Terrain roughness.

2.2. *Simulation Framework*

The simulation framework is built by combining Unreal Engine with AirSim, where Unreal Engine provides highly realistic environment rendering models, and AirSim offers comprehensive control application programming interfaces (APIs), binary interfaces (ABIs), and various sensor models. The confluence of these two constituents enables the creation of a reliable and authentic simulation environment for UAV flight path planning.

2.2.1. Unreal Engine

Unreal Engine is a cross-framework game engine developed by Epic Games. As simulation applications have been evolving. Unreal Engine has become a versatile tool used for developing virtual reality and augmented reality applications, movie special effects, industrial simulations, and more [31]. One notable research focus within Unreal Engine pertains to UAV flight path planning. Within Unreal Engine, numerous features are useful for UAV flight path planning. The terrain editor allows the creation of realistic terrains and scenes, further fostering the realism essential to successful simulations. Additionally, UE4 provides extensible plugins, such as virtual reality and networking plugins, which offer further functionalities and support for UAV flight path planning. Unreal Engine also boasts a powerful material editor, enabling the rendering of highly realistic textures, whose lighting, blueprint, and physics rendering features can be employed to implement various interaction and simulation designs, assisting in the creation, testing, and optimization of UAV flight path planning algorithms to meet developers' needs. Furthermore, Unreal Engine's cross-framework advantage allows it to run on various hardware and operating systems, providing a wide range of possibilities for UAV flight path planning applications. Utilizing Unreal Engine to create realistic environments and scenes, automate UAV control, and conduct UAV path planning aids in advancing UAV technology.

2.2.2. AirSim

A UAV simulator must create a suitable environment for UAV flight, facilitating the integration of various sensors, such as cameras, LiDAR, GPS, microphones, gas sensors, etc. It also necessitates the incorporation of physical aspects like accurate turbulence, air density, wind shear, clouds, precipitation, and other fluid dynamics constraints. Microsoft's AirSim is a high-fidelity virtual environment based on Unreal Engine that meets these requirements [32]. As an open-source simulation framework developed on Unreal Engine [33], AirSim aims to bridge the gap between simulation and reality, supporting the simulation of diverse vehicles, including UAVs and cars, thereby providing users with a remarkably realistic and immersive experience.

AirSim offers a wide array of callable APIs and ABI interfaces. Throughout the simulation process, AirSim supplies sensor information from the simulated environment to the UAV flight controller. This flight controller then processes the received data using appropriate algorithms and generates control signals for the UAV model, effectively implementing a complete UAV flight design. The API design of AirSim isolates the UAV and flight controller, thereby separating the mathematical model of the simulated UAV from the processing executed by the flight controller. Such design fosters a fully realistic simulation of real-world UAV flights, significantly enhancing the overall realism and effectiveness of the simulation. Additionally, AirSim provides the capability of interfacing with Mavlink, allowing users to employ Pixhawk firmware (e.g., Ardupilot and PX4) for software-in-the-loop (SITL) and hardware-in-the-loop (HITL) simulations. Figure 3 is an example of simulating a virtual drone flight example in the simulation framework.

Figure 3. An example of virtual drone flight simulation within the proposed simulation framework (windows below, from left to right, show the depth map, semantic segmentation map, and photographic image).

2.2.3. Texture Mapping

When rendering large-scale terrain scenes, the use of geometric models to represent natural elements such as grass, soil, and rocks can result in increased complexity in the terrain. To reduce the demands on memory and rendering time while simultaneously enhancing the scene's realism, texture mapping is employed to improve the rendering effect of images [34].

Textures are formed by arranging simple matrices of color data and brightness data [35,36]. The color of the landslide model's texture is determined by the diffuse reflection and ambient color of the terrain surface, following is the formula, where C represents the color of the landslide model's surface, $C_{ambient}$ is the ambient light color, and $C_{diffuse}$ is the color of the diffuse reflection on the landslide model's surface:

$$C = C_{ambient} + C_{diffuse} \tag{4}$$

Texture mapping refers to establishing a correspondence between the geometric information of objects and texture information based on the spatial position data of the triangle mesh in the model. This process segments the optimal texture mapping for each triangular face, achieving automatic texture mapping of the model and enhancing the visual realism of rendering without adding geometric details to the objects. In texture mapping, (u, v) represents a point in the texture space of the image, and (x, y) are coordinates in the texture image, $(w_{texture}, h_{texture})$ represent the width and height of the texture image, respectively. The formula is described as follows:

$$(u,\ v) = \left(\frac{x}{w_{texture}}, \frac{y}{h_{texture}}\right) \tag{5}$$

2.2.4. Normal Mapping

The level of surface detail depends on how light rays interact with the surface. To achieve a more realistic appearance, it is essential to simulate the irregularities present in real surfaces. The influence of wrinkles on the perception of surface irregularities primarily stems from their impact on the surface's normal direction. To enhance the 3D sense of the object's surface, this paper utilizes normal maps [37] to incorporate bump detail texture information into the material. The height of each texel is encoded using a height field, from which normals are obtained via normalization. Assuming Hg represents the height of the texel, Ha is the height above the texel, and Hr is the height to the right of the texel, the normal formula is as follows:

$$n = \frac{(H_g - H_r, H_g - H_a, 1)}{\sqrt{(H_g - H_r)^2 + (H_g - H_a)^2 + 1}} \tag{6}$$

Subsequently, the X, Y, and Z components of the normal are stored in the color channels R, G, and B, respectively. However, since normal vectors have signed values within the range of $[-1, 1]$, while the RGB range in the texture is $[0, 1]$ without signed values, it is necessary to compress the normal vector's range. This is accomplished by employing col to represent the compressed normal vector, and its formula is as follows:

$$col = 0.5 \times n + 0.5 \tag{7}$$

After applying the normal map to the texture, when light illuminates the object's surface, different normal directions will present various visual effects.

2.2.5. Lighting

In most cases, visible light illumination models only focus on considering the reflection phenomena of materials. Various simplified models in computer graphics, such as the Phong model [38], Blinn–Phong model [39], and Cook–Torrance model [40], are all based on the global visible light illumination model.

The Blinn–Phong model represents an advanced version of the Phong model, proposed by Blinn, which optimizes and enhances the traditional Phong lighting model. It incorporates the diffuse component of the Lambert model and standard specular mapping. In rendering, the Blinn–Phong model produces smoother and softer highlights compared to the Phong model, with faster calculation speed and heightened realism. Simplifying the incident light into three types: ambient light, diffuse reflection, and specular reflection [41], the Blinn–Phong lighting model is particularly effective in scenarios with a single light source. The calculation formula for the Blinn–Phong model, in such cases, is as follows:

$$I = I_{ambdiff} + I_{ldiff} + I_{spec} = k_a I_a + k_d I_l \cos\theta + k_s I_l \, (N \cdot H)^{n_s} \tag{8}$$

$$H = \frac{L + V}{2} \tag{9}$$

where I is the intensity of the reflected light, $I_{ambdiff}$ is the intensity of the interaction between the diffuse material and the ambient light, I_{diff} is the intensity of the interaction between the diffuse material and the directional light, and I_{spec} is the intensity of the interaction between the specular material and the directional light. k_a, k_d, and k_s ($0 < k < 1$) are the reflection coefficients for ambient light, diffuse reflection, and specular reflection, respectively. I_a represents the intensity of the point light source, θ represents the angle between the incident light direction and the vertex normal, n represents the specular exponent, and N represents the unit normal vector at the incident point. H denotes the intermediate vector between the light direction L and the view direction V.

2.2.6. Unreal Engine UAV Flight Simulation

Unreal Engine can provide a virtual environment for simulating UAVs' process. In this study, we initially utilized UE4 to simulate the topographical environment of the landslide (Section 2.1) and configure prebuilt scenes. Visualizing the motion of UAVs required adjustments to texture mapping materials and lighting to ensure a realistic simulation. It was essential to establish seamless communication between the constructed landslide model and the 3D environment. Following this, AirSim utilized modules designed for modeling camera sensors. Virtual UAVs were equipped with cameras and LiDAR sensors, placed within the landslide scenario, and sensor data synthesis or detection was achieved.

Subsequently, AirSim's API and ABI interfaces were called to provide simulated environmental sensor information to the UAV flight controller during the simulation process. The flight control layer then generated control signals for the UAV model. And the obtained model was stored in the flight system for subsequent route planning and acquisition of high-quality images from the simulated environment (Section 2.3).

2.3. *UAV Flight Route Planning*

2.3.1. Traditional Flight Route Planning

At present, there are various common UAV route planning schemes, such as single horizontal, vertical, and zigzag patterns [42]. These planning schemes can be applied to different terrain conditions and flight missions to meet various task requirements. Single horizontal and vertical line layouts are relatively straightforward but come with certain drawbacks, such as inadequate coverage and overlap, which can affect the quality and accuracy of map data. In some cases, diagonal layouts are necessary to accommodate irregularly shaped areas or complex terrain. The crisscross pattern involves laying out flight paths in a grid-like manner across the target area, allowing the UAV to fly sequentially over each intersection point to complete the entire area's mission. The crisscross patterns can be further refined based on the first two layouts to ensure both heading and lateral overlap, thereby enhancing image quality and effectively avoiding omissions and duplicate captures, thereby improving the efficiency and accuracy of the mission. However, it remains challenging to apply this method flexibly in complex terrain conditions. Figure 4 shows different kinds of traditional flight path planning methods.

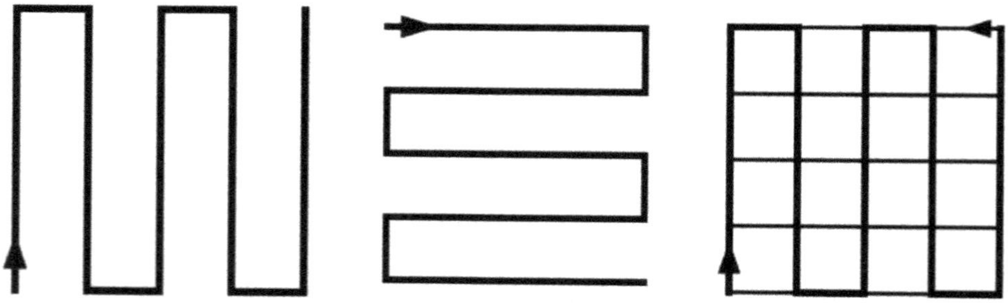

(a) (b) (c)

Figure 4. Traditional flight route planning methods: (**a**) single horizontal flight route; (**b**) vertical flight route; (**c**) grid or zigzag pattern flight route.

2.3.2. Novel Route Planning

Traditional UAV route planning methods fall short in capturing the vertical details of landslides and encounter issues such as the failure of 3D densification computation. In this study, a novel terrain-following flight approach is proposed. It necessitates continuous images with a specific ratio of heading and lateral overlap during the flight, and it demands simultaneous image capture of the landslide area to obtain higher-quality 3D textures. Otherwise, unrelated shadows or reduced visual disparities could degrade the model reconstruction quality. The method first utilizes UAV oblique photogrammetry to generate a digital elevation model (DEM) of the target area and subsequently generates contour lines with 30 m spacing to depict terrain contours optimally. Using contour lines to design UAV routes allows for better representation of variations in terrain elevation. Contour line density can be controlled by the route density, with higher contour line densities requiring more routes. Typically, DEM-generated contour lines exhibit numerous inflection points and complexity. Planning routes directly based on these contour lines would increase the UAV's energy consumption, thus reducing its flight endurance. Frequent changes in direction could also adversely affect flight safety. In practice, both flight endurance and safety are critical factors for UAVs. Therefore, contour lines must be smoothed to better support route planning and flights. This study employs the Douglas–Peucker algorithm [43] to smooth the contour lines, reducing the number of inflection points, lowering computational complexity, and enhancing route planning efficiency. Subsequently, contour lines are stretched based on factors such as object heights and UAV flight altitudes to achieve the conversion from contour lines to UAV routes. Figure 5 shows the key steps of the novel route planning method.

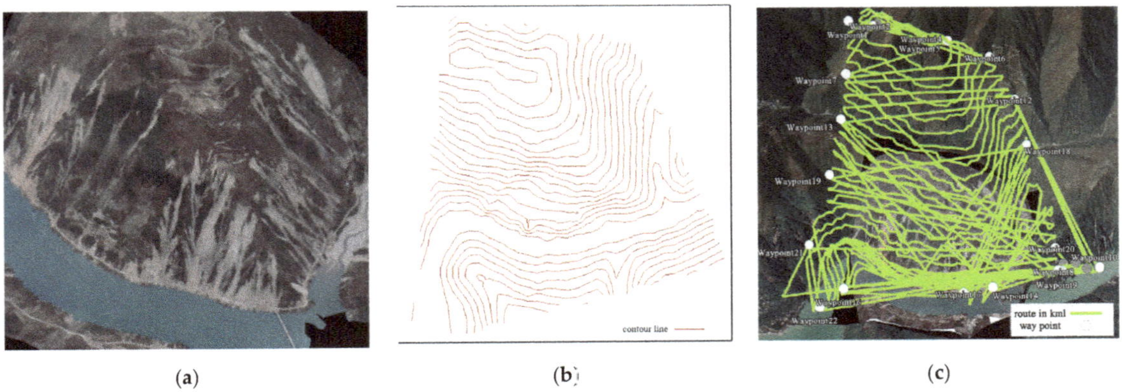

Figure 5. The main steps of the novel route planning method: (**a**) orthorectified image of the survey area; (**b**) contour map (in SHP format); (**c**) UAV flight route (in KML format).

3. Experiment and Results

To ensure the visual realism of the experimental scene, the safety of UAV flight, and to test the accuracy of the flight path planning method, this experiment combines the power of Unreal Engine and AirSim for validation. Firstly, landslide datasets are acquired and utilized for 3D reconstruction, creating a simulated terrain model. Subsequently, Unreal Engine is leveraged to fine tune the lighting and textures, enhancing the simulated environment to closely resemble reality, and AirSim is employed for UAV flight path simulation. Ultimately, validating the correctness of the flight path planning algorithm.

3.1. Data Set

In this study, two sets of landslide image data were obtained from the SkyPixel website [44]. These images capture two typical landslide incidents in the vicinity of Lianhe Village, Luding County, Ganzi Prefecture, Sichuan Province. Figure 4 shows the original images of the composite and steep types of landslides. The composite landslide is composed of a variety of landslide types such as notch, bulge, and fracture. They change from the slope slide to rock mass slide or collapse. The steep landslides are convex structures with steep slopes. With fast sliding speed, the sliding will be accompanied by large noise and vibration. The original videos possess a frame rate of 30 frames per second with a size of 1920×1080 pixels and last for a duration of 25 s. To reduce the processing workload of analyzing all frames in the video, 100 images were extracted from each video at a time interval of 0.25 s. Figure 6 shows the original images of the two types of landslide.

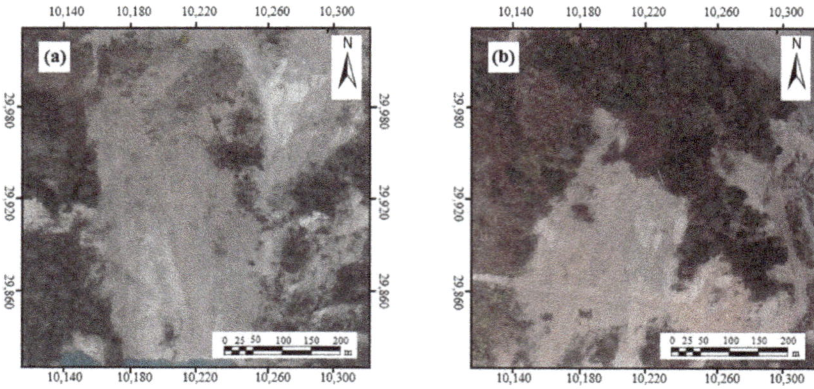

Figure 6. The original landslide image: (**a**) compound-type landslide; (**b**) steep-type landslide.

3.2. Landslide Model Construction

Firstly, aerial triangulation techniques were used to generate dense point clouds, and irregular triangulated meshes were created based on the point cloud data. Secondly, the texture of the landslide was obtained from the aerial images. However, there were noticeable color differences between the texture maps obtained from the landslide images and the terrain scene texture maps. These differences manifested as higher exposure, brighter colors, lower contrast, and lower saturation. To achieve color consistency between the two texture maps, the color matching method was employed, which successfully aligned the color information of the terrain scene texture map with that of the landslide texture map. Subsequently, the landslide model and its texture map were unified to the WGS-84 coordinate system, and texture mapping was employed to seamlessly apply the texture to the landslide model. Through this process, a final output of a highly realistic 3D model of the landslides was obtained.

To achieve seamless height blending between the landslide model and the terrain scene, as well as to apply the appropriate material to the landslide model in Unreal Engine, a material sphere was meticulously constructed and subsequently assigned to the landslide model. In cases where the model displays pronounced specular highlights under scene lighting, it becomes essential to fine tune the roughness and metallic parameters of the material to minimize the intensity of reflections. The resulting landslide model crafted through this experimental process, is illustrated in Figure 7.

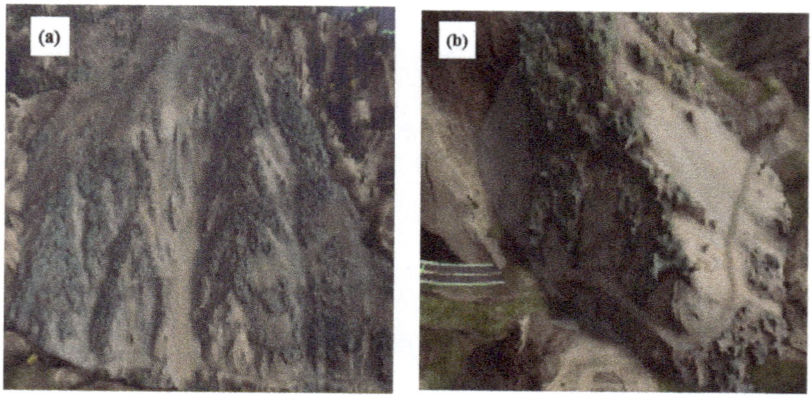

Figure 7. Slide model: (**a**) compound-type landslide; (**b**) steep-type landslide.

3.3. UAV Flight Path Planning Simulation Implementation

In this study, the flight path algorithm for the compound-type landslide was initially simulated and validated. Following this, a second validation was conducted using the steep-type landslide with the same novel method to ensure the algorithm's applicability across various landslide scenarios and to verify the realism and efficacy of the simulation framework.

Utilizing the previously constructed terrain scene, the UAV flight path planning method was introduced for simulation in this experiment. The UAV was tasked to follow the meticulously planned flight path, capturing image data of the simulated experimental scene during the flight. Subsequently, the captured image data was used for the 3D reconstruction of the simulated terrain scene. Firstly, flight paths were meticulously planned for both the composite-type and steep-type landslides using both the traditional horizontal flight surface mode and the novel terrain-following method proposed in this paper. Subsequently, the UAV followed the predefined flight paths and systematically collected images of the experimental scene at regular time intervals within the simulation framework to obtain DEM data of the landslide area.

During the image collection process, ensuring consistent heading overlap was of paramount importance, and the camera tilt angle was set to be vertically downward. The relevant parameters for UAV flight were thoughtfully configured, as illustrated in Table 2.

Table 2. Flight parameter setting.

Type of Landslide	Flying Height/m	Route Mode	Flight Runtime/s	Time Interval/s	Flight Distance/m	Ground Resolution/cm/px	Number of Images/Sheet
Compound type	0–360	traditional method	256	2	1024	10.6	128
		Novel method	250		1024	8	125
Steep type	0–200	traditional method	264	3	1024	11.92	88
		Novel method	255		1024	7	85

The obtained image data was processed to generate a real point cloud based on the actual images. Subsequently, a dense reconstruction process was employed to produce a high-resolution dense point cloud complemented by authentic textures, resulting in a 3D model with high-resolution and authentic textures. To evaluate the models reconstructed using the two flight path planning methods, a thorough examination of texture details was conducted. This analysis served to validate the advantages of the novel terrain-following flight path method and assess the overall quality of the simulation framework. Figure 8 presents the results of the 3D reconstruction using different methods.

3.4. Result

3.4.1. 3D Model Completeness

In this experiment, we initially evaluate the merits of the two different methods in a qualitative manner, and meticulously compared the 3D models of the landslides generated by the two different flight path planning methods. The evaluation focused on two crucial aspects: overall completeness and local feature details.

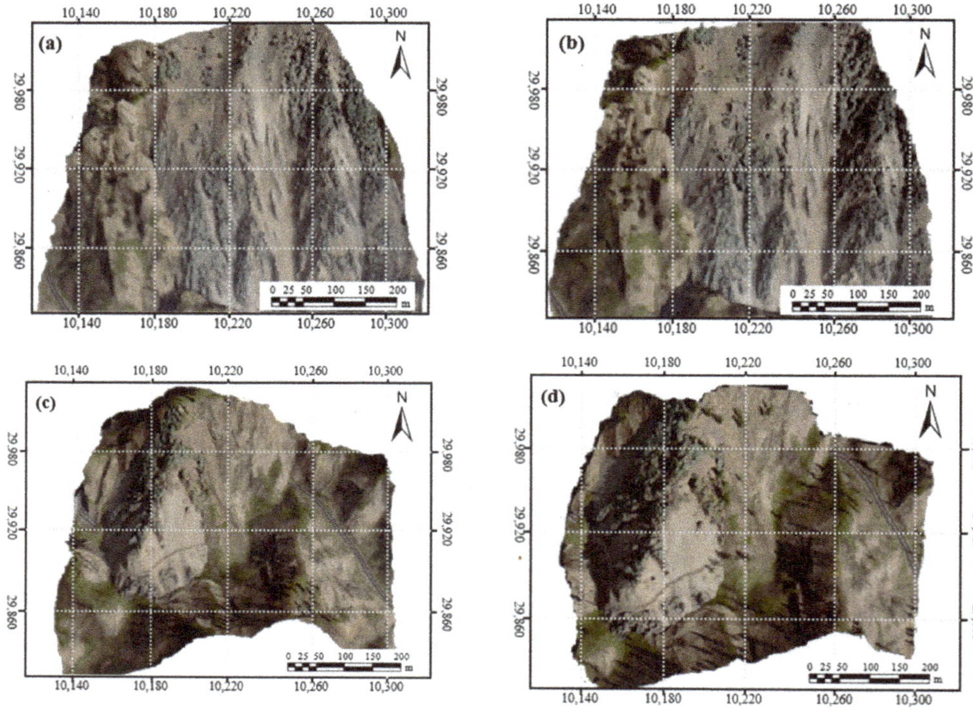

Figure 8. 3D reconstruction model: (**a**) model of compound-type landslide with traditional method; (**b**) model of compound-type landslide with novel method; (**c**) model of steed-type landslide with traditional method; (**d**) model of steed-type landslide with novel method.

In terms of overall completeness, both flight path planning methods accurately reproduced the overall shape of the landslides, without any significant details missing or shape distortions observed in either case. The models exhibited a faithful representation of the landslide topography, validating the effectiveness of both methods in capturing the general shape of the terrain. However, when evaluating local feature details, noteworthy differences emerged between the two approaches. The traditional terrain-following flight path method often resulted in slightly blurry ground information and exhibited some deformation in vegetation. In contrast, the 3D reconstruction results using the novel terrain-following flight path design method showed higher overall resolution and clearer ground details. The novel method remarkably captured vegetation coverage and rock distribution characteristics with exceptional fidelity, revealing minimal deformation in vegetation and rocks. These observations demonstrate the superior model reconstruction effects offered by the novel terrain-following flight path method. Figure 9 represents the two types of landslide local details.

The experiment highlights the advantages of the proposed terrain-following flight path design method in attaining higher-quality 3D reconstruction results, effectively capturing intricate local features and producing more realistic and visually appealing models of the landslides.

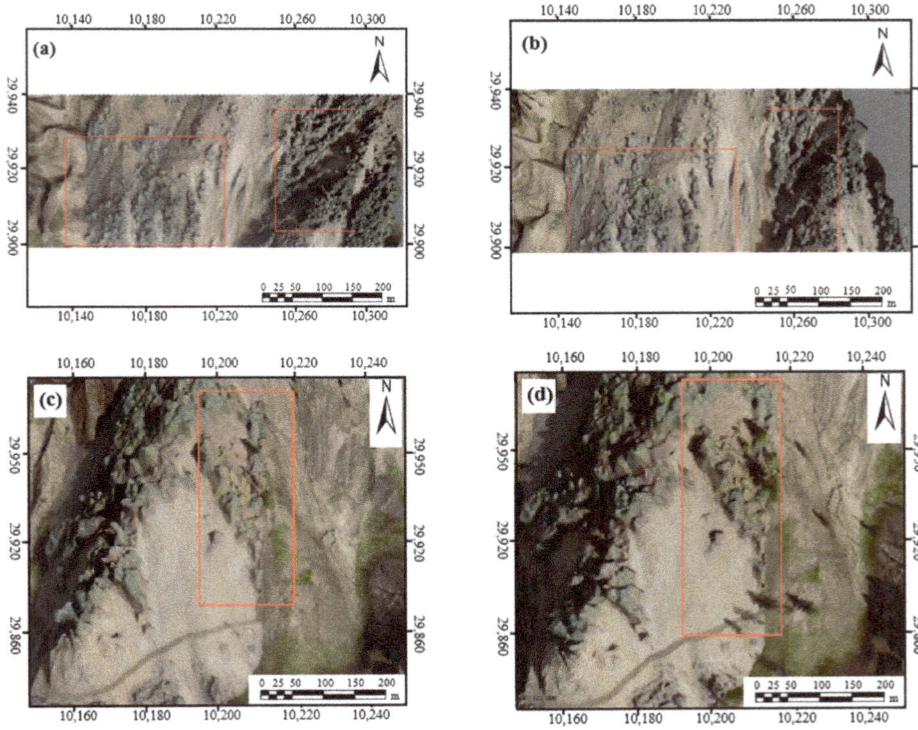

Figure 9. Landslide local details: (**a**) traditional method used in compound-type landslide; (**b**) novel method used in compound-type landslide; (**c**) traditional method used in steed-type landslide; (**d**) novel method used in steed-type landslide.

3.4.2. 3D Model Accuracy

Subsequently, we quantitatively compare the two different methods. We selected the RMSE as the analytical indicator. The most crucial aspect of the landslide model is to ensure its geometric accuracy while reproducing the real form. In this experiment, the length and width information of the landslides obtained from the image maps were taken as the actual values, while the corresponding geometric length values on the 3D models were considered as the measured values. By computing the root-mean-square error, the experiment was able to quantify the level of accuracy achieved by the 3D models in replicating the geometric attributes of the landslides, providing a quantitative measure of the model's fidelity to the real-world topography. The formula is as follows:

$$RMSE = \sqrt{\frac{\sum_{i=1}^{n}(l' - l)^2}{n}} \tag{10}$$

where $RMSE$ represents the root-mean-square Error, l denotes the actual value, and l' represents the measured value, n represents the number of measured edges.

The calculation results of the geometric length RMSE for different flight path planning methods are presented in Table 3. The table reveals that the 3D model accuracy of both methods ranging from 10 to 14 cm. Specifically, the traditional flight path approach results in model accuracy between 12 and 14 cm, while the novel flight path method improves model accuracy to the range of 10 to 11 cm. Notably, the 3D models generated using the novel terrain-following flight path method demonstrated significantly higher precision, with the novel method outperforming the traditional one by 2 to 3 cm in precision. Among them, the compound-type landslide model reconstructed using the novel terrain-following flight path algorithm achieved the highest accuracy, with an RMSE of 10.807 cm. Conversely, the 3D models generated using the traditional flight path planning approach displayed noticeable issues, including overall distortion, loss of texture, and displacement of details. As a result, these models exhibited larger measured errors in geometric length, indicating a comparatively lower level of accuracy in replicating the real-world topography.

Table 3. RMSE of 3D models generated via different routes.

Type of Landslide	Route Type	RMSE/cm
Compound type	Traditional method	12.457
	Novel method	10.807
Steep type	Traditional method	13.684
	Novel method	11.121

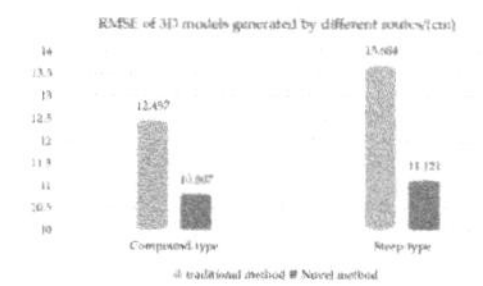

The observed improvement in RMSE is statistically significant, indicating the superiority of the proposed flight path approach in terms of monitoring precision. In the context of geological hazard monitoring, even minor improvements can have a crucial impact on accuracy, enabling monitoring agencies to better predict and respond to geological disasters. The refined accuracy offered by the novel flight path method is paramount in enhancing the overall efficacy of geological hazard monitoring efforts. Its 2 to 3 cm accuracy improvement is important for making quick decisions and taking action in emergency situations. Furthermore, the quantitative analysis using RMSE as the evaluation metric provides a robust foundation for assessing the performance of the two methods. The narrower range and lower values of RMSE associated with the novel flight path approach highlight its superiority in capturing the intricacies of the terrain and geological features. This reduction in RMSE reflects a more faithful representation of the actual landscape, emphasizing the method's capability to produce highly accurate three-dimensional models.

The results above clearly demonstrate the substantial improvement achieved by the novel terrain-following flight path method in terms of geometric precision, making contributions to attain more reliable and precise 3D reconstructions of landslide scenarios.

Additionally, the novel terrain-following flight path algorithm was found to reduce the total flight time by 9.3% compared to the traditional algorithm, which partly alleviates the issue of UAV endurance, allowing for more efficient and extended data collection periods during flight operations. Moreover, the simulation results for the steep-type landslide scene were found to be in line with those of the composite-type landslide scene. This observation underscores the versatility and applicability of the method employed in this study, demonstrating its effectiveness in addressing different landslide scenarios.

In conclusion, the combination of improved flight efficiency and consistent performance across diverse landslide scenarios highlights the potential of the novel terrain-following flight path algorithm as a valuable tool for UAV-based terrain data acquisition and 3D modeling in landslide monitoring and analysis applications, simultaneously confirming the practicability and authenticity of the simulation framework proposed in this paper.

4. Discussion

In this study, we propose a low-cost UAV flight path validation method based on Unreal Engine and AirSim. This method allows for the testing of various flight path algorithms within a preconstructed landslide simulation scene, ultimately resulting in safe flight paths for efficiently acquiring the necessary imagery for 3D modeling in complex environments. Compared to conducting UAV flights directly in the field with unvalidated flight paths, this approach offers high fault tolerance and cost effectiveness and significantly reduces the risk of UAV damage due to the complexity of the landslide scenario or potential parameter errors.

In contrast to some other UAV simulation frameworks, Unreal Engine stands out for its capability to create complex and highly realistic scenes, providing cross-framework compatibility across various hardware and operating systems. Combined with AirSim, it enables the creation of UAV motion planning with support for motion capture, providing the information caught by the sensors to UAV flight controllers obtained from the simulation environment, ensuring the realism and effectiveness of the simulation. In the landslide 3D reconstruction experiments, this study utilized two sets of typical landslide images from the vicinity of Lianhe Village, Luding County, Ganzi Prefecture, Sichuan Province, to construct high-accuracy compound-type and steep-type landslide scenes, meeting the requirements for subsequent UAV flight path planning simulations.

In the UAV flight path planning simulation experiments, flight path validation was conducted for both types of landslide scenarios, successfully demonstrating the applicability of our proposed method to different landslide scenes. Traditional contour-based UAV flight path planning leads to frequent sharp turns. To reduce computational complexity and enhance UAV flight efficiency, we applied the Douglas–Peucker algorithm to smooth the contour lines and stretch them to optimize flight paths within the landslide scenarios. The results indicate that both flight path design solutions are safe and accurately reproduce the overall morphology of the landslides. Compared to traditional flight path planning methods, the new approach is better suited for landslide terrain, resulting in higher-resolution and clearer ground detail models. Additionally, the new flight path requires less time by 9.3%, resulting in higher overall 3D model accuracy.

Apart from the studies discussed above, the safety of UAV is a critical issue. Prior studies have noted the importance of drone route safety. In the simulation framework of this study, adaptive adjustments can be made to UAV parameters, camera parameters, and the quality of generated images. Factors such as the flight speed of the UAV, safe clearance from on-site obstacles, and minimum altitude above ground can all be considered in the virtual scene. Due to the limited battery capacity of UAVs, which decreases with battery aging, the flight duration of UAVs is restricted.

Furthermore, the proposed method allows for further adjustments to the flight time and path, placing suitable image acquisition viewpoints at key locations to enhance the quality of model reconstruction. It can avoid occlusion or collision caused by on-site obstacles, guaranteeing the safety of the UAV and the quality of the captured images. Importing the optimized flight path parameters into the UAV effectively reduces costs and risks during actual flights, improving landslide monitoring efficiency and accuracy.

5. Conclusions

This study aimed to address the challenges and complexities associated with UAV flights in landslide areas. By integrating Unreal Engine and AirSim, the researchers successfully implemented UAV flight path planning and simulation. The simulation framework allowed for the creation of a realistic landslide model and enabled the design and execution of UAV flight paths within the simulated environment. The captured images during the UAV flight simulation were then utilized for precise 3D reconstruction, and the reconstructed models were evaluated based on their texture details. The experimental results demonstrated that the simulation framework developed in this study provided a favorable environment for conducting UAV flight path planning and simulation experiments.

Additionally, the proposed novel terrain-following UAV flight path planning method outperformed the traditional approach, resulting in finer texture details with an accuracy of 10.807 cm, which affirms the correctness of the flight path algorithm. The establishment of the UAV flight path simulation framework contributes to timely and efficient emergency response in the event of landslide disasters. Furthermore, the validated flight path algorithm ensures accurate flight path planning, leading to reduced costs and risks during real UAV flights, and enhances the efficiency of landslide monitoring. The application of this framework and validated flight path algorithm in natural disaster scenarios promises to make a valuable impact in mitigating and managing landslide events.

Author Contributions: Conceptualization, D.X., R.H. and C.W.; methodology, D.X., R.H. and C.W.; software, D.X. and R.H.; investigation, D.X. and R.H.; formal analysis, D.X. and R.H.; writing—original draft preparation, D.X. and R.H.; and writing—review and editing, D.X., R.H., C.W., C.Z., H.X. and Q.L. All authors have read and agreed to the published version of the manuscript.

Funding: The work is jointly supported by the Chang'an University (Xi'an, China) through the National Key Research and Development Program of China (Grant No. 2020YFC1512001), the Shenzhen Scientific Research and the Development Funding Programmes (Grant No. RCYX20210706092140076), the Open Research Fund from Guangdong Laboratory of Artificial Intelligence and Digital Economy (SZ) (Grant No. GML-KF-22-15), the National Natural Science Foundation of China (Grant No. 42374018) and Open Research Fund of State Key Laboratory of Subtropical Building and Urban Science (Grant No. 2022ZB04).

Data Availability Statement: The data generated and analyzed during this study are available from the corresponding author on request.

Conflicts of Interest: The authors declare no conflict of interest.

References

1. Yao, W.; Li, C.; Zhan, H.; Zhou, J.-Q.; Criss, R.E.; Xiong, S.; Jiang, X. Multiscale Study of Physical and Mechanical Properties of Sandstone in Three Gorges Reservoir Region Subjected to Cyclic Wetting–Drying of Yangtze River Water. *Rock. Mech. Rock. Eng.* **2020**, *53*, 2215–2231. [CrossRef]
2. Guzzetti, F.; Gariano, S.L.; Peruccacci, S.; Brunetti, M.T.; Marchesini, I.; Rossi, M.; Melillo, M. Geographical Landslide Early Warning Systems. *Earth-Sci. Rev.* **2020**, *200*, 102973. [CrossRef]
3. Gariano, S.L.; Guzzetti, F. Landslides in a Changing Climate. *Earth-Sci. Rev.* **2016**, *162*, 227–252. [CrossRef]
4. Nguyen, B.-Q.-V.; Kim, Y.-T. Regional-Scale Landslide Risk Assessment on Mt. Umyeon Using Risk Index Estimation. *Landslides* **2021**, *18*, 2547–2564. [CrossRef]
5. Chen, G.; Meng, X.; Qiao, L.; Zhang, Y.; Wang, S. Response of a Loess Landslide to Rainfall: Observations from a Field Artificial Rainfall Experiment in Bailong River Basin, China. *Landslides* **2018**, *15*, 895–911. [CrossRef]
6. Tang, Y.; Feng, F.; Guo, Z.; Feng, W.; Li, Z.; Wang, J.; Sun, Q.; Ma, H.; Li, Y. Integrating Principal Component Analysis with Statistically-Based Models for Analysis of Causal Factors and Landslide Susceptibility Mapping: A Comparative Study from the Loess Plateau Area in Shanxi (China). *J. Clean. Prod.* **2020**, *277*, 124159. [CrossRef]
7. Huang, Y.; Zhao, L. Review on Landslide Susceptibility Mapping Using Support Vector Machines. *Catena* **2018**, *165*, 520–529. [CrossRef]
8. Wang, C.; Chang, L.; Wang, X.; Zhang, B.; Stein, A. A Review of InSAR Statistical Inference in Deformation Measurement and Geophysical Inversion. *IEEE Geosci. Remote Sens. Mag.*.
9. Teo, T.-A.; Fu, Y.-J.; Li, K.-W.; Weng, M.-C.; Yang, C.-M. Comparison between Image-and Surface-Derived Displacement Fields for Landslide Monitoring Using an Unmanned Aerial Vehicle. *Int. J. Appl. Earth Obs. Geoinf.* **2023**, *116*, 103164. [CrossRef]
10. Kaleem, Z.; Rehmani, M.H. Amateur Drone Monitoring: State-of-the-Art Architectures, Key Enabling Technologies, and Future Research Directions. *IEEE Wirel. Commun.* **2018**, *25*, 150–159. [CrossRef]
11. Khachumov, M.; Khachumov, V. Optimization Models of UAV Route Planning For Forest Fire Monitoring. In Proceedings of the 2022 International Russian Automation Conference (RusAutoCon), Sochi, Russian, 4–10 September 2022; IEEE: New York, NY, USA, 2022; pp. 272–277.
12. Zhou, Z.; Feng, J.; Gu, B.; Ai, B.; Mumtaz, S.; Rodriguez, J.; Guizani, M. When Mobile Crowd Sensing Meets UAV: Energy-Efficient Task Assignment and Route Planning. *IEEE Trans. Commun.* **2018**, *66*, 5526–5538. [CrossRef]
13. Kim, S.-H.; Padilla, G.E.G.; Kim, K.-J.; Yu, K.-H. Flight Path Planning for a Solar Powered UAV in Wind Fields Using Direct Collocation. *IEEE Trans. Aerosp. Electron. Syst.* **2020**, *56*, 1094–1105. [CrossRef]

14. Battulwar, R.; Winkelmaier, G.; Valencia, J.; Naghadehi, M.Z.; Peik, B.; Abbasi, B.; Parvin, B.; Sattarvand, J. A Practical Methodology for Generating High-Resolution 3D Models of Open-Pit Slopes Using UAVs: Flight Path Planning and Optimization. *Remote Sens.* **2020**, *12*, 2283. [CrossRef]
15. D'Urso, F.; Santoro, C.; Santoro, F.F. An Integrated Framework for the Realistic Simulation of Multi-UAV Applications. *Comput. Electr. Eng.* **2019**, *74*, 196–209. [CrossRef]
16. Shao, X.; Shi, Y.; Zhang, W. Fault-Tolerant Quantized Control for Flexible Air-Breathing Hypersonic Vehicles with Appointed-Time Tracking Performances. *IEEE Trans. Aerosp. Electron. Syst.* **2020**, *57*, 1261–1273. [CrossRef]
17. Hentati, A.I.; Krichen, L.; Fourati, M.; Fourati, L.C. Simulation Tools, Environments and Frameworks for UAV Systems Performance Analysis. In Proceedings of the 2018 14th International Wireless Communications & Mobile Computing Conference (IWCMC), Limassol, Cyprus, 25–29 June 2018; IEEE: New York, NY, USA, 2018; pp. 1495–1500.
18. X-Plane 12 Flight Simulator—X-Plane. Available online: https://www.x-plane.com/ (accessed on 27 September 2023).
19. Wang, Z.; Li, J. 3D Simulation of Flight Control System for Quad Tilt Rotor UAV Based on Flightgear. *IOP Conf. Ser. Earth Environ. Sci.* **2020**, *440*, 052056. [CrossRef]
20. Gazebo. Available online: https://gazebosim.org/home (accessed on 27 September 2023).
21. Matlekovic, L.; Juric, F.; Schneider-Kamp, P. Microservices for Autonomous UAV Inspection with UAV Simulation as a Service. *Simul. Model. Pract. Theory* **2022**, *119*, 102548. [CrossRef]
22. Ling, H.; Luo, H.; Chen, H.; Bai, L.; Zhu, T.; Wang, Y. Modelling and Simulation of Distributed UAV Swarm Cooperative Planning and Perception. *Int. J. Aerosp. Eng.* **2021**, *2021*, 9977262. [CrossRef]
23. Fernando, H.; De Silva, A.T.A.; De Zoysa, M.D.C.; Dilshan, K.; Munasinghe, S.R. Modelling, Simulation and Implementation of a Quadrotor UAV. In Proceedings of the 2013 IEEE 8th International Conference on Industrial and Information Systems, Peradeniya, Sri Lanka, 17–20 December 2013; IEEE: New York, NY, USA, 2013; pp. 207–212.
24. Park, S.; Lee, S.; Im, B.; Lee, D.; Shin, S. Improvement of a Multi-Rotor UAV Flight Response Simulation Influenced by Gust. *Aerosp. Sci. Technol.* **2023**, *134*, 108156. [CrossRef]
25. Song, Y.; Naji, S.; Kaufmann, E.; Loquercio, A.; Scaramuzza, D. Flightmare: A Flexible Quadrotor Simulator. In Proceedings of the 2020 Conference on Robot Learning, PMLR, Cambridge MA, USA, 4 October 2021; pp. 1147–1157.
26. Benjamin, A.R.; O'Brien, D.; Barnes, G.; Wilkinson, B.E.; Volkmann, W. Improving Data Acquisition Efficiency: Systematic Accuracy Evaluation of GNSS-Assisted Aerial Triangulation in UAS Operations. *J. Surv. Eng.* **2020**, *146*, 05019006. [CrossRef]
27. Wen, X.; Xie, H.; Liu, H.; Yan, L. Accurate Reconstruction of the LoD3 Building Model by Integrating Multi-Source Point Clouds and Oblique Remote Sensing Imagery. *ISPRS Int. J. Geo-Inf.* **2019**, *8*, 135. [CrossRef]
28. Xiong, C.; Lu, X.; Huang, J.; Guan, H. Multi-LOD Seismic-Damage Simulation of Urban Buildings and Case Study in Beijing CBD. *Bull. Earthquake Eng.* **2019**, *17*, 2037–2057. [CrossRef]
29. Yijun, Z.; Jiadong, X.; Chen, L. A Fast Bi-Directional A* Algorithm Based on Quad-Tree Decomposition and Hierarchical Map. *IEEE Access* **2021**, *9*, 102877–102885. [CrossRef]
30. Chen, Q.; Liu, G.; Ma, X.; Mariethoz, G.; He, Z.; Tian, Y.; Weng, Z. Local Curvature Entropy-Based 3D Terrain Representation Using a Comprehensive Quadtree. *ISPRS J. Photogramm. Remote Sens.* **2018**, *139*, 30–45. [CrossRef]
31. Qiu, W.; Yuille, A. Unrealcv: Connecting Computer Vision to Unreal Engine. In Proceedings of the Computer Vision–ECCV 2016 Workshops, Amsterdam, The Netherlands, 8–10, 15–16 October 2016; Part III 14. Springer: Berlin/Heidelberg, Germany, 2016; pp. 909–916.
32. Shah, S.; Dey, D.; Lovett, C.; Kapoor, A. Airsim: High-Fidelity Visual and Physical Simulation for Autonomous Vehicles. In Proceedings of the Field and Service Robotics: Results of the 11th International Conference, Zurich, Switzerland, 12–15 September 2017; pp. 621–635.
33. AirSim. Available online: https://github.com/microsoft/AirSim/ (accessed on 28 September 2023).
34. Li, Z.; Zhang, Y.-D. 3D Reconstruction Method of Forest Landscape Based on Virtual Reality. *Multimed. Tools Appl.* **2020**, *79*, 16369–16383. [CrossRef]
35. Sanchez, G.M.E.; Van Renterghem, T.; Sun, K.; De Coensel, B.; Botteldooren, D. Using Virtual Reality for Assessing the Role of Noise in the Audio-Visual Design of an Urban Public Space. *Landsc. Urban. Plan.* **2017**, *167*, 98–107. [CrossRef]
36. Gil-Tena, A.; Aquilué, N.; Duane, A.; De Cáceres, M.; Brotons, L. Mediterranean Fire Regime Effects on Pine-Oak Forest Landscape Mosaics under Global Change in NE Spain. *Eur. J. For. Res.* **2016**, *135*, 403–416. [CrossRef]
37. Xu, Y.; Zhu, X.; Shi, J.; Zhang, G.; Bao, H.; Li, H. Depth Completion From Sparse LiDAR Data With Depth-Normal Constraints. In Proceedings of the 2019 IEEE/CVF International Conference on Computer Vision (ICCV), Seoul, Republic of Korea, 27 October–2 November 2019; pp. 2811–2820.
38. Shen, J.; Cashman, T.J.; Ye, Q.; Hutton, T.; Sharp, T.; Bogo, F.; Fitzgibbon, A.; Shotton, J. The Phong Surface: Efficient 3D Model Fitting Using Lifted Optimization. In *Computer Vision—ECCV 2020*; Vedaldi, A., Bischof, H., Brox, T., Frahm, J.-M., Eds.; Lecture Notes in Computer Science; Springer International Publishing: Cham, Switzerland, 2020; Volume 12346, pp. 687–703. ISBN 978-3-030-58451-1.
39. Gao, Y.; Li, Q.; Yan, B.; Guo, S. A Blinn-Phong Light Enhancement Algorithm Based on the Gradient of Voxel. In Proceedings of the 2019 International Conference on Computer, Network, Communication and Information Systems (CNCI 2019), Qingdao, China, 27–29 March 2019; Atlantis Press: Amsterdam, The Netherlands, 2019; pp. 17–23.

40. Sun, L.; Liang, Y. The Impact Factor Analysis on the Improved Cook-Torrance Bidirectional Reflectance Distribution Function of Rough Surfaces. In *Proceedings of the Fifth Euro-China Conference on Intelligent Data Analysis and Applications*; Krömer, P., Zhang, H., Liang, Y., Pan, J.-S., Eds.; Advances in Intelligent Systems and Computing; Springer International Publishing: Cham, Switzerland, 2019; Volume 891, pp. 463–470. ISBN 978-3-030-03765-9.
41. Jiddi, S.; Robert, P.; Marchand, E. Detecting Specular Reflections and Cast Shadows to Estimate Reflectance and Illumination of Dynamic Indoor Scenes. *IEEE Trans. Visual. Comput. Graphics* **2022**, *28*, 1249–1260. [CrossRef]
42. He, T.; Zeng, Y.; Hu, Z. Research of Multi-Rotor UAVs Detailed Autonomous Inspection Technology of Transmission Lines Based on Route Planning. *IEEE Access* **2019**, *7*, 114955–114965. [CrossRef]
43. Liu, J.; Li, H.; Yang, Z.; Wu, K.; Liu, Y.; Liu, R.W. Adaptive Douglas-Peucker Algorithm with Automatic Thresholding for AIS-Based Vessel Trajectory Compression. *IEEE Access* **2019**, *7*, 150677–150692. [CrossRef]
44. Skypixel. Available online: https://www.skypixel.com/ (accessed on 28 September 2023).

remote sensing

MDPI

Article

Coseismic Deformation, Fault Slip Distribution, and Coulomb Stress Perturbation of the 2023 Türkiye-Syria Earthquake Doublet Based on SAR Offset Tracking

Wan Wang [1,2], Yunhua Liu [1,*], Xiaoran Fan [1], Chao Ma [2] and Xinjian Shan [1]

[1] State Key Laboratory of Earthquake Dynamics, Institute of Geology, China Earthquake Administration, Beijing 100029, China; wangw@ies.ac.cn (W.W.); fbb1108@ies.ac.cn (X.F.); xjshan@163.com (X.S.)
[2] School of Surveying and Land Information Engineering, Henan Polytechnic University, Jiaozuo 454003, China; mac@hpu.edu.cn
* Correspondence: liuyunhua@ies.ac.cn; Tel.: +86-(10)-62009346

Abstract: The Türkiye-Syria earthquake doublet of 6 February 2023 (Mw 7.8 at 01:17 UTC and Mw 7.6 at 10:24 UTC) resulted in extensive damage and tens of thousands of casualties. We present the surface displacements of the two earthquakes from synthetic aperture radar (SAR) offset tracking measurements. We extracted the geometric parameters of the rupture faults from the surface displacements and early aftershock distribution, based on which we inverted the coseismic slip distributions. We then calculated Coulomb stress to investigate the triggering relationship between the earthquakes and stress transfer to neighbouring faults and regions. The coseismic ruptures of the earthquake doublet were predominantly left-lateral strike-slip motions distributed between 0 and 15 km depth. The maximum fault slip reached > 8 m (Mw 7.8) and almost 10 m (Mw 7.6). The coseismic deformation and fault slip motion are consistent with the overall westward extrusion of the Anatolian Plate relative to the Eurasian and Arabian plates. The Mw 7.8 earthquake increased Coulomb failure stress at the hypocenter of the Mw 7.6 earthquake, implying that the Mw 7.8 event had a strong positive causative effect. Moreover, coseismic stress perturbations revealed a positive Coulomb stress effect on the middle Puturge Fault, northern Dead Sea Fault Zone (DSFZ), Yesemek Fault, Antakya Fault, and Turkoglu Fault, indicating an increasing seismic hazard in these regions.

Keywords: 2023 Türkiye-Syria earthquake doublet; East Anatolian Fault Zone; SAR offset tracking; fault slip distribution; Coulomb stress changes

1. Introduction

A destructive earthquake doublet struck Türkiye and northern Syria on 6 February 2023. The powerful mainshock (Mw 7.8 at 01:17 UTC) triggered a series of aftershocks, including a magnitude Mw 7.6 earthquake that occurred ~9 h later at a distance of 95 km from the Mw 7.8 event. These events caused widespread damage and tens of thousands of casualties [1]. The Mw 7.8 earthquake initiated on the Narh Fault (NF) [2,3] and then ruptured bilaterally along the East Anatolian Fault Zone (EAFZ). The Mw 7.6 earthquake mainly occurred on the Cardak Fault (CF) and propagated bilaterally along the east-west direction [4–6]. The occurrence of two such large earthquakes (Mw > 7.5) on nearby faults within a few hours of each other is very rare.

This event follows a number of large earthquakes that occurred along the EAFZ in the 19th and 20th centuries, including the 1986 Mw 6.1, 2003 Mw 6.3, 2010 Mw 6.1, and 2020 Mw 6.8 earthquakes [7]. Most of these earthquakes occurred to the east of Erkenek [8]; in contrast, the fault to the west (the Pazarcık and Amanos segments) has been largely locked for more than a century and has accumulated a significant amount of energy.

Following the earthquake, comprehensive investigations have been undertaken to meticulously examine the rupture process and seismic tectonics of the twin earthquakes in Türkiye. Melgar et al. [5] used high-rate GNSS (HR-GNSS) recordings and synthetic aperture radar (SAR) images to perform a joint finite fault inversion and analyse rupture processes and velocities for the Mw 7.8 event. They found that the 2023 Mw 7.8 earthquake occurred in two phases and that a secondary structure (the NF) dominated the rupture onset. In addition, they discussed the supershear rupture states of both the Mw 7.8 and 7.6 earthquakes. Barbot et al. [4] used geodetic and seismic data to estimate the peak sliding, slip deficit fraction, and spatio-temporal characteristics of aftershocks for the Mw 7.8 and 7.6 earthquakes. Jia et al. [9] used HR-GNSS and strong motion data to determine the complex rupture histories, including sub-shear and supershear events. They mainly emphasised the role of fault interactions and the necessity of heterogeneous background stresses. Meng et al. [10] used long-range and local seismic data, HR-GNSS records, and SAR images to perform a joint finite fault inversion by means of slow-enhanced backpropagation in order to explore the rupture process of the Mw 7.8 earthquake. Through differential interferometric SAR (D-InSAR) processing of the 2023 Türkiye-Syria earthquake sequence, Mila et al. [11] provided an initial reference for ground deformation. Li et al. [12] analysed the surface displacement, co-seismic slip distribution, inter-seismic fault slip rates, locking depths, static Coulomb damage stress changes, and fault geometry using SAR images and Global Positioning System (GPS) data. An et al. [13] combined optical and SAR images to generate three-dimensional (3D) deformation fields for the two seismic events and focused on assessing the surface deformation.

These studies provide important constraints and account for the specificity of the 2023 earthquake sequence. However, further near-field observations are needed to refine the slip distribution, stress-triggering relationship between the earthquakes, and regional stress perturbations [14]. Moreover, analysing stress accumulation within this fault zone is needed to better understand the sequence of strong seismic activity and seismic hazards in the region. In this study, we used SAR data processed by pixel offset tracking technology to derive two-dimensional (2D) displacements of the 2023 Türkiye-Syria earthquake doublet (Figure 1). By analysing changes in displacements, we obtained the geometric characteristics and deformation magnitudes of the rupture faults. Then, we inverted the coseismic slip distribution of the earthquake sequence based on the homogeneous elastic half-space dislocation model. Finally, we analysed the fault motion, rupture patterns, and stress transfer. The results of this study provide new insights into the mechanisms of strong earthquakes and inter-plate motion in the EAFZ.

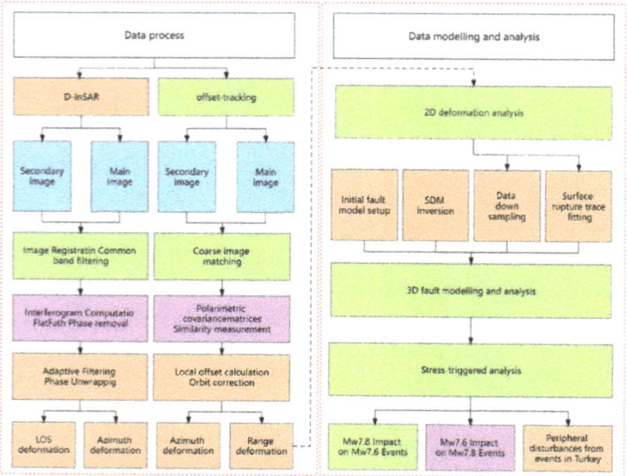

Figure 1. A workflow was used to study the 2023 Türkiye-Syria earthquake sequence. LOS deformation, line-of-sight deformation.

2. Materials and Methods

2.1. Tectonic Setting

The first event, which occurred at 01:17 UTC on 6 February 2023, had a magnitude of Mw 7.8, an epicentre located at 37.17°N and 37.03°E, and a focal depth of ~10 km (Table 1; https://earthquake.usgs.gov/, accessed on 20 February 2023). This powerful mainshock triggered a series of aftershocks, including a magnitude Mw 7.6 earthquake that occurred ~9 h later at a distance of 95 km from the Mw 7.8 event. Focal mechanism solutions indicate that the earthquake doublet was dominated by left-lateral strike-slip motion. The Mw 7.8 earthquake initiated on the NF [2,3] and then ruptured bilaterally along the EAFZ, consisting of two to four sub-events with a total duration of 20–80 s [8]. The Mw 7.6 earthquake mainly occurred on the Cardak Fault (CF) and propagated bilaterally along the east-west direction [4–6].

Table 1. Focal mechanism solutions for the 2023 Mw 7.8 Türkiye-Syria earthquake.

Orbit	Track	Azimuth Angle (°)	Incidence Angle (°)	Reference Image	Secondary Image
Ascending	T14	−22	39	28 January 2023	9 February 2023
	T116	−22	39	4 February 2023	28 February 2023
Descending	T21	−103	39	29 January 2023	10 February 2023

In terms of regional tectonics, the epicentral region is located near the triple junction of the Anatolian, Arabian, and Eurasian plates [11,12,15,16] (Figure 2). The Anatolian Plate, which lies between the other two plates, shows extrusive movement towards the Aegean Sea owing to the northward movement of the Arabian and Eurasian plates [4,17,18]. The active structures of Anatolia consist of the North Anatolian Fault Zone (NAFZ) and the EAFZ. As the boundary between the Anatolian and Eurasian plates, the NAFZ is dominated by left-lateral strike-slip motion [19]. Together with the EAFZ, it accommodates the counterclockwise movement of the Anatolian Plate towards the west. The EAFZ intersects the NAFZ at the Karliova triple junction and then extends southwestwards ~600 km to the Kahramanmaras triple junction near Antakya, where it joins the Dead Sea Fault Zone (DSFZ) [20]. The EAFZ mainly connects seven segments: Karlıova, Ilıca, Palu, Puturge, Erkenek, Pazarcık, and Amanos [20,21]. Slip rates vary across these fault zones owing to the influence of conjugate fractures, pullout basins, and their discontinuous nature. GPS and geological slip rates are consistent between the Karlıova and Puturge segments (8.3 mm/a) [22–24]. Influenced by the valley geomorphology, the slip rate of the Erkenek segment is ~6.5–7.0 mm/a [20]. The slip rate of the Pazarcık segment is more controversial: Westaway et al. [25] obtained a slip rate of 4.0–4.6 mm/a by considering the influence of serpentinite and drainage channel offsets; Karabacak et al. [26] found a slip rate of 9.18 mm/a based on paleoseismological data. Through radiometric dating of Quaternary volcanic rocks with serpentinite offsets in the vicinity of this section and GPS data of the lateral motion of the Arabian and African plates, Duman and Emre [20] calculated a slip rate of 5.57 mm/a for the Amano segment. Variable geological features and discontinuities between faults not only increase the complexity of the EAFZ but also have a controlling effect on the rupture locations of large earthquakes.

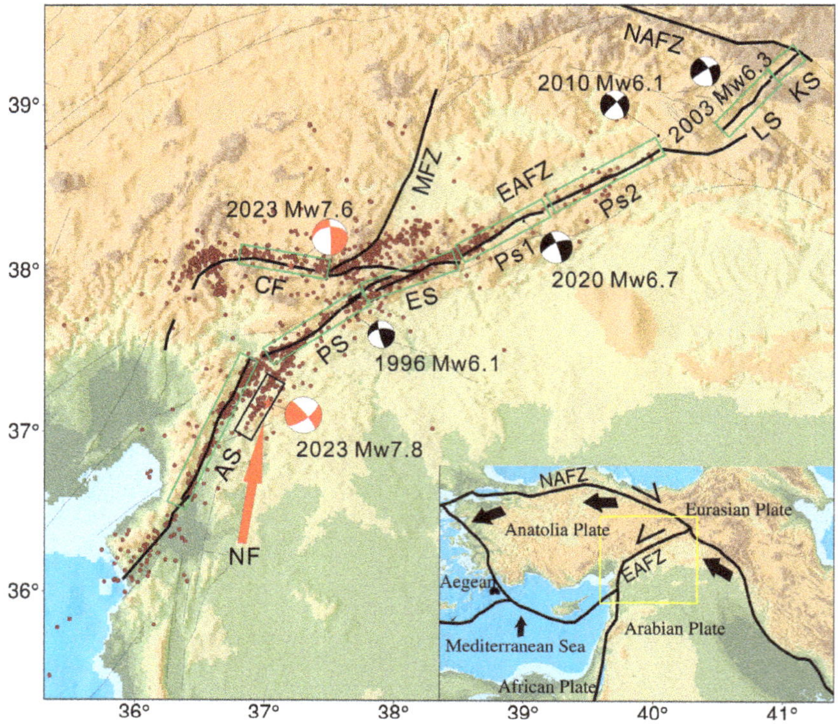

Figure 2. Tectonic setting of the 2023 Türkiye-Syria earthquake sequence. Red beach balls indicate the 2023 Mw 7.8 and 7.6 earthquakes on 6 February 2023. The yellow box denotes the study area. Black beach balls represent strong historical earthquakes along the EAFZ. Red stars represent the epicentres of the 2023 Mw 7.8 and 7.6 earthquakes. Green rectangular boxes represent the main active faults. The black rectangular box represents the Narh Fault [10]. The aftershock distributions of the 2023 Türkiye-Syria earthquake sequence are derived from Lomax [27]. The inset shows the motions of major tectonic units [28]. Abbreviations: EAFZ: East Anatolian Fault Zone, NAFZ: North Anatolian Fault Zone, MFZ: Malatya Fault Zone, AS: Amanos Fault, PS: Pazarcık Fault, ES: Erkenek Fault, Ps1: Puturge Fault, Ps2: Palu Fault, LS: Ilıca Fault, KS: Karlıova Fault, CF: Cardak Fault, NF: Narh Fault.

2.2. Data Collection and Analysis

Surface displacement, a direct manifestation of earthquakes, plays a pivotal role in earthquake hazard assessment, fault slip modelling, and understanding triggering mechanisms [29,30]. SAR, a remote sensing technology, effectively captures high-precision, high-spatial-resolution surface displacement fields by transmitting radar pulses to the ground and measuring the amplitude and phase of the reflected signals [31,32]. For a pair of SAR images, based on the phase information, D-InSAR [33] methods have been extensively employed for monitoring surface deformation resulting from moderate to strong earthquakes in recent years [34–37]. Additionally, SAR amplitude information enables the pixel tracking method [38], simulating the acquisition of surface displacements in both the line-of-sight (LOS) and azimuth (AZ) directions of the satellite. Notably, when the ground displacement exceeds half of a pixel's interference fringe, the offset tracking method serves as a valuable interferometric synthetic aperture radar (InSAR) complement [39,40]. Building on this foundation, we aimed to investigate the 2023 Türkiye-Syria earthquake sequence by employing two distinct methodologies: D-InSAR and SAR offset tracking.

The InSAR dataset in this study consisted of six SAR acquisitions. For ascending track T014, the master and slave images were acquired on 28 January 2023 and 9 February 2023 (gap of 12 days). For ascending track T116, the master and slave images were acquired on 4 February 2023 and 28 February 2023. For descending track T21, we chose image pairs on 29 January 2023 and 10 February 2023. The detailed parameters of the S1A data are shown in Table 2.

Table 2. Basic parameters of coseismic synthetic aperture radar (SAR) data of the 2023 Türkiye-Syria earthquake sequence.

Orbit	Track	Azimuth Angle (°)	Incidence Angle (°)	Reference Image	Secondary Image
Ascending	T14	−22	39	28 January 2023	9 February 2023
	T116	−22	39	4 February 2023	28 February 2023
Descending	T21	−103	39	29 January 2023	10 February 2023

By processing the available S1A Single Look Complex (SLC) images, we generated three D-InSAR interferograms using the GAMMA package with multi-look factors of 2 and 10 in the azimuth and range directions, respectively [41]. A 3-arc-second Shuttle Radar Topography Mission (SRTM) digital elevation model (DEM) was used to remove topographical effects. The interferograms were then filtered using a power spectrum method [42], followed by unwrapping with the minimum cost flow algorithm [43]. Finally, the unwrapped interferograms were geocoded into geodetic coordinates (Figure 3).

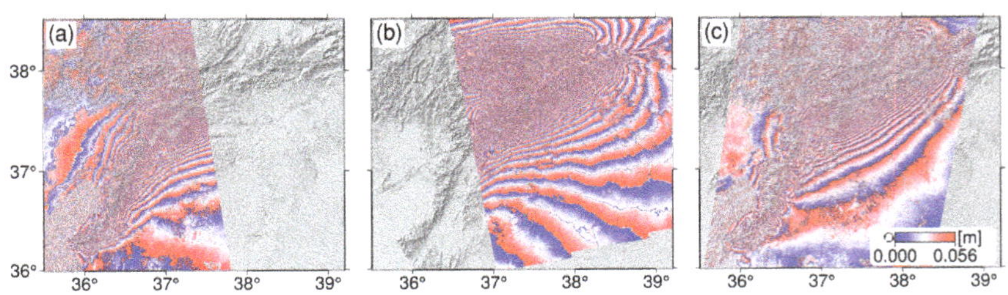

Figure 3. Interferograms of the 2023 Turkey sequence. (**a**) Interferogram of ascending track T14 based on the differential interferometric synthetic aperture radar (D-InSAR) method. (**b**) Interferogram for ascending track T116 based on the D-InSAR method. (**c**) Interferogram for descending track T21 based on the D-InSAR method.

The unwrapping results suffered from many fringes and areas of decorrelation. The reasons for this included: (1) large deformation gradients in the source region, with phase differences between adjacent elements in the centre of the deformation region exceeding π (i.e., 1/2 period) and coherence that was often very low or even completely out of phase [37,44]; (2) the double shock and medium-intensity aftershock occurring in a short period of time led to deconvolution failure. Multiple earthquakes cause phases to overlap, and existing algorithms have difficulty distinguishing the overlapping phases or interference fringes [45]. Therefore, the D-InSAR results of the Sentinel data were not analysed or adopted in the source modelling.

The pixel offset tracking technique uses the amplitude information of SAR images to compute ground displacements in both azimuth and range directions [12,46,47]. This method is unaffected by phase coherence and phase unwrapping [48,49]. It was therefore particularly suitable for the 2023 Türkiye-Syria seismic sequence. We first aligned the images to the pre- and post-earthquake data, and then the single-look SAR images were segmented into smaller blocks. We selected a search window of 64 × 192 pixels (range × azimuth) to calculate the offset between the corresponding blocks using the intensity correlation method. Finally, we converted the estimated offsets into displacements in both the azimuth and range directions.

3. Results

3.1. Offset Deformation Results

Using pixel offset tracking analysis, we measured ground displacements in the vicinity of the fault traces [50]. The most notable features were the sharp discontinuities for both events.

For the Mw 7.8 earthquake, the location of the surface rupture zone was mainly concentrated on the southern branch of the EAFZ. The coseismic deformation patterns in the ascending displacement fields (T14 and T116) were basically the same, while the descending displacement field showed a diametrically opposite deformation pattern (T21) (Figure 4a–c): positive (negative) displacement was seen in descending (ascending) deformation maps for the north-wall of the fault, suggesting that the earthquakes generated deformation mainly in the horizontal direction, which is consistent with the characteristics of strike-slip earthquakes. Moreover, this is in agreement with the focal mechanism from the Global Centroid-Moment-Tensor (GCMT). To the southwest of the Mw 7.8 event, the rupture trace could be fitted based on the T121 displacement gradient; to the northeast, the rupture trace was mainly fitted based on the T116 displacement gradient. According to seismic wave data and the 24-h post-earthquake aftershock distribution, the dashed line in Figure 4a represents the original rupture fault of the earthquake.

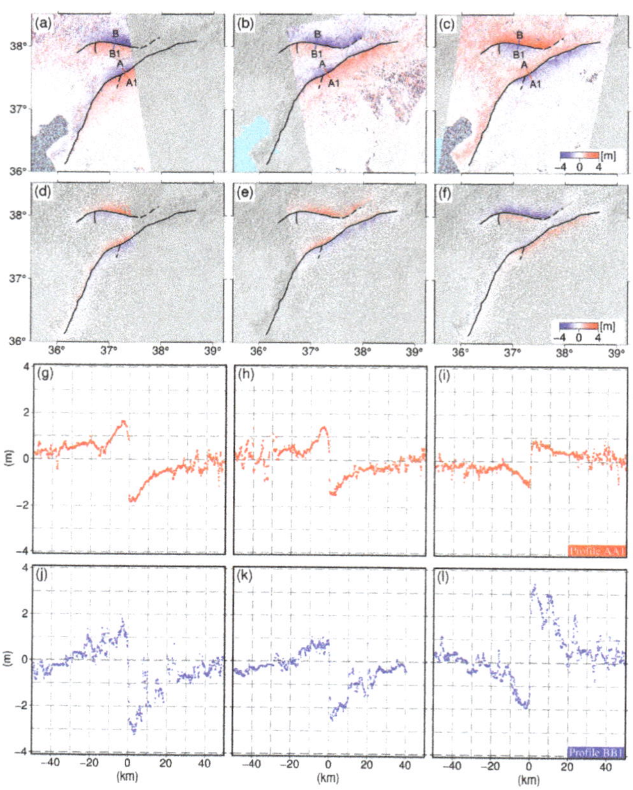

Figure 4. (**a**–**c**) Coseismic deformation of the 2023 Türkiye-Syria seismic sequence along the range direction for ascending tracks T14 and T116 and descending track T21. Black lines represent fault rupture traces based on surface deformation. (**d**–**f**) Downsampled points for ascending tracks T14

and T116 and descending track T21. (**g–i**) Profiles of ascending tracks T14 and T116 and descending track T21 (red, AA1 profile). (**j–k**) Profiles of ascending tracks T14 and T116 and descending track T21 (blue, BB1 profile). AA1 indicates a 30 km long by 0.1 km wide section line along the southern branch of the EAFZ (the main rupture zone of the Mw 7.8 earthquake rupture), and BB1 indicates a 30 km long by 0.1 km wide section line along the northern branch of the EAFZ (the main rupture zone of the Mw 7.6 earthquake rupture).

For the Mw 7.6 earthquake, the surface rupture zone was mainly located on the Carkdak Fault, which is the northern branch of the EAFZ. The T21 displacement gradient showed a distinct vertical branch to the west of the event. We identified the rupture northeast of the Mw 7.6 event from the spatial distributions of aftershocks (Figure 1).

To better define the surface rupture characteristics of the Türkiye-Syria earthquake sequence, we took a profile 30 km long and 0.1 km wide perpendicular to the fault strike (Figure 4h,i), centred on the identified rupture trace (Figure 4c). The ascending displacement range was greater than the descending displacement range. For ascending displacement during the Mw 7.8 earthquake, profiles AA1 and BB1 showed displacements of 5 and 3.5 m (T14) and 2.9 and 3.3 m (T116), respectively (Table 3). In contrast, for the same position on the descending track (T21), deformation was only 2.0 and 5.3 m.

Table 3. Seismic sequence profile line variables of the 2023 Türkiye-Syria seismic sequence. AA1 is located on the southern branch of the East Anatolian Fault Zone (EAFZ), and BB1 is located on the northern branch of the EAFZ. The exact locations are shown in Figure 4a.

Track	ASCT14		ASCT16		DSCT21	
Profile	AA1	BB1	AA1	BB1	AA1	BB1
max (m)	1.8	1.7	1.4	0.9	0.9	3.4
min (m)	−3.2	−1.8	−1.5	−2.4	−1.1	−1.9

3.2. Fault Model and Slip Distribution Inversion

3.2.1. Rupture Trace Fitting

In this study, we first combined the gradient of the displacement field with the spatial distribution of aftershocks (as shown in Figure 2) to produce a fault trace with a SW-NE strike for the Mw 7.8 event and an east-west strike for the Mw 7.6 event (black lines in Figure 4c). The rupture trace of the south-west branch of the Mw 7.8 event was fitted mainly with reference to the displacement field of descending track T21, while the north-east branch was fitted mainly in combination with the displacement field of ascending track T116. Based on the results of Lomax et al. [27], the rupture started from the NF and then ruptured bilaterally along the EAFZ (represented as the dotted line in Figure 4a).

The rupture trace of the Mw 7.6 event was located on the Carkdak Fault and was fitted based on the deformation field. The branch rupture west of the Mw 7.6 event was fitted using the T21 deformation field. The rupture at the eastern end of the Carkdak Fault, which is parallel to the EAFZ, was fitted based on the spatial distribution of aftershocks.

3.2.2. Data Downsampling

Continuous deformation fields consist of hundreds of millions of points, which is computationally expensive and can lead to difficulty in convergence of the results owing to noise interference [50]. Therefore, before inversion, the deformation field data were downsampled using the Delaunay triangulation method [51]. This method retains more points in the region of large near-field deformation and gradually reduces the sampling points for far-field data, which ensures data quality and improves sampling efficiency. The final data set consisted of 8600 points (Figure 4d–f).

3.2.3. Constructing the Initial Fault Model

By comparing the results of the field geological study, seismological study, and offset and optical remote sensing image deformation fields, a three-segmented geometric fault surface rupture model (S1–S3) was established for the southern main branch of the EAFZ. In most places, this fault segmentation model is consistent with the surface rupture of the field geological survey of the Mw 7.8 earthquake, which started at NF. For the Mw 7.6 earthquake, we divided the Carkdak Fault into a two-fault segmentation model (S4, S5) according to changes in rupture strike; in addition, we also considered a small vertical fault branch Cf1 (black dashed branch to the left of profile BB1 in Figure 4c), which was observed by combining the distribution of aftershocks with the descending deformation field. Focal mechanism solutions provided by several organisations show that the dip is between 64° and 89°, and the rake angle varies between −1° and 11°. Most of the aftershocks were located at a depth of 20 km. Combining these parameters, we used a four-segment fault model for the Mw 7.8 event and a three-segment model for the Mw 7.6 event to invert the slip distributions. The lower boundary of the fault model was located at a depth of 30 km, and the rake angle was set to (−20°, 20°), taking into account that both ruptures were left-lateral strike-slip motions. The simulated fault for the Mw 7.8 earthquake extended from 36.14° E and 36.12°N (southwest point) to 38.67°E and 38.09°N (northeast point). The modelled fault for the Mw 7.6 earthquake extended from 36.36°E and 37.89°N (the western point) to 38.15°E and 38.24°N (the eastern point). Along the strike and depth directions, we discretised the fault surface into 4 × 4 km patches and constructed the fault model in an elastic and homogeneous half-space.

A linear inversion method, the Steepest Descent Method (SDM) [52], was used to invert the coseismic slip distribution of the Türkiye-Syria earthquake sequence. The mathematical formula for the inversion is:

$$F(x) = ||Gm(x) - y||^2 + \alpha^2 ||Hm||^2 \quad (1)$$

where G is the elastic half-space Green's function, $m(x)$ is the sliding vector matrix, H is the Laplace operator, y is the surface observation matrix, α is the smoothing factor, and Hm is the weighting factor of the associated displacement magnitude with the Laplace operator finite difference approximation, and is the roughness of the fault slip. In this inversion, the Green's function of the uniform elastic half-space model was calculated using the method described in Okada [53], assuming a Poisson's ratio of 0.25.

3.2.4. Coseismic Slip Distribution

The main rupture of the Mw 7.8 earthquake was located on the southern branch of EAFZ. Coseismic slip was concentrated at depths of 0–10 km and tapered off at depths of 11–15 km (Figure 5b). This is in accordance with the EAFZ being prone to shallow-source earthquakes [54]. Along the strike, coseismic slip was high in the centre and low on either side. The maximum rupture depths of the S1, S2, and S3 fault segments were 5.6, 8.4, and 7.1 m, corresponding to depth ranges of 0–5, 0–15, and 0–10 km, respectively. The rupture initiation bifurcation fault had a maximum slip of ~2.7 m. The coseismic slip on the Cardark Fault was mainly caused by the Mw 7.6 shock. The rupture depth ranged from 0 to 15 km, the average slip was 2.6 m, and the rake was 3.4°. The maximum slip was 9.6 m, which was concentrated on the western side of the source.

The total moment magnitude of the two earthquakes obtained from the inversion was Mw 7.9, which is higher than those of the GCMT and United States Geological Survey (USGS). This is probably because the coseismic deformation field includes the contribution of short-term deformation after the earthquake.

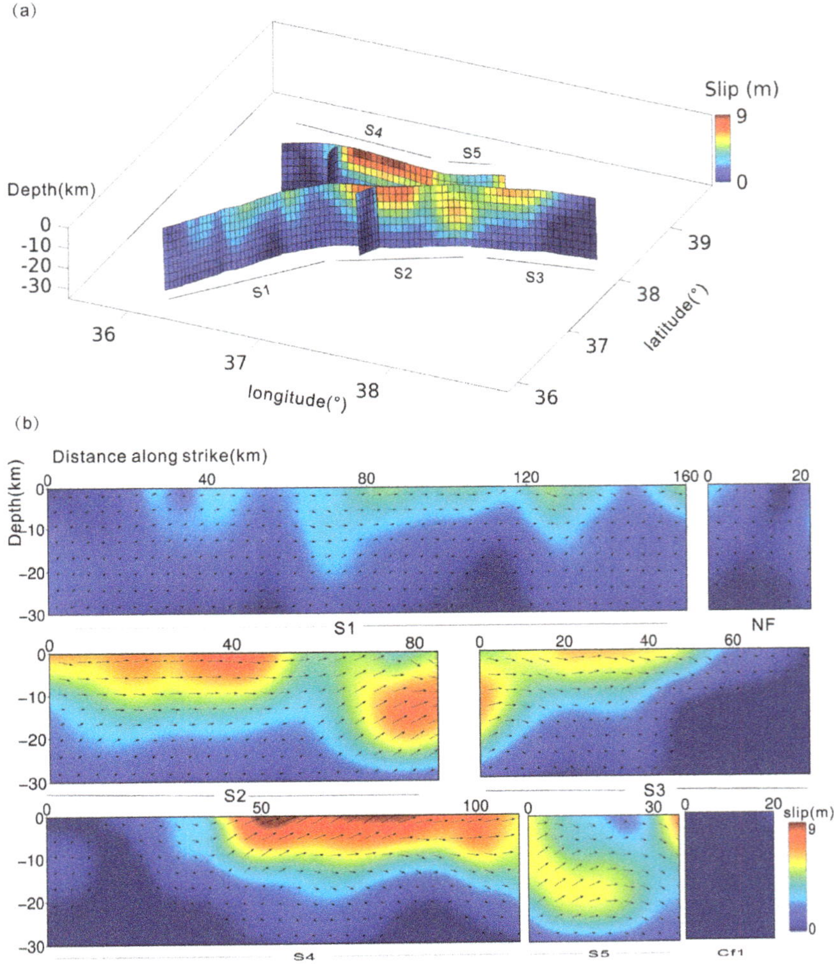

Figure 5. Rupture model of the 2023 Türkiye-Syria seismic sequence. (**a**) Three-dimensional (3D) rupture model of the 2023 Türkiye-Syria seismic sequence. Black solid line segments (S1–S5) indicate the segmented fault numbers used for inversion in the synthetic aperture radar (SAR) data. Colours denote the total slip magnitude (in metres); the red colour saturates at 9 m in S4 with a maximum slip of 9.6 m. (**b**) Two-dimensional (2D) distribution of cumulative coseismic fault slips.

The residuals between the observed and modelled results (Figure 6) suggest that simulated and observed displacements are in good agreement. However, we observed some significant discrepancies, particularly in the near-field of the fault, where the fault geometry and strike change. Moreover, sources of error can also include observational noise, inelastic deformation, and simplification of seismogenic faults [44].

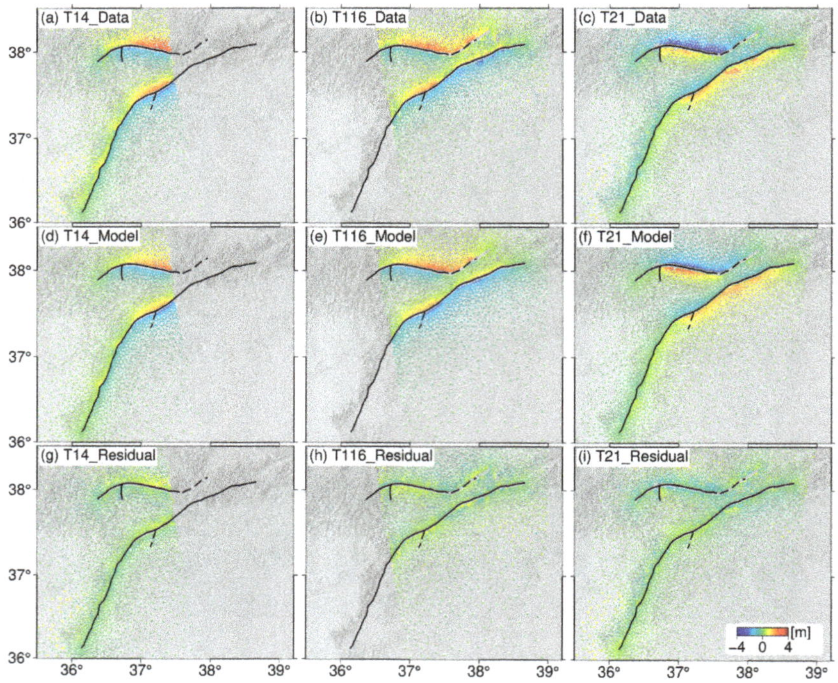

Figure 6. Observed and modelled parameters of the 2023 Türkiye-Syria earthquake sequence. (**a–c**) Synthetic aperture radar (SAR) observations for ascending ((**a**) T14, (**b**) T116) and descending ((**c**) T21) tracks. (**d–f**) SAR model calculations for ascending ((**d**) T14, (**e**) T116) and descending ((**f**) T21) tracks. (**g–i**) Residuals for ascending ((**g**) T14, (**h**) T116) and descending ((**i**) T21) tracks. Black lines denote surface rupture traces.

4. Discussion

4.1. Interaction between Plates

Both the Mw 7.8 and 7.6 earthquakes ruptured on faults of the EAFZ and exhibited left-lateral slip motion. Such an earthquake doublet, with two earthquakes rupturing nearby faults with almost identical rupture patterns, is rare. The most similar previous examples include the 2019 Mw 7.2 Ridgecrest earthquake and the 2012 Mw 8.6 Indian Ocean earthquake. For the 2023 Türkiye-Syria earthquake sequence, the identical movement patterns are inextricably linked to the westward motion of the Anatolian Plate. For the Mw 7.8 earthquake, the main faults that ruptured were EAFZ segments (Erkenek, Pazarcık, and Amanos). Influenced by the rapidly changing relative motions between the Anatolian and Arabian plates, these fault motions were mainly dominated by left-lateral strike-slip [15,54]. Relative movement between faults accelerated after the earthquakes. Moreover, the rupture motion of the Mw 7.6 earthquake was also dominated by left-lateral slip, which was precisely matched to the rightward motion of the Cardak Fault and the leftward motion of the EAFZ. These movements are consistent with the counterclockwise extrusion of the Anatolian Plate into the Aegean Sea.

4.2. Stress-Triggering Relationship between the Mw 7.8 and 7.6 Earthquakes

According to Coulomb failure law, when an earthquake occurs, it modulates the stress state of surrounding active ruptures, which in turn triggers or inhibits the seismic hazard of ruptures in the vicinity [55,56]. Coulomb failure stress (∇CFS) is an important indicator of the probability of earthquake triggering:

$$\nabla CFS = \nabla \tau_s + \mu(\nabla \sigma_n + \nabla \mathrm{p}) \tag{2}$$

where $\nabla \tau_s$ is the change in shear stress resolved in the slip direction of a fault that may fail in a subsequent earthquake, $\nabla \sigma_n$ is the change in normal stress due to the first earthquake perpendicular to the plane of the subsequent earthquake fault (positive for extension), $\nabla \mathrm{p}$ is the change in pore pressure, and μ is the coefficient of friction, which is typically set to 0.4 for left-lateral strike-slip movement.

First, we used the distributed slip models of the EAFZ and NF faults to calculate the stress transferred by the Mw 7.8 mainshock. We set the rake angle to 0° to match the characteristics of a left-lateral strike-slip fault. As shown in Figure 7, the distribution of stresses generated by the Mw 7.8 earthquake on the EAFZ was the opposite of the slip distribution; that is, areas of high slip mainly show stress suppression, which corresponds to the distribution of stresses on the fault. The stress generated by the Mw 7.8 earthquake revealed a significant segmentation effect on the Cardak Fault. Stress was negative on the left of S4 but positive on the right, and completely negative for S5. The Mw 7.8 mainshock increased the Coulomb failure stress at the hypocenter of the Mw 7.6 shock to over 2 bar, increasing the probability of the second event (Figure 7a).

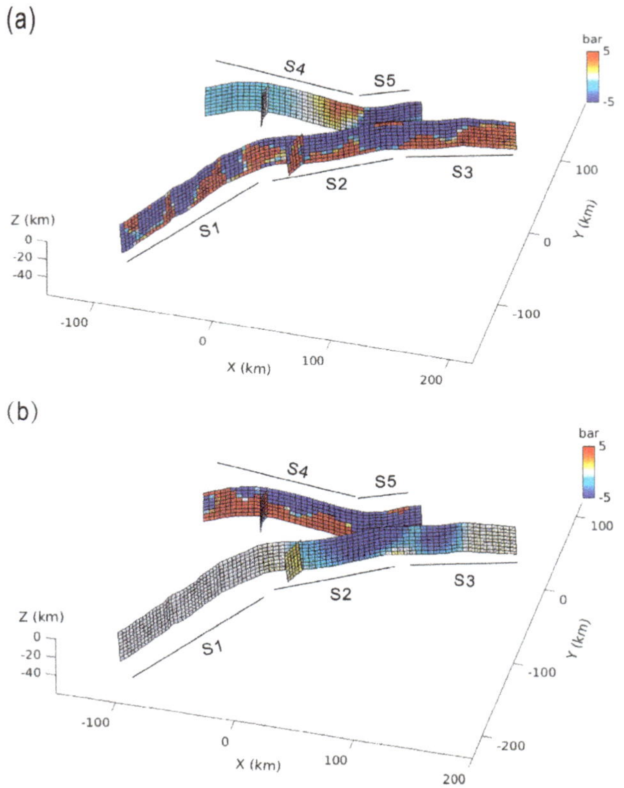

Figure 7. Stress transfer to surrounding faults by the two earthquakes of the 2023 Türkiye-Syria earthquake sequence. Black solid line segments (S1–S5) indicate the segmented fault numbers used for inversion in the synthetic aperture radar (SAR) data. the dots in the colored squares resprent represent grids, each of size 4 × 4 km. (**a**) Stress transfer to surrounding faults by the Mw 7.8 earthquake. (**b**) Stress

transfer to surrounding faults by the Mw 7.6 earthquake. As first described by Harris et al. [57], the blue region had the greatest fault slip, the lowest remaining stress, and the lowest future earthquake risk. In contrast, the red region, also known as the trigger zone, continues to experience high stress and a high risk of future earthquakes.

We then used the distributed slip model obtained from the Mw 7.6 earthquake to calculate stress on the EAFZ (Figure 7b). The majority of the energy in the Cardak Fault was released after the earthquake, and the stress caused by the Mw 7.6 earthquake had little effect on S1. However, significant negative stress changes were estimated along S2 and west of S3, corresponding to areas with small numbers of aftershocks (as shown in Figure 8).

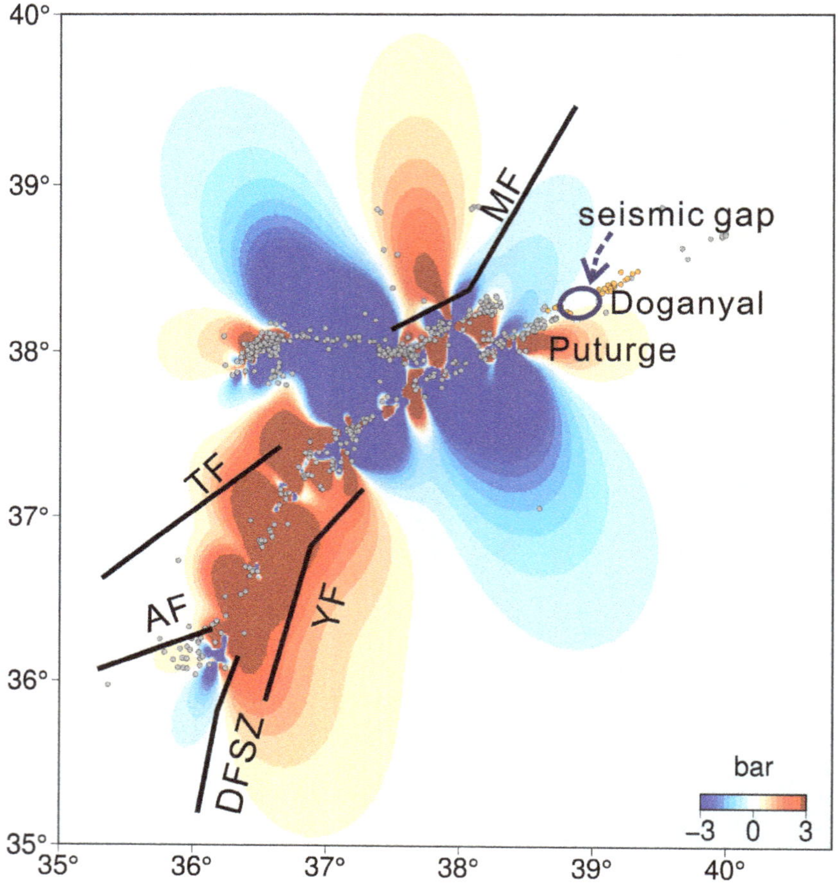

Figure 8. Coulomb failure stress (CFS) changes on surrounding faults of the 2023 Türkiye-Syria earthquake sequence. MF: Malatya Fault; TF: Turkoglu Fault; AF: Antakya Fault; YF: Yesemek Fault; DSFZ: Dead Sea Fault Zone. Grey circles denote aftershocks of the 2023 Turkey earthquake sequence (Mw > 4 within 3 months); orange circles denote aftershocks of the 2020 Turkey Mw 6.8 earthquake (Mw > 4).

4.3. Stress Perturbations in the Vicinity of the Türkiye-Syria Earthquake Sequence

Seismic gaps remain along the EAFZ following the Türkiye-Syria earthquake sequence [20,58]. Therefore, it is crucial to analyse the stress changes in the surrounding faults created by the seismic sequence. We simplified the geometry of the receiving fault by combining historical event source mechanisms and the fault strike. The receiver fault (strike = 277°, dip = 78°, rake = 4°) was based on the GCMT. According to the regional geological background and Coulomb stress research, we adopted $\mu = 0.4$ for the calculation. In the southwestern section of the Malatya Fault, the stress conditions displayed a cyclical pattern of alternating positive and negative states. The middle Puturge Fault, northern DSFZ, Yesemek Fault, Antakya Fault, and Turkoglu Fault are under strong positive stress and remain at high risk of large earthquakes (Figure 8).

By comparing the distribution of aftershocks (Mw > 4) following the 2023 earthquake sequence with that following the 2020 Mw 6.8 earthquake (orange circles in Figure 8), we found a moderately strong seismic gap along the west-central earthquake-prone Puturge Fault. The distribution of earthquakes is related to the inhomogeneity of the stress field. For strain-expanding regions, there is mostly a normal rupture component, whereas the reverse component is mainly distributed in strain-compressed regions. From east to west along the Puturge Fault, the average dip gradually shallows from 70° to 40°. The corresponding strains are almost vertical in the east, gradually flatten out in the central-western area, and gradually change from horizontal to vertical near Gokdere. According to Bletery et al. [54], the maximum moment release was mainly concentrated on the east-west boundary curve of the Puturge Fault, which may be one reason why no major earthquakes have occurred along the middle-western Puturge Fault segment.

The aftershock sequence of the Türkiye-Syria earthquake doublet almost coincided with that of the 2020 Mw 6.8 earthquake on the Puturge segment. Additionally, studies have shown that nearly repetitive earthquakes occur throughout the region within 10 km along the Puturge segment [59]. This overlap may be associated with interseismic coupling [21]. Blettery et al. [54] showed that coupling is low along the eastern Puturge section but is high further west. The aftershock overlap zone is mainly in the transition zone between high and low coupling [60]. For small convex, partially or fully coupled faults, persistent creep-slip results in a uniform spatial distribution of earthquakes. As such, repeated areas of aftershocks also occur.

5. Conclusions

In this study, we utilised pixel offset tracking to record surface displacements resulting from the 2023 Türkiye-Syria earthquake sequence. Analysing these displacement changes provided insights into the geometric characteristics and deformation magnitudes of the fault ruptures. We then employed a homogeneous elastic half-space dislocation model to invert and map the distribution of coseismic slip during the earthquake sequence. Finally, we determined the dynamics of fault motion, rupture patterns, and stress transfer. The main conclusions are as follows: (1) The D-InSAR method faced challenges owing to near-surface incoherence, while SAR offset-tracking excelled at capturing near-field deformation details. (2) The cumulative deformation caused by the Mw 7.6 earthquake slightly exceeds that of the Mw 7.8 event. Furthermore, the ascending track displays slightly larger deformations compared with the descending track at the same location. (3) Both earthquakes predominantly exhibit left-lateral slip motion, with the depth of slip ranging from 0 to 20 km. Specifically, the Mw 7.8 earthquake mainly triggered slip in the east-central part of the southern EAFZ (S2 and S3), while the Mw 7.6 event induced slip concentrated on the western section of the northern EAFZ (S4). (4) The Mw 7.8 earthquake triggered the Mw 7.6 earthquake, while conversely, the Mw 7.6 earthquake strongly suppressed the central section (S2) of the southern branch of the EAFZ. (5) Following the Mw 7.6 earthquake, Coulomb stress is strongly loaded on the central Puturge Fault, northern DSFZ, Yesemek Fault, Antakya Fault, and Turkoglu Fault.

Author Contributions: Conceptualization, C.M. and Y.L.; methodology, W.W. and X.F.; validation, C.M., Y.L. and X.S.; formal analysis, W.W. and X.F.; investigation, Y.L. and X.F.; data curation, W.W.; writing-original draft preparation, W.W.; writing-review and editing, W.W. and X.F.; visualisation,

W.W.; supervision, X.F.; project administration, Y.L.; funding acquisition, Y.L. and X.S. All authors have read and agreed to the published version of the manuscript.

Funding: This work was co-supported by Grants from the National Nonprofit Fundamental Research of Institute of Geology, China Earthquake Administration (Grant No. IGCEA2005) and the National Science Foundation of China (Grant No. 42274046, 41874027).

Data Availability Statement: The Sentinel-1 SAR data were acquired and processed by the European Space Agency Copernicus program (https://scihub.copernicus.eu/, accessed on 24 February 2023) and were retrieved from the Alaska Satellite Facility Distributed Active Archive Center (https://vertex.daac.asf.alaska.edu, accessed on 24 February 2023). The preliminary surface ruptures of the Turkey earthquake sequence based on analysis of post-seismic satellite data were obtained from USGS (https://usgs.maps.arcgis.com/apps/webappviewer/indexhtml?id=5229bb842bd64b688d769abbefe43b46, accessed on 26 March 2023). The relocated aftershocks of the 2023 Turkey earthquake sequence were archived from Zenodo (https://zenodo.org/record/7699882#.ZEKnT3ZBy3A, accessed on 26 March 2023). The aftershocks of the 2020 Turkey earthquake sequence were archived from the AFAD catalog (https://deprem.afad.gov.tr/event-catalog, accessed on 26 March 2023).

Acknowledgments: We thank the editor and the three anonymous reviewers for their constructive suggestions that significantly improved the quality of the manuscript.

Conflicts of Interest: The authors declare no conflict of interest.

References

1. Mai, P.M.; Aspiotis, T.; Aquib, T.A.; Valero Cano, E.; Castro Cruz, D.A.; Espindola-Carmona, A.; Li, B.; Li, X.; Liu, J.; Matrau, R.; et al. The Destructive Earthquake Doublet of 6 February 2023 in South-Central Türkiye and Northwestern Syria: Initial Observations and Analyses. *Seism. Rec.* **2023**, *3*, 105–115. [CrossRef]
2. Emre, Ö.; Duman, T.Y.; Özalp, S.; Elmaci, H. *Active Fault Map of Turkey with an Explanatory Text 1: 1,250,000 Scale*; special publication series 30; General Directorate of Mineral Research and Exploration: Ankara, Turkey, 2013; p. 89.
3. Gülen, L.; Barka, A.; Toksöz, M.N. Continental collision and related complex deformation: Maras triple junction and surrounding structures, SE Turkey. *Hacet. Univ. Earth Sci. J.* **1987**, *14*, 319–336.
4. Barbot, S.; Weiss, J.R. Connecting subduction, extension and shear localization across the Aegean Sea and Anatolia. *Geophys. J. Int.* **2021**, *226*, 422–445. [CrossRef]
5. Melgar, D.; Taymaz, T.; Ganas, A.; Crowell, B.; Öcalan, T.; Kahraman, M.; Tsironi, V.; Yolsal-Çevikbilen, S.; Valkaniotis, S.; Irmak, T.S.; et al. Sub-and super-shear ruptures during the 2023 Mw 7.8 and Mw 7.6 earthquake doublet in SE Türkiye. *Seismica* **2023**, *2*. [CrossRef]
6. Zahradník, J.; Turhan, F.; Sokos, E.; Gallovič, F. Asperity-like (segmented) structure of the 6 February 2023 Turkish earthquakes. *Earth ArXiv* **2023**. [CrossRef]
7. Jiao, X.; Liu, C.; Xiong, X. Source process of the 24 January 2020 Mw 6.7 East Anatolian fault zone, Turkey, earthquake. *Seismol. Res. Lett.* **2020**, *91*, 3120–3128.
8. Lin, X.; Hao, J.; Wang, D.; Chu, R.; Zeng, X.; Xie, J.; Zhang, B.; Bai, Q. Coseismic Slip Distribution of the 24 January 2020 Mw 6.7 Doganyol Earthquake and in Relation to the Foreshock and Aftershock Activities. *Seism. Res. Lett.* **2020**, *92*, 127–139. [CrossRef]
9. Jia, Z.; Jin, Z.; Marchandon, M.; Ulrich, T.; Gabriel, A.-A.; Fan, W.; Shearer, P.; Zou, X.; Rekoske, J.; Bulut, F.; et al. The complex dynamics of the 2023 Kahramanmaraş, Turkey, Mw 7.8–7.7 earthquake doublet. *Science* **2023**, *381*, 985–990. [CrossRef]
10. Meng, L.; Xu, L.; Mohanna, S.; Ji, C.; Ampuero, J.; Yunjun, Z.; Hasnain, M.; Chu, R. The 2023 Mw7.8 Kahramanmaraş, Turkey Earthquake: A Multi-segment Rupture in A Mil-lennium Supercycle. *Res. Sq. pre-print.* [CrossRef]
11. Atanasova, M.; Raykova, P.; Nikolov, H. Determining the Deformations of the Earth's Surface after the Earthquakes in Turkey-Syria of 06 February 2023—Initial Results. *C. R. Acad. Bulg. Sci.* **2023**, *76*, 554–562. [CrossRef]
12. Li, S.; Wang, X.; Tao, T.; Zhu, Y.; Qu, X.; Li, Z.; Huang, J.; Song, S. Source Model of the 2023 Turkey Earthquake Sequence Imaged by Sentinel-1 and GPS Measurements: Implications for Heterogeneous Fault Behavior along the East Anatolian Fault Zone. *Remote Sens.* **2023**, *15*, 2618. [CrossRef]
13. An, Q.; Feng, G.; He, L.; Xiong, Z.; Lu, H.; Wang, X.; Wei, J. Three-Dimensional Deformation of the 2023 Turkey Mw 7.8 and Mw 7.7 Earthquake Sequence Obtained by Fusing Optical and SAR Images. *Remote Sens.* **2023**, *15*, 2656. [CrossRef]
14. Zhang, G.; Qu, C.; Shan, X.; Song, X.; Zhang, G.; Wang, C.; Hu, J.-C.; Wang, R. Slip distribution of the 2008 Wenchuan Ms 7.9 earthquake by joint inversion from GPS and InSAR measurements: A resolution test study. *Geophys. J. Int.* **2011**, *186*, 207–220. [CrossRef]
15. Reilinger, R.; McClusky, S. Nubia-Arabia-Eurasia plate motions and the dynamics of Mediterranean and Middle East tectonics. *Geophys. J. Int.* **2011**, *186*, 971–979. [CrossRef]

16. Sboras, S.; Lazos, I.; Bitharis, S.; Pikridas, C.; Galanakis, D.; Fotiou, A.; Chatzipetros, A.; Pavlides, S. Source model-ling and stress transfer scenarios of the October 30, 2020 Samos earthquake: Seismotectonic implications. *Turk. J. Earth Sci.* **2021**, *30*, 699–717. [CrossRef]
17. Jolivet, L.; Faccenna, C.; Huet, B.; Labrousse, L.; Le Pourhiet, L.; Lacombe, O.; Lecomte, E.; Burov, E.; Denèle, Y.; Brun, J.-P.; et al. Aegean tectonics: Strain localisation, slab tearing and trench retreat. *Tectonophysics* **2013**, *597*, 1–33. [CrossRef]
18. Faccenna, C.; Becker, T.W.; Auer, L.; Billi, A.; Boschi, L.; Brun, J.P.; Capitanio, F.A.; Funiciello, F.; Horvàth, F.; Jolivet, L.; et al. Mantle dynamics in the Mediterranean. *Rev. Geophys.* **2014**, *52*, 283–332. [CrossRef]
19. Gallovič, F.; Zahradník, J.; Plicka, V.; Sokos, E.; Evangelidis, C.; Fountoulakis, I.; Turhan, F. Complex rupture dynamics on an immature fault during the 2020 Mw 6.8 Elazığ earthquake, Turkey. *Commun. Earth Environ.* **2020**, *1*, 40. [CrossRef]
20. Duman, T.Y.; Ömer, E. *The East Anatolian Fault: Geometry, Segmentation and Jog Characteristics*; Geological Society; London, Special Publications: London, UK, 2013; Volume 372, pp. 495–529.
21. Güvercin, S.E.; Karabulut, H.; Konca, A.; Doğan, U.; Ergintav, S. Active seismotectonics of the East Anatolian Fault. *Geophys. J. Int.* **2022**, *230*, 50–69. [CrossRef]
22. Herece, E. *Doğu Anadolu Fayı (DAF) Atlası [East Anatolian Fault (EAF) Atlas]*; MTA: Ankara, Turket, 2008; Volume 359.
23. Reilinger, R.; McClusky, S.; Vernant, P.; Lawrence, S.; Ergintav, S.; Cakmak, R.; Ozener, H.; Kadirov, F.; Guliev, I.; Stepanyan, R.; et al. GPS constraints on continental deformation in the Africa-Arabia-Eurasia continental collision zone and implications for the dynamics of plate interactions. *J. Geophys. Res. Solid Earth* **2006**, *111*, B5. [CrossRef]
24. Aktug, B.; Ozener, H.; Dogru, A.; Sanbucu, A.; Turgut, B.; Halicioglu, K.; Yilmaz, O.; Havazli, E. Slip rates and seis-mic potential on the East Anatolian Fault System using an improved GPS velocity field. *J. Geod.* **2016**, *94–95*, 1–12.
25. Westaway, R.O.B.; Arger, J.A.N. The Gölbai basin, southeastern Turkey: A complex discontinuity in a major strike-slip fault zone. *J. Geol. Soc.* **1996**, *153*, 729–744. [CrossRef]
26. Karabacak, V.; Yönlü, Ö.; Altunel, E.; Yalçıner, C.Ç.; Akyüz, H.S.; Kıyak, N.G. Doğu Anadolu Fay Zonu güneybatı uzanımının paleosismolojisi ve ilk kayma hızı bulguları. In *ATAG-15 (Aktif Tektonik Araştırma Grubu 15. Çalıştayı) Bildiri Özleri Kitabı*; Çukurova Üniversitesi: Adana, Turkey, 2011.
27. Lomax, A. Precise, NLL-SSST-Coherence Hypocenter Catalog for the 2023 Mw 7.8 and Mw 7.6 SE Turkey Earthquake Sequence. Zenodo. 2023. Available online: https://zenodo.org/records/7727678 (accessed on 20 October 2023).
28. Armijo, R.; Meyer, B.; Hubert, A.; Barka, A. Westward propagation of the North Anatolian fault into the northern Aegean: Timing and kinematics. *Geology* **1999**, *27*, 267–270. [CrossRef]
29. Hu, J.; Liu, J.; Li, Z.; Zhu, J.; Wu, L.; Sun, Q.; Wu, W. Estimating threedimensional coseismic deformations with the SM-VCE method based on heterogeneous SAR observations: Selection of homogeneous points and analysis of observation combinations. *Remote Sens. Environ.* **2021**, *255*, 112298. [CrossRef]
30. Liu, J.; Hu, J.; Li, Z.; Ma, Z.; Wu, L.; Jiang, W.; Feng, G.; Zhu, J. Complete three-dimensional coseismic displacements due to the 2021 Maduo earthquake in Qing-hai Province, China from Sentinel-1 and ALOS-2 SAR images. *Sci. China Earth Sci.* **2022**, *65*, 687–697. [CrossRef]
31. Bürgmann, R.; Schmidt, D.; Nadeau, R.M.; D'Alessio, M.; Fielding, E.; Manaker, D.; McEvilly, T.V.; Murray, M.H. Earthquake Potential Along the Northern Hayward Fault, California. *Science* **2000**, *289*, 1178–1182. [CrossRef]
32. Li, Y.; Bürgmann, R. Partial Coupling and Earthquake Potential Along the Xianshuihe Fault, China. *J. Geophys. Res. Solid Earth* **2021**, *126*, e21406. [CrossRef]
33. Gabriel, A.K.; Goldstein, R.M.; Zebker, H.A. Mapping small elevation changes over large areas: Differential radar inter-ferometry. *J. Geophys. Res.* **1989**, *94*, 9183–9191. [CrossRef]
34. Shan, X.-J.; Qu, C.-Y.; Gong, W.-Y.; Zhao, D.-Z.; Zhang, Y.-F.; Zhang, G.-H.; Song, X.-G.; Liu, Y.-H.; Zhang, G.-F. Coseismic deformation field of the Jiuzhaigou MS7.0 earthquake from Sentinel-1A InSAR data and fault slip inversion. *Chin. J. Geophys.* **2017**, *60*, 4527–4536. (In Chinese)
35. Zhao, D.; Qu, C.; Bürgmann, R.; Gong, W.; Shan, X. Relaxation of Tibetan Lower Crust and Afterslip Driven by the 2001 Mw7.8 Kokoxili, China, Earthquake Constrained by a Decade of Geodetic Measurements. *J. Geophys. Res. Solid Earth* **2021**, *126*, e2020JB021314. [CrossRef]
36. Fan, X.; Zhang, G.; Zhao, D.; Xie, C.; Huang, C.; Shan, X. Fault geometry and kinematics of the 2021 Mw 7.3 Maduo earthquake from aftershocks and InSAR observations. *Front. Earth Sci.* **2022**, *10*, 993984. [CrossRef]
37. Chen, H.; Qu, C.; Zhao, D.; Ma, C.; Shan, X. Rupture Kinematics and Coseismic Slip Model of the 2021 Mw 7.3 Maduo (China) Earthquake: Implications for the Seismic Hazard of the Kunlun Fault. *Remote Sens.* **2021**, *13*, 3327. [CrossRef]
38. Michel, R.; Avouac, J.-P.; Taboury, J. Measuring ground displacements from SAR amplitude images: Application to the Landers Earthquake. *Geophys. Res. Lett.* **1999**, *26*, 875–878. [CrossRef]
39. Wang, L.; Deng, K.; Zheng, M. Research on ground deformation monitoring method in mining areas using the probability integral model fusion D-InSAR, sub-band InSAR and offset-tracking. *Int. J. Appl. Earth Obs. Geoinf.* **2020**, *85*, 101981. [CrossRef]
40. Fan, H.; Gao, X.; Yang, J.; Deng, K.; Yu, Y. Monitoring Mining Subsidence Using A Combination of Phase-Stacking and Off-set-Tracking Methods. *Remote Sens.* **2015**, *7*, 9166–9183. [CrossRef]
41. Werner, C.; Wegmüller, U.; Strozzi, T.; Wiesmann, A. Gamma SAR and interferometric processing software. In Proceedings of the Ersenvisat Symposium, Gothenburg, Sweden, 16–20 October 2000; Volume 1620.

42. Goldstein, R.M.; Werner, C.L. Radar interferogram filtering for geophysical applications. *Geophys. Res. Lett.* **1998**, *25*, 4035–4038. [CrossRef]
43. Lo, R.W.; Levitt, K.N.; Olsson, R.A. MCF: A malicious code filter. *Comput. Secur.* **1995**, *14*, 541–566. [CrossRef]
44. Zhao, D.; Qu, C.; Shan, X.; Gong, W.; Zhang, Y.; Zhang, G. InSAR and GPS derived coseismic deformation and fault model of the 2017 Ms7. 0 Jiuzhaigou earthquake in the Northeast Bayanhar block. *Tectonophysics* **2018**, *726*, 86–99. [CrossRef]
45. Li, Z.; Song, G.; Yu, C.; Xiao, R.; Chen, L.; Luo, H.; Dai, K.; Ge, D.; Ding, Y.; Zhang, Y.; et al. Application of satellite radar remote sensing in landslide disaster detection and monitoring: Challenges and countermeasures. *J. Wuhan Univ. (Inf. Sci. Ed.)* **2019**, *44*, 967–979. [CrossRef]
46. Rott, H.; Stuefer, M.; Siegel, A.; Skvarca, P.; Eckstaller, A. Mass fluxes and dynamics of Moreno Glacier, Southern Patagonia Icefield. *Geophys. Res. Lett.* **1998**, *25*, 1407–1410. [CrossRef]
47. Gray, A.; Short, N.; Mattar, K.; Jezek, K. Velocities and Flux of the Filchner Ice Shelf and its Tributaries Determined from Speckle Tracking Interferometry. *Can. J. Remote Sens.* **2001**, *27*, 193–206. [CrossRef]
48. Liu, Y.; Qu, C.; San, X. Obtaining two-dimensional deformation field of Wenchuan earthquake based on SAR image offset. *J. Geophys.* **2012**, *55*, 3296–3306.
49. Strozzi, T.; Luckman, A.; Murray, T.; Wegmuller, U.; Werner, C. Glacier motion estimation using sar offset-tracking procedures. *IEEE Trans. Geosci. Remote Sens.* **2002**, *40*, 2384–2391. [CrossRef]
50. Feng, G.; Li, Z.; Shan, X.; Zhang, L.; Zhang, G.; Zhu, J. Geodetic model of the 2015 April 25 Mw 7.8 Gorkha Nepal Earthquake and Mw 7.3 aftershock estimated from InSAR and GPS data. *Geophys. J. Int.* **2015**, *203*, 896–900. [CrossRef]
51. Corzo, G.; Varouchakis, E.A. (Eds.) *Spatiotemporal Analysis of Extreme Hydrological Events*; Elsevier: Amsterdam, The Netherlands, 2018.
52. Wang, R.; Parolai, S.; Ge, M.; Jin, M.; Walter, T.R.; Zschau, J. The 2011 Mw 9.0 Tohoku Earthquake: Comparison of GPS and Strong-Motion Data. *Bull. Seism. Soc. Am.* **2013**, *103*, 1336–1347. [CrossRef]
53. Okada, Y. Surface deformation due to shear and tensile faults in a half-space. *Bull. Seism. Soc. Am.* **1985**, *75*, 1135–1154. [CrossRef]
54. Bletery, Q.; Cavalié, O.; Nocquet, J.; Ragon, T. Distribution of Interseismic Coupling Along the North and East Anatolian Faults Inferred from InSAR and GPS Data. *Geophys. Res. Lett.* **2020**, *47*, e2020GL087775. [CrossRef]
55. Harris, R.A. Introduction to Special Section: Stress Triggers, Stress Shadows, and Implications for Seismic Hazard. *J. Geophys. Res. Solid Earth* **1998**, *103*, 24347–24358. [CrossRef]
56. Shan, X.; Li, Y.; Gao, Z.; Hua, J.; Huang, X.; Gong, W.; Qu, C.; Zhao, D.; Chen, J.; Huang, C.; et al. Co-seismic deformation characteristics of the 2022 Luding M_S6.8 earthquake and the risk of strong earthquakes in the vicinity. *Sci. Bull.* **2023**, *68*, 944–953.
57. Harris, R.A.; Simpson, R.W. In the shadow of 1857—The effectof the great Ft. Tejon earthquake on subsequent earthquakes insouthern California. *Geophys. Res. Lett.* **1996**, *23*, 229–232. [CrossRef]
58. Gülerce, Z.; Shah, S.T.; Menekşe, A.; Özacar, A.A.; Kaymakci, N.; Çetin, K. Probabilistic Seismic-Hazard Assessment for East Anatolian Fault Zone Using Planar Fault Source Models. *Bull. Seism. Soc. Am.* **2017**, *107*, 2353–2366. [CrossRef]
59. Konca, A.Ö.; Karabulut, H.; Güvercin, S.E.; Eskiköy, F.; Özarpacı, S.; Özdemir, A.; Floyd, M.; Ergintav, S.; Doğan, U. From Interseismic Deformation with Near-Repeating Earthquakes to Co-Seismic Rupture: A Unified View of the 2020 Mw6. 8 Sivrice (Elazığ) Eastern Turkey Earthquake. *J. Geophys. Res. Solid Earth* **2021**, *126*, e2021JB021830. [CrossRef]
60. Metois, M.; Vigny, C.; Socquet, A. Interseismic coupling, megathrust earthquakes and seismic swarms along the Chilean subduction zone (38–18 S). *Pure Appl. Geophys.* **2016**, *173*, 1431–1449. [CrossRef]

remote sensing

MDPI

Article

Study of the Interseismic Deformation and Locking Depth along the Xidatan–Dongdatan Segment of the East Kunlun Fault Zone, Northeast Qinghai–Tibet Plateau, Based on Sentinel-1 Interferometry

Shuai Kang, Lingyun Ji *, Liangyu Zhu, Chuanjin Liu, Wenting Zhang, Ning Li, Jing Xu and Fengyun Jiang

The Second Monitoring and Application Center, China Earthquake Administration, 316 Xiying Road, Xi'an 710054, China

* Correspondence: jilingyun@smac.ac.cn; Tel.: +86-13992856879

Abstract: The East Kunlun fault zone (EKFZ), located northeast of the Qinghai–Tibet Plateau, has experienced several strong earthquakes of magnitude seven or above since 1900. It is one of the most active fault systems and is characterized by left-lateral strike-slip. However, the Xidatan–Dongdatan segment (XDS) of the East Kunlun fault zone (EKFZ) has had no earthquakes for many years, and the Kunlun Mountains M_S 8.1 earthquake has a stress loading effect on this segment, so it is widely regarded as a high-risk earthquake gap. To this end, we collected the Sentinel-1 data of the XDS of the EKFZ from July 2014 to July 2019 and obtained the high-precision interseismic deformation field by the Interferometric Synthetic Aperture Radar (InSAR) technique to obtain the slip rate and locking depth of the XDS of the EKFZ, and the seismic potential of the segment was analyzed. The results are as follows: (1) The LOS deformation field of the XDS of the EKFZ was obtained using Sentinel-1 data of ascending and descending orbits, which indicated that the XDS of the EKFZ is dominated by horizontal motion. Combined with the interference results, it is shown that the strike-slip rate dominates the deformation information of the XDS of the EKFZ. The deep strike-slip rate of the fault is about 6 mm/yr, the deep dip-slip rate is about 2 mm/yr, and the slip-deficit rate on the fault surface is about 6 mm/yr; (2) Combined with the spiral dislocation theory model, the slip rate of the XDS to Xiugou Basin of the EKFZ has a gradually increasing trend, with an average slip rate of 9.6 ± 2.3 mm/yr and a locking depth of 29 ± 5 m; (3) The stress accumulation is about 483 ± 92 years in the XDS of the EKFZ, indicating that the cumulative elastic strain energy of the XDS can produce an M_W 7.29 $\pm$ 0.1 earthquake in the future.

Keywords: East Kunlun fault zone; Xidatan–Dongdatan segment; InSAR; interseismic deformation; slip rate; locking depth; seismogenic depth

1. Introduction

The East Kunlun fault zone is one of the famous faults and is accompanied by a left-lateral strike-slip structure in mainland China. It stretches for more than a thousand kilometers and traverses the central part of Qinghai Province from east to west. It starts from the west of Whale Lake (the border between Qinghai Province and Xinjiang Province), through Kusai Lake, Xidatan–Dongdatan, Xiugou Basin, Alag Hu, Tuosuo Lake, Xiadawu, and Maqin in the east and extends to the east of Maqu in Gansu Province [1]. Up to now, about 70 paleoseismic events have been discovered in the EKFZ in Qinghai Province, and these earthquakes are approximately evenly distributed in various segments between Katabanfeng and Maqu, forming a vast earthquake surface fracture zone and stretching nearly 1000 km. Through the analysis of the paleoseismic catalog, it is concluded that the number of historical earthquakes in the EKFZ accounts for about 3/4 of the entire Bayanhar Mountains seismic zone, and it is the central active region of the Bayanhar

Mountains seismic zone. The frequency of the EKFZ seismic activity from high to low is as follows: the west segment, the east segment, the middle west segment, and the middle east segment [2–4].

Since 1900, the EKFZ has experienced several strong earthquakes of magnitude seven or above, such as the 1937 Huashixia M_S 7.5 earthquake, the 1963 Dulan M_S 7.0 earthquake, the 1973 Mani M_S 7.3 earthquake, the 1997 Mani M_S 7.5 earthquake, and the 2001 Kunlun Mountains M_S 8.1 earthquake. These earthquakes are mainly concentrated in the western and middle eastern segments of the EKFZ [5,6]. Among them, the 2001 Kunlun Mountains M_S 8.1 earthquake had a stress loading effect on the Xidatan–Dongdatan segment (XDS) of the EKFZ [7–12]. Therefore, the XDS of the EKFZ is worthy of attention for future strong earthquakes. Scholars have also verified this view through paleoseismic identification, earthquake repetition interval determination, and model probability calculation (e.g., [3,7–10]). Based on a variety of basic methods such as seismic geology, geodesy, and geophysics, the Working Group of Seismic Situation in Mainland China gives the determination results of key earthquake risk areas in China from 2021–2030, among which the XDS of EKFZ is one of the key risk areas (red dashed circle in Figure 1a; [11,12]). At present, the study of the tectonic movement characteristics of the EKFZ mainly focuses on the long-term slip rate on the eastern and western members, such as, from west to east, the slip rates of the EKFZ are 10.0–2.0 mm/yr [13] and 14.8–9.4 mm/yr [14]; the slip rate of Maqin since the late Pleistocene is 12.5 mm/yr [15]; from late Pleistocene to Holocene, the slip rate of the Maqu segment is 10.15–2.0 mm/yr, and it is speculated that the slip rate of the Maqu segment shows the gradient attenuation [16–19]. On the west segment of the EKFZ, the slip rate is 10–12 mm/yr [20], and in the Mani earthquake of the west segment of EKFZ, the interseismic slip rate is 10.2 mm/yr [21]. However, there is less research on the XDS, which is a large earthquake gap with a higher future earthquake risk.

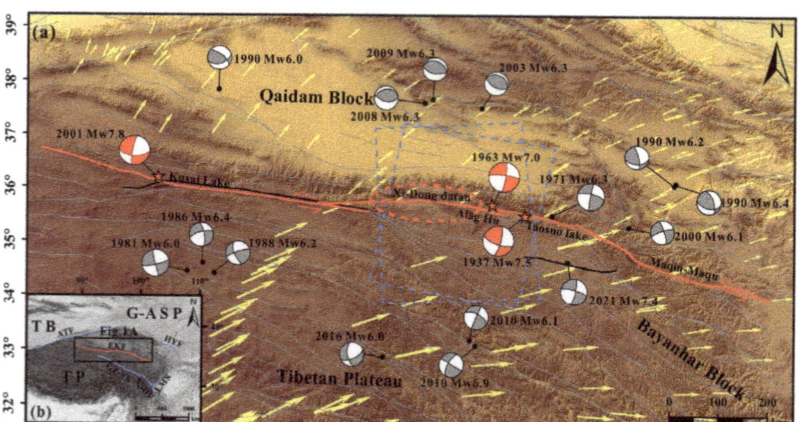

Figure 1. Seismotectonic background map of the East Kunlun Fault Zone (EKFZ). Faults are modified from [22] and are superimposed on the Digital Elevation Models (DEMs) from the Shuttle Radar Topography Mission (STRM). (**a**) The red dashed circle is the middle and long danger zone from 201–2030. The bold red line represents the EKFZ. The red five-pointed stars represent the historical earthquakes of the EKFZ. The dashed blue box indicates the InSAR data coverage. The black lines represent the rough surface rupture of the historical earthquakes [23,24]. The black dots are the historical earthquakes surrounding the EKFZ. The gray lines represent secondary faults around the study area. The yellow arrows represent GPS velocity fields at the regional. (**b**) Macroscopic distribution of the study area. T B is the Tarim Basin. G-A S P is the Gobi-Ala Shan Platform. T P is the Tibetan Plateau. The blue lines show the main faults around the EKFZ. Altyn Tagh Fault (ATF), Haiyuan Fault (HYF), Ganzi–Yushu Fault (GZ-YS), Xianshuihe Fault (XSHF), Longmenshan Fault (LMS).

The XDS of the EKFZ is located between the 2001 Kunlun Mountains M_S 8.1 earthquake and the 1963 Dulan M_S 7.0 earthquake, and it is a seismic gap in the EKFZ and an earthquake risk region in Mainland China (Figure 1a). It is of great practical significance to study the current locking degree and slip deficit characteristics of the XDS for further understanding of earthquake risk in this region and more scientific and practical earthquake prevention and disaster reduction. In recent years, with the accumulation of InSAR data and the continuous updating of data processing technology, not only can we obtain the crustal deformation field during interseismic periods in fault zones but also timely and effectively obtain large-range high-precision deformation and strain accumulation characteristics of fault by InSAR technology (e.g., [19,25–30]). As shown in Figure 1a, the altitude of the study area is relatively high, resulting in less GNSS measurement data, but SAR satellite data can comprehensively cover it. From July 2014 to July 2019, there are data on both the ascending and descending orbits on the XDS of the EKFZ, which can ensure the integrity of the data and no earthquakes occurred during this period, which can ensure the reliability of the results of the interseismic deformation field of the XDS of the EKFZ. Therefore, we collected the Sentinel-1 data of the XDS of EKFZ from July 2014 to July 2019 to study the kinematic characteristics (such as the locking depth and the slip rate) of the XDS combined with InSAR technology. Based on this, the sectional activity of the XDS of the EKFZ and the difference in tectonic movement among each segment are discussed, and the seismic potential or magnitude in this area is analyzed.

2. InSAR Data and Interseismic Velocity Field

2.1. InSAR Data

Interferometric Synthetic Aperture Radar (InSAR) was first proposed by L.C. Graham [31]. It is a three-dimensional imaging concept and is used as a spatial geodetic technology developed in recent decades. Unlike traditional geodesy techniques (GPS, Leveling, etc.), InSAR technology can measure crustal deformation fields with high spatial resolution [31–35]. At present, SAR satellite data are rich, have high precision, are not constrained by time and climate, etc., and are widely used in monitoring geological disasters, earthquake disasters, volcanic activities, city subsidence, and railway subsidence (e.g., [36–43]). This paper uses data from the European Space Agency (ESA) Sentinel-1 satellite. Compared with other satellites, Sentinel-1 has the advantages of a short revisit period and high orbital accuracy [33]. Since the launch of the satellite, Sentinel-1 data have been widely used in the study of coseismic deformation, such as the 2014 Napa California M_W 6.1 earthquake [38,44,45], the 2015 Nepal M_S 8.1 earthquake [39,46], and the 2017 Jiuzhaigou M_S 7.0 earthquake [40,47]. With the accumulation of SAR satellite data over the years and the continuous improvement of InSAR data processing technology, InSAR technology should also obtain an extensive range and high-resolution fault tectonic deformation field (e.g., [19,25,27–30,48,49]).

2.2. InSAR Data Processing Method

In this paper, InSAR data are processed using the GAMMA commercial software platform [50]. The interseismic deformation field was mainly obtained from the Sentinel-1 SAR satellite data by using the Stacking method. The method was proposed by Wright et al. [51] in 2001. It is a sequential InSAR algorithm that utilizes linear stacking of multiple unwrapped differential interferometry phase graphs to minimize atmospheric errors and improve the accuracy of the deformation rate [51–53]. The principle of the Stacking method assumes that in an independent interferogram, the error phase of atmospheric disturbance is random, and the deformation rate is linear. Then, the average deformation rate in the superposition time range of the study area can be obtained by calculating the average superposition of the phases unwinding corresponding to multiple independent interferograms [51–56]. The specific data processing flow is shown in Figure 2.

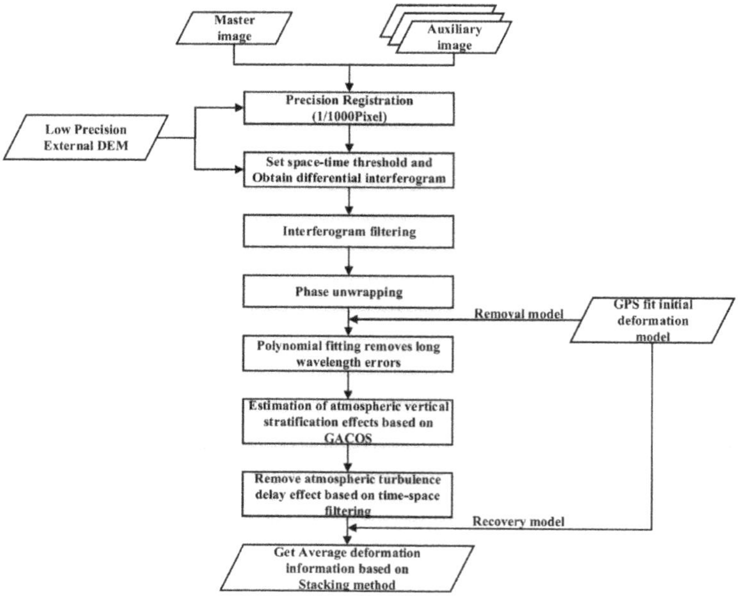

Figure 2. Sequential InSAR algorithm processing flow [55,57].

In this study, a total of 136 Sentinel-1 SAR images covering the XDS of the EKFZ were obtained from July 2014 to July 2019, with 64 ascending and 72 descending orbit images. The spatial range of these data was centered on XDS, 330 km in the NS directions and 280 km in the EW directions (Figure 1a; Table 1). We set the multi-look factor of the interferogram to 100:30, and the corresponding pixel size was about 420 m × 420 m, from which pixels with a coherence degree of about 0.2 were selected for phase unwrapping. Interferograms spanning a short time interval tend to have higher coherence. However, they make small tectonic signals, such as those across the XDS of the EKFZ, more difficult to detect. To minimize geometric decorrelation and errors due to the topography and maximize the deformation signal in the interferogram [25,51–53], we selected pairs of images by constraining the perpendicular and temporal baselines simultaneously. So, to improve the signal-to-noise ratio of interseismic deformation, we selected interferograms based on two criteria (Table 2; Figure 3). (1) Image pairs with temporal baselines of different Days were employed to maximize the deformation signal in the interferograms. (2) Due to the topography of the XDS of the EKFZ being very undulating, spatial baselines (separation between orbits) of less than 10 m, 100 m, and 200 m were used to minimize topography error influences, respectively. As can be seen from Table 2, the temporal and perpendicular baselines are coordinating relations and should be met simultaneously. (1) When the temporal baseline is less than 90 days, the perpendicular baselines must be less than 10 m; (2) When the temporal baselines are between 275 and 455 days, the perpendicular baselines must be less than 100 m; (3) When the temporal baselines between $n + 275$ and $n + 455$ days (n is an integer multiple of 365), the perpendicular baselines must be less than 200 m.

Table 1. Sentinel-1 SAR image and interferogram count.

Flight Direction	Track Number	Number of Images	Number of Selected Image Number	Number of Interferograms	Number of Selected Interferograms
A *	172	64	63	662	165
D *	004	72	41	974	304

* A is the ascending orbit, and D is the descending orbit.

Table 2. Constraint Criteria of Temporal and Perpendicular Baselines.

No.	Temporal Baseline (Days) ΔT	Perpendicular Baseline (Meter) ΔP
1	ΔT < 90 Days	ΔP ≤ 10 m
2	275 Days < ΔT < 455 Days	ΔP ≤ 100 m
3	*n* + 275 Days < ΔT < *n* + 455 Days *	ΔP < 200 m

* *n* is an integer multiple of 365.

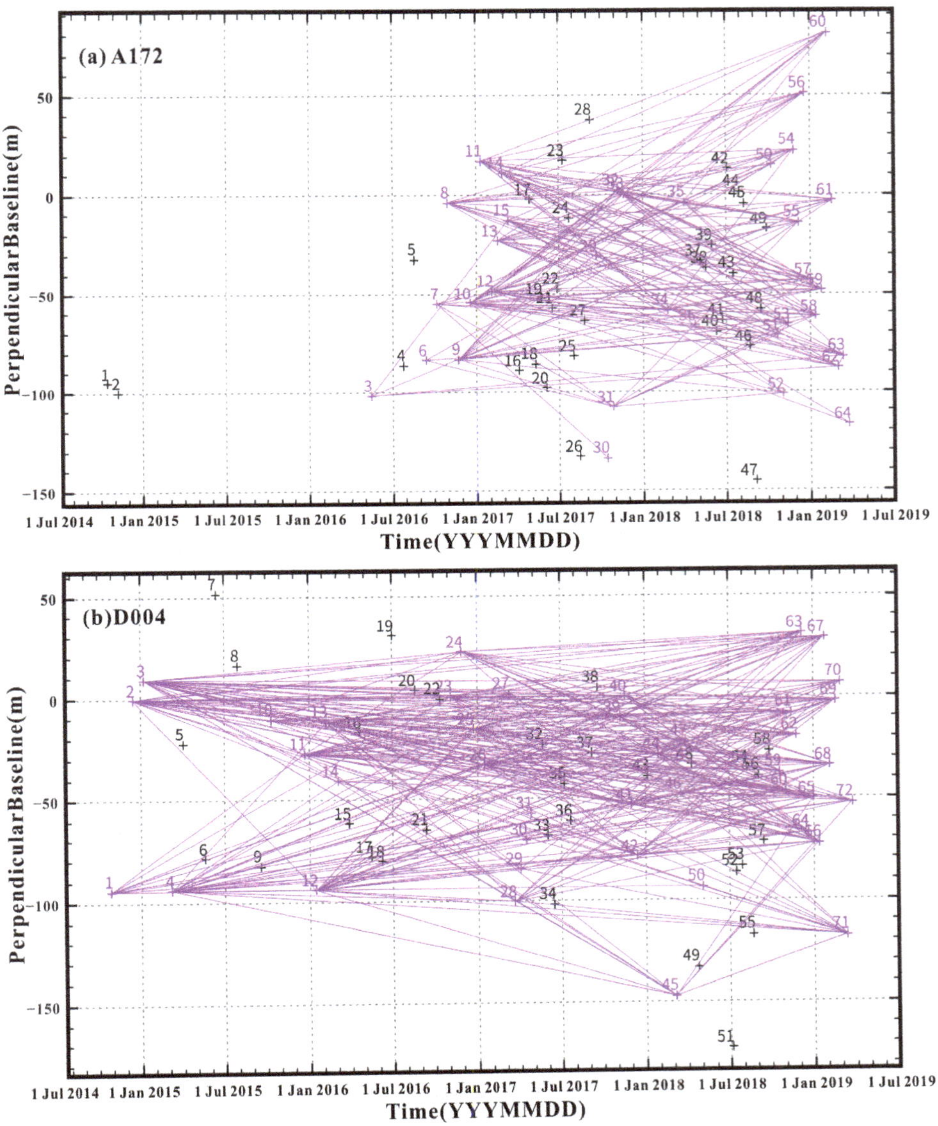

Figure 3. Distribution of temporal and perpendicular baselines of the interferogram. The images included in the inversion calculations are represented by the purple + labels. The images not included in the inversion calculations are represented by the black + labels. The interferograms are represented by purple lines. (**a**) The ascending orbit 172; (**b**) The descending orbit 004.

2.3. InSAR Inversion Interseismic Velocity Field

The inverse slip dislocation theory is a commonly used method to describe slip rate distribution in the interseismic period [58,59]. This theory assumes that the movement of all points inside the fault is determined by the rotation of the fault and the deformation inside the fault, and then the surface deformation caused by the slip deficit is determined by the blocking depth at the fault surface. Therefore, based on the inverse slip dislocation theory, various models (such as the angular dislocation model, rectangular dislocation model, elasticity model, viscoelasticity model, and layered viscoelasticity model) developed to simulate the observed velocities in the interseismic period by researchers and implemented them with code and software, such as TDEFMPDE code [60], Blocks code [61,62], and the software of viscoelastic model layered [63,64]. Since the viscoelastic properties of the crustal medium have no significant influence on the observed interseismic velocity [19,64], the slip rate of the XDS of the EKFZ in the interseismic period was estimated using the elastic medium.

As shown in Figure 1a, multiple branch faults in the XDS of the EKFZ are distributed, and the tectonic background is complex [19,65], so the far-field loading rate [66] or geological slip rate [67] could determine the long-time slip rate of the XDS of the EKFZ. On this basis, combined with the inverse slip dislocation theory, it can be seen that the locking degree of the fault interseismic period is a quotient of the interseismic slip-deficit rate and the interseismic long-time slip rate [19,59]. Therefore, we assume that the interseismic deformation observed by InSAR expresses the loading rate of the far field [61,62,67–71]. A reliable and more informative constrained least square method is used to invert the interseismic slip distribution of the XDS of EKFZ [19,72]. Then, the degree of current fault surface occlusion is estimated.

3. Study of the Interseismic Velocity Field in the XDS

3.1. InSAR Interseismic Velocity Field Analysis

Sentinel-1 SAR data processing mainly involves several critical problems: (1) In image precision registration, to ensure the accuracy of image registration, orbit information, external Digital Elevation Model (DEM), and intensity map should first be used for initial registration, and then enhanced spectral diversity should be used for azimuth registration to achieve fine registration [54,73]; (2) When generating differential interferogram, use the 30 m spatial resolution SRTM DEM released by NASA to simulate and eliminate terrain phase; (3) Considering that dense vegetation, snow and ice cover, climate variability, and other factors in the study area lead to poor coherence of the interferogram, it is necessary to conduct multi-view processing and filtering processing on the interferogram. In the interferogram process, two multi-look processes are adopted: the first multi-look factor was set to 10:3, and the second multi-look factor was set to 100:30. After multi-view processing, the Goldstein filter was used to improve the coherence further [74]; (4) Based on prior fault information, the initial deformation model was constructed to estimate and remove orbit errors; (5) The Generic Atmospheric Correction Online Service (GACOS) was used to estimate the effects of atmospheric vertical stratification, and time-domain high-pass and spatial-domain low-pass filtering were used to estimate the effects of atmospheric turbulence delay [75,76]. Finally, the high accuracy and high spatial resolution mean deformation rate field was obtained in the study area based on the mature temporal InSAR technology Stacking (Figure 4).

As shown in Figure 4, the ascending orbit deformation is opposite to the descending orbit deformation direction, indicating that horizontal movement is the primary movement in this area. In the vicinity of the XDS of the EKFZ, there is the maximum difference in the InSAR deformation field of ascending and descending orbits, and they accord with the movement characteristics of a left-lateral strike-slip fault, indicating that the XDS of the EKFZ mainly influences the crustal deformation in this area. In Figure 4a, the InSAR deformation field in the LOS direction of the A172 has a significant velocity difference of about 2–5 mm/yr along the fault and its extension, and the velocity step is mainly near the

XDS of the EKFZ. There is no significant large-scale difference in other faults. Figure 4b shows that the InSAR deformation field in the LOS direction of the D004 shows this feature and a minor velocity difference of about 1–4 mm/yr near the fault. Therefore, the overall deformation characteristics of the XDS of the EKFZ are small near-field movement and large far-field movement, which is a typical feature of strike-slip fault [19,58].

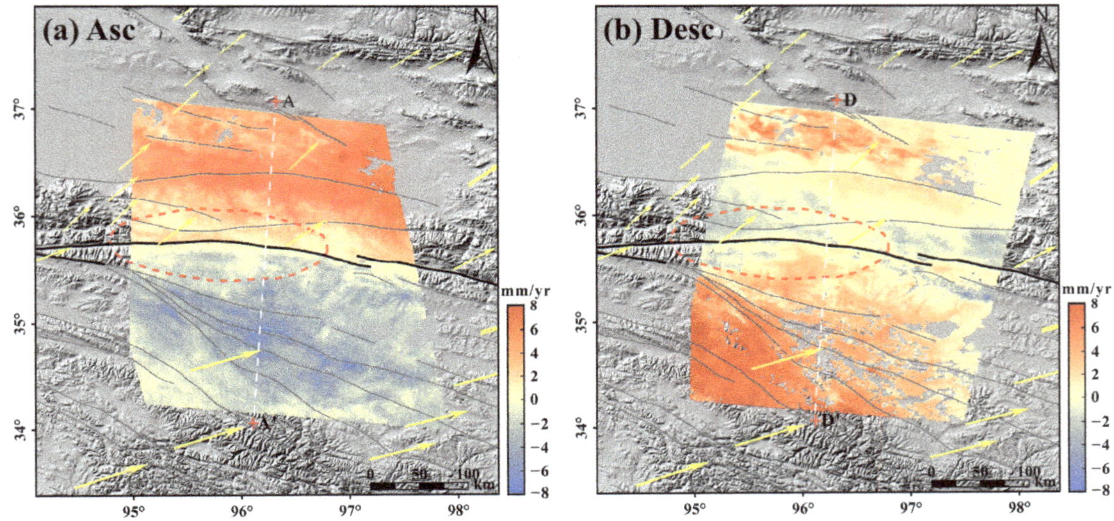

Figure 4. InSAR interseismic velocity field of the XDS. The red dotted circle represents the danger zone (same as in Figure 1). The black line represents the main fault of the EKFZ, The yellow arrows represent GPS velocity fields at the regional, and the gray lines represent the faults around the EKFZ [22]. (**a**) The ascending orbit 172, AA': the profile line of the ascending orbit. (**b**) The descending orbit 004, DD': the profile line of the descending orbit.

3.2. Accuracy Evaluation of InSAR Interseismic Velocity Field

There are two main methods to appraise the precision of the InSAR interseismic deformation results. The first method compares it with GPS results; the second method calculates the standard deviation (SD) of the velocity differences in the overlapping area of adjacent independent orbits [19,30,54,77,78]. This paper used the image data of the ascending and the descending, so the accuracy was by GPS results. We extracted the profile line of the ascending orbit (AA') (Figure 4a) and the descending orbit (DD') (Figure 4b), respectively, to compare the GPS and InSAR results. The profile line position is shown in Figure 4. The profile line length was 150 km on each side of the fault. GPS data were extracted within 120 km on each side of the profile line. InSAR data were extracted within a 50 km width on each side of the profile line. Since InSAR data and GPS data respectively represent deformation rates in different directions, and the activity of the EKFZ is a left-lateral strike-slip, we can ignore the vertical motion component of the EKFZ [19,79]. Therefore, before data extraction, we used the mathematical Formula (1) to convert the GPS-observed data into the deformation rate in the LOS direction using the flight azimuth and radar incidence angle [56,80].

$$D_{LOS} = (-\sin\theta\cos\alpha) \times D_{EW} + \sin\theta\sin\alpha \times D_{NS} \quad (1)$$

where D_{LOS} is the deformation rate in the LOS direction of radar, D_{EW} and D_{NS} are the horizontal east–west deformation rate and north–south deformation rate of GPS, α is the flight azimuth angle, and θ is the radar incidence angle. Secondly, to correct the offset between the GPS data and the reference datum of the InSAR data, the average value corrects the extracted GPS rate. It is compared with the deformation rate in the InSAR LOS direction. The profile of GPS and InSAR deformation rate is shown in Figure 5. From the perspective of visual effect, the two independent data sets of GPS and InSAR have a high degree of agreement. The independent horizontal GPS measurements agree well with the InSAR measurements, which not only supports the hypothesis of minimum vertical deformation but also confirms that the EKFZ movement is mainly horizontal [19,79]. Finally, the SD is 1.87 mm/yr between the InSAR deformation rate of the ascending LOS and GPS, and the SD is 2.45 mm/yr between the InSAR deformation rate of the descending LOS and GPS. Therefore, it can be concluded that the measurement accuracy of the InSAR interseismic velocity field is better than 3 mm/yr.

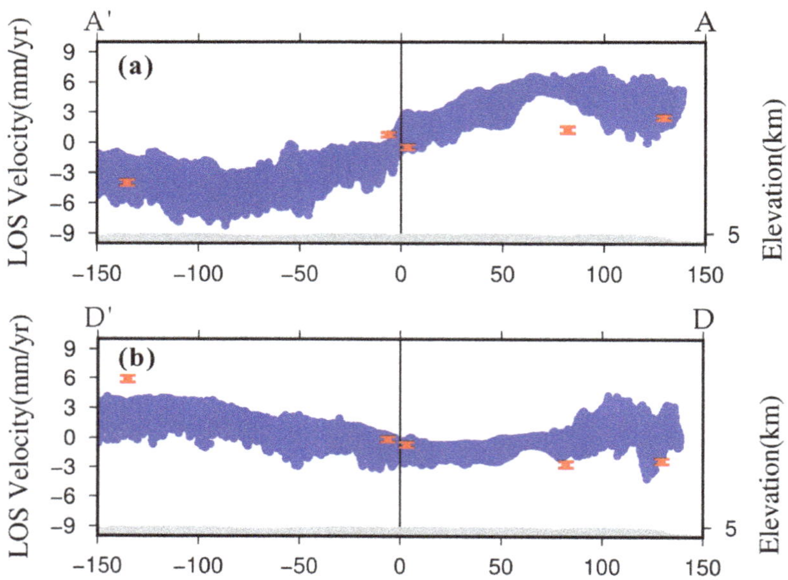

Figure 5. Accuracy evaluation showing the profile of GPS and InSAR deformation rates. The GPS measuring results are represented by red diamonds with error bars. The InSAR measuring results are represented by blue circles. The locations of the EKFZ are represented by the black vertical lines. The topographic information is represented by the gray areas. (**a**) AA′ profile in the ascending orbit and (**b**) DD′ profile in the descending orbit.

4. Interseismic Deformation Modeling Based on InSAR

4.1. Parameters and Smoothing Factors of the Fault Geometry Model

The geometric model parameters of the fault should be determined before the interseismic deformation model based on the InSAR-derived model. The following reasons should be considered before establishing the geometric models of the XDS of the EKFZ. (1) From Figure 4, we can see that the EKFZ mainly influences all the deformation information in the research area, so we do not need to consider the effects of other faults during the inversion process; (2) According to the previous studies, the dip of the XDS of EKFZ ranges from 70° to 90° [19,81]. We performed some search calculations to determine the fault dip angle. After varying the fault dip angle intervals and calculations several times, the results are shown in Figure 6a, and if the fault dip angle of the XDS of the EKFZ was set to 90°, the fitting residual was the smallest. Therefore, the fault dip angle of the XDS of the EKFZ was set to 90° when the fault model was established (Figure 6b); and (3) According to the inverse slip dislocation theory, the fault planes can be divided into upper and lower parts [71,82]. The upper part is responsible for the near-field deformation signal and is assumed to be the seismogenic fault. Its depth is determined to be 20 km by the source depth of the repositioned earthquake. The lower part is responsible for the far-field deformation signal and is assumed to be an elastic layer, and its depth is set to 80 km according to the depth of the lower boundary of the lithosphere [83]. In addition, we tested the slip rate distribution at depths of 20 km, 40 km, 60 km, and 80 km, respectively, and concluded that the slip rate distribution varied little when the section depth was about 40 km.

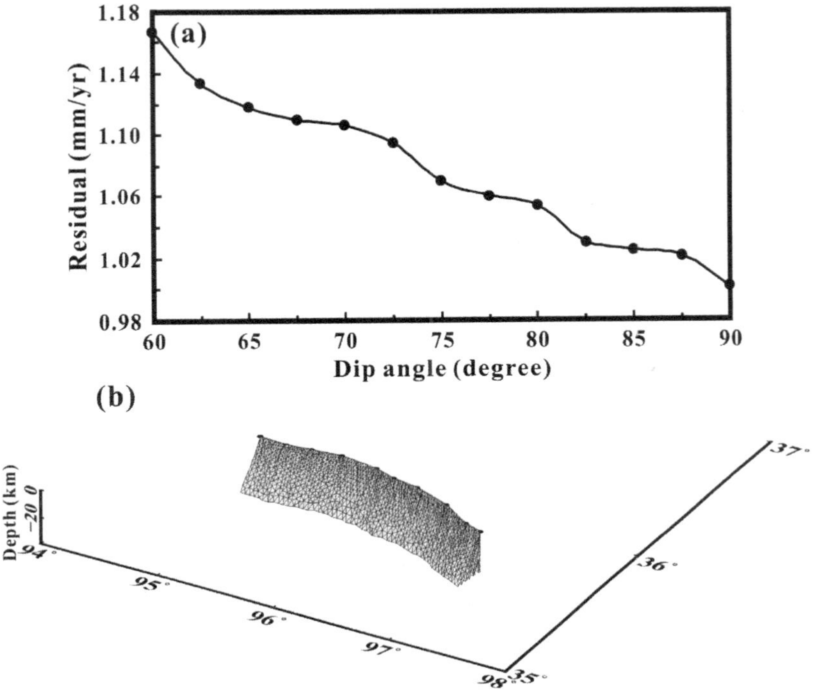

Figure 6. Results of the fault dip angle residual search and effect diagram of fault modeling. (**a**) Variation of the residual with different fault dip angles. (**b**) Variation of fault geometry with different fault dip angles.

4.2. Modeling Effects and Locking Degree Distribution in the XDS

The angular dislocation model can not only depict complex fault planes well but also avoid tearing caused by strike-slip direction deformation [64,68,84]. Therefore, the interseismic slip rate distribution in the XDS of the EKFZ was inverted with the InSAR average velocity field as a constraint (Figure 4). Figure 7 shows the interferogram fitting results, in which Figure 7a,d show the InSAR observation results of the ascending and descending orbits; Figure 7b,e show the interference results of the ascending and descending orbits; Figure 7c,f show the residual results of observation results and interference results; Figure 7g,h show the residual histograms of Figure 7c,f respectively; and Figure 7i shows the curve of model roughness and fitting residual L, with the optimal smoothing factor of 0.5. The overall fitting is reasonable, combined with the deformation characteristics of the region and the deformation characteristics of the near field of the fault. However, because some artifact signals in the local far-field signals were not entirely removed in the preprocessing stage and could not be fitted, they were deducted. Even if they were true deformation signals, they were too far from the XDS of the EKFZ to have anything to do with the movement of the XDS of the EKFZ.

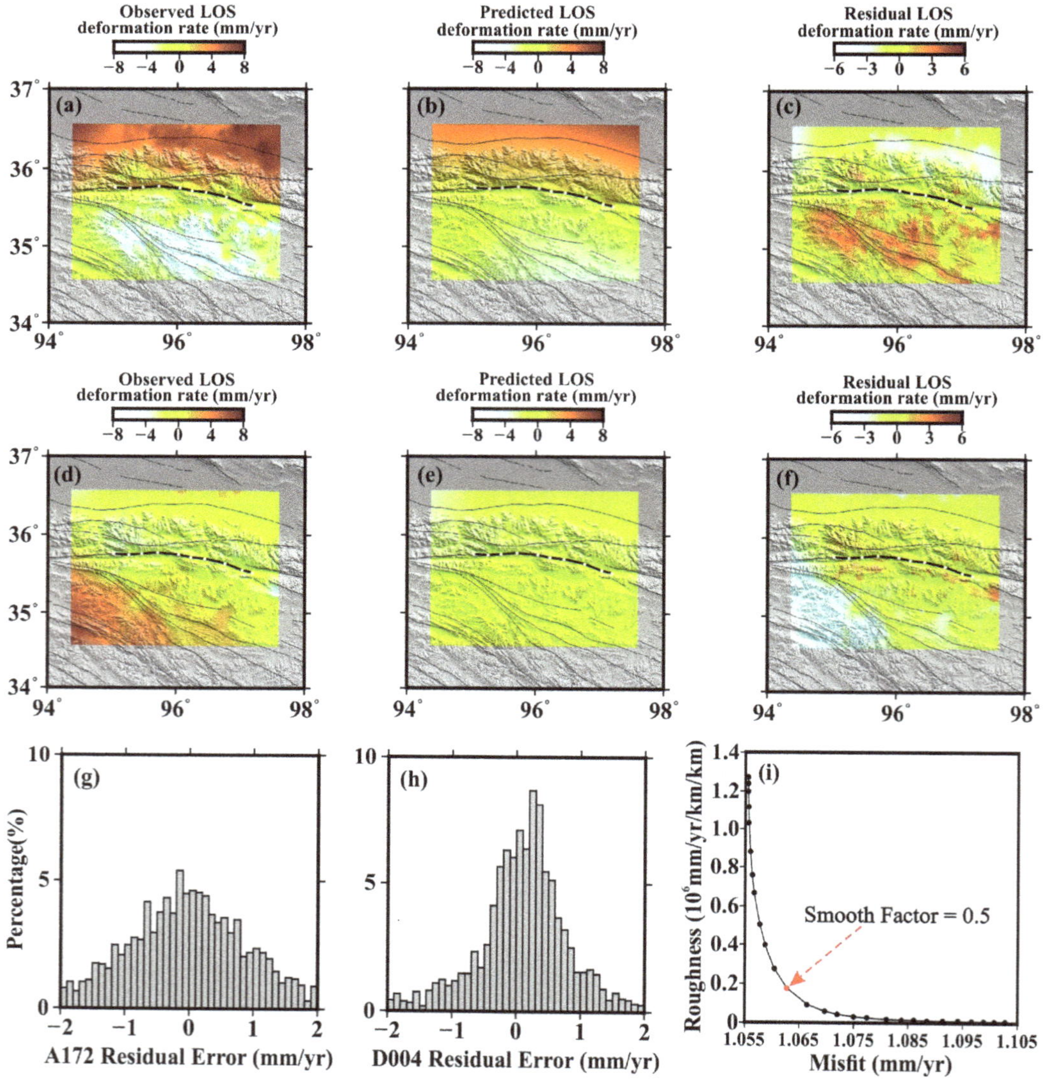

Figure 7. Modeling results and error statistics. The black line represents the main fault of the XDS of the EKFZ. (**a**,**d**) The InSAR observation results of the ascending and descending orbits. (**b**,**e**) The interference-fitting results of the ascending and descending orbits. (**c**,**f**) The residuals of the two results. (**g**,**h**) The residual histograms of (**c**,**f**). (i) The L-curve of model roughness and fitted residual, and the red dot represents the optimal smoothing factor.

Figure 8 shows the distribution of the slip rates on the fault plane, and the fault is in motion in the depth range. In Figure 8a, the deformation information of XDS of the EKFZ is dominated by the strike-slip rate. The deep strike-slip rate of the fault is about 6 mm/yr, and the maximum locked depth is about 30 km. In Figure 8b, the distribution of the dip-slip rate is limited to 2 mm/yr in the fault deep. In Figure 8c, the distribution of the slip loss is about 6 mm/yr on the fault surface.

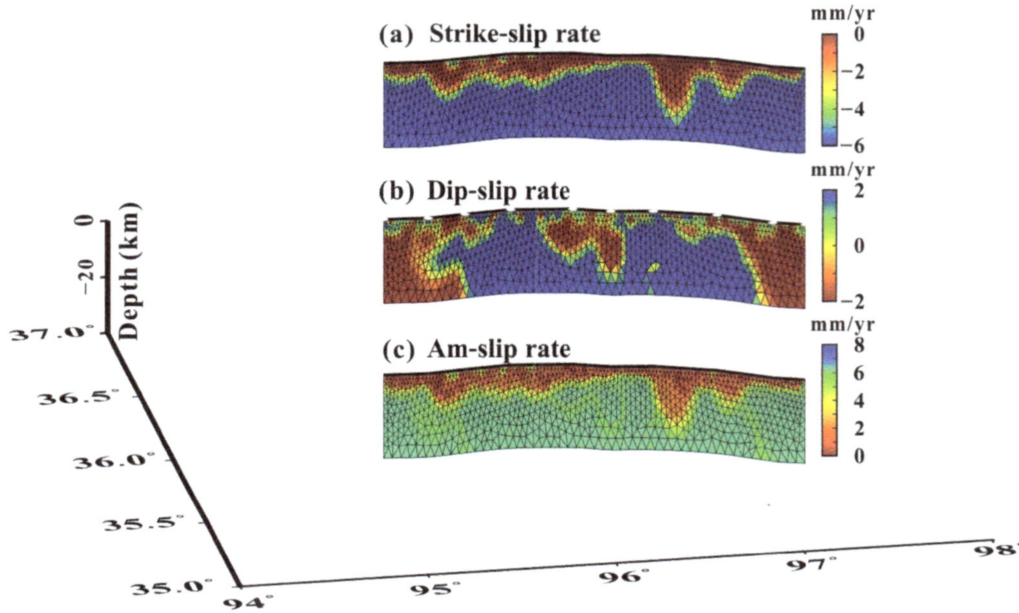

Figure 8. Interseismic slip distribution of the fault plane. (**a**) Strike-slip rate, in which negative values indicate left-lateral strike-slip motion to the east. (**b**) Dip-slip rate, in which the red (negative) values represent downward motion. White (positive) values indicate upward motion. (**c**) Am-slip rate represents the distribution of the slip-deficit rate on the fault plane.

5. Discussion

5.1. Present-Day Strain Distribution around the XDS of the EKFZ

It can be seen from Figure 4 that the InSAR deformation field captured the deformation gradient of the XDS of the EKFZ. However, there are other large local deformation gradients in the deformation field, which may be related to glacier, landslide, seasonal frozen soil, or other non-tectonic factors [85]. Therefore, the three-dimensional deformation field of the XDS of the EKFZ was constructed by integrating the previously published GNSS observations [86,87] combined with the InSAR deformation observations obtained from the ascending and descending orbits (Figure 9a–c). Figure 9a shows the E-W velocity component in the study area, and a velocity gradient was observed along the XDS of the EKFZ, indicating that a shear strain rate concentration is located in this region. Figure 9b shows the N-S velocity component in the study area, and there is no obvious velocity gradient along the XDS of the EKFZ. Figure 9c shows the velocity component in the vertical direction, and there is no obvious velocity gradient along the XDS of the EKFZ.

The strain rate field is one of the important constraints on tectonic deformation and allows for assessing seismic risks [19,42,88–90]. In this study area, we obtained the second strain rate invariant of the XDS of the EKFZ based on the three-dimensional deformation field (Figure 9d). As can be seen from Figure 9d, the accumulation of strain is mainly concentrated in the southeast direction of the Kusai Lake segment of EKFZ (F1-1), the XDS of the EKFZ (F1-2), and Tuosuo Lake segment (F1-3), with the accumulation amount of about 80 nano-strain, and other regions are diffused. It can be inferred that the EKFZ dominates the strain model in the Qinghai–Tibet area and that the 2001 Kunlun Mountains M_S 8.1 earthquake has a loading effect on the strain accumulation of F1-1 and extends to the southeast direction.

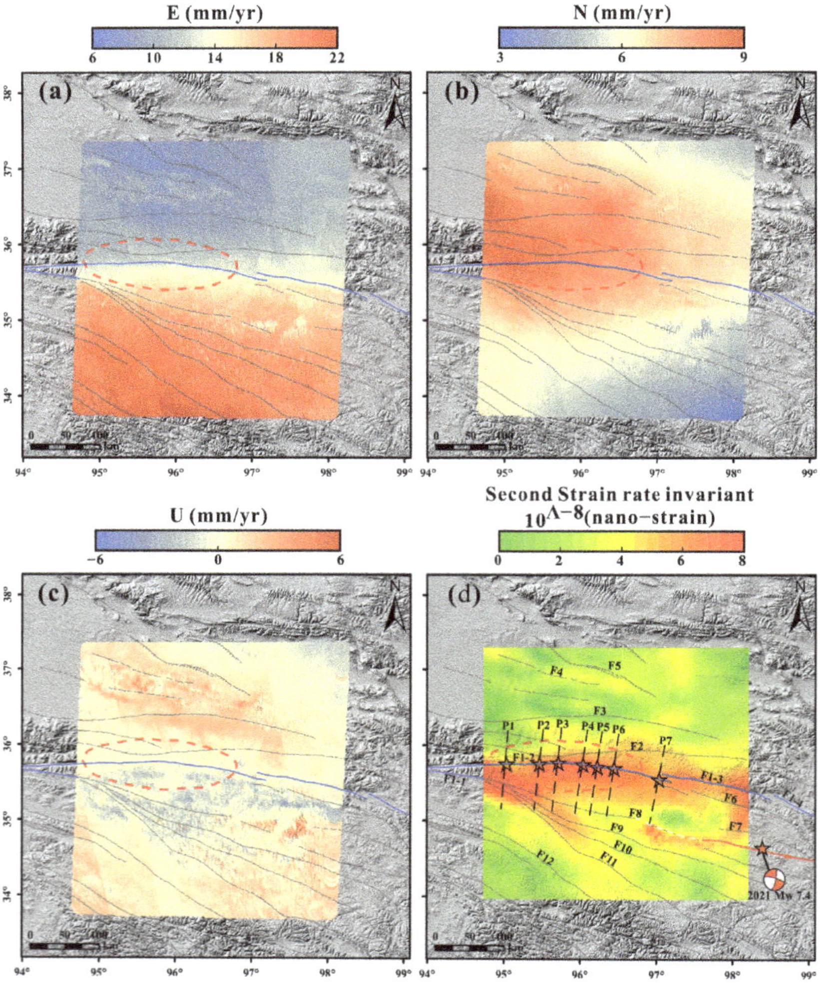

Figure 9. The three-dimensional deformation field and second invariants of the strain rates of the XDS. The blue line is the main fault of the EKFZ, and the gray line represents faults (same as in Figure 4) [22]. The red dotted circle represents the danger zone (same as in Figure 1). (**a**) Velocity in the eastern direction. (**b**) Velocity in the northern direction. (**c**) Velocity in the vertical direction. (**d**) Second invariants of the strain rates (The black five-pointed star is the fault position obtained by the inversion of spiral dislocation. The black dashed line is the position of the fit profile. The red five-pointed star is the 2021 Maduo M_W 7.4 earthquake. The white dotted line is presumed to be the extension direction of the Jiangcuo fault. The red line is the Maduo surface rupture [24]). (F1-1: Kusai Lake segment of EKFZ, F1-2: the XDS of EKFZ, F1-3: Tuosuo Lake segment of EKFZ, F1-4: Maqin–Maqu segment of EKFZ, F2: Middle Kunlun fault, F3: Qaidam south margin fault, F4: Qaidam north central fault, F5: Qaidam north margin fault, F6: Dagou–Changmahe fault, F7: Maduo–Gande fault, F8: Jiangcuo fault, F9: Dari fault, F10: Bayanqala fault, F11: Wudaoliang–Changsha Gongma fault, F12: Wudaoliang–Qumalai fault).

In the strain rate diagram (Figure 9d), we noticed that the strain variables east of the XDS of the EKFZ are not concentrated on a single fault, such as the Middle Kunlun fault (F2), Dagou–Changmahe fault (F6), and Maduo-Gande fault (F7). This dense strain rate field also accords with the diffuse distribution, and it can be seen that the strain rate is absorbed not only by the fault systems but also by the deformation of the small blocks separated by faults. The faults north of the EKFZ include the Qaidam south margin fault (F3), Qaidam north central fault (F4), and Qaidam north margin fault (F5), and they are collectively referred to as the Qaidam fault. The strain rate is not significantly at the Qaidam fault but cannot be ignored. The faults south of the EKFZ include Jiangcuo fault (F8), Dari fault (F9), Bayanqala fault (F10), Wudaoliang–Changsha Gongma fault (F11), and Wudaoliang–Qumalai fault (F12). It is noteworthy that the strain rates of Jiangcuo, Dari, Bayanqala, and Wudaoliang–Changsha Gongma faults are significant, which may be mainly caused by the 2001 Kunlun Mountains M_S 8.1 earthquake. From a regional perspective (Figure 1a), the Jiangcuo fault belongs to the secondary fault on the south side of the EKFZ, and its westward extension could be connected with the 2001 Kunlun Mountains M_S 8.1 earthquake, so the predecessor also referred to the two as Kunlun Mountain Pass–Jiangcuo fault [91]. The Maduo earthquake occurred in 2021, and field research showed that the earthquake produced a coseismic surface rupture zone with the characteristics of a left-lateral strike-slip in a field of about 151 km (Red line in Figure 9d). Based on this, it is inferred that the Jiangcuo fault extends along the southeast direction (white dotted line in Figure 9d) and is connected with the surface rupture generated by the 2021 Maduo M_W 7.4 earthquake. Further, it confirms that the 2021 Maduo M_W 7.4 earthquake resulted from the further southeast migration of the strain energy of the 2001 Kunlun Mountains M_S 8.1 earthquake along the EKFZ [24].

5.2. Seismogenic Potential of the XDS of the EKFZ

In the introduction, a detailed description was given of the scholars' analysis and study of various seismic data [7–9], model method [10], and coulomb stress variation [92–95], all of which indicate that with the occurrence of strong earthquakes in the surrounding area of the XDS of EKFZ, the possibility of strong earthquakes in this area increases significantly. Therefore, it is necessary to study the seismic potential of the XDS of the EKFZ.

The interseismic fault-locking technology has been widely used in focal fault risk assessment and earthquake potential magnitude estimation. During interseismic periods, the strengthening of fault contraction indicates that the coupling degree between fault planes in this region is high, increasing strain accumulation. Therefore, it can be considered that there is a high-incidence area of earthquakes in this region [19,30,96]. The interseismic locking area is constrained using the high precision and high-density geodetic observation data, and the approximate range of coseismic slip is determined based on it. Based on the long-term fault slip rate and the time of the recent earthquake, we can estimate accurately the potential magnitude of the earthquake in this study area. According to the distribution of the slip-deficit rate shown in Figure 8c, the moment accumulation (M_0) can be calculated through the first-order relation [29,30]. The relationship (Formula (2)) is as follows:

$$M_0 = \mu U A \tag{2}$$

where A represents the area of the fault patch, μ represents the shear modulus, set to be 30 GPa, and U represents the slip-deficit rate from the inversion. The XDS of EKFZ is a large seismic void region, but through geological mapping and dating, scholars have revealed that there have been at least six paleoseismic events in this section since the Holocene, and the last paleoseismic event was 1540 ± 92 aB.P. [3,7,15,97,98], so we surmised that the stress accumulation in the XDS of EKFZ lasted about 483 ± 92 years. Over 483 years, the cumulative elastic strain energy of the XDS of the EKFZ can produce an M_W 7.29 ± 0.1 earthquake in the future. However, by using quantitative geological data and other methods, the former people speculated that there is an M (7.5~8.0) earthquake risk in the XDS of the EKFZ [3,9,15,81], which is different from the research results in this paper. According to the literature review, the reasons may be as follows: (1) This paper does not consider the stress loading effect of the left-lateral slip of the 2001 Kunlun Mountains M_S 8.1 earthquake on the XDS of EKFZ [7,92,93,97]; (2) The time of earthquake recurrence may be inconsistently defined due to faulting habits and the incompleteness of paleoseismic events [3,9,15,81], and the time definition in this paper is small; (3) Combined with the statistical slip rate in Table 3, it can be inferred that the slip rate of InSAR inversion in this paper is smaller than that of geological estimation [15,99,100]. To sum up, the XDS is undoubtedly the most dangerous area for future large earthquakes in the EKFZ, which needs special attention.

Table 3. The slip rate from XDS to Xiugou Basin of EKFZ.

Position	Dislocation Maker	Method	Age (ka)	Dislocation Distance (m)	Slip Rate (mm/yr)	Reference
XDS	Terrace dislocation	Cosmogenic nuclide	2.4~11.8	23~174	10-15	[99,101]
XDS	Terrace dislocation	Cosmogenic nuclide	1.8~8.1	24~110	11.7 ± 1.5	[15,81,98]
XDS	Terrace dislocation	Thermo luminescence	262~335	2970 ± 30	11.6 ± 0.9	[100]
XDS	NA	InSAR	NA	NA	9.8 ± 2.3	This study
Xiugou west	Alluvial fan dislocation	Thermo luminescence	297 ± 19	2970 ± 30	10.1 ± 0.8	[100,102]
Xiugou middle	Terrace dislocation	Cosmogenic nuclide	6.3~8.1	90 ± 5	12.9 ± 2.9	[15,81,98,100]
Xiugou	NA	InSAR	NA	NA	8 ± 3	This study

5.3. Variations of the Present-Day Slip Rate in the XDS of the EKFZ

In this paper, there are some errors in the data collection and processing of the ascending and descending orbit. Therefore, to ensure the accuracy of data processing in advance, based on the discrete GPS data and the InSAR deformation rate field of the ascending and descending orbits, we obtained the three-dimensional crustal deformation field in the study area (Figure 9a–c), and the fault movement characteristics in the study area were obtained by inversion fitting. It can be seen that most regions have been uplifted, but the localization of this phenomenon is remarkable from Figure 9c, indicating that the vertical motion may contain a large number, including non-tectonic deformation. Therefore, we only considered the horizontal motion components and ignored the vertical motion components in this study. Since the InSAR deformation measurement is based on the reference range of radar LOS, it should first be converted into the deformation rate in the parallel fault direction through Formula (3), and the profile location was selected, as shown in Figure 9. The fault strike parameters at the profile were set to 90°, 88.95°, 94.96°, 104°, 97.20°, 100.5°, and 105.62°, which were all perpendicular to the fault strike. Secondly, according to Savage et al., the theoretical model formula of spiral dislocation (Formula (4)) was given to invert the current active motion characteristics of the study area [58]. The final fitting results in the parallel direction of the fault are shown in Figure 10.

$$D_{fault} = V_n \cos\beta + V_e \sin\beta \tag{3}$$

$$V_0 = V_{ref} + V * a\tan((X_0 - X)/D)/PI \tag{4}$$

where in Formula (2), D_{fault} represents the parallel deformation rate, V_n represents the north deformation rate, V_e represents the east deformation rate, and β represents the fault strike. In Formula (3), V_0 represents the observed value, V_{ref} represents the overall offset, V represents the fitting slip rate, X_0 represents the distance between the observed value and the fault, X represents the distance between the fitting value and the fault, and PI is π.

In this study, by using the discrete GPS data and the InSAR deformation rate field, the three-dimensional crustal deformation field of the XDS of the EKFZ was obtained. Using seven profiles of the InSAR deformations as constraints, the spiral dislocation model used estimated the locking depth of the XDS to be 29 ± 6 m, the average slip rate of the XDS (P1–P6) to be 9.8 ± 2.3 mm/yr, the locking depth of Xiugou Basin to be 26 m, and the average slip rate of Xiugou Basin (P7) slip to be 8 ± 3 mm/yr, among which the fitted locking depth is basically consistent with the previous modeling results (Figure 8).

The results of this paper are compared with the slip rate obtained by previous geological mapping and dating (Table 3, e.g., [15,99,100]). The average slip rate of the XDS to Xiugou Basin of EKFZ obtained by this study is basically consistent with them and is also close to the 10~12 mm/yr slip rate of the EKFZ observed by GPS today [20,86]. It can be seen from Figure 10 that the slip rate of the XDS gradually increases from west to east, and the fitting values of P1, P2, and P3 are relatively small, which may be caused by the sparse observed number of the InSAR deformation at these three profile locations, but it does not affect the accuracy of the results.

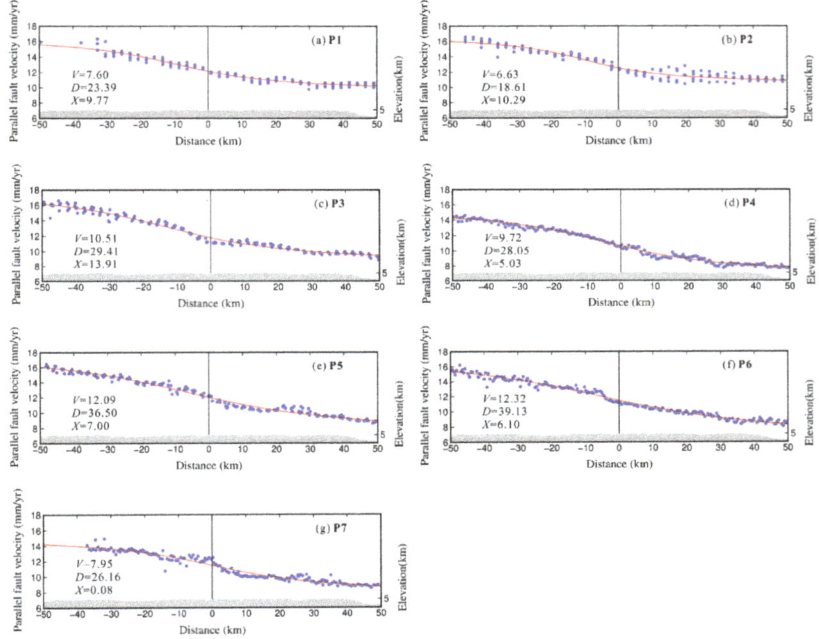

Figure 10. Section view of the XDS of the EKFZ along the parallel direction in Figure 9. The blue dots represent InSAR observations, the red line segments represent the best-fit values, the black vertical lines represent the location of the EKF (same as in Figure 5), and the gray areas represent topographic information (same as in Figure 5). The best fitting parameters are marked in the lower left corner of (**a–g**). *V* represents the modeled slip rate at depth (mm/year), *D* represents locking depth (km), and *X* represents the distance from fault location (km).

6. Conclusions

In this study, InSAR technology was used to obtain the InSAR interseismic deformation field of the XDS of the EKFZ based on the Sentinel-1 SAR data of the ascending and descending orbits, and the deformations were in good agreement with the GPS observations. Based on these constraints, the slip rate and locking depth of the region were derived by combining the triangular dislocation model and the spiral dislocation theoretical model, and the seismic potential of the XDS of the EKFZ was estimated.

The following conclusions could be drawn from this study: (1) The LOS deformation field of the XDS of the EKFZ was obtained by using Sentinel-1 data of ascending and descending orbits, which indicated that the XDS of the EKFZ is dominated by horizontal movement. Combined with the interference results, it is shown that the strike-slip rate dominates the deformation information of the XDS of the EKFZ. The deep strike-slip rate of the fault is about 6 mm/yr, the deep dip-slip rate is about 2 mm/yr, and the slip-deficit rate on the fault surface is about 6 mm/yr; (2) Combined with the spiral dislocation theory model, the slip rate of the XDS to Xiugou Basin of the EKFZ has a gradually increasing trend, with an average slip rate of 9.6 ± 2.3 mm/yr and a locking depth of 29 ± 5 m; (3) The stress accumulation is about 483 ± 92 years in the XDS of EKFZ and indicates that the cumulative elastic strain energy of the XDS of the EKFZ can produce an M_W 7.29 ± 0.1 earthquake in the future, which needs special attention.

Author Contributions: All the authors participated in editing and reviewing the manuscript. Conceptualization, L.J. and L.Z.; methodology, S.K. and N.L.; software, S.K. and J.X.; validation, F.J.; formal analysis, S.K. and L.J.; investigation, S.K. and L.Z.; resources, S.K. and J.X.; data curation C.L. and W.Z.; writing—original draft preparation, S.K.; writing—review and editing, S.K., L.J., L.Z., C.L. and W.Z.; visualization, S.K. and W.Z.; supervision, L.J. and N.L.; project administration, S.K., C.L. and J.X.; funding acquisition, S.K. and J.X. All authors have read and agreed to the published version of the manuscript.

Funding: This research was funded by the Natural Science Foundation of Shaanxi Province, China (Nos. 2023-JC-QN-0329, 2023-JC-QN-0292, and 2023-JC-QN-0296), the National Natural Science Foundation of China (No. 42104061), and the Spark Programs of Earthquake Sciences granted by the China Earthquake Administration (No. XH23059YA).

Data Availability Statement: The Sentinel-1 data used in this study are downloaded from the European Space Agency (ESA) through the ASF Data Hub website https://vertex.daac.asf.alaska.edu/.

Conflicts of Interest: The authors declare no conflict of interest.

References

1. Qinghai Earthquake Agency, China Earthquake Administration; Institute of Crustal Dynamics, China Earthquake Administration. *The East Kunlun Active Fault Belt*; Earthquake: Beijing, China, 1999. (In Chinese)
2. Li, C.F.; He, Q.L.; Zhao, G.G. Paleoearthquake studies on the Eastern section of The Kunlun Fault. *Acta Seismol. Sin.* **2005**, *27*, 60–67. (In Chinese)
3. Hu, D.G.; Ye, P.S.; Wu, Z.H.; Wu, Z.H.; Zhao, X.T.; Liu, Q.S. Research on holocene paleoearthquakes on the Xidatan segment of the East Kunlun fault zone in Northern Tibet. *Quat. Sci.* **2006**, *26*, 1012–1020. (In Chinese)
4. Xia, Y.S.; Li, Z.M.; Tu, H.W.; Yao, J.J. Ancient earthquake research of east Kunlun fault zone. *Prog. Geophys.* **2013**, *28*, 146–154. (In Chinese)
5. Peltzer, G.; Crampé, F.; King, G. Evidence of Nonlinear Elasticity of the Crust from the Mw7.6 Manyi (Tibet) Earthquake. *Science* **1999**, *286*, 272–276. [CrossRef] [PubMed]
6. Xu, X.W. Scientific investigation on the Mani, northern Tibet earthquake. In *1999 China Earthquake Yearbook*; Seismological Press: Beijing, China, 2000. (In Chinese)
7. Li, J.J.; Zhang, J.L.; Cai, Y.Y. Investigation of Historical Earthquakes, Paleo-earthquakes and Seismic Gap in the Eastern Kunlun Fautl Zone. *Earthqauke* **2017**, *37*, 103–111. (In Chinese)
8. Hu, D.G.; Wu, Z.H.; Wu, Z.H.; Zhao, X.T.; Ye, P.S. Late quaternary paleoseismic history on the Kusai Lake segment of East Kunlun Fautl zone in northern Tibet. *Quat. Sci.* **2007**, *27*, 27–34. (In Chinese)
9. Hu, D.G.; Ye, P.S.; Wu, F.; Zhang, Y.L.; Wu, Z.H.; Liu, Q.S.; Wu, Z.H. Late quaternary seismic history on the Xidatan segment of East Kunlun Fault zone in northern Tibet. *Quat. Sci.* **2008**, *28*, 214–221. (In Chinese)
10. Cai, Y.Y.; Zhang, J.L. Repeating Intervals and Potentials of Earthquakes in the Eastern Kunlun Fault Zone. *Earthquake* **2018**, *38*, 58–65. (In Chinese)
11. Shao, Z.G.; Wu, Y.Q.; Ji, L.Y.; Diao, F.Q.; Shi, F.Q.; Li, Y.J.; Long, F.; Zhang, H.; Zhu, L.Y.; Chen, C.Y.; et al. Comprehensive determination for the late stage of the interseismic period of major faults in the boundary zone of active tectonic blocks in Chinese mainland. *Chin. J. Geophys.* **2022**, *65*, 4643–4658. (In Chinese)
12. Wang, P.; Shao, Z.G.; Liu, X.X.; Yin, X.F. Ten-years probability of strong earthquakes on major faults in boundaries of active blocks in Chinese continent. *Chin. J. Geophys.* **2022**, *65*, 3829–3843. (In Chinese)
13. Loveless, J.P.; Meade, B.J. Partitioning of localized and diffuse deformation in the Tibetan Plateau from joint inversions of geologic and geodetic observations. *Earth Planet. Sci. Lett.* **2011**, *303*, 11–24. [CrossRef]
14. Li, Y.H.; Cu, D.X.; Hao, M. GPS-Constrained Inversion of Slip Rate on Majior Active Faults in the Northeastern Margin of Tibet Plateau. *Earth Sci.-J. China Univ. Geosci.* **2015**, *40*, 1767–1780. (In Chinese)
15. Jerome, V.D.W.; Paul, T.; Frederick, J.R.; Anne-Sophie, M.; Bertrand, M.; Yves, G.; Robert, C.F.; Marc, W.C.; Zhao, G.G.; Xu, Z.Q. Uniform postglacial slip-rate along the central 600 km of the Kunlun Fault (Tibet), from ^{26}Al, ^{10}Be, and ^{14}C dating of riser offsets, and climatic origin of the regional morphology. *Geophys. J. Int.* **2002**, *3*, 356–388.
16. Ma, Y.S.; Shi, W.; Zhang, Y.Q.; Yang, N.; Zhang, C.S.; Zhang, H.P. Characteristics of the activity of the Maqu segment of the East Kunlun active fault belt and its eastward extension. *Geol. Bull. China* **2005**, *24*, 30–35. (In Chinese)
17. Kirby, E.; Harkins, N.; Wang, E.; Shi, X.; Fan, C.; Burbank, D. Slip rate gradients along the eastern Kunlun fault. *Tectonics* **2007**, *26*, C2010–C2011. [CrossRef]

18. Harkins, N.; Kirby, E. Fluvial terrace riser degradation and determination of slip rates on strike-slip faults: An example from the Kunlun fault, China. *Geophys. Res. Lett.* **2008**, *35*, 94–96. [CrossRef]
19. Zhu, L.; Ji, L.; Liu, C. Interseismic slip rate and locking along the Maqin–Maqu Segment of the East Kunlun Fault, Northern Tibetan Plateau, based on Sentinel-1 images. *J. Asian Earth Sci.* **2021**, *211*, 104703. [CrossRef]
20. Zhang, P.; Shen, Z.; Wang, M.; Gan, W.; Burgmann, R.; Molnar, P.; Wang, Q.; Niu, Z.; Sun, J.; Wu, J.; et al. Continuous deformation of the Tibetan Plateau from global positioning system data. *Geol. Soc. Am. Bull.* **2004**, *116*, S809. [CrossRef]
21. Sun, J.B.; Xu, X.W.; Shen, Z.K.; Shi, Y.L.; Liang, F. Parameter inversion of the 1997 Mani earthquake from InSAR coseismic deformation field based on linear elastic dislocation model-I. Uniform slip inversion. *Chin. J. Geophys.* **2007**, *50*, 1091–1110. (In Chinese)
22. Deng, Q.D.; Zhang, P.Z.; Ran, Y.K.; Yang, X.P.; Min, W. Basic characteristics of active tectonics of China. *Sci. China Ser. D* **2002**, *32*, 1020–1030. (In Chinese)
23. Xu, X.; Yu, G.; Klinger, Y.; Tapponnier, P.; Van Der Woerd, J. Reevaluation of surface rupture parameters and faulting segmentation of the 2001 Kunlunshan earthquake (Mw 7.8), northern Tibetan Plateau, China. *J. Geophys. Res. Solid Earth* **2006**, *111*, B05316.
24. Pan, J.W.; Bai, M.K.; Li, C.; Liu, F.C.; Li, H.B.; Liu, D.L.; Chevalier, M.L.; Wu, K.G.; Wang, P.; Lu, H.J.; et al. Coseismic surface rupture and seismogenic structure of the 2021-05-22 Maduo (Qinghai) M_S 7.4 earthquake. *Acta Geol. Sin.* **2021**, *95*, 1655–1670. (In Chinese)
25. Wang, H.; Wright, T.J.; Biggs, J. Interseismic slip rate of the northwestern Xianshuihe fault from InSAR data. *Geophys. Res. Lett.* **2009**, *36*, 139–145. [CrossRef]
26. Wang, H.; Peng, J.H. Test on InSAR atmospheric delay correction using ECMWF model. *J. Guangdong Univ. Technol.* **2014**, *31*, 74–77. (In Chinese)
27. Chaussard, E.; Johnson, C.W.; Fattahi, H.; Bürgmann, R. Potential and limits of InSAR to characterize interseismic deformation independently of GPS data: Application to the southern San Andreas Fault system. *Geochem. Geophys. Geosyst.* **2016**, *17*, 1214–1229. [CrossRef]
28. Shirzaei, M.; Bürgmann, R.; Fielding, E.J. Applicability of Sentinel-1 Terrain Observation by Progressive Scans multitemporal interferometry for monitoring slow ground motions in the San Francisco Bay Area. *Geophys. Res. Lett.* **2017**, *44*, 2733–2742. [CrossRef]
29. Liu, C.; Ji, L.; Zhu, L.; Zhao, C. InSAR-Constrained Interseismic Deformation and Potential Seismogenic Asperities on the Altyn Tagh Fault at 91.5–95°E, Northern Tibetan Plateau. *Remote Sens.* **2018**, *10*, 943. [CrossRef]
30. Zhu, L.; Ji, L.; Liu, C.; Xu, J.; Liu, X.; Liu, L.; Zhao, Q. The 8 January 2022, Menyuan Earthquake in Qinghai, China: A Representative Event in the Qilian-Haiyuan Fault Zone Observed Using Sentinel-1 SAR Images. *Remote Sens.* **2022**, *14*, 6078. [CrossRef]
31. Graham, L.C. Synthetic interferometer radar for topographic mapping. *Proc. IEEE* **2005**, *62*, 763–768. [CrossRef]
32. Xu, C.; Liu, Y.; Wen, Y.; Wang, R. Coseismic Slip Distribution of the 2008 Mw 7.9 Wenchuan Earthquake from Joint Inversion of GPS and InSAR Data. *Bull. Seismol. Soc. Am.* **2010**, *100*, 2736–2749. [CrossRef]
33. Salvi, S.; Stramondo, S.; Funning, G.J.; Ferretti, A.; Sarti, F.; Mouratidis, A. The Sentinel-1 mission for the improvement of the scientific understanding and the operational monitoring of the seismic cycle. *Remote Sens. Environ.* **2012**, *120*, 164–174. [CrossRef]
34. Wang, R.; Parolai, S.; Ge, M.; Jin, M.; Walter, T.R.; Zschau, J. The 2011 Mw 9.0 Tohoku Earthquake: Comparison of GPS and Strong-Motion Data. *Bull. Seismol. Soc. Am.* **2013**, *103*, 1336–1347. [CrossRef]
35. Zhang, Q.Y.; Zhang, J.F.; Li, Y.S.; Li, B.Q.; Luo, S.M.; Ma, Q.Z. Acquisition of Three Dimensional Deformation Field of Bam Earthquake. *Sci. Technol. Eng.* **2021**, *21*, 2179–2185. (In Chinese)
36. Massonnet, D.; Rossi, M.; Carmona, C.; Adragna, F.; Peltzer, G.; Feigl, K.; Rabaute, T. The displacement field of the Landers earthquake mapped by radar interferometry. *Nature* **1993**, *364*, 138–142. [CrossRef]
37. Lu, Z.; Wicks, C.; Dzurisin, D.; Power, J.A.; Moran, S.C.; Thatcher, W. Magmatic inflation at a dormant stratovolcano: 1996-1998 activity at Mount Peulik volcano, Alaska, revealed by satellite radar interferometry. *J. Geophys. Res. Solid Earth* **2002**, *107*, ETG 4-1–ETG 4-13. [CrossRef]
38. Li, Y.S.; Feng, W.P.; Zhang, J.F.; Li, Z.H.; Tian, Y.F.; Jiang, W.L.; Luo, Y. Coseismic slip of the 2014 Mw 6.1 Napa, California Earthquke revealed by Sentinel-1 A InSAR. *Chin. J. Geophys.* **2015**, *58*, 2339–2349. (In Chinese)
39. Qu, C.Y.; Zuo, R.H.; Shan, X.J.; Zhang, G.H.; Song, X.G.; Liu, Y.H.; Yu, L. Coseismic deformation field of the Nepal Ms 8.1 earthquake from Sentinel-1 A InSAR data fault slip inversion. *Chin. J. Geophys.* **2017**, *60*, 151–162. (In Chinese)
40. Ji, L.Y.; Liu, C.J.; Xu, J.; Liu, L.; Long, F.; Zhang, Z.W. InSAR observation and inversion of the seismogenic fault for the 2017 Jiuzhaigou M_S 7.0 earthquake in China. *Chin. J. Geophys.* **2017**, *60*, 4069–4082. (In Chinese)
41. Zhang, Q.; Li, Y.; Zhang, J.; Luo, Y. InSAR technique applied to the monitoring of the Qinghai–Tibet Railway. *Nat. Hazard. Earth Syst. Sci.* **2019**, *19*, 2229–2240. [CrossRef]
42. Wang, Y.; Yang, J.; Liu, Y.P.; Tian, S.; Huang, X.D. Landslide Monitoring of Wuming Mountain in Jizhou, Tianjin based on DInSAR and Precise Leveling. *J. Catast.* **2020**, *35*, 108–112.
43. Zhang, Q.; Wu, Y.; Guo, N.; Chen, C. Research on deformation characteristics of the 2021 Qinghai Maduo MS7.4 earthquake through coseismic dislocation inversion. *Adv. Space Res.* **2022**, *69*, 3059–3070. [CrossRef]
44. Elliott, J.R.; Elliott, A.J.; Hooper, A.; Larsen, Y.; Marinkovic, P.; Wright, T.J. Earthquake monitoring gets boost from new satellite. *Eos* **2015**, *96*, 14–18. [CrossRef]

45. Guangcai, F.; Zhiwei, L.; Xinjian, S.; Bing, X.; Yanan, D. Source parameters of the 2014 Mw 6.1 South Napa earthquake estimated from the Sentinel 1A, COSMO-SkyMed and GPS data. *Tectonophysics* **2015**, *655*, 139–146. [CrossRef]
46. Feng, G.; Li, Z.; Shan, X.; Zhang, L.; Zhang, G.; Zhu, J. Geodetic model of the 2015 April 25 Mw 7.8 Gorkha Nepal Earthquake and Mw 7.3 aftershock estimated from InSAR and GPS data. *Geophys. J. Int.* **2015**, *203*, 896–900. [CrossRef]
47. Sun, J.; Yue, H.; Shen, Z.; Fang, L.; Zhan, Y.; Sun, X. The 2017 Jiuzhaigou Earthquake: A Complicated Event Occurred in a Young Fault System. *Geophys. Res. Lett.* **2018**, *45*, 2230–2240. [CrossRef]
48. Sreejith, K.M.; Sunil, P.S.; Agrawal, R.; Saji, A.P.; Rajawat, A.S.; Ramesh, D.S. Audit of stored strain energy and extent of future earthquake rupture in central Himalaya. *Sci. Rep.* **2018**, *8*, 16697. [CrossRef]
49. Zhao, N.; Ji, L.; Zhang, W.; Xu, X.; Wang, J. Present-day kinematics and seismic potential of the Ganzi-Yushu fault, eastern Tibetan plateau, constrained from InSAR. *Front. Earth Sci.* **2023**, *11*, 1123711. [CrossRef]
50. Werner, C.; Wegmüller, U.; Strozzi, T.; Wiesmann, A. GAMMA SAR and interferometric processing software. *Gothenburg* **2000**, 16–20.
51. Wright, T.; Parsons, B.; Fielding, E. Measurement of interseismic strain accumulation across the North Anatolian Fault by satellite radar interferometry. *Geophys. Res. Lett.* **2001**, *28*, 2117–2120. [CrossRef]
52. Zebker, H.A.; Rosen, P.A.; Hensley, S. Atmospheric effects in interferometric synthetic aperture radar surface deformation and topographic maps. *J. Geophys. Res.* **1997**, *102*, 7547–7563. [CrossRef]
53. Biggs, J.; Wright, T.; Lu, Z.; Parsons, B. Multi-interferogram method for measuring interseismic deformation: Denali Fault, Alaska. *Geophys. J. Int.* **2007**, *170*, 1165–1179. [CrossRef]
54. Lyons, S.; Sandwell, D. Fault creep along the southern San Andreas from interferometric synthetic aperture radar, permanent scatterers, and stacking. *J. Geophys. Res. Solid Earth* **2003**, *108*, B1. [CrossRef]
55. Simons, M.; Rosen, P.A. Interferometric Synthetic Aperture Radar Geodesy. *Treatise Geophys.* **2007**, *3*, 391–447.
56. Zhang, W.; Ji, L.; Zhu, L.; Liu, C.; Jiang, F.; Xu, X. Current Slip and Strain Rate Distribution Along the Ganzi-Yushu-Xianshuihe Fault System Based on InSAR and GPS Observations. *Front. Earth Sci.* **2022**, *10*, 821761. [CrossRef]
57. Li, Y.S.; Zhang, J.F.; Luo, Y.; Gong, L.X. InSAR deformation time series analysis using Small-Baseline Approach. *2013 Int. Geosci. Remote Sens. Symp.* **2013**, 1352–1355. [CrossRef]
58. Savage, J.C.; Burford, R.O. Geodetic Determination of Relative Plate Motion in Central California. *J. Geophys. Res.* **1973**, *78*, 832–845. [CrossRef]
59. Matsu'Ura, M.; Jackson, D.D.; Cheng, A. Dislocation Model for Aseismic Crustal Deforamtion at Hollister, California. *J. Geophys. Res.* **1986**, *91*, 12661–12674. [CrossRef]
60. McCaffrey, R.; Qamar, A.I.; King, R.W.; Wells, R.; Khazaradze, G.; Williams, C.A.; Stevens, C.W.; Vollick, J.J.; Zwick, P.C. Fault locking, block rotation and crustal deformation in the Pacific Northwest. *Geophys. J. Int.* **2007**, *169*, 1315–1340. [CrossRef]
61. Meade, B.J.; Hager, B.H. Block models of crustal motion in southern California constrained by GPS measurements. *J. Geophys. Res.* **2005**, *110*, B3. [CrossRef]
62. Meade, B.J.; Loveless, J.P. Block Modeling with Connected Fault-Network Geometries and a Linear Elastic Coupling Estimator in Spherical Coordinates. *Bull. Seismol. Soc. Am.* **2009**, *99*, 3124–3139. [CrossRef]
63. Johnson, K.M.; Fukuda, J. New methods for estimating the spatial distribution of locked asperities and stress-driven interseismic creep on faults with application to the San Francisco Bay Area, California. *J. Geophys. Res.* **2010**, *115*, B12. [CrossRef]
64. Jiang, G.; Xu, X.; Chen, G.; Liu, Y.; Fukahata, Y.; Wang, H.; Yu, G.; Tan, X.; Xu, C. Geodetic imaging of potential seismogenic asperities on the Xianshuihe-Anninghe-Zemuhe fault system, southwest China, with a new 3-D viscoelastic interseismic coupling model. *J. Geophys. Res. Solid Earth* **2015**, *120*, 1855–1873. [CrossRef]
65. Zheng, W.; Liu, X.; Yu, J.; Yuan, D.; Zhang, P.; Ge, W.; Pang, J.; Liu, B. Geometry and late Pleistocene slip rates of the Liangdang-Jiangluo fault in the western Qinling mountains, NW China. *Tectonophysics* **2016**, *687*, 1–13.
66. Schmidt, D.A.; Bürgmann, R.; Nadeau, R.M.; Dalession, M.A. Distribution of aseismic slip rate on the Hayward fault inferred from seismic and geodetic data. *J. Geophys. Res.* **2005**, *110*, 1–15. [CrossRef]
67. Jouanne, F.; Mugnier, J.L.; Sapkota, S.N.; Bascou, P.; Pecher, A. Estimation of coupling along the Main Himalayan Thrust in the central Himalaya. *J. Asian Earth Sci.* **2017**, *133*, 62–71. [CrossRef]
68. Meade, B.J. Present-day kinematics at the India-Asia collision zone. *Geology* **2007**, *35*, 81–84. [CrossRef]
69. Pousse Beltran, L.; Pathier, E.; Jouanne, F.; Vassallo, R.; Reinoza, C.; Audemard, F.; Doin, M.P.; Volat, M. Spatial and temporal variations in creep rate along the El Pilar fault at the Caribbean-South American plate boundary (Venezuela), from InSAR. *J. Geophys. Res. Solid Earth* **2016**, *121*, 8276–8296. [CrossRef]
70. Jolivet, R.; Simons, M.; Agram, P.S.; Duputel, Z.; Shen, Z.K. Aseismic slip and seismogenic coupling along the central San Andreas Fault. *Geophys. Res. Lett.* **2015**, *42*, 297–306. [CrossRef]
71. Reinoza, C.; Jouanne, F.; Audemard, F.A.; Schmitz, M.; Beck, C. Geodetic exploration of strain along the El Pilar Fault in northeastern Venezuela. *J. Geophys. Res. Solid Earth* **2015**, *120*, 1993–2013. [CrossRef]
72. Moreno, M.; Rosenau, M.; Oncken, O. 2010 Maule earthquake slip correlates with pre-seismic locking of Andean subduction zone. *Nature* **2010**, *467*, 198–202. [CrossRef]
73. Lundgren, P.; Usai, S.; Sansosti, E.; Lanari, R.; Tesauro, M.; Fornaro, G.; Berardino, P. Modeling surface deformation observed with synthetic aperture radar interferometry at Campi Flegrei caldera. *J. Geophys. Res.* **2001**, *106*, 19355–19366. [CrossRef]

74. Goldstein, R.M.; Werner, C.L. Radar interferogram filtering for geophysical applications. *Geophys. Res. Lett.* **1998**, *25*, 4035–4038. [CrossRef]
75. Peltzer, G.; Crampé, F.; Hensley, S.; Rosen, P. Transient strain accumulation and fault interaction in the Eastern California shear zone. *Geology* **2001**, *29*, 975–978. [CrossRef]
76. Pritchard, M.E.; Simons, M. An aseismic slip pulse in northern Chile and along-strike variations in seismogenic behavior. *J. Geophys. Res.* **2006**, *111*, B8. [CrossRef]
77. Walters, R.J.; Parsons, B.; Wright, T.J. Constraining crustal velocity fields with InSAR for Eastern Turkey: Limits to the block-like behavior of Eastern Anatolia. *J. Geophys. Res. Solid Earth* **2014**, *119*, 5215–5234. [CrossRef]
78. Zheng, G.; Wang, H.; Wright, T.J.; Lou, Y.; Zhang, R.; Zhang, W.; Shi, C.; Huang, J.; Wei, N. Crustal Deformation in the India-Eurasia Collision Zone From 25 Years of GPS Measurements. *J. Geophys. Res. Solid Earth* **2017**, *122*, 9290–9312. [CrossRef]
79. Garthwaite, M.C.; Wang, H.; Wright, T.J. Broadscale interseismic deformation and fault slip rates in the central Tibetan Plateau observed using InSAR. *J. Geophys. Res. Solid Earth* **2013**, *118*, 5071–5083. [CrossRef]
80. Ji, L.; Zhang, W.; Liu, C.; Zhu, L.; Xu, J.; Xu, X. Characterizing interseismic deformation of the Xianshuihe fault, eastern Tibetan Plateau, using Sentinel-1 SAR images. *Adv. Space Res.* **2020**, *66*, 378–394. [CrossRef]
81. Van der Woerd, J.; Ryerson, F.J.; Tapponnier, P.; Meriaux, A.S.; Gaudemer, Y.; Meyer, B.; Finkel, R.C.; Caffee, M.W.; Guoguang, Z.; Zhiqin, X. Uniform Slip-Rate along the Kunlun Fault: Implications for seismic behaviour and large-scale tectonics. *Geophys. Res. Lett.* **2000**, *27*, 2353–2356. [CrossRef]
82. Jolivet, R.; Lasserre, C.; Doin, M.P.; Guillaso, S.; Peltzer, G.; Dailu, R.; Sun, J.; Shen, Z.K.; Xu, X. Shallow creep on the Haiyuan Fault (Gansu, China) revealed by SAR Interferometry. *J. Geophys. Res. Solid Earth* **2012**, *117*. [CrossRef]
83. Pasyanos, M.E.; Masters, T.G.; Laske, G.; Ma, Z. LITHO1.0: An updated crust and lithospheric model of the Earth. *J. Geophys. Res. Solid Earth* **2014**, *119*, 2153–2173. [CrossRef]
84. Dal Zilio, L.; Jolivet, R.; Dinther, Y. Segmentation of the Main Himalayan Thrust Illuminated by Bayesian Inference of Interseismic Coupling. *Geophys. Res. Lett.* **2020**, *47*, e2019GL086424. [CrossRef]
85. Daout, S.; Dini, B.; Haeberli, W.; Doin, M.; Parsons, B. Ice loss in the Northeastern Tibetan Plateau permafrost as seen by 16 yr of ESA SAR missions. *Earth Planet. Sci. Lett.* **2020**, *545*, 116404. [CrossRef]
86. Wang, M.; Shen, Z.K. Present-Day Crustal Deformation of Continental China Derived From GPS and Its Tectonic Implications. *J. Geophys. Res. Solid Earth* **2020**, *125*, e2019JB018774. [CrossRef]
87. Liang, S.; Gan, W.; Shen, C.; Xiao, G.; Liu, J.; Chen, W.; Ding, X.; Zhou, D. Three-dimensional velocity field of present-day crustal motion of the Tibetan Plateau derived from GPS measurements. *J. Geophys. Res. Solid Earth* **2013**, *118*, 5722–5732. [CrossRef]
88. Xu, J.; Liu-Zeng, J.; Yuan, Z.D.; Yao, W.Q.; Zhang, J.Y.; Ji, L.Y.; Shao, Z.G.; Han, L.F.; Wang, Z.J. Airborne LiDAR-Based Mapping of Surface Ruptures and Coseismic Slip of the 1955 Zheduotang Earthquake on the Xianshuihe Fault, East Tibet. *Bull. Seismol. Soc. Am.* **2022**, *112*, 3102–3120. [CrossRef]
89. England, P.; Molnar, P. Late Quaternary to decadal velocity fields in Asia. *J. Geophys. Res.* **2005**, *110*. [CrossRef]
90. Wang, H.; Wright, T.J. Satellite geodetic imaging reveals internal deformation of western Tibet. *Geophys. Res. Lett.* **2012**, *39*. [CrossRef]
91. Deng, Q.D.; Ran, Y.K.; Yang, X.P.; Min, W.; Chu, Q.Z. *Active Structure Map of China (1:400.000)*; Seismological Press: Beijing, China, 2007. (In Chinese)
92. Shen, Z.K.; Wan, Y.G.; Gan, W.J.; Zeng, Y.H.; Ren, Q. Viscoelastic triggering among large earthquakes along the East Kunlun Fault system. *Chin. J. Geophys.* **2003**, *46*, 786–795. (In Chinese) [CrossRef]
93. Liu, L.; Li, Y.J.; Zhu, L.Y.; Ji, L.Y. Influence of the 1947 Dari M7.7 earthquake on stress evolution along the boundary fault of the Bayan Har block: Insights from numerical simulation. *Chin. J. Geophys.* **2021**, *64*, 2221–2231. (In Chinese)
94. Li, Y.J.; Huang, L.Y.; Ding, R.; Yang, S.X.; Liu, L.; Zhang, S.M.; Liu, H.Q. Coulomb stress changes associated with the M7.3 Maduo earthquake and implications for seismic hazards. *Nat. Hazard Res.* **2021**, *1*, 95–101. [CrossRef]
95. Liu, L.; Li, Y.; Ji, L.; Zhu, L. Finite element simulation of stress change for the MS7.4 Madoi earthquake and implications for regional seismic hazards. *Earthq. Res. Adv.* **2022**, *2*, 100046. [CrossRef]
96. Lay, T.; Kanamori, H. Earthquake doublets in the Solomon Islands. *Phys. Earth Planet. Inter.* **1980**, *21*, 283–304. [CrossRef]
97. Xu, X.W.; Chen, W.B.; Yu, G.H.; Ma, W.T.; Dai, H.G.; Zhang, Z.J.; Chen, Y.M.; He, W.G.; Wang, Z.J.; Dang, G.M. Characteristic features of the surface ruptures of the Hou Saihu (Kunlun Shan) earthquake (M_S 8.1) northern Tibetan plateau, China. *Seismol. Geol.* **2002**, *24*, 1–13. (In Chinese)
98. Guo, J.; Lin, A.; Tadashi, M.; Zheng, J.; Sun, G. New Constraints on Recent Large Earthquakes along the Xidatan-Dongdatan Segment of the Kunlun Fault, Western China. *Bull. Seismol. Soc. Am.* **2006**, *96*, 48–58. [CrossRef]
99. Ren, J.W.; Wang, Y.P.; Wu, Z.M. Holocene earthquake deformation zones and their displacement and slip rate along the XIdatan-Dongdatan of Kusaihu-Maqu fault in northern Qinghai-Xizang Plateau. *Seismol. Geol.* **1993**, *15*, 285–288. (In Chinese)
100. Yang, S.H.; Fu, B.H.; Shi, P.L. Late quaternary structural deformation and tectono-geomorphic features along the Xiugou Basin segment, Eastern Kunlun fault zone. *Quat. Sci.* **2012**, *32*, 921–930. (In Chinese)

101. Kidd, W.S.F.; Molnar, P. Quaternary and active faulting observed on the 1985 Academia Sinica-Royal Society Geotraverse of Tibet. *Philos. Trans. R. Soc. London. Ser. A* **1988**, *327*, 337–363.
102. Yongqiu, W.; Zhijiu, C.; Ge, D.; Jiarun, Y.; Qinghai, X.; Pang, Q. Quaternary geomorphological evolution of the Kunlun Pass area and uplift of the Qinghai-Xizang (Tibet) Plateau. *Geomorphology* **2001**, *36*, 203–216.

remote sensing

MDPI

Article

Coupling the Relationship between Land Subsidence and Groundwater Level, Ground Fissures in Xi'an City Using Multi-Orbit and Multi-Temporal InSAR

Xing Zhang [1], Zhengfeng Cheng [2], Bei Xu [3], Rong Gui [1,*], Jun Hu [1,4], Changjiang Yang [2], Qiuhong Yang [1] and Tao Xiong [5]

1 School of Geosciences and Info-Physics, Central South University, Changsha 410083, China; lzxlzhangxing@csu.edu.cn (X.Z.)
2 The Central Southern China Electric Power Design Institute, Wuhan 430071, China
3 The Xi'an Institute of Surveying and Mapping, Xi'an 710054, China
4 Hunan Geological Disaster Monitoring, Early Warning and Emergency Rescue Engineering Technology Research Center, Changsha 410004, China
5 The College of Geographic Sciences, Hunan Normal University, Changsha 410081, China
* Correspondence: ronggui@csu.edu.cn

Abstract: The Xi'an region of China has been suffering from groundwater depletion, ground fissure hazards, and surface subsidence for a long time. Due to the complex tectonics and frequent human and natural activities, land deformation in the region is aggravated, posing a threat to infrastructure and human life. This study adopted the multi-orbit and multi-temporal InSAR technology to measure multi-dimensional displacements and time-series displacements in Xi'an City. Through the multi-dimensional deformation verification, it was found that the control of groundwater flow direction by ground fissures is the cause of horizontal deformation. On the contrary, the flow direction of groundwater from west to east was inferred using multi-dimensional deformation. Further analysis was performed by calculating the deformation gradient of the cumulative deformation to obtain differential land subsidence and angular distortions, and it was quantitatively determined that the threshold for the generation of ground fissures caused by differential subsidence is 1/500. Then, through the mutual verification of the time series data and the groundwater level, a positive correlation was obtained. However, due to the inconsistent geological conditions and soil layers at the monitoring positions of Well 2 and Well 3, the lag time was 64 days and 4 days, respectively. Finally, the relationship between the surface deformation and the groundwater in the sustained uplift areas was explored. The Well 1 groundwater-level data with a monitoring period of 22 years and the corresponding monitoring points' time series data were modeled; it was concluded that, in the future, the groundwater level will continue to rise and surface deformation will mainly increase, without a slowing trend. Therefore, research on the impact of surface uplift on infrastructure should be strengthened. By quantifying the relationship between land subsidence, ground fissures, and the groundwater level in Xi'an, the results of this study provide a reference for groundwater monitoring and management.

Keywords: Xi'an; land subsidence; multi-dimensional deformation; time-series displacements; angular distortion; groundwater level

1. Introduction

Land subsidence caused by groundwater overexploitation has become a global problem. As a geological environmental disaster, land subsidence has affected at least 200 regions worldwide in the past century due to its harmfulness, wide range of impact, and long duration [1]. These areas include not only the California Basin [2–5], the Mexico Basin [6–9], the Iran Basin [10,11], Indonesia [12], and Egypt [13], but also include in the North China

Plain [14–17] and the Fenwei Basin [18,19]. Especially in large cities, such as Beijing [20,21], Shanghai [22], Suzhou [23], Wuhan [24], and Xi'an [25], land subsidence is more severe. The rapid growth of the population and increasing exploitation of groundwater resources aggravate the existing phenomenon of land subsidence, which can lead to surface cracking, uneven settlement, tilting of buildings, and damage to other urban infrastructure.

Due to human activities and complicated geological conditions, Xi'an has suffered a huge impact from land subsidence in the past 60 years. According to historical data during 1960–1996, the maximum subsidence reached 2.6 m, and according to existing InSAR monitoring results, the maximum subsidence also reached 1 m between 1996 and 2021 [25], with a total surface subsidence of 3.6 m. This is mainly due to excessive groundwater exploitation and urban development and construction. Because there is less rainfall in the Xi'an region, it is difficult to meet the demand for groundwater recharge, leading to the depletion of its groundwater aquifer system and ultimately exacerbating surface subsidence. Long-term subsidence will lead to surface fractures at the discontinuities of aquifers or geological soil layers, especially in Xi'an, where special tectonic ground fissures have formed. According to a previous geological survey report, there were 10 ground fissures before 2000, and 3 new ones developed between 2000 and 2001; this finding is consistent with the intensification seen in surface subsidence. Ground fissures may cause significant damage to infrastructure, such as buildings, transportation facilities, and underground pipelines.

Interferometric synthetic aperture radar (InSAR) is one of the most effective techniques for studying surface deformation. Previous research has proven that InSAR can be used to study the relationship between land deformation and changes in the groundwater level [26–28]. Combining the groundwater level with InSAR deformation monitoring can help researchers understand the compaction phenomenon of aquifers related to groundwater overextraction [29–31]. Many of the existing studies were conducted in the Xi'an region.

Although previous studies have successfully measured Xi'an's subsidence using techniques such as MT-InSAR, they have neglected the influence of faults or ground fissures. Land subsidence is not only vertical deformation, but also presents three-dimensional deformation. This phenomenon also occurs in California due to the obstruction of groundwater flow by faults, resulting in three-dimensional deformation [32]. In the presence of ground fissures or faults, multi-dimensional deformation monitoring is required in order to obtain real surface deformation.

In this study, by analyzing the complete SAR data of the descending orbit TerraSAR (2017–2019) and the ascending orbit Sentinel-1 (2015–2022), we investigated the present-day deformation trend in Xi'an from the perspective of surface displacement mapping. We first applied the small baseline subset (SBAS) technique as a data processing method [33,34] to obtain ground deformation maps of Xi'an City. The accuracy of the InSAR displacement was verified by using real-data validation of eight levels in Xi'an. Secondly, angular distortions were obtained via the calculation of the land subsidence gradient, and the location and prediction of ground fissures were identified. We further used cross-correlation analysis to quantify the time delay effect between displacement and the groundwater level and determined their causal relationship. Using data obtained from 22 years of monitoring of groundwater-level changes and the InSAR displacement analysis, we concluded that surface deformation in the future will mainly be caused by uplift deformation and there is no sign of a slowing trend. We used the groundwater-level change curves and InSAR deformations to comprehensively analyze the temporal and spatial evolution of natural surface displacement after groundwater extraction or recharge. In addition, multiple observation geometries were used to estimate the multi-dimensional deformation, such as horizontal and vertical displacements, thereby enhancing our knowledge of the three-dimensional surface deformation that affects cities. This is another novelty of this study, as the combination of different orbital data to obtain multi-dimensional deformation has not been previously studied in the Xi'an region.

By obtaining the multi-dimensional surface deformation in Xi'an and studying the relationship between surface deformation and ground fissures, the faults and changes in the groundwater level can be used to evaluate the efficiency of groundwater management policies implemented to restore the over-developed aquifer system in Xi'an in the years to come.

2. Study Area and Data

2.1. Overview of the Study Area

Xi'an is located in the middle of the Guanzhong Plain. The main urban area is located at the junction of different tectonic units in the Weihe River Basin, with complex engineering geological conditions and abundant faults, such as the Lintong Chang'an Fault (LT-CA Fault). Additionally, Xi'an City has developed 13 ground fissures, roughly in a northeast-to-southeast direction, with the longest fissure, f7, exceeding 14 km (Figure 1a). As it is affected by these ground fissures, the funnel area with land subsidence is oval and expands rapidly to one side [35].

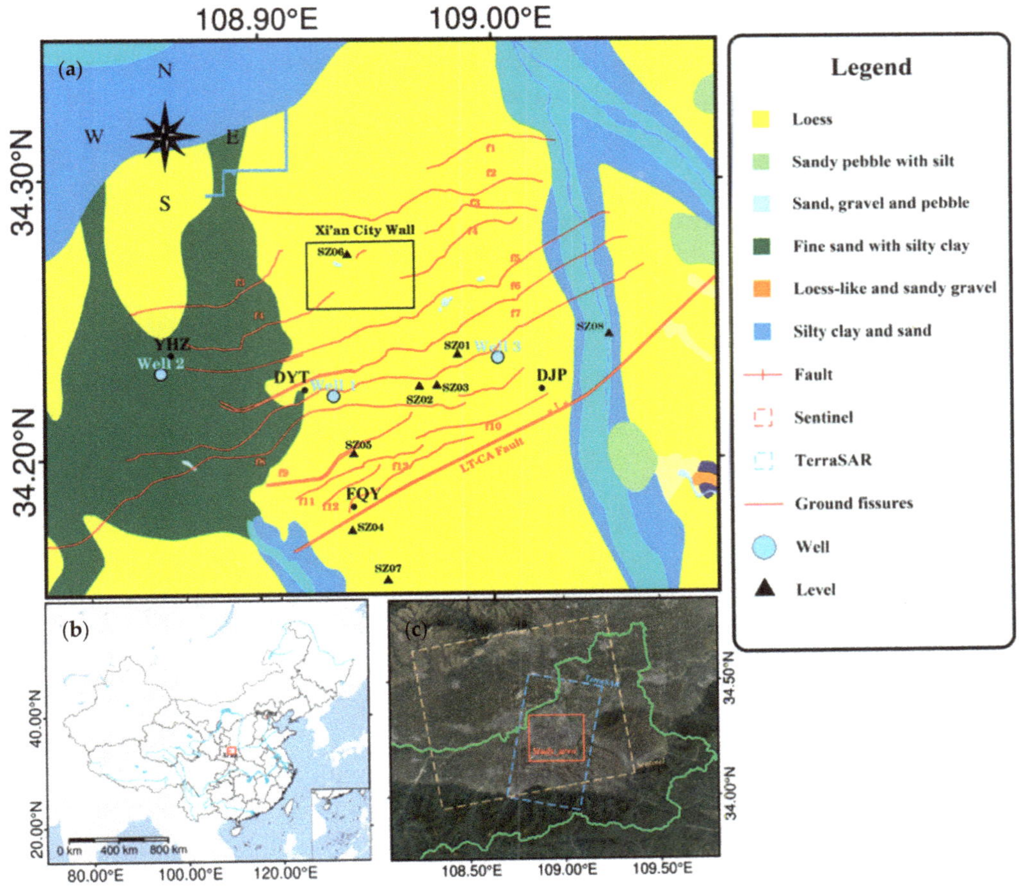

Figure 1. Overview of the research area. (**a**) Geological map of Xi'an, China, where tectonic faults and ground fissures are superimposed [25]. (**b**) Location of Xi'an in China. (**c**) Location of the research area and the SAR data coverage used in this study.

Figure 1 shows the geological map of the main urban area of Xi'an, where structural faults and ground fissures overlap [25]. Since the Cenozoic era, the deposits in this area have mainly consisted of sand, alluvial soil layer, proluvial sediments, and lacustrine deposits formed by loess accumulation and water flow [35]. The accumulation layer is relatively thick, especially with the loess accumulation layer exceeding 100 m. Loess is prone to surface deformation due to its unique soil properties.

2.2. Data

2.2.1. InSAR Datasets

In order to obtain the true spatial–temporal characteristics of deformation in the entire Xi'an region from 2015 to 2022, we used the SAR data from two sensors, including 25 TSX images from May 2017 to April 2019 and 187 S1 images from June 2015 to July 2022, totaling 208 images. The coverage range of the two sensors' SAR images is shown in Figure 1c. The basic parameters of the two SAR datasets are presented in Table 1. The external DEM data were provided by NASA's space shuttle radar terrain mission-1 (SRTM), with a spatial resolution of 30 m, for simulating and eliminating the terrain phase [36].

Table 1. Data of Sentinel-1 and TerraSAR.

Sensor	Band	Wavelength (cm)	Incidence Angle (°)	Heading (°)	Track	Polarization	Pass Direction	Number of Images	Date Range
S1	C	5.6	39.3	−12.9	84	VV	Ascending	187	20 June 2015–25 July 2022
TSX	X	3.1	28.6	190.6	13	HH	Descending	25	12 May 2017–16 April 2019

2.2.2. Field Datasets

(1) Hydraulic head

In the Xi'an study area, the relationship between the groundwater level and surface deformation was explored using three long-term observations of groundwater monitoring data. The hydraulic head observation frequency is once a month. The recorded depths of the three wells are 80–130 m from the ground, indicating that groundwater exploitation occurs in deep confined aquifers (Figure 1a).

(2) Level

There are eight level stations located within our study area (Figure 1a), obtained from two periods, 2015–2016 and 2020–2021, respectively, and used for InSAR data accuracy verification.

3. Method

3.1. SBAS-InSAR Data Processing

The SBAS-InSAR has become the most commonly used time-series deformation processing algorithm since 2002 [33]. After acquiring N SAR images of repeated observations and setting a spatio-temporal baseline threshold to form M interferograms, differential interferometry and phase unwrapping were performed on selected interferometric pairs, which were finally geocoded to obtain the final unwrapped interferogram. Next, we utilized the final unwrapped interferogram with a short baseline as the observation value, and considered the sequential interferometric phase as the unknown parameter; then, the relationship between the two can be expressed as:

$$\delta\varphi = B\varphi \tag{1}$$

where $\delta\varphi = [\delta\varphi_1, \delta\varphi_2, \cdots, \delta\varphi_M]^T$ represents the known vector of the unwrapped phases of M differential interferograms, $\varphi = [\varphi_1, \varphi_2, \cdots, \varphi_N]^T$ represents the N parameters to be solved, and B is the design matrix. The unknown parameters φ can be solved by the least square (LS) and singular value decomposition (SVD) method:

$$\varphi = \left(B^T B\right)^{-1} B^T \, \delta\varphi \tag{2}$$

Finally, we obtained the average deformation rate map and time series maps.

In this study, GAMMA software was used to process the data from the Sentinel-1 and TerraSAR satellites, and the SBAS-InSAR technology was utilized separately for each dataset. After generating the differential interferograms, NASA's 30 m resolution digital surface model (DSM) for the space shuttle radar terrain mission (SRTM) was used to remove registration errors caused by terrain phases and fluctuations, phase unwrapping was performed using minimum-cost flow (MCF), and the atmospheric phase delay and removal related to altitude were calculated. Finally, the least squares and singular value decomposition (SVD) were used to estimate the land subsidence based on the Sentinel-1 data from 2015 to 2022 and the TerraSAR data from 2017 to 2019.

3.2. Multi-Dimensional Deformation Method

The InSAR-monitored deformation over each point of each frame is a one-dimensional (1D) projection along the LOS direction (d_{LOS}) of the three-dimensional (3D) surface displacement (east–west component (d_e), north–south component (d_n), and up component (d_u)) [37]. Its estimation is as follows:

$$d^i_{LOS} = cos\theta^i \cdot d_u - sin\theta^i sin\left(\alpha^i_{azi} - 3\pi/2\right) \cdot d_e - sin\theta^i cos\left(\alpha^i_{azi} - 3\pi/2\right) \cdot d_n \tag{3}$$

where θ^i, α^i_{azi}, and $\alpha^i_{azi} - 3\pi/2$ represent the i SAR satellite incidence angle, the included angle between the i SAR satellite's flight direction and the north direction, and the included angle between the range direction and the north direction, respectively.

Due to the nearly north–south flight direction of the existing SAR satellites, their monitoring results are less sensitive to north–south displacement; therefore, the north–south displacement has a low contribution to the LOS value and can be ignored. When there are both ascending and descending data in the study area, the assumption that $d_n = 0$ is made, and the d_u and d_e components are solved as follows:

$$\begin{cases} d^{asc}_{LOS} = cos\theta^{asc} \cdot d_u - sin\theta^{asc} sin\left(\alpha^{asc}_{azi} - 3\pi/2\right) \cdot d_e \\ d^{dsc}_{LOS} = cos\theta^{dsc} \cdot d_u - sin\theta^{dsc} sin\left(\alpha^{dsc}_{azi} - 3\pi/2\right) \cdot d_e \end{cases} \tag{4}$$

When the study area covers only one geometric observation (ascending or descending), we can solve for the d_u component as follows:

$$d_u = \frac{d^i_{LOS}}{cos\theta^i} \tag{5}$$

3.3. Angular Distortions and Differential Subsidence

Differential subsidence at the edge of the surface deformation zones often occurs at the discontinuity of an aquifer structure, which is the main origin of shallow fault development, cracks, and urban infrastructure damage [38]. When evaluating the harm caused by land subsidence, we can measure the harm based not only on the annual average deformation rate or total subsidence, but also based on the different settlement Δd_{ui} between the two points under consideration [39], and then the value can be transformed into an angular distortion β. The solution is as follows:

$$\beta = \frac{\Delta d_{ui}}{l} \tag{6}$$

where l is the distance between the two points.

The calculation process of Equation (4) can be considered as fitting the slope of the central pixel in a 3 × 3 unit window with the plane of the surrounding 8 units, which is consistent with the standard method used for evaluating digital elevation data in GIS [40]. This process is calculated using the average maximum technique, as shown in Figure 2.

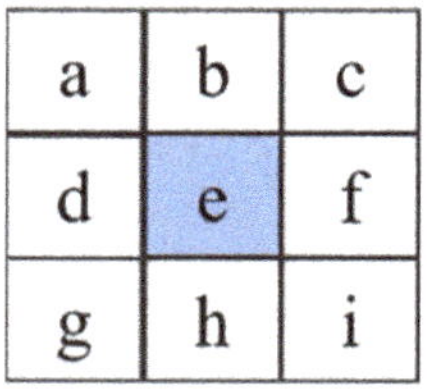

Figure 2. Schematic diagram of the gradient calculation method.

The data processing procedure consists of two steps (Figure 3). Step one estimates the land subsidence via an InSAR time-series analysis of the multi-orbit SLC data stacks. Step two jointly analyzes the groundwater level, ground fissures, and land subsidence to explore their relationship.

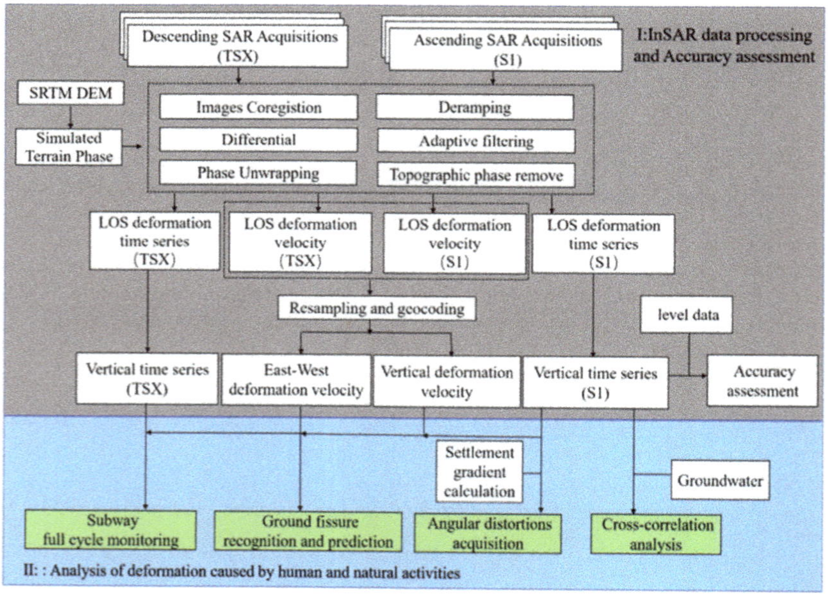

Figure 3. Flowchart of the data processing procedure (TSX: TerraSAR and S1: Sentinel-1).

4. Results

A short baseline interferometric measurement network was created using the Sentinel-1A data for the ascending orbit and the TerraSAR data for the descending orbit, and interferogram pairs were generated, as shown in Figure 4. The resolution of the Sentinel interferogram is approximately 20 m × 20 m; five rounds of multi−look generation at distance and one multi−look generation at azimuth were performed. The resolution of the TerraSAR interferogram is also 20 m × 20 m; the Goldstein filtering method was used to eliminate noise from the interferogram, and the MCF was used to unfold the interferogram. To reduce data processing errors, we selected interferograms with a coherence greater than the average threshold of 0.5. We used time-domain high-pass filtering to remove some high-frequency turbulent atmospheric data. Finally, we used the LS method to convert the short baseline interference phase into a sequence interference phase, and we multiplied the phase by a constant, $-\lambda / 4\pi$, to obtain the deformation time series.

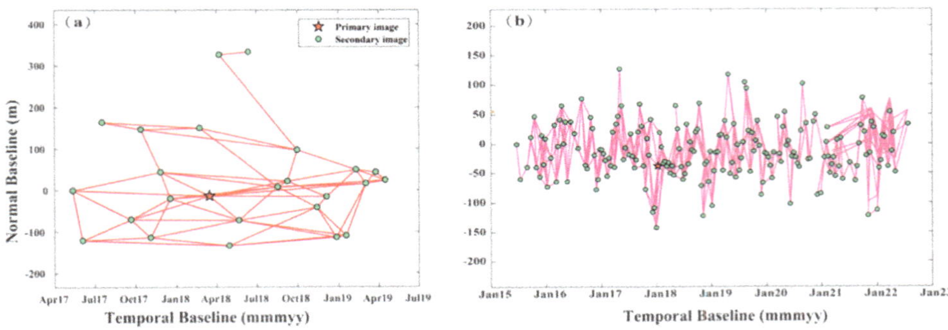

Figure 4. Temporal and perpendicular baseline combinations for the SAR datasets from the two SAR sensors used in this study: (**a**) TSX and (**b**) Sentinel-1A.

4.1. InSAR Monitoring Velocity Map

Figure 5 shows the map of deformation rate in the study area from 2015 to 2022. It can be seen clearly that there are five subsidence funnels with a maximum settlement rate exceeding 40 mm/yr, and an uplift zone with a maximum uplift rate exceeding 15 mm/yr.

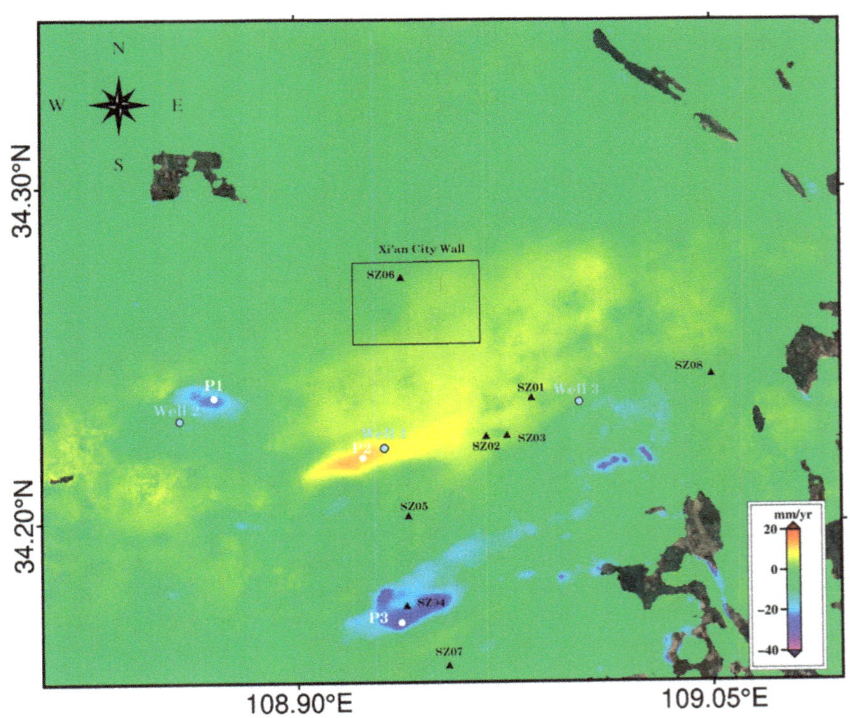

Figure 5. The map of S1 mean deformation rate in the Xi'an region from 2015 to 2022.

In addition, in order to obtain the true spatial–temporal characteristics of deformation, we calculated the vertical deformation rate field for different years. Figure 6a–f shows the deformation patterns of 2016, 2017, 2018, 2019, 2020, and 2021–2022, respectively. The spatial pattern of deformation from 2015 to 2022 was inconsistent, and the deformation rate varied over time. From 2016 to 2017, settlement was still the main deformation, with a maximum deformation rate exceeding −150 mm/yr. From 2018 to 2019, the phenomenon of surface subsidence disappeared, leading to surface uplift, with a maximum rate of 40 mm/yr. The uplift phenomenon is related to groundwater recovery. In 2020, the surface slightly uplifted, with a relatively small amplitude of uplift. The spatial–temporal characteristics are most obvious from 2021 to 2022, with the largest uplift amplitude and deformation rate exceeding 60 mm/yr. Due to the fact that most areas of the surface have risen rather than sunk, there is a trend of uplift. Based on the available research in the area, it can be inferred that the groundwater in this aquifer has achieved significant recharge over the past seven years. However, the rate of deformation recovery is less than settlement, and, finally, the overall effect still manifests as settlement. Therefore, it is inferred that irreparable non-elastic compression deformation occurs in the aquifer.

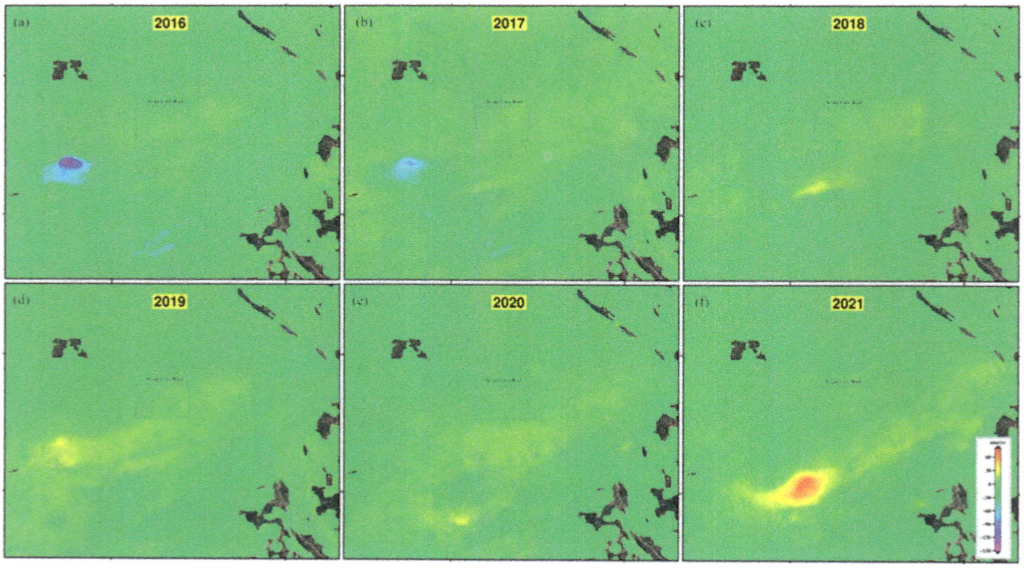

Figure 6. Maps of mean vertical deformation in Xi'an for different years: (**a**) 2016, (**b**) 2017, (**c**) 2018, (**d**) 2019, (**e**) 2020, and (**f**) 2021.

Figure 7 shows the map of the vertical deformation rate based on the TerraSAR data in the study area from 2017 to 2019, which is consistent with the deformation spatial distribution of the Sentinel-1 data shown in Figure 6. It is also evident that there are multiple subsidence funnels with a maximum subsidence rate exceeding −45 mm/yr, and two uplift zones with a maximum subsidence rate exceeding 30 mm/yr. The difference from the Sentinel-1's results is that there is a linear surface uplift area, which is referred to as the "Happiness Forest Belt Development Area", a large-scale urban development project. Large-scale urban infrastructure construction can also bring about surface deformation.

To further analyze the spatiotemporal evolution patterns of key regions, we selected three subsidence center points (P1–P3) shared by the Sentinel-1 and TerraSAR results, as shown in Figure 8. P1 is located in the YHZ area, where groundwater was overexploited from 2015 to 2018, leading to the most severe land subsidence. The rapid rebound phenomenon in October 2018 occurred due to the implementation of artificial water injection. P2 is located in the DYT area and showed an uplift phenomenon from 2015 to 2022; the uplift phenomenon occurred more rapidly from 2021 to 2022. P3 is located in the FQY area, and after a long period of continuous settlement, it started to rebound in 2021. With the issuance of the start of artificial water injection projects, the completion of water transfer hub projects, and groundwater extraction restrictions, land deformation in the Xi'an region continues to rebound, and in the future, land deformation in Xi'an City will mainly be uplifted.

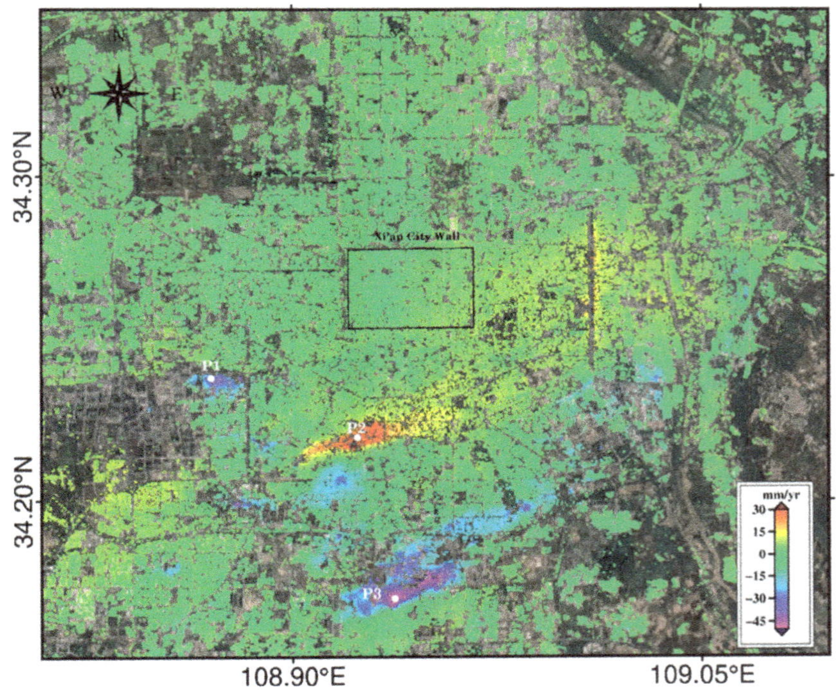

Figure 7. Map of TerraSAR mean deformation rate in the Xi'an region from 2017 to 2019.

4.2. Accuracy Assessment

To validate the InSAR results, we used leveling data from 2016 and 2020 to verify the accuracy of the InSAR results. Figure 1a shows the position of the level stations. Figure 9 shows a comparison of the level measurement results in 2016 and 2020. The STD of the differences is 3.1 and 2.5 mm in 2016 and 2020, respectively. Meanwhile, a field survey was also conducted, as shown in Figure 10. There are cracks in the houses in the subsidence funnel area, and large cracks appear on the surface, as shown in Figure 10a,b. In the area with ground cracks, there are also two sides falling away from an arching phenomenon in the middle, as shown in Figure 10d, further verifying the accuracy of the monitoring results. Overall, the precision of the InSAR measurement is high enough to investigate land subsidence.

In addition, a cross−comparison verification of the vertical InSAR results for S1 and TSX was also conducted, and the results are shown in Figure 11. The root mean square error (RMSE) is 2.3 mm/yr, and the correlation coefficient (R^2) is 0.73. Due to the low correlation coefficient, it can be inferred that surface deformation not only involves vertical deformation, but also horizontal deformation.

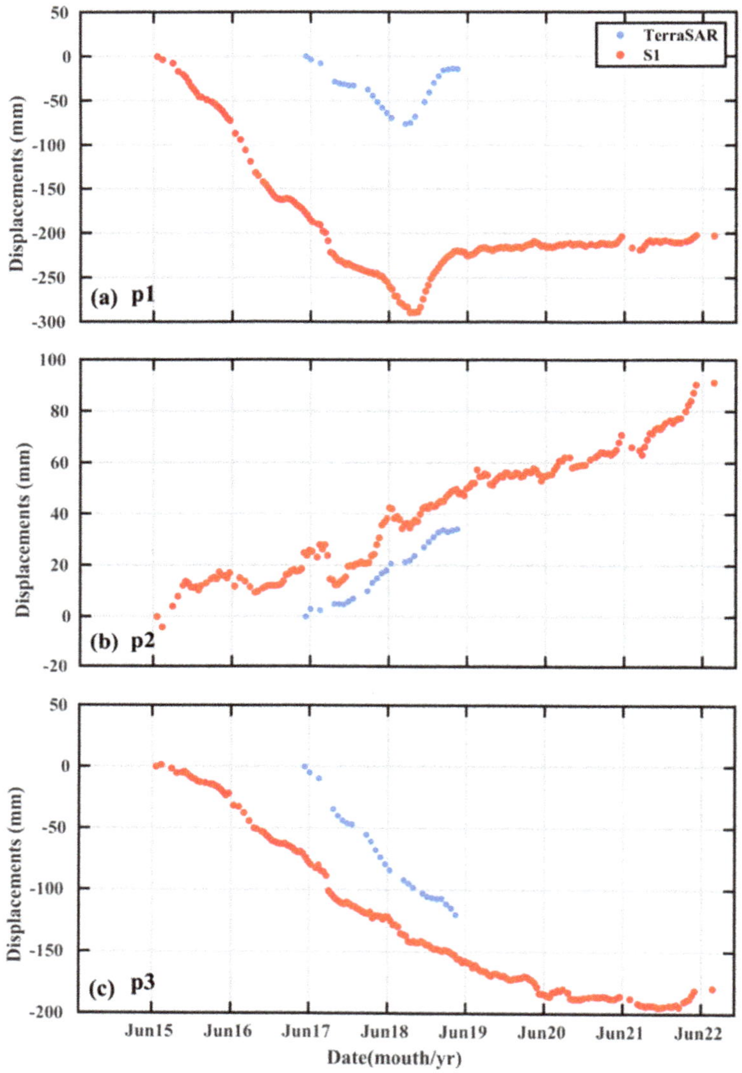

Figure 8. Deformation time series at points P1–P3 from 2015 to 2022.

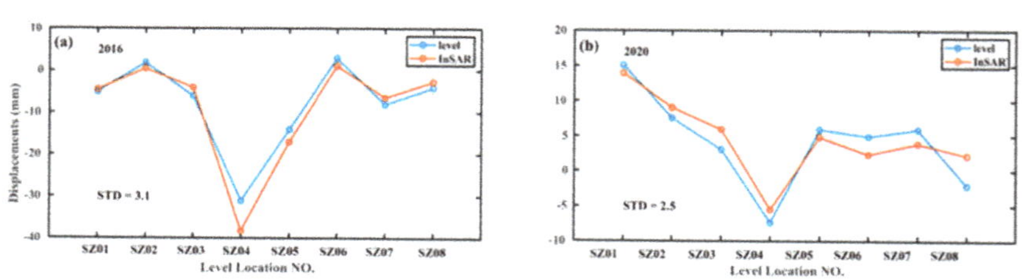

Figure 9. Comparison of the InSAR measurements with the level measurements (**a**) in 2016 and (**b**) in 2020.

Figure 10. Field survey results.

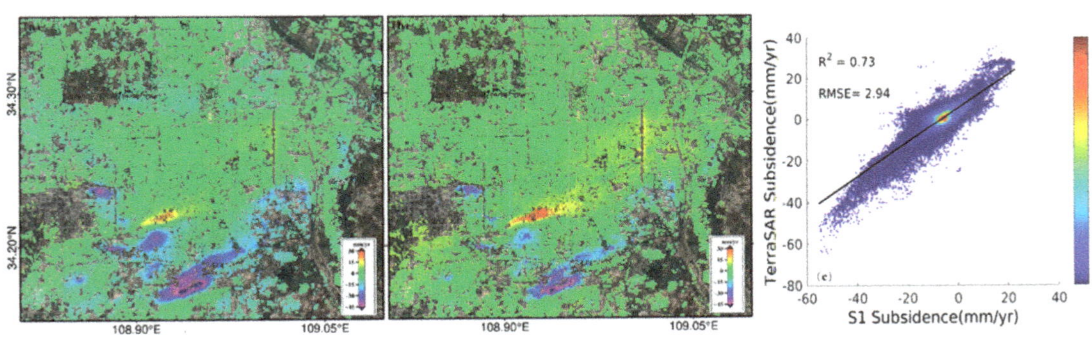

Figure 11. Cross-comparison between S1 vertical deformation rate and TSX vertical deformation rate: (**a**) S1 vertical deformation rate, (**b**) TSX vertical deformation rate, and (**c**) cross−comparison results.

4.3. InSAR Multi-Dimensional Deformation

From the cross-validation, it was found that surface deformation in Xi'an has not only vertical deformation, but also horizontal deformation. We solved the multi-dimensional deformation using the S1 data of the ascending orbit and the TSX data of the descending orbit. Under the premise of ignoring the north–south deformation, a two-dimensional deformation rate field was obtained, which is shown in Figure 12, and based on this, the ground fissure and fault data were superimposed. As shown in Figure 12a, it can be concluded that surface deformation in Xi'an City is mainly vertical deformation, and the multiple deformation boundaries formed are consistent with the boundaries of ground fissures, especially between the f7 and f8 ground fissures, where there is a clear surface uplift boundary. As shown in Figure 12b, it can be concluded that there is a significant narrow horizontal deformation in Xi'an, especially between the f7 and f8 ground fissures, where there is a horizontal deformation moving eastward. Based on the analysis of the hydrogeological data, it can be concluded that the direction of the groundwater flow is affected by ground fissures, which hinder the diffusion of groundwater and force the direction of the groundwater flow to follow the direction of the ground fissures, leading to horizontal deformation.

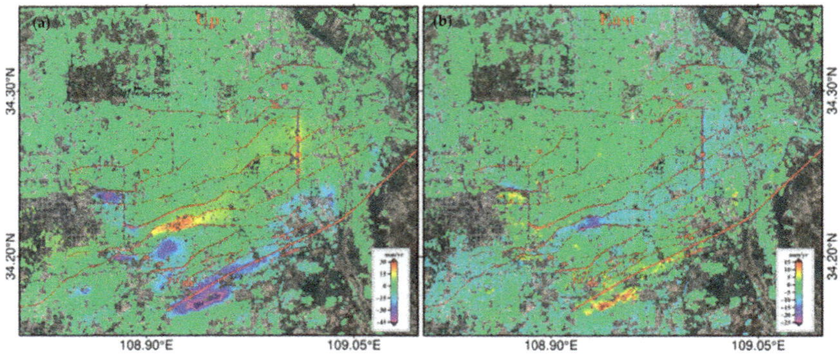

Figure 12. Multi-dimensional deformation: (**a**) up deformation and (**b**) east deformation.

5. Discussion

5.1. The Relationship between Subway Construction and Deformation

Ground subsidence has a negative impact on the construction and operation of urban rail transit systems, as it is considered the most serious type of disaster. Ground subsidence affects the stability of a subway system and its surrounding infrastructure. Identifying land subsidence during construction and operation is crucial for the safety of subways. This study used long-term time-series displacement to study the impact of ground subsidence caused by underground earthwork excavation during subway construction and surface deformation caused by groundwater extraction on subway lines. We analyzed the distribution of subway ground subsidence and quantified the time-series variation characteristics of deformation throughout the entire period, including construction and operation. The subway displacement rates obtained using the Sentinel-1 data from 2015 to 2022 and the TerraSAR data from 2017 to 2019 are shown in Figure 13. A statistical analysis was conducted on the maximum displacement and average displacement rates of six subway lines, and the results are shown in Table 2. From the deformation maps and statistical data, it can be concluded that the Xi'an subway lines are relatively stable, and only the deformation of the ground subsidence funnel area is large. For example, Line 2, Line 3, and Line 5 cross the ground subsidence funnel area in the YHZ District of the Yanta District and the FQY District of the Changan District. The average deformation rate of Line 2, Line 3, and Line 5 ranges from −24 mm/yr to −33 mm/yr.

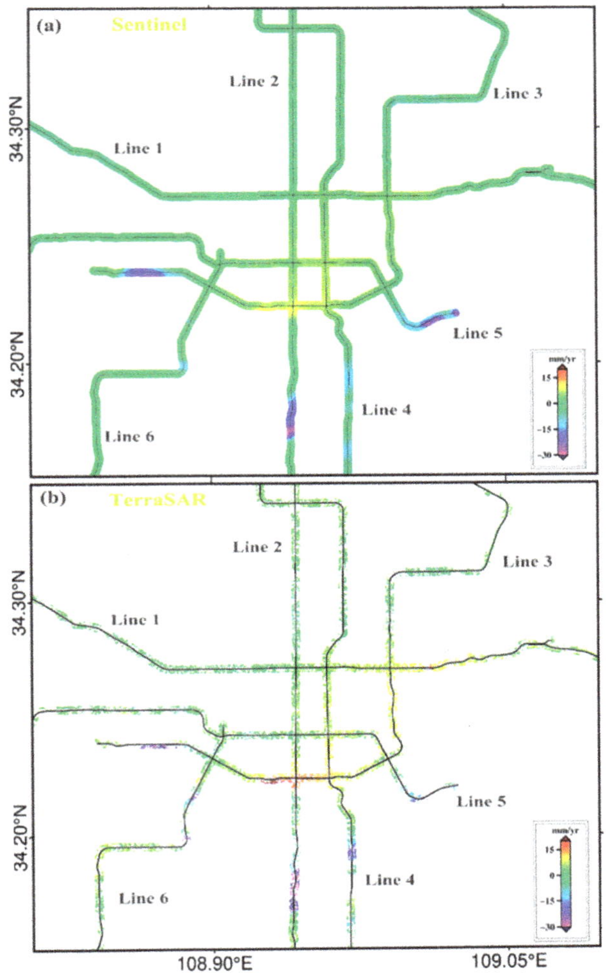

Figure 13. Deformation rates along Xi'an subway lines. (**a**) Sentinel; (**b**) TerraSAR.

Table 2. Properties of the subway lines in the study area.

Name	First Opening Date	Sentinel-1 Average Deformation Rate (mm/yr)	Sentinel-1 Maximum Deformation Rate (mm/yr)	TerraSAR Average Deformation Rate (mm/yr)	TerraSAR Maximum Deformation Rate (mm/yr)
Line 1	15 September 2013	−2	−9	−4	−11
Line 2	29 September 2006	−3	−30	−4	−32
Line 3	08 November 2016	−2	−24	−2	−15
Line 4	26 December 2018	−1	−14	−3	−14
Line 5	28 December 2020	−4	−33	−3	−21
Line 6	28 December 2020	−2	−14	−1	−9

The construction period of Line 5 Phase I was from January 2016 to December 2020. We combined the construction period and the operation period as the "life cycle" of the subway line, with the construction period of Line 5 from January 2016 to December 2020 and the operation period of Line 5 from December 2020 to July 2022. We obtained the "life cycle" deformation monitoring results, as shown in Figure 14, and we selected typical P1 points and plotted the time series deformation, as shown in Figure 15. The land deformation during the construction period showed linear subsidence and the cumulative deformation reached −138 mm in December 2020. Then, during the operation period from January 2021 to July 2022, for a total of 19 months, the ground subsidence was −22 mm, and the deformation still existed, but a slowing trend was obvious, which was in line with the natural sedimentation pattern. Comparing the optical images of 2017 and 2022, it can be concluded that the reason for the severe deformation area of the subway system here is caused by the excavation construction of the subway line, as shown in Figure 16.

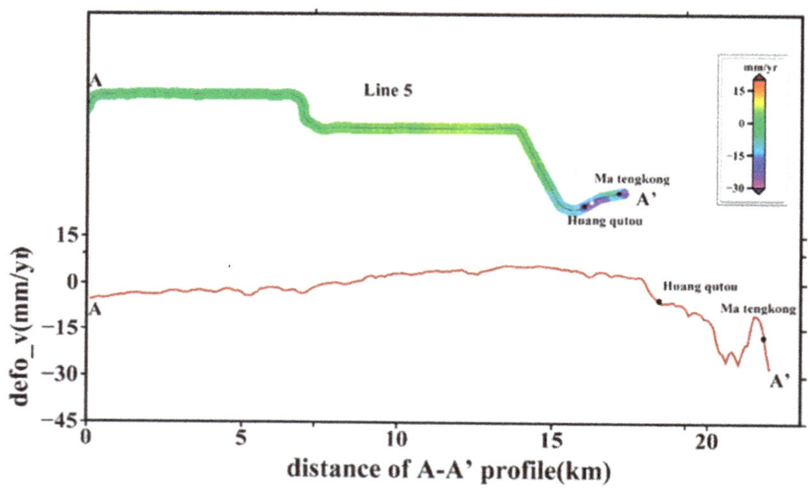

Figure 14. Deformation rate profile of Line 5.

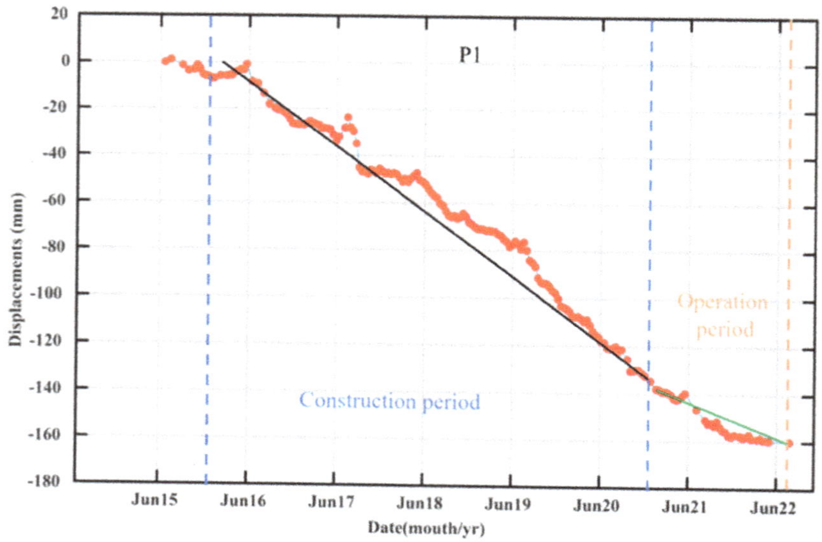

Figure 15. Time series displacement of P1.

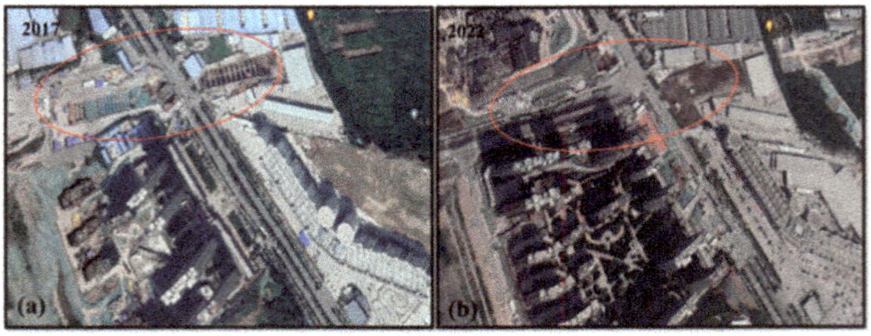

Figure 16. Optical map: (**a**) 2017 and (**b**) 2022.

5.2. The Relationship between Ground Fissures and Deformation

Figure 17a shows the cumulative deformation results in Xi'an City from 2015 to 2022. It can be seen that most of the area presents as an uplift area, which also includes multiple settlement funnel centers and multiple settlement boundaries. To better reflect the deformation boundary, the deformation map was separated into an uplift and a subsidence map. Figure 17c shows that the subsidence funnels have obvious boundaries, Moreover, as shown in Figure 17b, it can be seen that the uplift area presents a linear shape that matches the ground fissures, and there are clear boundaries in the uplift area between ground fissures f7 and f8. Discontinuities in deformation often present the most hazardous areas. Further calculation of the differential subsidence and acquisition of angular distortions is needed.

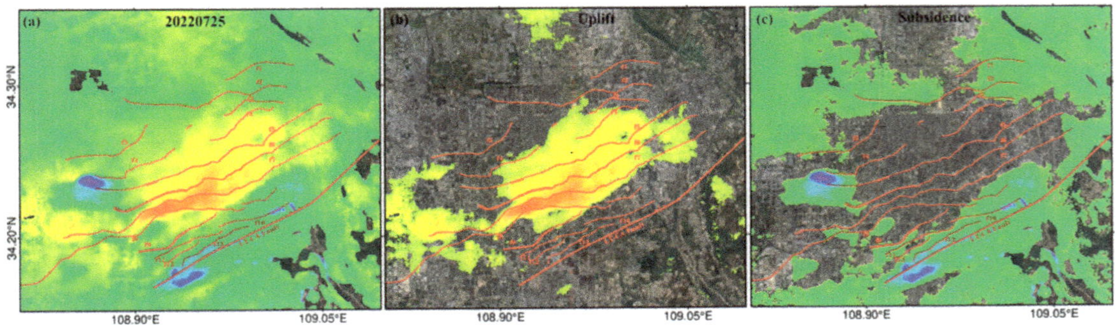

Figure 17. (**a**) Cumulative subsidence map, (**b**) uplift, and (**c**) subsidence.

According to the subsidence difference calculation method adopted in this study, the differential subsidence and angular distortions were extracted from the total subsidence (Figure 17a), and the results of the angular distortions were obtained, as shown in Figure 18. It can be seen clearly that there are two significant differences in deformation, as well as significant angular distortions, located in the YHZ area and the DJP area, respectively.

In these areas, within seven years, the differential subsidence has exceeded 25 cm, with a resolution unit of 100 m (0.25%), which is converted into an angular deformation β of 1/400 (i.e., 0.14°). We need to further determine the critical settlement gradient threshold related to the generation of ground fissures in order to quantitatively assess the harmfulness of the ground fissures. We established four hazard level categories based on β: low ($\beta \leq 1/3000$), medium ($1/3000 < \beta \leq 1/1500$), high ($1/1500 < \beta \leq 1/500$), and very high ($\beta > 1/500$) [41], as shown in Figure 19, indicating an increasing likelihood of damage, therefore compromising the serviceability of the urban infrastructure affected. The zone of very high hazard is around the YHZ area. In this study, we statistically analyzed the two regions with the largest angular deformations, and the result shows that severe surface fissures have begun to occur with an angular distortion of 1/500, which is consistent with the study of ground fissures in Mexico City [41].

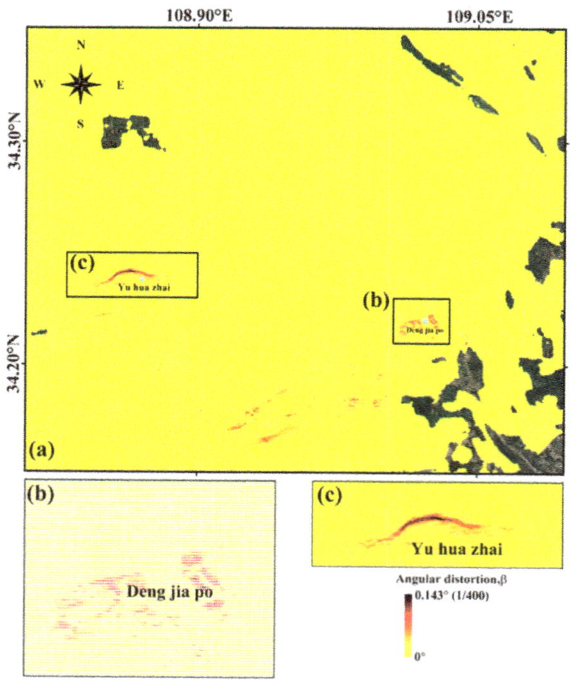

Figure 18. Analysis of subsidence-induced ground fissure hazards in Xi'an City from 2015–2022 from S1 results: (**a**) angular distortions, (**b**) angular distortions in the YHP area, and (**c**) angular distortions in the DJP area.

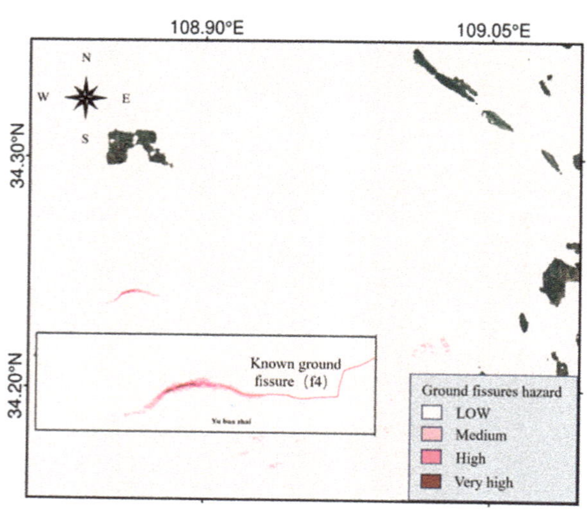

Figure 19. Analysis of subsidence-induced ground fissure hazards in Xi'an City from 2015–2022 from S1 results: derived classification of hazard levels.

Based on the research above, we believe that there is an undiscovered ground fissure in the YHZ area; thus, we identified the deformation boundary and angular damage area of the YHZ area as the location of the ground fissure, as shown in Figure 20. The red dashed line represents the predicted ground fissure, and the red solid line represents the existing ground fissure in Xi'an. This study can provide a dual quantitative and qualitative evaluation for the study of ground fissures in Xi'an.

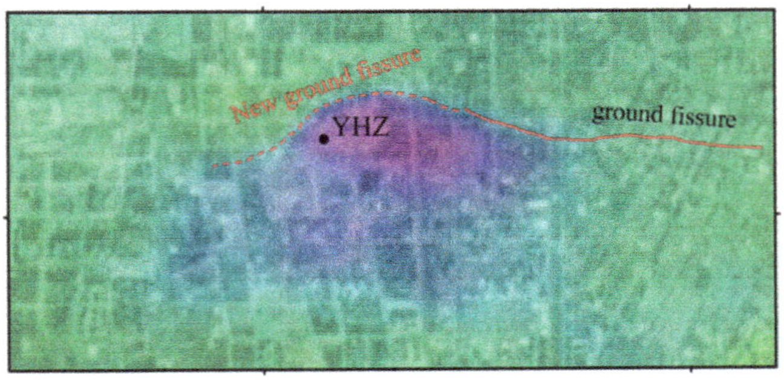

Figure 20. Prediction results of ground fissures (the red dashed line predicts a new ground fissure, and the red solid line shows an existing ground fissure).

5.3. The Relationship between Groundwater and Deformation

The measurement of surface displacement can serve as a supplement to groundwater monitoring, as the surface displacement reflects changes in the groundwater reserves, benefiting from the high resolution of the InSAR technology. Data on the groundwater level can also be used to reveal the causes of surface deformation. We selected the groundwater level curves of Well 2 and Well 3 presented in Figure 1 and the time series results of the nearest InSAR monitoring point. As shown in Figure 21a, the groundwater level of Well 2 first decreases and then rapidly increases. The reason for the rapid increase is due to human water injection, which causes the water level to quickly rise. At the same time, the surface also shifts from surface subsidence to surface elevation. During the period from 2015 to 2018, the groundwater level decreased by 22 m and the surface subsidence was 200 mm. However, during the period from 2018 to 2021, the groundwater level rose by 30 m and the surface elevation was 76 mm, indicating that most of the displacement at the Well 2 site area was inelastic. As shown in Figure 21b, the groundwater level of Well 3 shows an upward trend, and the corresponding surface also shows an upward phenomenon. Based on Figure 21, it can be seen that their changes over time have good consistency, and there is a positive correlation between the groundwater level and the displacement time series, indicating that the land uplift and subsidence in Xi'an are controlled by the groundwater injection and exploitation processes.

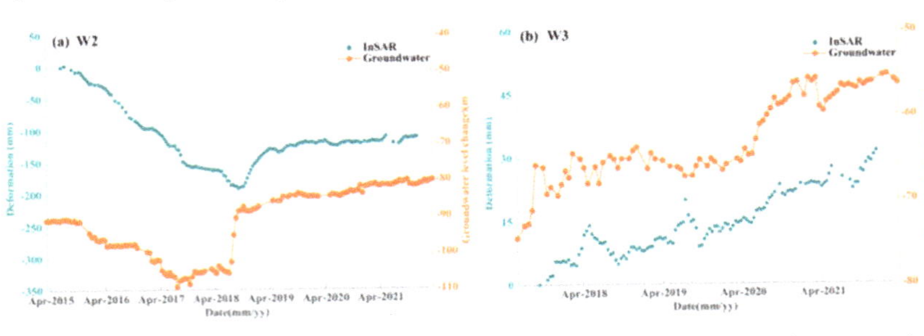

Figure 21. Comparison between the time series of vertical deformation and the time series of groundwater-level change at two water wells: (**a**) Well 2 and (**b**) Well 3.

Through the cross-correlation analysis, we determined the relationship between the vertical deformation time series and the groundwater level, which can quantify the impact of groundwater level fluctuations on land displacement. We obtained the cross−correlation coefficient parameters of two sequences, which can explain well the correlation between the land displacement time series and the groundwater level. The correlation coefficients between the groundwater data of Well 2 and Well 3 and the corresponding InSAR data are shown in Figure 22. Figure 22a shows a positive correlation between the displacement and groundwater level in Well 2, with a lag of 64 days. Figure 22b shows a positive correlation between the displacement and groundwater level in Well 3, with a lag of four days, evidencing the rapid response of land displacement to groundwater level fluctuation. Why there is a significant difference in the lag days between Well 2 and Well 3? This is because W3 well is located in a loess layer with a thickness of 100 m, while Well 2 well is located in an area with fine sand and gravel, thus leading to the different responses.

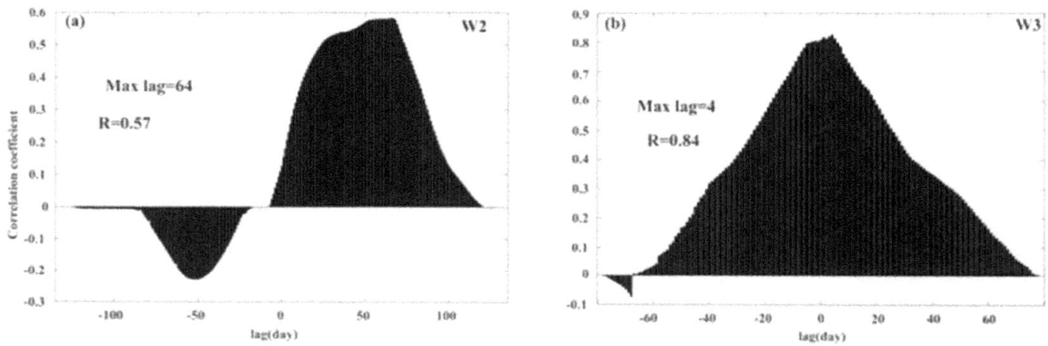

Figure 22. Correlation analysis between the times series of vertical deformation and groundwater-level change at two water wells: (**a**) Well 2 and (**b**) Well 3.

Since 2002, Xi'an has been supplied with water through the Heihe Reservoir, which greatly alleviates the phenomenon of groundwater depletion in Xi'an. As shown in Figure 23a, it is evident that the groundwater level of Well 1 well has been showing an upward trend. We further quantitatively evaluated the relationship between the secular variation in the groundwater level and the deformation of the uplifted area. The rebound of the groundwater level and the land uplift follow an exponential function curve [42,43]. We conducted an exponential regression of the groundwater level and displacement at the Well 1 site using the following equation:

$$def(t) = M\left(e^{kt} - 1\right) \tag{7}$$

where $def(t)$ is the vertical deformation time series, M is the value that characterizes the cumulative displacement, and $k \in [-1, 0]$. Firstly, the groundwater-level curve and the exponential function are well matched (Figure 23a, green line, RMSE = 4.8), showing that the groundwater level tends to be stable but is still rising. Secondly, the curve of the deformation time series and the exponential function have a good fitting (Figure 23b, red line, RMSE = 5.2), showing that the observed uplift can be explained by the elastic rebound of the pores in the aquifer system due to the groundwater level recovery. The surface uplift in Xi'an has become the main mode of surface deformation, and the harm caused by the uplift is uncertain. More research is needed in the future.

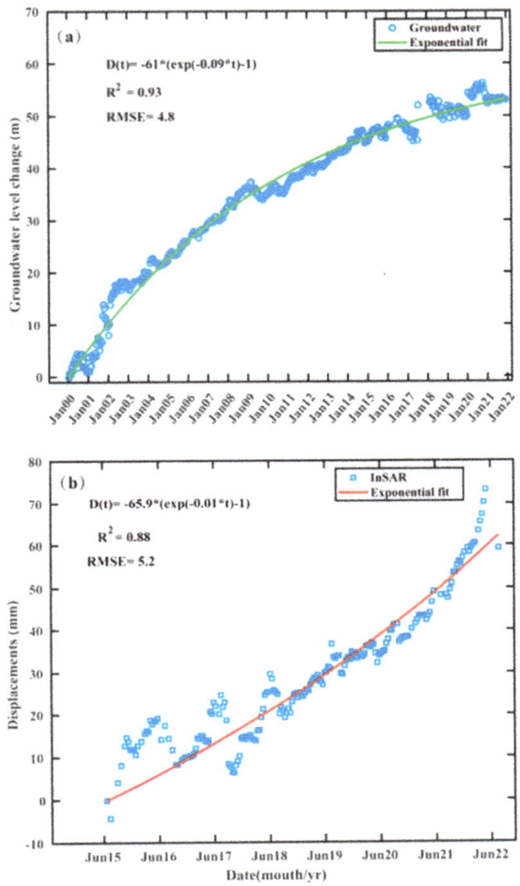

Figure 23. (**a**) Groundwater-level change at Well 1 between 2000 and 2021 and (**b**) ground uplift at this location between 2015 and 2022 based on the S1 data.

6. Conclusions

The Xi'an region has been suffering from long-time problems of groundwater depletion, ground fissure hazards, and surface subsidence. By using the multi-temporal InSAR technology and ascending C-band Sentinel-1 SAR data from 2015 to 2022, and descending X-band TerraSAR SAR data from 2017 to 2019, the land deformation was investigated and analyzed in a Xi'an urban area. There are multiple subsidence funnel areas and a narrow and long uplift area extending from the southwest to the southeast in Xi'an, and through annual deformation extraction, it can be observed that land subsidence had shifted from subsidence to an uplift phenomenon. The deformation time series is highly correlated with the variation in the groundwater level in aquifers, evidencing that surface deformation changes are controlled by fluctuations in the groundwater level. There are positive correlations between the vertical deformation time series and the groundwater levels, with lags of 64 days in Well 2 and 4 days in Well 3. Further, through the modeling and analysis of the 22-year Well 1 groundwater level and the InSAR time series data of the adjacent uplift area, it is shown that the groundwater recharge has not yet reached a stable state, and the deformation uplift has not slowed down. It can be imagined that under the implementation of the "Water Diversion Project from Han to Wei", the uplift phenomenon in the main urban area of Xi'an will be more significant, and attention should be paid to the harm of surface uplift to infrastructure in the later stage.

Through multi-dimensional deformation research, it has been shown that, due to the obstruction of groundwater diffusion by ground fissures, the flow direction of the groundwater is forced to be consistent with the direction of the ground fissures, leading to the occurrence of horizontal surface deformation in Xi'an. This study also demonstrated that by solving the deformation gradient and angular deformation, the critical conditions for the generation of ground fissures caused by uneven settlement were quantitatively evaluated, and new ground fissures in the YHZ region were predicted.

Our research results indicate that multi-dimensional deformation results and time-series deformation using InSAR have significant advantages in quantitatively evaluating the harm of ground fissures and the loss of groundwater reserves, which helps us to understand the relationship between ground fissures and surface deformation and evaluate the future of groundwater resource reserves in Xi'an under the background of large-scale water transfer projects.

Author Contributions: Methodology, X.Z., Z.C., R.G. and J.H.; Software, X.Z., B.X. and Q.Y.; Formal analysis, X.Z.; Resources, X.Z.; Writing—original draft, X.Z.; Writing—review & editing, R.G., C.Y. and T.X. All authors have read and agreed to the published version of the manuscript.

Funding: This work was supported by the National Natural Science Foundation of China under Grants 42030112 and 42201432, and the Technology and Fundamental Research Funds for the Central Universities of Central South University under Grant 2020zzts190.

Data Availability Statement: The data presented in this study are available from the corresponding author upon request.

Acknowledgments: The authors would like to thank the European Space Agency (ESA) for providing the Sentinel-1 data. The authors would like to thank the Xi'an Institute of Surveying and Mapping for providing the TerraSAR images, the leveling data, and the groundwater data.

Conflicts of Interest: The authors declare no conflict of interest.

References

1. Herrera-Garcia, G.; Ezquerro, P.; Tomas, R.; Bejar-Pizarro, M.; Lopez-Vinielles, J.; Rossi, M.; Mateos, R.M.; Carreon-Freyre, D.; Lambert, J.; Teatini, P.; et al. Mapping the global threat of land subsidence. *Science* **2021**, *371*, 34–36. [CrossRef] [PubMed]
2. Jeanne, P.; Farr, T.G.; Rutqvist, J.; Vasco, D.W. Role of agricultural activity on land subsidence in the San Joaquin Valley, California. *J. Hydrol.* **2019**, *569*, 462–469. [CrossRef]
3. Murray, K.D. Short-lived pause in Central California subsidence after heavy winter precipitation of 2017. *Sci. Adv.* **2018**, *4*, eaar8144. [CrossRef]
4. Chaussard, E.; Farr, T.G. A New Method for Isolating Elastic From Inelastic Deformation in Aquifer Systems: Application to the San Joaquin Valley, CA. *Geophys. Res. Lett.* **2019**, *46*, 10800–10809. [CrossRef]
5. Hoffmann, J.; Galloway, D.L.; Zebker, H.A. Inverse modeling of interbed storage parameters using land subsidence observations, Antelope Valley, California. *Water Resour. Res.* **2003**, *39*, 1031. [CrossRef]
6. Amelung, C.C. Land subsidence in central Mexico detected by ALOS InSAR time-series. *Remote Sens. Environ.* **2014**, *140*, 94–106.
7. Cabralcano, E.; Solano Rojas, D.E.; Olivercabrera, T.; Salazartlaczani, L.; Wdowinski, S.; Demets, C.; Pacheco, J. Subsidence and associated shallow faulting hazard assessment in central Mexico using InSAR and GPS. In Proceedings of the Agu Fall Meeting, San Francisco, CA, USA, 15–19 December 2014.
8. Castellazzi, P.; Martel, R.; Rivera, A.; Huang, J.; Pavlic, G.; Calderhead, A.I.; Chaussard, E.; Garfias, J.; Salas, J. Groundwater depletion in Central Mexico: Use of GRACE and InSAR to support water resources management. *Water Resour. Res.* **2016**, *52*, 5985–6003. [CrossRef]
9. Cigna, F.; Tapete, D. Satellite InSAR survey of structurally-controlled land subsidence due to groundwater exploitation in the Aguascalientes Valley, Mexico. *Remote Sens. Environ.* **2021**, *254*, 112254. [CrossRef]
10. Motagh, M.; Shamshiri, R.; Haghighi, M.H.; Wetzel, H.U.; Akbari, B.; Nahavandchi, H.; Roessner, S.; Arabi, S. Quantifying groundwater exploitation induced subsidence in the Rafsanjan plain, southeastern Iran, using InSAR time-series and in situ measurements. *Eng. Geol.* **2017**, *218*, 134–151. [CrossRef]
11. Haghighi, M.H.; Motagh, M. Ground surface response to continuous compaction of aquifer system in Tehran, Iran: Results from a long-term multi-sensor InSAR analysis. *Remote Sens. Environ.* **2019**, *221*, 534–550. [CrossRef]

12. Chaussard, E.; Amelung, F.; Abidin, H.; Hong, S.-H. Sinking cities in Indonesia: ALOS PALSAR detects rapid subsidence due to groundwater and gas extraction. *Remote Sens. Environ.* **2013**, *128*, 150–161. [CrossRef]
13. Halipu, A.; Wang, X.; Iwasaki, E.; Yang, W.; Kondoh, A. Quantifying Water Consumption through the Satellite Estimation of Land Use/Land Cover and Groundwater Storage Changes in a Hyper-Arid Region of Egypt. *Remote Sens.* **2022**, *14*, 2608. [CrossRef]
14. Gong, H.; Pan, Y.; Zheng, L.; Li, X.; Zhou, C. Long-term groundwater storage changes and land subsidence development in the North China Plain (1971–2015). *Hydrogeol. J.* **2018**, *26*, 1417–1427. [CrossRef]
15. Shi, M.; Gong, H.; Gao, M.; Chen, B.; Zhou, C. Recent Ground Subsidence in the North China Plain, China, Revealed by Sentinel-1A Datasets. *Remote Sens.* **2020**, *12*, 3579. [CrossRef]
16. Wei, F.; Wang, C.; Mu, D.; Min, Z.; Xu, H. Groundwater storage variations in the North China Plain from GRACE with spatial constraints. *Chin. J. Geophys.* **2017**, *60*, 1630–1642.
17. Guo, H.; Zhang, Z.; Cheng, G.; Li, W.; Li, T.; Jiao, J.J. Groundwater-derived land subsidence in the North China Plain. *Environ. Earth Sci.* **2015**, *74*, 1415–1427. [CrossRef]
18. Dong, Y.; Zhang, M.; Liu, J.; Zhang, X.; Feng, L. Coupling relationship between groundwater and ground fissures of land subsidence in Xi'an city and risk prevention and control technology. *Northwest. Geol.* **2019**, *52*, 95–102.
19. Qu, W.; Lu, Z.; Zhang, Q.; Li, Z.; Peng, J.; Wang, Q.; Drummond, J.; Zhang, M. Kinematic model of crustal deformation of Fenwei basin, China based on GPS observations. *J. Geodyn.* **2014**, *75*, 1–8. [CrossRef]
20. Bai, Z.; Wang, Y.; Balz, T. Beijing Land Subsidence Revealed Using PS-InSAR with Long Time Series TerraSAR-X SAR Data. *Remote Sens.* **2022**, *14*, 2529. [CrossRef]
21. Chen, B.; Gong, H.; Chen, Y.; Li, X.; Zhou, C.; Lei, K.; Zhu, L.; Duan, L.; Zhao, X. Land subsidence and its relation with groundwater aquifers in Beijing Plain of China. *Sci. Total Environ.* **2020**, *735*, 139111. [CrossRef]
22. Zhang, Y.; Wu, J.; Xue, Y.; Wang, Z.; Yao, Y.; Yan, X.; Wang, H. Land subsidence and uplift due to long-term groundwater extraction and artificial recharge in Shanghai, China. *Hydrogeol. J.* **2015**, *23*, 1851–1866. [CrossRef]
23. Shi, G.; Ma, P.; Hu, X.; Huang, B.; Lin, H. Surface response and subsurface features during the restriction of groundwater exploitation in Suzhou (China) inferred from decadal SAR interferometry. *Remote Sens. Environ.* **2021**, *256*, 112327. [CrossRef]
24. Han, Y.; Zou, J.; Lu, Z.; Qu, F.; Kang, Y.; Li, J. Ground deformation of wuhan, china, revealed by multi-temporal insar analysis. *Remote Sens.* **2020**, *12*, 3788. [CrossRef]
25. Li, G.; Zhao, C.; Wang, B.; Peng, M.; Bai, L. Evolution of spatiotemporal ground deformation over 30 years in Xi'an, China, with multi-sensor SAR interferometry. *J. Hydrol.* **2023**, *616*, 128764. [CrossRef]
26. Amelung, F.; Galloway, D.L.; Bell, J.W.; Zebker, H.A.; Laczniak, R.J. Sensing the ups and downs of Las Vegas: InSAR reveals structural control of land subsidence and aquifer-system deformation. *Geology* **1999**, *27*, 483–486. [CrossRef]
27. Castellazzi, P.; Longuevergne, L.; Martel, R.; Rivera, A.; Brouard, C.; Chaussard, E. Quantitative mapping of groundwater depletion at the water management scale using a combined GRACE/InSAR approach. *Remote Sens. Environ.* **2018**, *205*, 408–418. [CrossRef]
28. Bell, J.W. Permanent scatterer InSAR reveals seasonal and long-term aquifer-system response to groundwater pumping and artificial recharge. *Water Resour. Res.* **2008**, *44*, W02407. [CrossRef]
29. Chaussard, E.; Bürgmann, R.; Shirzaei, M.; Fielding, E.J.; Baker, B. Predictability of hydraulic head changes and characterization of aquifer-system and fault properties from InSAR-derived ground deformation. *J. Geophys. Res. Solid Earth* **2014**, *119*, 6572–6590. [CrossRef]
30. Chaussard, E.; Bürgmann, R. Remote Sensing of Ground Deformation for Monitoring Groundwater Management Practices: Application to the Santa Clara Valley during the 2012–2015 California Drought: Groundwater Monitoring with InSAR. *J. Geophys. Res. Solid Earth* **2017**, *122*, 8566–8582. [CrossRef]
31. Jiang, L.; Bai, L.; Zhao, Y.; Cao, G.; Wang, H.; Sun, Q. Combining InSAR and Hydraulic Head Measurements to Estimate Aquifer Parameters and Storage Variations of Confined Aquifer System in Cangzhou, North China Plain. *Water Resour. Res.* **2018**, *54*, 8234–8252. [CrossRef]
32. Murray, K.D.; Lohman, R.B.; Kim, J.; Holt, W.E. An Alternative Approach for Constraining 3D-Displacements With InSAR, Applied to a Fault-Bounded Groundwater Entrainment Field in California. *J. Geophys. Res. Solid Earth JGR* **2021**, *126*, e2020JB021137. [CrossRef]
33. Berardino, P.; Fornaro, G.; Lanari, R.; Sansosti, E. A New Algorithm for Surface Deformation Monitoring Based on Small Baseline Differential SAR Interferograms. *IEEE Trans. Geosci. Remote Sens.* **2002**, *40*, 2375–2383. [CrossRef]
34. Hooper, A. A multi-temporal InSAR method incorporating both persistent scatterer and small baseline approaches. *Geophys. Res. Lett.* **2008**, *35*, 96–106. [CrossRef]
35. Peng, M.; Zhao, C.; Zhang, Q.; Lu, Z.; Li, Z. Research on Spatiotemporal Land Deformation (2012–2018) over Xi'an, China, with Multi-Sensor SAR Datasets. *Remote Sens.* **2019**, *11*, 664. [CrossRef]
36. Wright, T.J.; Parsons, B.E.; Lu, Z. Toward mapping surface deformation in three dimensions using InSAR. *Geophys. Res. Lett.* **2004**, *31*. [CrossRef]
37. Hu, J.; Li, Z.W.; Ding, X.L.; Zhu, J.J.; Zhang, L.; Sun, Q. Resolving three-dimensional surface displacements from InSAR measurements: A review. *Earth Sci. Rev.* **2014**, *133*, 1–17. [CrossRef]
38. Bouwer, H. Land Subsidence and Cracking Due to Ground-Water Depletion. *Ground Water* **1977**, *15*, 358–364. [CrossRef]
39. Macdonald, D.H.; Skempton, A.W. The Allowable Settlements of Buildings. *ICE Proc. Eng. Div.* **1956**, *5*, 727–768.

40. Mcdonnell, R.A.; Lloyd, C.; Burrough, P. *Principles of Geographical Information Systems*; Oxford University Press: Oxford, UK, 1998.
41. Cigna, F.; Tapete, D. Present-day land subsidence rates, surface faulting hazard and risk in Mexico City with 2014–2020 Sentinel-1 IW InSAR. *Remote Sens. Environ.* **2021**, *253*, 112161. [CrossRef]
42. Terzaghi, K. Principles of soil mechanics: IV Settlement and consolidation of clay. *Eng. News Rec.* **1925**, *95*, 874–878.
43. Hu, X.; Bürgmann, R. Aquifer deformation and active faulting in Salt Lake Valley, Utah, USA. *Earth Planet. Sci. Lett.* **2020**, *547*, 116471. [CrossRef]

remote sensing

MDPI

Article

Deformation Evaluation of the South-to-North Water Diversion Project (SNWDP) Central Route over Handan in Hebei, China, Based on Sentinel-1A, Radarsat-2, and TerraSAR-X Datasets

Siting Xiong [1], Zhichao Deng [1], Bochen Zhang [2,3], Chisheng Wang [1,3,4,*], Xiaoqiong Qin [2] and Qingquan Li [1,2,3]

1 Guangdong Laboratory of Artificial Intelligence and Digital Economy (SZ), Shenzhen 518107, China; xiongsiting@gml.ac.cn (S.X.); 2210273112@email.szu.edu.cn (Z.D.)
2 College of Civil and Transportation Engineering, Shenzhen University, Shenzhen 518060, China; zhangbc@szu.edu.cn (B.Z.); liqq@szu.edu.cn (Q.L.)
3 MNR Key Laboratory for Geo-Environmental Monitoring of Great Bay Area & Guangdong Key Laboratory of Urban Informatics & Shenzhen Key Laboratory of Spatial Smart Sensing and Services, Shenzhen University, Shenzhen 518060, China
4 School of Architecture & Urban Planning, Shenzhen University, Shenzhen 518060, China
* Correspondence: wangchisheng@szu.edu.cn

Abstract: The South-to-North Water Diversion Project (SNWDP) is a megaproject which has been constructed to alleviate imbalanced water resource distribution between northern and southern China. It encompasses three routes distributed in the east, central, and west of China, respectively. The central route (CR) of the SNWDP starts from the Danjiangkou Reservoir and ends in Beijing and Tianjin, running through Hubei, Henan, and Hebei Provinces; it has been in service since December 2014. For this type of megaproject, efficient and effective safety monitoring during its operation is highly challenging to the management department. Multitemporal interferometric synthetic aperture radar (MT-InSAR) has been widely applied in monitoring land deformation, especially in a wide area. However, its ability to show the deformation of one specific facility along the SNWD has not been deeply investigated. This study investigates the capability of MT-InSAR in monitoring the deformation of the canal and ancillary facilities along the SNWD-CR over Handan, Hebei Province, in China, using Sentinel-1, Radarsat-2, and TerraSAR-X datasets. Deformation rates from March 2015 to March 2016 are obtained by applying permanent scatterers (PS)-InSAR to these three SAR datasets. After combining the deformation rates derived by the three datasets, deformation along the SNWDP-CR is evaluated using a method encompassing median absolute deviation (MAD) calculation and heatmap. The evaluation result reveals that one part of the western embankment of the open canal is subsiding at up to 10 mm/year, which may be associated with overirrigation. Besides this location, the most dangerous areas assessed by the proposed method are related to ancillary facilities, mainly aqueducts and crossing-canal bridges.

Keywords: multitemporal interferometric SAR; the South-to-North Water Diversion Project (SNWD); infrastructure safety; damage detection

1. Introduction

China's economy has been soaring in the last few decades, accompanied by many new and large-scale infrastructure projects constructed domestically. The South-to-North Water Diversion Project (SNWDP) is one typical example, which aims to alleviate the water imbalance between northern prosperous regions and southern water-rich regions [1,2]. Running 1276 km from the Danjiangkou Reservoir to Beijing, the SNWDP-CR transferred 30 billion cubic metres of water from the Danjiangkou Reservoir to the northern cities by 3 June 2020 [3,4]. Starting from the Danjiangkou Reservoir, which is about 146 m high, water flows almost by gravity along the SNWDP-CR, which is primarily artificial canals [5].

Construction of the SNWDP-CR includes primarily open canals and intersecting structures, such as aqueducts, siphons, culverts, sluices, and bridges [5]. The canal embankments are made from concrete and shaped like a dam embankment.

For this type of mega-infrastructure, challenges reside not only in its construction but also in safety monitoring during its operational period, which is the focus of its management departments. Conventionally, point-wise measurements and human visual inspection are carried out to investigate the safety status of the infrastructure. Nowadays, sensors such as accelerometers and strain gauges, GPS receivers, fibre optical sensing, image-based monitoring, etc., are used to improve inspection efficiency [6–8]. However, the expense of these systems is significantly high when applied to large-scale infrastructures. In this case, satellite observations can provide a low-cost complementary tool that vastly improves the efficiency of safety control of the SNWDP.

Interferometric synthetic aperture radar (InSAR) is now a widely applied satellite remote sensing technique to detect land deformation at millimetre accuracy over large areas [9]. Many multitemporal (MT)-InSAR methods have been developed to extract time series of land deformation from repeat-pass satellite datasets [10,11]. With these methods, long-term land deformations caused by earthquakes, volcanoes, landslides, groundwater withdrawal, etc., can be obtained in an effective and efficient way [12–15]. MT-InSAR has been successfully applied to monitor land deformation associated with the SNWDP-CR. It has been reported that additional groundwater supply sourced from the SNWDP-CR has primarily led to the alleviation of land subsidence in Beijing [16–22]. For example, Zhu et al. analysed the land subsidence in Beijing three years after the SNWDP-CR commenced by integrating hydrogeologic information, piezometric records, permanent scatterer (PS)-InSAR, and levelling [16]. They reported that a certain decrease (up to 10 mm/year) in the subsidence rates was observed in the central portion of the north Beijing plain, but the land subsidence continued to increase in the rest of the region [16]. Lyu et al. processed long-time-series Envisat ASAR (2004–2010), Radarsat-2 (2011–2014), and Sentinel-1 (2015–2017) of one central part of Beijing [17]. Their results show that over 57% of the area within the 25 mm/year contour line show decelerating subsidence after 2014, when the SNWDP started to supply water to Beijing [17]. Dong et al. retrieved land subsidence measurements over the past decades (1992–2022) by integrating multisensor C-band InSAR measurements into a logistic model, revealing three major subsidence funnels surrounding downtown in the north, northeast, and east of Beijing [22]. Dong et al. carried out multiscale deformation monitoring along the SNWDP-CR based on the Sentinel-1 dataset. They remarked that the canal bypassed the giant subsidence funnel in the southeast part of Hebei Province while exhibiting overall stability apart from a few sections affected by significant embankment deformation or land subsidence [23].

Apart from regional land deformation monitoring, InSAR techniques have also been increasingly used in direct deformation measurement of various types of infrastructure, such as buildings, bridges, railways, etc. [24–26]. These types of infrastructure, made from concrete, provide ideal persistent scatterers, which manifest as high signal-to-noise ratio (SNR) in radar signals. Nevertheless, they are sensitive to temperature variation, leading to a thermal effect on the deformation results [27–30]. As a water conservancy infrastructure, the thaw and freeze of water running in the canal of the SNWDP may be a cause of the distress in the embankment. This triggers the question of whether we can use satellite SAR observations to measure the deformation of the SNWDP infrastructure and to detect hazards or even dangerous regions.

In this study, we focus on the deformation monitoring of the SNWDP-CR canal and ancillary facilities based on multiple SAR datasets, including Sentinel 1-A (S1A), Radarsat-2 (RSAT2), and TerraSAR-X (TSX) over Handan in Hebei Province, China. The results derived by applying PS-InSAR to these three datasets are combined using a Z-score standardisation. The standardised deformation rates are combined and then evaluated using a median absolute deviation (MAD)-based weighted heatmap to highlight the dangerous areas with large deformation [31,32]. The following section introduces the study area, datasets, and methods. In Section 3, the PS-InSAR results of the study area and close-ups of typical ancillary facilities are presented. Based on these results, the deformation is evaluated, and the derived heatmap is displayed to show the dangerous areas. Finally, the discussion and conclusions based on the results are summarised in Sections 4 and 5, respectively.

2. Materials and Methods

2.1. Study Area and Datasets

This study focuses on one segment of the SNWDP-CR crossing Handan, as shown in Figure 1, which is in southern Hebei Province, China, at the boundary of the Taihang Mountains. West of the SNWDP-CR, mining activities led to land deformation of up to 90 cm as measured by SAR observations during the period of July 2015 to April 2016 [33]. The SNWD-CR expands about 80 km across Handan, running from Anyang through Zhang River into Ci County in Handan, bypassing Dongwushi Reservoir, then west, parallel to the Jingguang railway, and north into Xingtai through Yongnian County, as shown by the red line in Figure 1. Most parts of the Handan segment are open canals, along which the bottom width of the embankments is 19–31 m, and the surface width is about 100 m. The maximum water depth is intended to be 6 m, with the flow speed designed to be 235 m^3/s [34]. Since beginning operation in 2014, it provides 352 million cubic metres of water per year to Handan, of which the per capita water resources reach 192 cubic metres, accounting for only 8.4% of the national average. The SNWDP-CR is designed to provide water resources for eastern Handan City and 13 counties, including 0.6 million people occupying a total area of 7384 km^2 [34].

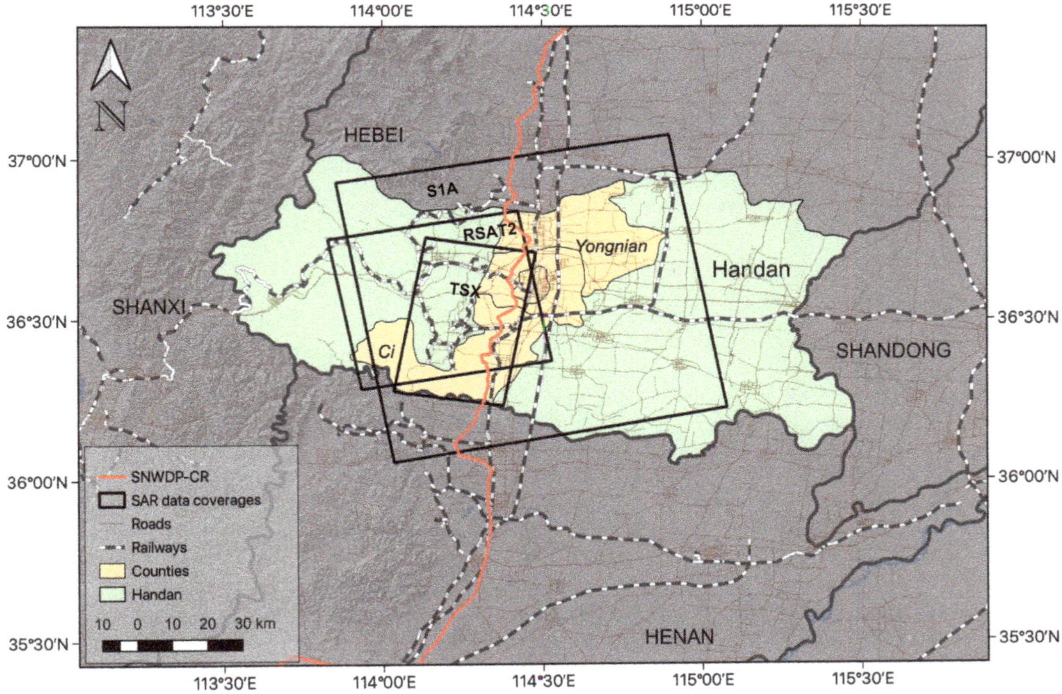

Figure 1. Geographical location of the study area and coverages of SAR datasets.

Over the study area, we collected three satellite SAR datasets, and their spatial coverages are presented by the black boxes in Figure 1. The S1A dataset fully covers the SNWD-CR in Handan, while the TSX dataset covers that in Ci County and Handan County, and the RSAT2 dataset covers that in Handan County and Yongnian County. Detailed information about these datasets is listed in Table 1; the RSAT2 and TSX datasets were commercially obtained over a span of only one year. Apart from these two commercial datasets, we also collected 18 Sentinel-1A images, which span from June 2015 to March 2016, to cross-validate results derived from the other two datasets.

Table 1. Detailed information of the three satellite SAR datasets.

	Sentinel-1A (S1A)	Radarsat-2 (RSAT2)	TerraSAR-X (TSX)
Wavelength	C-band (5.6 cm)	C-band (5.6 cm)	X-band (3.2 cm)
Range pixel spacing	2.3 m	2.7 m	1.4 m
Azimuth pixel spacing	13.9 m	2.9 m	1.9 m
Heading (α)	347°	349°	190°
Incident angle (θ)	39°	35.5°	41°
Repeat orbit	12 days	24 days	11 days
Orbit direction	ascending	ascending	descending
Polarizations	VV	HH	HH
Time period	20150617–20160331	20150404–20160305	20150524–20160212
Reference image	20151003	20150826	20151014
No. of images	18	14	15

2.2. PS-InSAR Processing

SAR images record both the amplitude and phase of the microwave signals returned from ground targets. With multiple repeat-orbit acquisitions, the movement of the target can be measured at an accuracy of millimetres. Phases between two acquisitions contain several components, i.e., topographic phase ϕ_{top}, deformation phase ϕ_{dis}, orbital phase (inaccuracy of orbital ephemeris) ϕ_{orb}, atmospheric phase (caused by different delays between acquisitions) ϕ_{atm}, noise phase (caused by thermal noise or incoherent scattering) ϕ_{noi}, etc., as listed in Equation (1).

$$\phi = \phi_{top} + \phi_{dis} + \phi_{orb} + \phi_{atm} + \phi_{noi} \tag{1}$$

With a priori knowledge of the surface height, the topographic phase ϕ_{top} can be removed and the deformation of the target can be estimated, as shown in Equation (2).

$$d = -\frac{\lambda}{4\pi}\phi_{dis} \tag{2}$$

where d is the deformation of the target and λ is the wavelength.

One drawback of the InSAR technique is that it is influence by the phase decorrelation phenomenon, i.e., the phase is incoherent due to changing scattering mechanisms of the target, and the atmospheric effect, i.e., the time delay difference of acquisitions contributes to the atmospheric phase, which is very difficult to detangle from the deformation phase. Two classic methods were proposed to deal with these problems: PS-InSAR and small-baseline subset (SBAS). The former method is used to select pixels with a dominant scattering mechanism, whose phase is stable and whose phase noise is ignorable, allowing for the derivation of more reliable long-time-series displacements [35,36]. In this method, interferograms are formed with one common reference acquisition. The latter method selects interferograms with short temporal and spatial baselines [37]; hence, it can deal with datasets with a limited number of acquisitions. In SBAS, multiple reference images are used as reference acquisitions, and resampling of the acquisitions and interferograms is usually needed. Compared to PS-InSAR, which is suitable for urban areas because many artificial targets are permanent scatterers, SBAS is suitable for applications involving rural areas and wide coverage. Since resampling of the original image is carried out during the interferogram formation in SBAS processing, the resolution after resampling is not favourable to reflect the detailed deformation of the SNWDP-CR constructs. Therefore, PS-

InSAR is chosen to be applied to the three SAR datasets. PS-InSAR processing encompasses the first two modules shown in Figure 2.

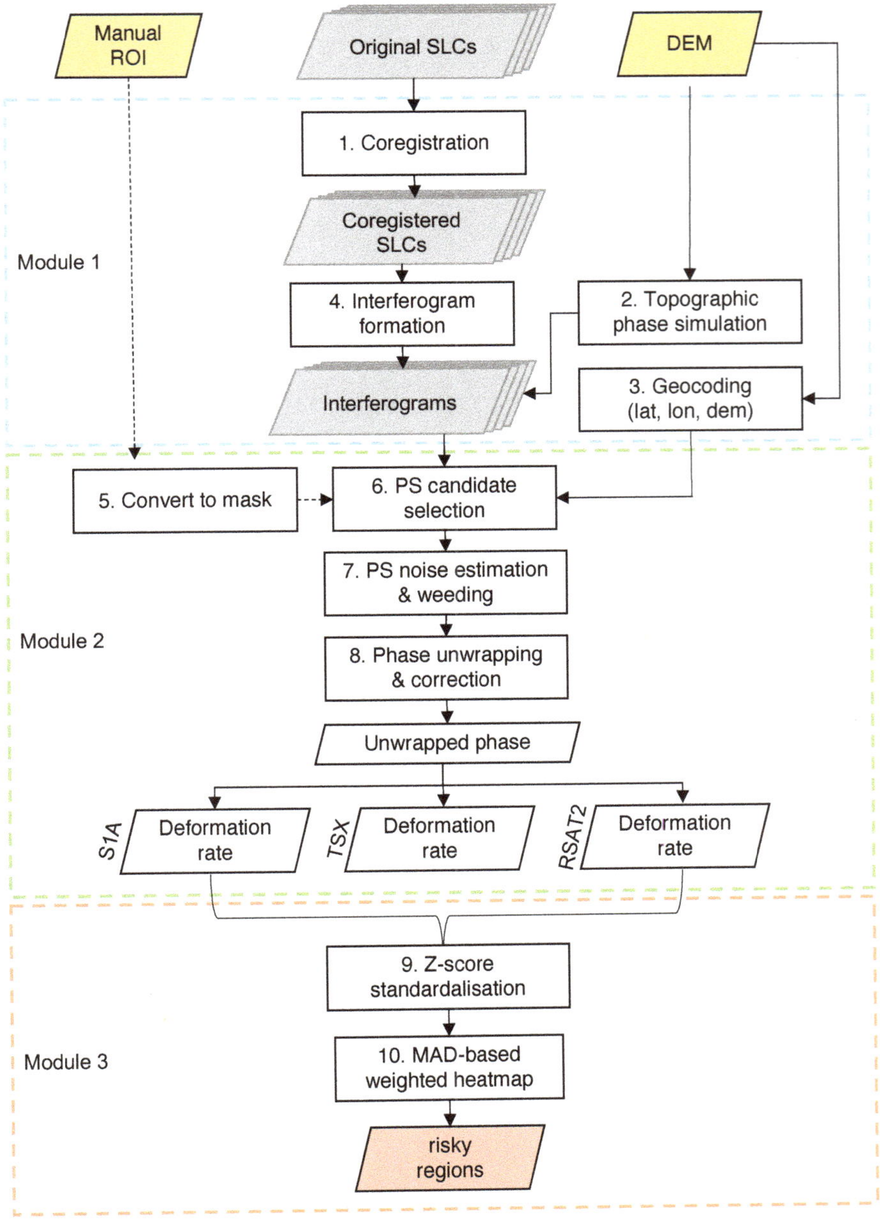

Figure 2. The flowchart encompasses three modules: (1) the MT-InSAR processing in the dash blue box, (2) the time-series analysis in the dash green box, and (3) the deformation evaluation in the dash orange box. The ROI is the buffer area along the SNWDP-CR, and the buffer area is set to be 1 km around the route in this study. The coloured boxes annotate the input to the first module and final output from the last module.

The first module is InSAR processing, during which the input multitemporal SAR acquisitions are coregistered to one common acquisition. With the external shuttle radar terrain mapping (SRTM) digital elevation model (DEM), the coregistered SAR stack is then used to form single reference interferograms, and the geocode information (lat, lon, and dem) can be derived. The first module includes steps 1–4, which are realised based on GAMMA software [38]. The output from the first module is then fed to the second module, which is the Stanford method for PS analysis (StaMPS) [39] with an optional manual delineated region of interest (ROI) to select PS candidates with amplitude dispersion as steps 5 and 6. In the case of the SNWDP, this ROI is selected as a buffer area of 1 km around the central route. In step 7, the phase noises are estimated and used to exclude noisy points. The final step of the PS analysis is phase unwrapping and correction. The key parameters of the PS-InSAR analysis are listed in Table 2.

Table 2. Key parameters of the PS-InSAR analysis.

Parameters of PS-InSAR	Values
amplitude dispersion index	0.4
filter_grid_size	50
density_rand	20
weed_standard_dev	1.0
weed_max_noise	1.0
unwrap_method	3D
unwrap_prefilter_flag	yes
unwrap_grid_size (m)	200
unwrap_gold_n_win	32
unwrap_time_win (d)	730

2.3. Deformation Evaluation Based on Combined PS-InSAR Results

The third module consists of a result combination using the Z-score standardisation and the deformation evaluation using the MAD-based weighted heatmap. The Z-score standardisation returns a normalized value based on the mean and the standard deviation. It is used for standardising scores on the same scale by dividing a score's deviation by the standard deviation in a dataset. Results derived by using different SAR observations may follow different distributions. Z-score standardisation is used to transform the results to the same scale. For each of the S1A, RSAT2, and TSX results, the expectation and standard deviation of the normal distribution are fitted using the deformation rates v. Then, each deformation rate v in this result is standardised using Equation (3).

$$v' = \frac{v - \mu}{\sigma} \tag{3}$$

After standardisation, v' is not the physical deformation measured using InSAR processing, although it should follow the trend of the target's deformation. The three standardised results are then combined directly to be evaluated using the MAD-based weighted heatmap [31]. The MAD-based weighted heatmap is a heatmap derived based on the MAD evaluation of standardised deformation rates, which are weighted using inversion of neighbouring point numbers. Firstly, a MAD is calculated for each point in the combined results using standardised deformation rates. For the ith point in the combined result, we search the nearest points within a radius R, resulting in a set of N_i standardised deformation rates, $v' = \left[v'_1, v'_2, \ldots, v'_{N_i}\right]$. With this set, the MAD for the ith point can be calculated as Equation (4) [32].

$$MAD_i = bM\left(\left|v' - M(v')\right|\right) \tag{4}$$

where b is a constant set to 1.4826, according to [32], and $M(\cdot)$ is the median operator. Based on the calculated MAD, a risk index γ_i and a risk label $\mathcal{L}_i$ for the ith point can be derived using Equations (5) and (6), respectively. Then, a heatmap with a quartic kernel shape and a radius of 50 m is produced to reflect the density of risky points. The set of the radius is arbitrary but should be smaller than the buffer distance. To include the different significance of the risky levels and justify the spatial inhomogeneity of the PS points, the heatmap is weighted by the inversion of the neighbouring point number. The weight is calculated as $w_i = \mathcal{L}_i / N_i$. The heatmap value is approximately zero for the clustered points, with $\mathcal{L}_i = 0$. The larger the number of the risk label $\mathcal{L}_i$, the more significance it contributes to the heatmap value. However, for an isolated point with a large risk label value, the weighted heatmap value should be high, and this is the aim to introduce inversion of the neighbouring point numbers.

$$\gamma_i = \left| \frac{v'_i - M(v')}{MAD_i} \right| \tag{5}$$

$$\mathcal{L}_i = \begin{cases} 0 & \gamma_i < 2 \\ 1 & 2 < \gamma_i < 2.5 \\ 2 & 2.5 < \gamma_i < 3 \\ 3 & \gamma_i > 3 \end{cases} \tag{6}$$

3. Results

3.1. PS-InSAR Results Derived from Different SAR Datasets

The deformation rates derived by by PS-InSAR analysis on each of the the three datasets within the overlapping area are demonstrated in Figure 3. The deformation is measured along the line of sight (LOS) direction of the spaceborne SAR. The positive values indicate the targets moving towards the sensors, while the negative values indicate moving away.

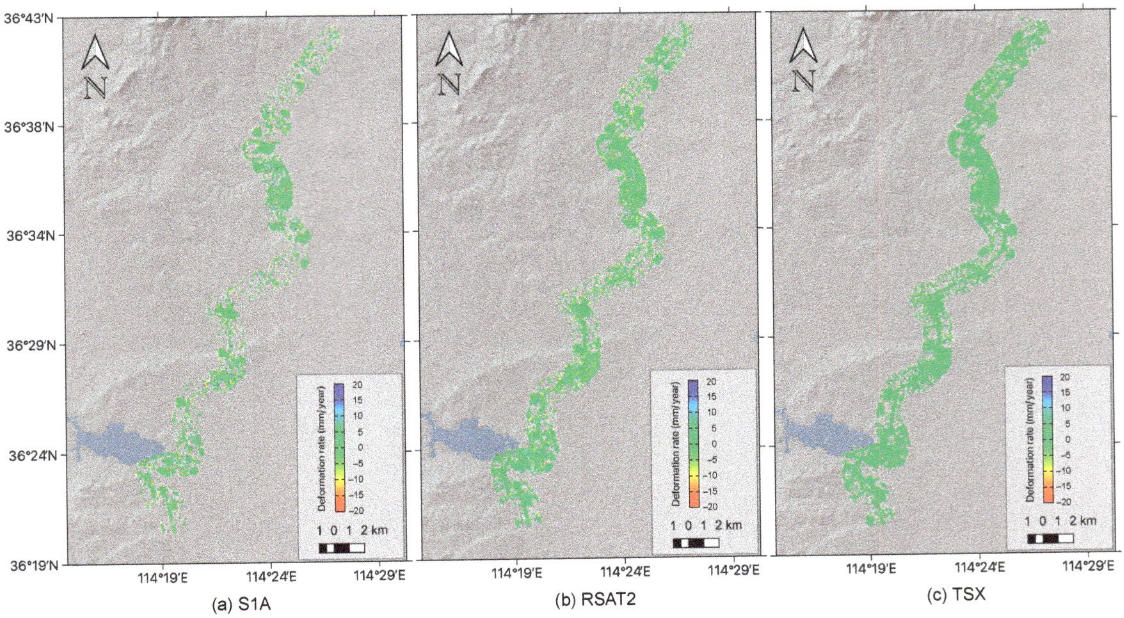

Figure 3. Deformation rate derived from PS-InSAR processing of (**a**) S1A, (**b**) RSAT2, and (**c**) TSX datasets.

For S1A, RSAT2, and TSX results shown in the Figure 3, 30, 439, 163, 497, and 433, 741 points remained after filtering using phase stability, respectively. The deformation rates are in the range of −27.39~24.16 mm/year when using the S1A dataset, while this range is comparative to −15.95~15.67 mm/year for the RSAT2 dataset and −14.40~12.54 mm/year for the TSX dataset. All three datasets are processed using the same parameters listed in Table 2, resulting in much fewer PS points selected in the S1A results than the other two results. However, relaxing the criteria for PS selection resulted in much noisier PS points in the S1A result; therefore, we retained the current parameter setting. It can be seen from Figure 3 that the SNWD-CR over Handan is overall stable, with deformation rates primarily ranging between −10 and 10 mm/year. However, subtle deformation can still be observed in some specific areas. In this study, we do not focus on the buildings surrounding the route; instead, we will pay attention to the canal embankment and ancillary facilities in the following subsection.

3.1.1. The Open Canal

The main canal of the SNWD-CR is excavated to be inverted trapezoidal, with the embankment filled with earth and lined with concrete. Along the SNWD-CR in the study area, some locations appear unstable, as revealed by the PS-InSAR results. One example is plotted in Figure 4, from which we can observe a subsiding region annotated with P1. This subsidence occurs on the western embankment of the SNWD-CR south of the Dongwushi Reservoir. In this region, the subsiding rate exceeds 10 mm/year in both S1A and RSAT2 results.

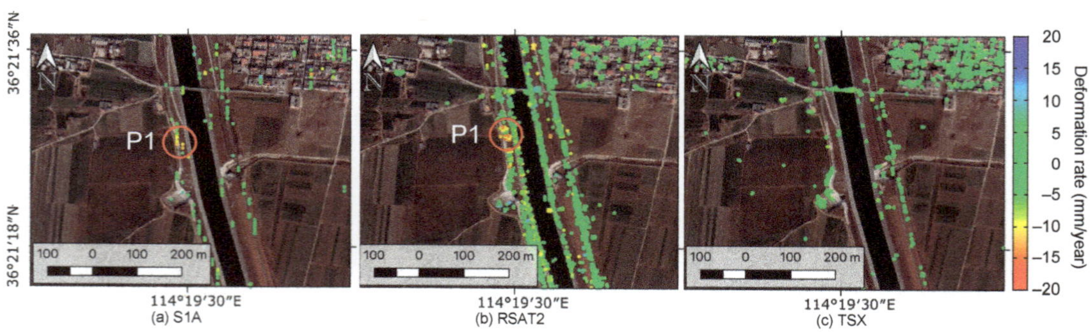

Figure 4. Close-ups of one subsiding area on the western embankment of the SNWDP-CR. The red circles highlight PSs in the S1A and RSAT2 results. The background images are satellite images from Google Earth.

The Google satellite map is inspected to investigate the land surface of this region, and its archived images spanning from 26 November, 2016 to May 2, 2019 are shown in Figure 5. Comparing these images reveals an obvious land collapse in the region denoted by red circles. In Figure 5a,b, this region remained intact, while an apparent damaged area can be observed in Figure 5c,d. This damage seems to be repaired with side slope tactionion tools in Figure 5e, and fully repaired in Figure 5f. This region is about 60 m south of the P1 region along the western embankment. Considering that the temporal coverage of the RSAT2 dataset is from 4 April 2015 to 5 March 2016, and the S1A temporal coverage is from 17 June 2015 to 31 May 2016, the large deformation rate at P1 in Figure 4 should have indicated the deforming process underground before the collapse occurred on the land surface.

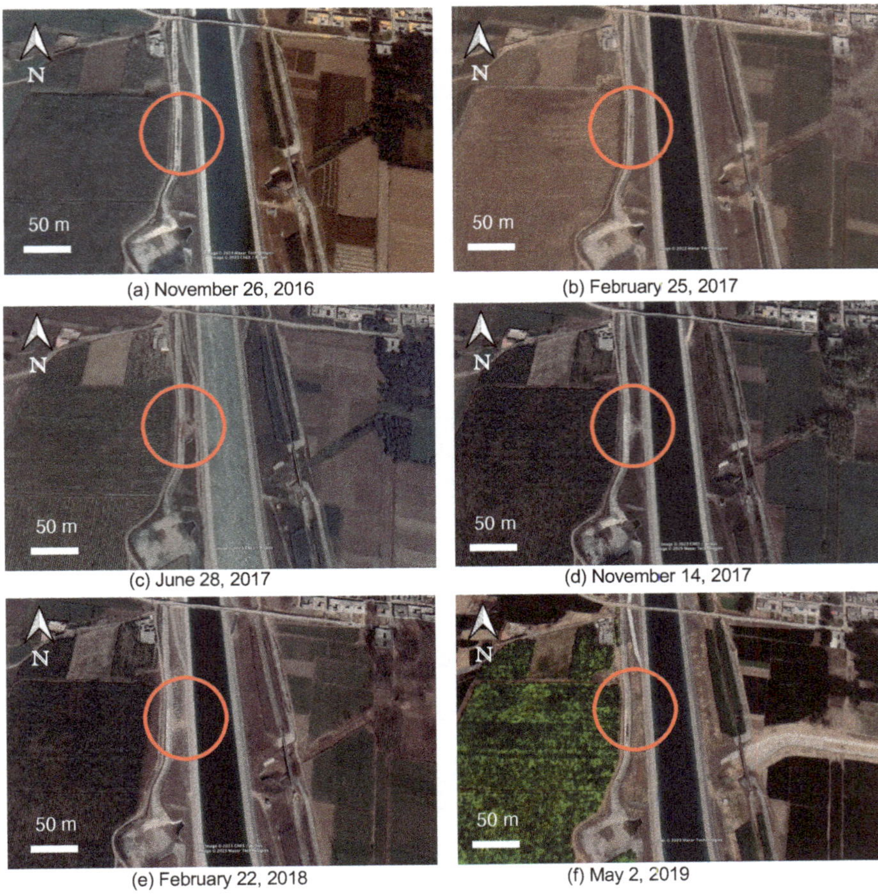

Figure 5. Satellite images from Google Earth showing the change in one land collapse south of P1 location. The red circles in (**a**–**f**) annotate the location where a land collapse evolving on the western embankment. The land surface damage occurred between 25 February 2017 and 28 June 2017. It was repaired on 22 February 2018.

3.1.2. Ancillary Facilities

Apart from the main canal, hundreds of various ancillary facilities have been built to support the daily operation of the SNWDP-CR in Handan, among which are 78 crossing-canal bridges that have been constructed in the suburbs [40]. In the following sections, we show detailed results of three main types of these ancillary facilities, including aqueducts, crossing-canal bridges, and siphons.

One important type of facility along the SNWDP-CR is the aqueduct, which is a canal built aloft, supported by pillars, for conveying water. Figure 6 shows one aqueduct which is oriented S–N in the study area. S1A and RSAT2 capture the deformation of the western side, while TSX captures the eastern side. The aqueduct is overall stable, except that the two ends that connect with the open canal appear to be slightly subsiding. From the S1A result, P2 and P3 are suffering subsidence at a rate above 10 mm/year. The RSAT2 result shows that the subsiding rate is above 10 mm/year at P3 and ranges between 5 and 10 mm/year at P2. However, the measurements of these deformation rates are smaller in the TSX result.

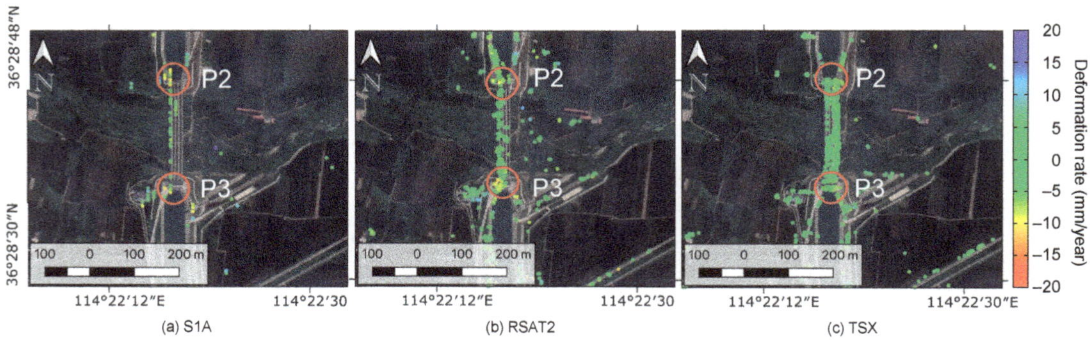

Figure 6. Close-ups of deformation rates of one aqueduct oriented in the south-to-north direction. Red circles are two ends of the aqueduct. The background images are satellite images from Google Earth.

Bridges, which are transportation facilities that cross the open canal to connect roads and railways, are frequently seen along the SNWDP-CR. Figure 7a–c show the three results of one arch bridge crossing the canal, as shown in the red circle. In the RSAT2 result, the western side of the bridge shows a trend of subsidence, while in the TSX result, this part seems to be slightly uplifting. These two opposite deforming directions are confirmed to be a planar movement of the bridge arch, since RSAT2 and TSX are of different orbit directions.

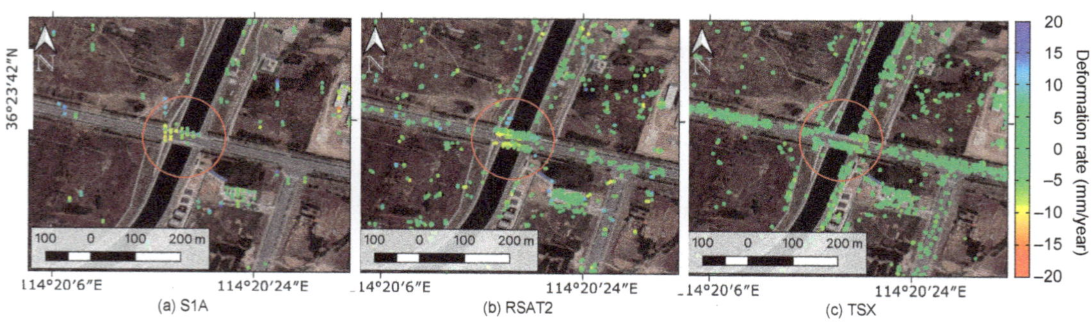

Figure 7. Close-ups show the deformation rates of one crossing-canal arch bridge derived from (**a**) S1A, (**b**) RSAT2, and (**c**) TSX datasets. Red circles highlight the bridge area. The background images are satellite images from Google Earth.

Figure 8a–c show another two bridges whose displacements are captured in the RSAT2 and TSX results, as denoted by the red circles. In the former, there is no result in the middle bridge, while the latter captured more points on the bridge. These two crossing-canal bridges are overall stable, with deformation rates of −5~5 mm/year.

Figure 9 shows one siphon that controls the transfer of water under a river. More PS points are selected on the western embankment and the northern culverts, while more PS points are on the eastern embankment and the southern culverts. The deformation rates of these two results show that the siphon and related culverts are overall stable, except for a small region on the eastern side of the embankment of the northern culverts, which is slightly subsiding at a rate of around 8 mm/year.

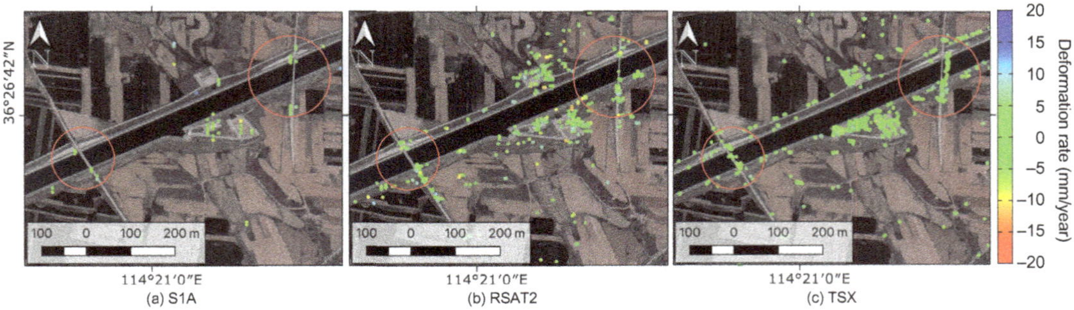

Figure 8. Close-ups show the deformation rates of two crossing-canal dam bridges derived from (**a**) S1A, (**b**) RSAT2, and (**c**) TSX datasets. Red circles highlight the bridge areas. The background images are satellite images from Google Earth.

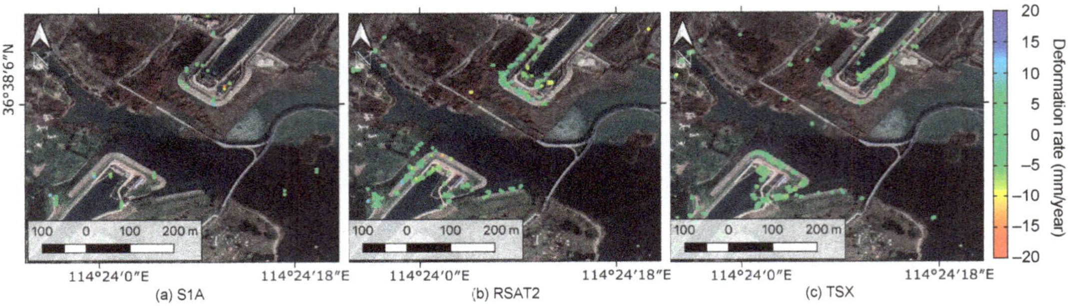

Figure 9. Close-ups show the deformation rates of one siphon derived from (**a**) S1A, (**b**) RSAT2, and (**c**) TSX datasets. The background images are satellite images from Google Earth.

3.2. Deformation Evaluation Combining the three Datasets

S1A, RSAT2, and TSX are of different heading angles, especially TSX, which is of a descending orbit while the other two have ascending orbits; this may lead to different scattering locations of the same target and a significant difference in the number of selected PSs, especially when the canal is at a favourable orientation to one SAR but not to the others. For example, in Figure 4, we can see that many more PS targets are selected when the canal segments are oriented perpendicular to the RSAT2 LOS direction, which is not favourable to the TSX observation. In addition, the different SAR measurements play as different rulers for the same land deformation, as the histograms in Figure 10a–c show different distributions of these three datasets. After standardisation using Equation (3), there are $\mu = 0$ and $\sigma = 1$ for the three data distributions, which are plotted in Figure 10d. In this subfigure, the red curve is the fitted normal distribution for the standardised and combined deformation rates.

With the standardised and combined deformation rates, the stability of the SNWD-CR is evaluated using a MAD-based weighted heatmap, as shown in Figure 11. Heatmaps of four segments of the central route are presented in Figure 11a–d. The weighted heatmap reflects not only the density of the risky points but also the significance of the risk. The higher the heatmap value, the higher the risk. The white and yellow lines seen on the Google satellite map are roads and railways, respectively. Apart from the two regions located at the canal embankments denoted by green boxes, most risky regions are associated with roads and railways, as denoted by the red boxes. In addition, aqueducts and siphons are other ancillary facilities at high risk of deformation.

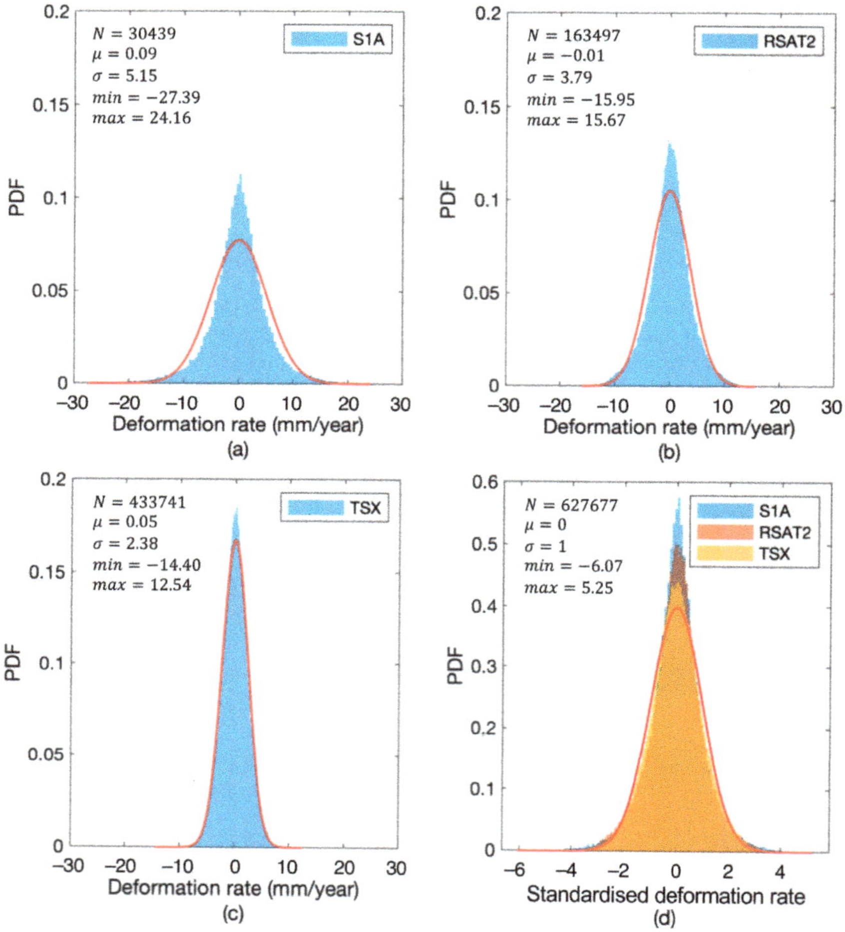

Figure 10. Histograms showing the deformation rate distributions of (**a**) S1A, (**b**) RSAT2, and (**c**) TSX results (units for μ, σ, min and max are mm/year), as well as (**d**) the distributions of the standardised deformation rates of the three results. The red curves in (**a–c**) are fitted normal distributions for the three results, respectively. The red curve in (**d**) is the fitted normal distribution for the standardised and combined deformation rates.

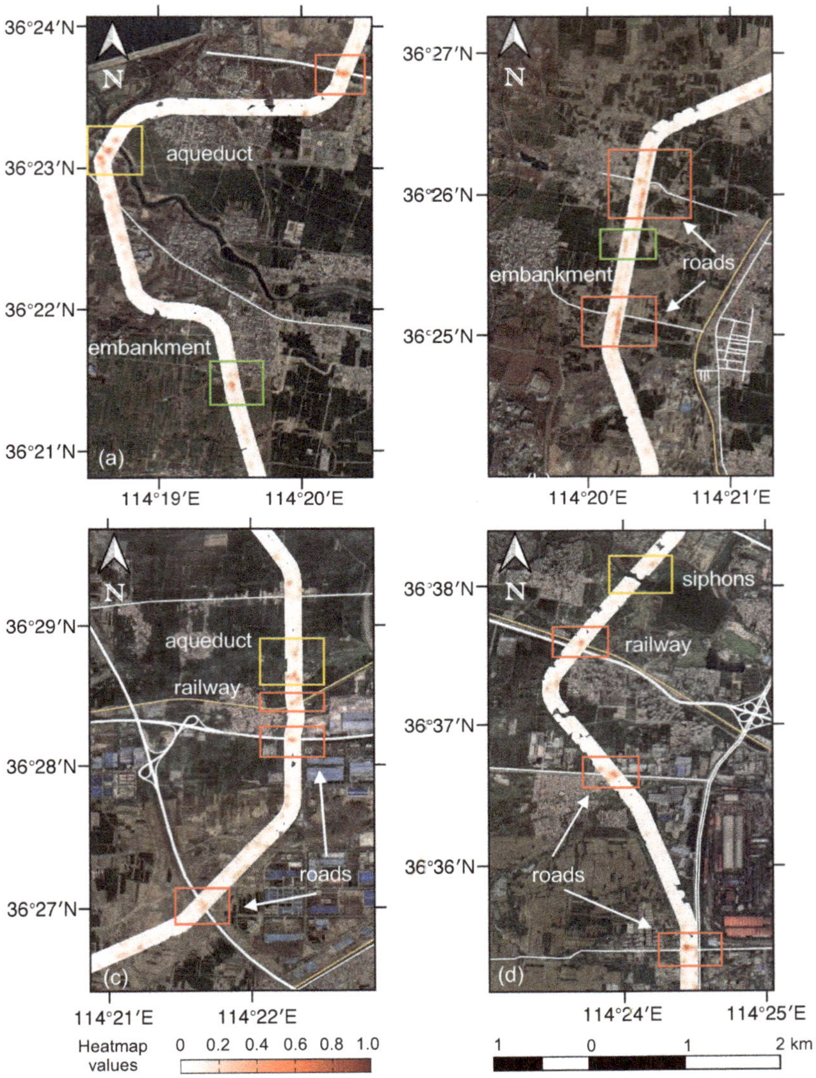

Figure 11. Stability evaluation based on the combined results along (**a**–**d**) four segments from south to north. Dangerous areas related to canal embankment, roads/railways, and aqueducts/siphons are denoted using green, red, and yellow boxes, respectively. The white lines and the yellow lines on the Google Satellite map are roads and railways, respectively.

3.3. Influence from Different Orbit Directions

It is worthwhile noting that heading angles of the SAR systems largely influence the results, including not only the number of selected PS points, as mentioned in the previous sections, but also the measured deformation direction. Figure 12a,b illustrate three cases (I, II, and III) of measured deformation by S1A/RSAT2 and TSX. In case I, shown in Figure 12a, there is a dominant downward deformation, and the measured deformation is negative for both ascending and descending orbits. The situation is different for cases II and III, shown in Figure 12b, in which the planar movement is dominant. In case II, the measured deformation is positive for the descending orbit and negative for the ascending orbit when the actual deformation occurs in the east direction. In case III, with a westward deformation, the signs of the measured deformation become opposite to those in case II.

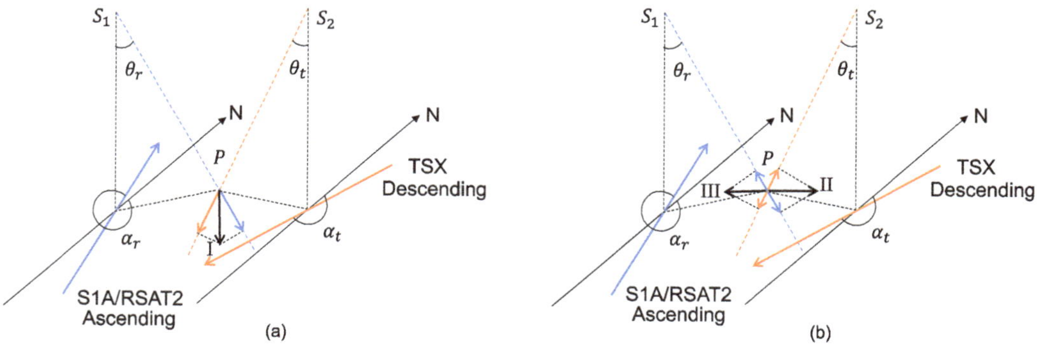

Figure 12. Schematic map shows measured LOS deformation of (**a**) vertical movement (case I shown as the black arrow) and (**b**) horizontal movement (cases II and III indicated as the black arrows) from ascending (the blue arrows showing S1A/RSAT2) and descending (the yellow arrows showing TSX) orbits.

The deformations of the aqueduct and the crossing-canal bridge analysed in Section 3.1 are typical examples illustrating the influence of different orbit directions. Figure 13 shows the standardised and combined results of these two facilities. In case I, the sign of the TSX deformation at the two ends of the aqueduct do not need to be changed in the combination, as shown in Figure 13a. However, the sign needs to be changed for the deformation measured on the crossing-canal bridge in Figure 13b. The deforming parts are two arches of the beam–arch hybrid bridge. The western side of the arches is subsiding, which corresponds to case II, and the eastern side corresponds to case III, implying a contraction of the arches.

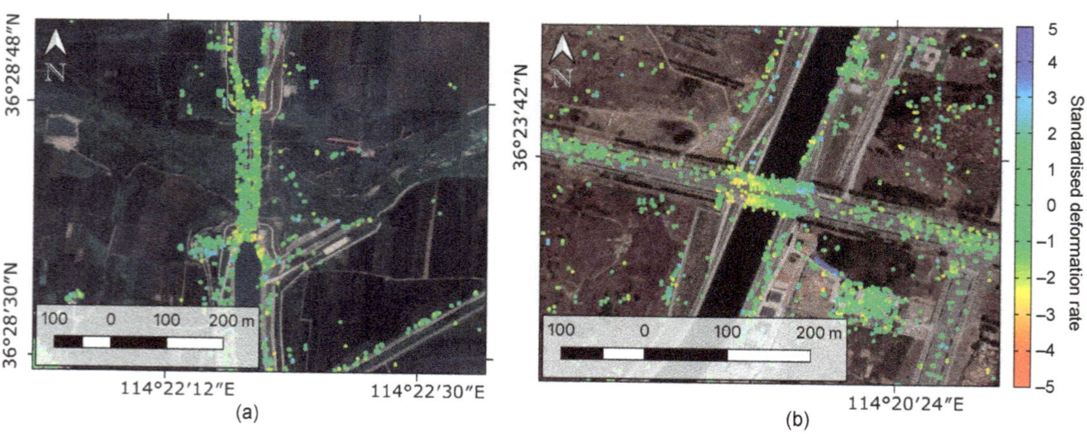

Figure 13. The standardised deformation rates of the merged result of (**a**) the aqueduct and (**b**) the crossing-canal bridge.

4. Discussion

This study presents an application of multitemporal and multifrequency satellite SAR observations to monitor and evaluate deformations of the SNWDP-CR. With the same parameter settings in PS-InSAR processing, RSAT2 and TSX results contain many more PS points than the S1A result, implying better performance of the high-resolution SAR data. Due to the different frequencies and phase noises, the three results follow different distributions, which cannot be directly combined. Another difference between the three SAR observations is the different heading angles. The SNWD is a line structure spanning a wide area from south to north, and its orientation significantly influence the PS-InSAR results. Firstly, the number of selected PSs is considerably larger when the canal orients favourably to the SAR system. The best orientation is when the canal is parallel to the orbit path, and the LOS direction is perpendicular to the canal. Secondly, different aspects of the same target are monitored by ascending and descending orbits. The aqueduct is a good example, for which more PS points are selected on the western side in the RSAT2 result, while more are selected on the eastern side in the TSX result. Thirdly, even if the same deformation occurs on the target being captured, their signs may differ in the ascending and descending orbits. For a dominant vertical deformation, measured deformations are of the same sign. However, when it comes to a planar deformation, the signs are opposite in results from ascending and descending orbits.

To evaluate the deformation and stability of the SNWD-CR over the study area, we combined the three results using a Z-score standardisation and a MAD-based weighted heatmap. The derived heatmap highlights the risky regions as more significant deformation is observed, and the dangerous areas are primarily related to crossing-canal bridges for connecting roads and railways. Aqueducts and siphons are two further types of risky ancillary facilities. The demonstrated example of the aqueduct in Figure 13a subsides at its two ends, which may be related to the pillars at the ends. Another example in Figure 13b is one crossing-canal beam–arch hybrid bridge whose two arches are contracting, which may be associated with the deflection of the beam part. When the deflection occurs, the central beam moves downward, and the sides of the beam move upward; this can push the arches to contract. The main canal is overall stable except for two risky regions on the western embankment. One of them is inferred to be associated with a land collapse which occurred in 2017 by checking the archived images in Google Earth.

Unfortunately, we could not execute any in situ measurements along the SNWD-CR to validate the PS-InSAR results, but the risky evaluation should not be influenced as PS-InSAR results are relative measurements, and risk is a concept about relativity in this study. In addition, we only used the deformation rate derived by using PS-InSAR processing, which also outputs time-series deformation for each PS point. In the future, more advanced methods should be developed to investigate the deformation process utilising time-series deformation, especially regarding long-term deformation monitoring. With the MAD-based weighted heatmap, the dominant direction of the deformation is ignorable in evaluating the risk. Risky targets are then selected based on this heatmap. However, the dominant direction needs to be determined before combining the three results, which still depends on manual comparison in this study. This calls for a way to deal with this task with higher efficiency.

5. Conclusions

This study investigated the application of satellite observations to monitor the deformation of the SNWDP-CR, including S1A, RSAT2, and TSX observations. PS-InSAR was applied to each of the three datasets, and they were standardised and combined to be evaluated with the proposed method for producing a MAD-based weighted heatmap. This heatmap highlighted the risky regions where relatively more significant deformation was developing. Based on the PS-InSAR results and the derived weighted heatmap, the risky deformation along the SNWD-CR was found to be primarily associated with crossing-canal bridges for connecting roads and railways. It was found that one beam–arch hybrid bridge was likely to be suffering from subsidence, causing the arches to deform at a rate of up to 9~10 mm/year. Aqueducts were found to be another type of risky facility, with one example showing a deformation rate of up to 9~10 mm/year at the two ends of the overhead structure. The main canal is overall stable, except for two subsiding regions which were founded on the western embankment of the SNWD-CR. One of these is likely associated with a land collapse occurring about 60 m to the south, which happened in 2017, according to the archived satellite images in Google Earth. This region was subsiding at a rate of up to 15 mm/year.

Although without validation data, we evaluated the deformation of the SNWD canal and its ancillary facilities based on the three PS-InSAR results derived from S1A, RSAT2, and TSX datasets. In practical applications that call for absolute deformation values, in situ validation must be carried out. We expect this to be carried out in future work. Results in this study show that in the specific application scenario of the SNWD, the heading angle and orientation of the construction play an essential role in the results. This calls for more studies in the future that fuse observations from different orbits and frequencies to obtain a comprehensive deformation of the structure. In this study, the observations span only one year, thus only accounting for tens of acquisitions. In the future, observations with a long period up to several years can be processed, and in this case, time-series information is worthwhile to be investigated to show the deformation evolution of risky regions.

Author Contributions: Conceptualization, S.X. and B.Z.; methodology, S.X. and B.Z.; software, S.X., B.Z. and Z.D.; validation, B.Z.; formal analysis, S.X. and B.Z.; investigation, S.X. and B.Z.; resources, S.X., C.W. and B.Z.; data curation, B.Z. and C.W.; writing—original draft preparation, S.X.; writing—review and editing, S.X., B.Z., C.W. and X.Q.; visualization, S.X.; supervision, C.W. and Q.L.; project administration, S.X.; funding acquisition, S.X., B.Z. and C.W. All authors have read and agreed to the published version of the manuscript.

Funding: This research was funded by Shenzhen Scientific Research and Development Funding Programme under Grants JCYJ20190808120005713 and RCYX20210706092140076, and the Guangdong Basic and Applied Basic Research Foundation under Grants 2022A1515110861 and 2021A1515011427. The authors are also grateful for the funding support from the National Natural Science Foundation of China under Grants 41974006 and 42104012, the Open Research Fund from Guangdong Laboratory of Artificial Intelligence and Digital Economy (SZ) under Grant GML-KF-22-15, and the Open Research Fund from MNR Key Laboratory for Geo-Environmental Monitoring of Great Bay Area & Guangdong Key Laboratory of Urban Informatics & Shenzhen Key Laboratory of Spatial Smart Sensing and Services.

Data Availability Statement: The datasets used in this study are available as requested from the third author B.Z. (zhangbc@szu.edu.cn).

Acknowledgments: The authors would like to thank the German Aerospace Centre (DLR) for the TerraSAR-X data under the PI project LAN2979, MDA for the Radarsat-2 data, and Google for the satellite images in Google Earth.

Conflicts of Interest: The authors declare no conflict of interest.

References

1. Liu, J.; Zang, C.; Tian, S.; Liu, J.; Yang, H.; Jia, S.; You, L.; Liu, B.; Zhang, M. Water conservancy projects in China: Achievements, challenges and way forward. *Glob. Environ. Change* **2013**, *23*, 633–643. [CrossRef]
2. Liu, J.; Cao, G.; Zheng, C. Sustainability of groundwater resources in the North China Plain. In *Sustaining Groundwater Resources: A Critical Element in the Global Water Crisis*; Springer: Dordrecht, The Netherlands, 2011; pp. 69–87.
3. Zhao, Z.Y.; Zuo, J.; Zillante, G. Transformation of water resource management: A case study of the South-to-North Water Diversion project. *J. Clean. Prod.* **2017**, *163*, 136–145. [CrossRef]
4. Ministry of Water Resources of People's Republic of China. 2020. Available online: http://www.mwr.gov.cn/xw/slyw/202006/t20200603_1406672.html (accessed on 22 February 2021).
5. Office of the South-to-North Water Diversion Project Construction Committee, State Council, PRC. The South-to-North Water Diversion Project. *Engineering* **2016**, *2*, 265–267. [CrossRef]
6. Hassani, S.; Dackermann, U. A Systematic Review of Advanced Sensor Technologies for Non-Destructive Testing and Structural Health Monitoring. *Sensors* **2023**, *23*, 2204. [CrossRef]
7. Im, S.B.; Hurlebaus, S.; Kang, Y.J. Summary Review of GPS Technology for Structural Health Monitoring. *J. Struct. Eng.* **2023**, *139*, 1653–1664. [CrossRef]
8. Hassani, S.; Dackermann, U. A Systematic Review of Optimization Algorithms for Structural Health Monitoring and Optimal Sensor Placement. *Sensors* **2023**, *23*, 3293. [CrossRef] [PubMed]
9. Gabriel, A.K.; Goldstein, R.M.; Zebker, H.A. Mapping small elevation changes over large areas: Differential radar interferometry. *J. Geophys. Res.* **1989**, *94*, 9183–9191. [CrossRef]

10. Crosetto, M.; Monserrata, O.; Cuevas-González, M.; Devanthéry, N.; Crippa, B. Persistent Scatterer Interferometry: A review. *ISPRS J. Photogramm. Remote Sens.* **2016**, *115*, 78–89. [CrossRef]
11. Jia, H.; Liu, L. A technical review on persistent scatterer interferometry. *J. Mod. Transp.* **2016**, *24*, 153–158. [CrossRef]
12. Massonnet, D.; Rossi, M.; Carmona, C.; Adragna, F.; Peltzer, G.; Feigl, K.; Rabaute, T. The displacement field of the landers earthquake mapped by radar interferometry. *Nature* **1993**, *364*, 138–142. [CrossRef]
13. Lazecký, M.; Spaans, K.; González, P.J.; Maghsoudi, Y.; Morishita, Y.; Albino, F.; Elliott, J.; Greenall, N.; Hatton, E.; Hooper, A.; et al. LiCSAR: An automatic InSAR tool for measuring and monitoring tectonic and volcanic activity. *Remote Sensing.* **2020**, *12*, 2430. [CrossRef]
14. Zhao, C.; Lu, Z. Remote Sensing of Landslides—A Review. *Remote Sens.* **2018**, *10*, 279. [CrossRef]
15. Qin, H.; Andrews, C.B.; Tian, F.; Cao, G.; Luo, Y.; Liu, J.; Zheng, C. Groundwater-pumping optimization for land-subsidence control in Beijing plain, China. *Hydrogeol. J.* **2018**, *26*, 1061–1081. [CrossRef]
16. Zhu, L.; Gong, H.; Chen, Y.; Wang, S.; Ke, Y.; Guo, G.; Li, X.; Chen, B.; Wang, H.; Teatini, P. Effects of water diversion project on groundwater system and land subsidence in Beijing, China. *Eng. Geol.* **2020**, *276*, 105763. [CrossRef]
17. Lyu, M.; Ke, Y.; Guo, L.; Li, X.; Zhu, L.; Gong, H.; Constantinos, C. Change in regional land subsidence in Beijing after South-to-North Water Diversion Project observed using satellite radar interferometry. *GISci. Remote Sens.* **2019**, *57*, 140–156. [CrossRef]
18. Guo, L.; Gong, H.; Li, J.; Zhu, L.; Xue, A.; Liao, L.; Sun, Y.; Li, Y.: Zhang, Z.; Hu, L.; et al. Understanding uneven land subsidence in Beijing, China, using a novel combination of geophysical prospecting and InSAR. *Geophys. Res. Lett.* **2020**, *47*, e2020GL088676. [CrossRef]
19. Du, Z.; Ge, L.; Ng, A.H.-M.; Lian, X.; Zhu, Q.; Horgan, F.G.; Zhang, Q. Analysis of the impact of the South-to-North water diversion project on water balance and land subsidence in Beijing, China between 2007 and 2020. *J. Hydrol.* **2021**, *603*, 126990. [CrossRef]
20. Zhang, X.; Chen, B.; Gong, H.; Lei, K.; Zhou, C.; Lu, Z.; Zhao, D. Inversion of Groundwater Storage Variations Considering Lag Effect in Beijing Plain, from RadarSat-2 with SBAS-InSAR Technology. *Remote Sens.* **2022**, *14*, 991. [CrossRef]
21. Zheng, Y.; Peng, J.; Chen, X.; Huang, C.; Chen, P.; Li, S.; Su, Y. Spatial and Temporal Evolution of Ground Subsidence in the Beijing Plain Area Using Long Time Series Interferometry. *IEEE J. Sel. Top. Appl. Earth Obs. Remote Sens.* **2023**, *16*, 153–165. [CrossRef]
22. Dong, J.; Guo, S.; Wang, N.; Zhang, L.; Ge, D.; Liao, M.; Gong, J. Tri-decadal evolution of land subsidence in the Beijing Plain revealed by multi-epoch satellite InSAR observations. *Remote Sens. Environ.* **2023**, *286*, 113446. [CrossRef]
23. Dong, J.; Lai, S.; Wang, N.; Wang, Y.; Zhang, L.; Liao, M. Multi-scale deformation monitoring with Sentinel-1 InSAR analyses along the Middle Route of the South-North Water Diversion Project in China. *Int. J. Appl. Earth Obs. Geoinf.* **2021**, *100*, 102324. [CrossRef]
24. Qin, X.; Liao, M.; Zhang, L.; Yang, M. Structural health and stability assessment of high-speed railways via thermal dilation mapping with time-series InSAR analysis. *IEEE J. Sel. Top. Appl. Earth Obs. Remote Sens.* **2017**, *10*, 2999–3010. [CrossRef]
25. Ma, P.; Li, T.; Fang, C.; Lin, H. A tentative test for measuring the sub-millimeter settlement and uplift of a high-speed railway bridge using COSMO-SkyMed images. *ISPRS J. Photogramm. Remote Sens.* **2019**, *155*, 1–12. [CrossRef]
26. Milillo, P.; Giardina, G.; Perissin, D.; Milillo, G.; Coletta, A.; Terranova, C. Pre-collapse space geodetic observations of critical infrastructure: The Morandi Bridge, Genoa, Italy. *Remote Sens.* **2019**, *11*, 1403. [CrossRef]
27. Wegmüller, U.; Werner, C. Mitigation of thermal expansion phase in persistent scatterer interferometry in an urban environment. In Proceedings of the 2015 Joint Urban Remote Sensing Event (JURSE), Lausanne, Switzerland, 30 March 2015–1 April 2015; pp. 3–6. [CrossRef]
28. Crosetto, M.; Monserrat, O.; Cuevas-González, M.; Devanthéry, N.; Luzi, G.; Crippa, B. Measuring thermal expansion using X-band persistent scatterer interferometry. *ISPRS J. Photogramm. Remote Sens.* **2015**, *100*, 84–91. [CrossRef]
29. Xiong, S.; Wang, C.S.; Qin, X.Q.; Zhang, B.C.; Li, Q.Q. Time-Series Analysis on Persistent Scatter-Interferometric Synthetic Aperture Radar (PS-InSAR) Derived Displacements of the Hong Kong–Zhuhai–Macao Bridge (HZMB) from Sentinel-1A Observations. *Remote Sens.* **2021**, *13*, 546. [CrossRef]
30. Qin, X.; Zhang, L.; Yang, M.; Luo, H.; Liao, M.; Ding, X. Mapping surface deformation and thermal dilation of arch bridges by structure-driven multi-temporal DInSAR analysis. *Remote Sens. Environ.* **2018**, *216*, 71–90. [CrossRef]
31. Zhang, B.; Liao, X.; Zhang, J.; Xiong, S.; Wang, C.; Wu, S.; Zhu, C.; Zhu, J.; Li, Q. Megalopolitan-scale ground deformation along metro lines in the Guangdong-Hong Kong-Macao Greater Bay Area, China, revealed by MT-InSAR. *Int. J. Appl. Earth Obs. Geoinf.* 2023; *in press*.
32. Leys, C.; Ley, C.; Klein, O.; Bernard, P.; Licata, L. Detecting outliers: Do not use standard deviation around the mean, use absolute deviation around the median. *J. Exp. Soc. Psychol.* **2013**, *49*, 764–766. [CrossRef]
33. Zhang, B.; Wu, S.; Ding, X.; Wang, C.; Zhu, J.; Li, Q. Use of multiplatform SAR imagery in mining deformation monitoring with dense vegetation coverage: A case study in the Fengfeng mining area, China. *Remote Sens.* **2021**, *13*, 3091. [CrossRef]
34. Wang, B.; Zhao, X.M. Handan Segment of the South to North Water Diversion Project Kicked Off. Available online: https://news.sina.com.cn/c/2010-01-13/073516923855s.shtml (accessed on 12 June 2023). (In Chinese)
35. Ferretti, A.; Prati, C.; Rocca, F. Nonlinear subsidence rate estimation using permanent scatterers in differential SAR interferometry. IEEE Trans. Geosci. *Remote Sens.* **2001**, *38*, 2202–2212. [CrossRef]

36. Ferretti, A.; Prati, C.; Rocca, F. Permanent scatterer in SAR interferometry. *IEEE Trans. Geosci. Remote Sens.* **2001**, *39*, 8–20. [CrossRef]
37. Berardino, P.; Fornaro, G.; Lanari, R.; Sansosti, E. A new algorithm for surface deformation monitoring based on small baseline differential SAR interferograms. *IEEE Trans. Geosci. Remote Sens.* **2002**, *40*, 2375–2384. [CrossRef]
38. Wegnüller, U.; Werner, C.; Strozzi, T.; Wiesmann, A.; Frey, O.; Santoro, M. Sentinel-1 support in the GAMMA software. *Procedia Comput. Sci.* **2016**, *100*, 1305–1312. [CrossRef]
39. Hooper, A.; Zebker, H.; Segall, P.; Kampes, B. A new method for measuring deformation on volcanoes and other natural terrains using InSAR persistent scatterers. *Geophys. Res. Lett.* **2004**, *31*, L23611. [CrossRef]
40. Zhao, Y. Construction of 78 Bridges Across the Middle Route of the South-to-North Water Diversion Project in Handan. Available online: https://hebei.hebnews.cn/2011-03/02/content_1694586.htm (accessed on 3 July 2023). (In Chinese)

remote sensing

MDPI

Article

Evaluation of Post-Tunneling Aging Buildings Using the InSAR Nonuniform Settlement Index

Yuzhou Liu [1,2,3], Wenxi Cao [1,2,3], Zhongqi Shi [1,2,3,*], Qingrui Yue [1,2,3,4], Tiandong Chen [1,2,3], Lu Tian [1,2,3], Rumian Zhong [1,2,3] and Yuke Liu [1,2,3]

1 Shenzhen Technology Institute of Urban Public Safety, Shenzhen 518000, China; yuzhouliu@link.cuhk.edu.hk (Y.L.)
2 National Science and Technology Institute of Urban Safety Development, Shenzhen 518000, China
3 Key Laboratory of Urban Safety Risk Monitoring and Early Warning, Ministry of Emergency Management, Shenzhen 518055, China
4 Research Institute of Urbanization and Urban Safety, School of Civil and Resource Engineering, University of Science and Technology Beijing, Beijing 100083, China
* Correspondence: shizq@szsti.org

Abstract: Tunneling work, including the construction of municipal tunnels and metro lines, may disturb the structural health of aging buildings in densely built urban areas. Deformation monitoring and risk assessments of aging buildings are crucial to mitigate incidents and prevent losses of people's lives and properties. Time-series InSAR reveals spatio-temporal information about observed targets by extracting persistent scatterers of the structures, which can achieve the wide-range monitoring of buildings and infrastructure. However, solely relying on InSAR-derived general parameters (deformation rates and time series of specific points) cannot objectively assess the safety conditions of buildings. To address this issue, this study proposes an InSAR Nonuniform Settlement Index. First, the point targets of buildings are extracted through time-series InSAR processing. Then, using the points as inputs, the Nonuniform Settlement Index calculates the 3D settlement plane and the inclination angle of the plane corresponding to each building. In this way, the proposed Nonuniform Settlement Index acts as a subsequent analysis method of time-series InSAR to characterize the safety statuses of buildings. In our study, 147 scenes of COSMO-SkyMed images from 2013 to 2022 were used to inverse the nine-year deformation evolution of the tested area. After time-series InSAR processing and index analysis based on the above SAR datasets, cross-validation was implemented with static-level and manual investigation data. The approach was to use one aging, collapsed building affected by tunneling work, as well as the eight adjacent aging buildings. The results showed high consistency with the in situ data, which proves the efficiency of the proposed approach.

Keywords: aging building; risk evaluation; time-series InSAR; Nonuniform Settlement Index; tunneling work

1. Introduction

In recent years, the urbanization processes of emerging super-large agglomerations have accelerated rapidly, and the disturbance caused by human activities to the environment has been increasing. In subway and large-diameter shield tunneling projects, underground space is constantly being developed to create the spatial layout required in regional development. Among the world's 25 most advanced large-diameter shield machines, 18 are in China, and 6 are in Shenzhen. In 2020, more than 200 shield machines were being used to carry out underground projects in Shenzhen. Large-scale underground construction brings about potential threats to aging buildings. In Shenzhen, the total number of historical illegally built buildings exceeds 50%, and 7.38 million residents live in 1836 urban villages in the city. Most buildings in urban villages are aging, and densely built areas can easily be affected by multiple risks, such as subway construction, concealed culverts, and geo-hazards. In August 2019, a settlement and inclination incident occurred in a seven-story aging building in Hepingxinju, Shenzhen, due to underground construction. When the accident happened, the eastern side of the building inclined into the western structure (as shown in Figure 1). Personnel in the building were evacuated in advance, and fortunately, no casualties were caused. In this situation, establishing a monitoring and evaluation method for post-tunneling building damage is particularly important to ensure the safety of people's lives and properties.

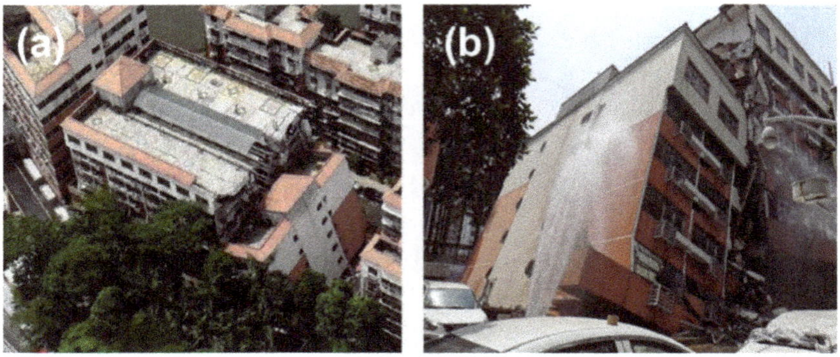

Figure 1. Site of building settlement and inclination incident: Hepingxinju. (**a**) Top view; (**b**) head-up view.

Traditional monitoring techniques for buildings and infrastructure are generally divided into manual inspection and in situ monitoring techniques. While the accuracy of both means is reliable, only a small number of structures can be monitored consistently in the long-term. Nowadays, with the development of Earth observation technologies, satellite remote sensing can be used in conjunction with traditional monitoring techniques to provide multi-scale information about buildings and infrastructures.

Interferometric Synthetic Aperture Radar (InSAR) measures relative surface displacement within the sensor's LOS (line of sight), whose imagery is not affected by daylight or cloud cover [1,2]. Thus, InSAR has attracted attention from scholars in the field of Earth sciences for a long time [3–5]. To solve several problems that limit the accuracy and reliability of traditional differential InSAR, time-series InSAR has been developed and popularized [6,7]. The algorithms mainly fall into two main categories: one is persistent scatterer InSAR (PSI), with a single image as the primary image [8–10]; the other is small baseline subsets (SBAS), with multiple images as the primary image [11,12]. Other algorithms developed on the basis of PSI are IPTA [13], PSP [14], etc. In addition to SBAS, TCP-InSAR [15], PSIG [16], etc., have been developed on the basis of small baselines. StaMPS [17] exists, which is a hybrid approach incorporating PSI and SBAS. These algorithms have been effectively used in traditional subsidence and deformation monitoring application scenarios, such as volcanic activity [18], earthquake and faulting activity [19], landslide instability [20], groundwater and mining exploitation [21], and urban land subsidence [22]. With the increase in image resolution, these methods are gradually being applied to research into buildings and infrastructure, including railways and highways [23,24], buildings [25,26], bridges [26,27], and transportation hubs [28,29]. Despite the wide range of applications, the interpretations and analyses based on existing time-series InSAR techniques still separate themselves from directly indicating the risk conditions of buildings and infrastructure, which obstruct time-series InSAR techniques from having effective operational applications.

In this study, we addressed the above problems by developing a subsequent analysis method of time-series InSAR. First, a Nonuniform Settlement Index was developed by generating a 3D settlement plane and calculating the inclination angle on the basis of time-series InSAR processing. Next, we tested the performance of the proposed Nonuniform

Settlement Index using an inclined aging building (Hepingxinju), whose safety condition had been disturbed by tunneling works. The deformation conditions of the overall surface along the tunnel and the test buildings were revealed using COSMO-SkyMed acquisitions. Finally, the inclination and settlement trend revealed using the InSAR Nonuniform Settlement Index are cross-compared with in situ investigations in other aging buildings, which verifies the efficiency of the proposed methodology.

2. Methodology

Time-series InSAR has been applied not only to the large-scale geological processes, but also to the refined monitoring of a single building or structure by inversing the general parameters of persistent scatterers (PSs), such as deformation rate and time series. Nevertheless, it is impossible to determine the safety condition of buildings and infrastructures by relying solely on these parameters. We developed the Nonuniform Settlement Index (NSI) as an evaluation method of time-series InSAR. First, PSInSAR is used to process high-resolution SAR images to determine spatio-temporal trends in the test area. The monitoring result is cross-validated by static level. Then, NSI is introduced to calculate the 3D settlement plane and inclination angle with InSAR-derived spatio-temporal information of the test buildings. The workflow of the proposed methodology is given in Figure 2.

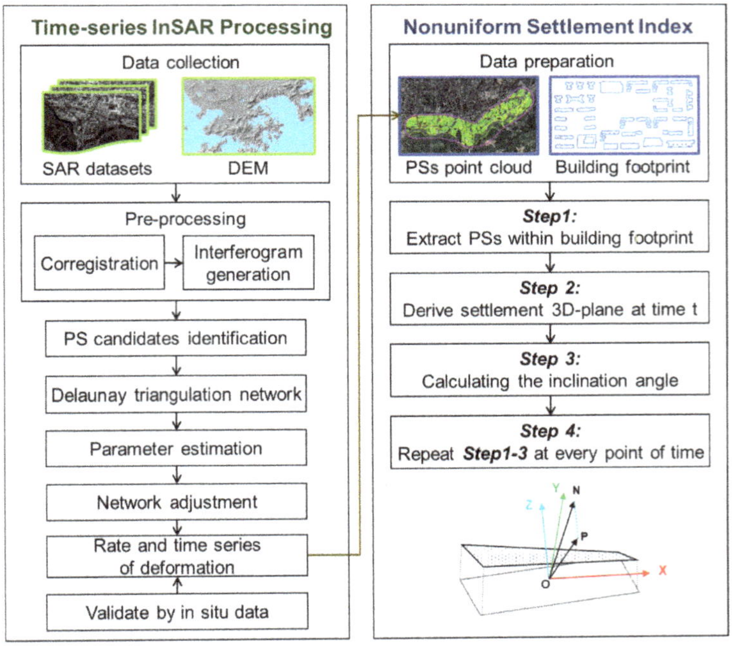

Figure 2. Workflow of the proposed method.

2.1. Time-Series InSAR Monitoring

2.1.1. Time-Series InSAR Processing

In this study, we employed an improved time-series InSAR algorithm [29] to extract the PSs of the study area. Using a stack of M + 1 SAR images, M interferograms were generated by master–slave pairs. Then, the interferometric pairs were used as the input of the detecting workflow for PS target detection. First, the amplitude dispersion index (ADI) [8,9] and averaging coherence coefficient were jointly adopted to select PS candidates. Second, the Delaunay triangulation network was formed, consisting of arcs with PS candidates on the endpoints. Third, values of velocity and height were calculated through the comprehensive use of beamforming and M-estimator, to robustly estimate the parameters of the PSs [25]. To further determine the density of the measuring points, adaptive densification and omnidirectional expansion were applied to densify the PSs [30]. Finally, the derived deformation rate along the satellite line of sight was projected to the vertical direction to characterize the uneven situation of the buildings.

2.1.2. Validation

A static level is a fine instrument for measuring subsidence; it is commonly used in Structural Health Monitoring. It obtains the relative subsidence between the measuring points by recording the change in liquid level in connected pipes. In our study, the processing results of time-series InSAR were validated by static level. The measuring points by static level were installed on the corners of the building roofs. Two issues should be stressed by cross-comparing data from these two measuring systems.

The first issue is spatio-temporal alignment. Since InSAR monitors a longer period with a lower temporal sampling frequency compared with the static level, accuracy evaluations are carried out within the sensing period of static level, and each time point is basically based on time-series InSAR. For the geolocation inconsistency of the static level points and PSs, clusters of PSs around static level points are processed by Kriging interpolation so that the geolocation of the representatives of the PSs is consistent with static level points.

The other one is the inconsistency of the physical significance of the measured parameters. Time-series InSAR calculates the deformation rate relative to the reference point (with a deformation rate of 0 mm/year), which is often selected on a stable target in the centered position of the SAR image. A static level measures the subsidence of the roof corners by choosing one corner as the reference. Supposing A–B–C–D are the corners of a tested building, and A is the reference point of static level, then the deformation of corner B–C–D by static level can be written as:

$$L_{Ai} = L_i - L_A \tag{1}$$

$$i = B, C, and\ D. \tag{2}$$

The measurement by InSAR is K_i, $i = B, C, and\ D$. Then, the transferring can be given as:

$$K_{Ai} = K_i - K_A \tag{3}$$

Additionally, the error of time-series InSAR can be expressed as:

$$\Delta_i = K_{Ai} - L_{Ai}. \tag{4}$$

However, due to specific side-looking angle, the results of time-series InSAR may exhibit a lack of PSs around the reference point of static level. Therefore, double difference should be made by transferring the benchmark of the two techniques. Assuming there is a lack of PSs around corner A, and the benchmark for comparison is transferred to corner B, double difference can be made as:

$$L_{Bi} = L_{Ai} - L_{AB} = L_i - L_A - L_B + L_A = L_i - L_B \tag{5}$$

$$K_{Bi} = K_i - K_B. \tag{6}$$

In this case, the error of time-series InSAR can be expressed as:

$$\Delta_i = K_{Bi} - L_{Bi}. \tag{7}$$

The accuracy analysis is evaluated by two indexes, mean error and root mean square error, which are formulated by:

$$\overline{\Delta} = \pm \frac{\sum_{i=1} |\Delta_i|}{n} \tag{8}$$

$$m = \pm\sqrt{\frac{\sum_{i=1} \Delta_i^2}{n-1}} \quad (9)$$

where $\overline{\Delta}$ is the mean error, m is the root mean square error, and n is the number of the time points. To this end, the validated PSs are generated as an input of index analysis to further analyze the safety conditions of the buildings.

2.2. Nonuniform Settlement Index (NSI)

2.2.1. Problem Description

On the basis of the time-series InSAR processing described above, in the SAR monitoring area, a point cloud dataset consisting of N + 1 PSs is obtained, which is denoted as:

$$\{x_i, y_i, z_i, s_i^t\},\ i = 0, 1, 2 \ldots N,\ t = t_0, t_1, \ldots, t_M \quad (10)$$

where x_i, y_i, z_i represent the three-dimensional coordinates of PSs, respectively, and the observed deformation variable of the point at time t is denoted as s_i^t. At the same time, the vector footprint layer of the buildings in the SAR monitoring area is georeferenced in the same coordinate system as the PSs. The problem that needs to be solved is to utilize the available PSs point cloud and the building footprint vector data to classify the ground buildings into two types of building risk categories: risky or non-risky.

2.2.2. Algorithm Description

Aiming at the problems raised above, this paper proposes the use of Nonuniform Settlement Index (NSI) to identify building risk categories. The calculation of the designed index is as follows.

Step 1: In order to characterize the settlement information of a single building, it is necessary to segment the input PSs point cloud according to the geographical coordinates of each individual building provided by the building footprint vector data. To this end, we define the spatial relationship between each single building footprint vector and each PS as follows. A PS is inside, outside, or at the edge of the single building footprint, and one of the three must be chosen. Based on this spatial relationship, a subset of point clouds inside the corresponding building vector box, j, can be extracted by further screening the height of the PSs compared with surrounding PSs on the ground, denoted as $\{x_i, y_i, z_i, s_i^t\},\ i = 0, 1, 2 \ldots N_j,\ t = t_0, t_1, \ldots, t_M$.

Step 2: The next step is to use the extracted point cloud subset to find the settlement plane of the single building at time t. To this end, the z component representing the elevation information in the coordinates of each point in the point cloud is replaced by the component representing the settlement information. Using the modified point cloud data, a parametric 3D plane can be estimated based on the least-square principle, which is formulated as follows:

$$\{a^t, b^t, c^t, d^t\} = \operatorname{argmin}\left(\sum_{i=0}^{N_j} \left|a^t x + by + c^t s^t + d^t\right|^2\right) \quad (11)$$

where a^t, b^t, c^t, d^t are the fitting parameters of the plane.

Step 3: The 3D fitting plane obtained in step 2 can already represent the inclination degree of the corresponding single building at time t, but it is still not convenient to directly compare the plane parameters obtained at different times to represent the change information of the single building inclination over time. Therefore, the tangent value of the plane inclination angle is calculated through the plane equation parameters, which reflects the inclination degree of the single building at time t with respect to the horizontal direction:

$$\tan(\theta^t) = c^t / \sqrt{(a^t)^2 + (b^t)^2 + (c^t)^2}. \quad (12)$$

Step 4: Repeat steps 1 to 3 for each different time t to obtain the entire time series of the plane inclination of a single building, followed by calculation of the acceleration rate of the index in order to more intuitively observe the rate of change in the plane inclination over time.

Notably, the precision of the evaluated result in the previous introduced algorithm highly relies on the precision of the sample points used and their spatial distribution; we cannot guarantee that the settings are always optimal. In this way, we modified the traditional least-square principle to improve the estimation accuracy in two ways. First, we estimated the parameters repeatedly rather than only once. In each iteration step, the Huber loss function [31] is used to evaluate the residual of sample data and assign the weight factor accordingly for the next iteration. In this way, the influence of most singular samples is mitigated. Second, the calculation of the matrix inverse is conducted via singular value decomposition (SVD) to handle the numerical issues. Mathematically, a symmetric matrix can be decomposed by SVD as follows:

$$P = U\begin{pmatrix} h_1 & 0 & 0 \\ 0 & h_2 & 0 \\ 0 & 0 & h_3 \end{pmatrix} V^T \tag{13}$$

where $h_i,\ (i = 1, 2, 3)$ are the singular values of matrix P, and the columns of orthogonal matrices U and V are formed by the left- and right-singular vectors of P. Thus, the matrix inverse via SVD has following form:

$$P^{-1} = V\begin{pmatrix} {h_1}^{-1} & 0 & 0 \\ 0 & {h_2}^{-1} & 0 \\ 0 & 0 & {h_2}^{-1} \end{pmatrix} U^T. \tag{14}$$

We analyzed the singular values and compared their values to determine whether the rank of the design matrix was not full. In this situation, the ratio between the smallest and the largest singular values is near zero, and an empirical threshold (ratio = 0.1) is used to identify this situation. If this is the case, we set the reciprocal of the smallest singular value to zero during the calculation of inverse matrix. In this way, we imposed a rank constraint to the calculation of matrix inverse and mitigated numeric inaccuracies.

Through NSI calculation, when the acceleration rate was greater than a preset threshold, it was determined that the corresponding single building belonged to the risky category; otherwise, it was determined to be the non-risk category. In practice, the threshold should be determined based on trial calculations of a multitude of deformed and inclined samples of buildings, which is not easy to require due to limited samples. In preliminary practice, the risky conditions can be considered by comparison with buildings in assured safety status.

3. Test Site and Data

3.1. Test Site

3.1.1. The Aging Buildings

Nine aging buildings, including the inclined Hepingxinju located in the Luohu District of Shenzhen, were chosen as our test sites. Figure 3 illustrates the spatial distribution of the tested buildings, and Table 1 gives the basic information of the sites. The surrounding environment of the buildings belongs to the early development and construction area in Shenzhen. In this old urban area, aging buildings with a service time of more than 20 years are widely distributed; these structures are prone to external disturbances, especially large-diameter-tunneling-induced deformation. As shown in Figure 3b, the purple line denotes the centerline of Chunfeng Tunnel, which was the largest diameter shield tunnel when its construction started in 2019.

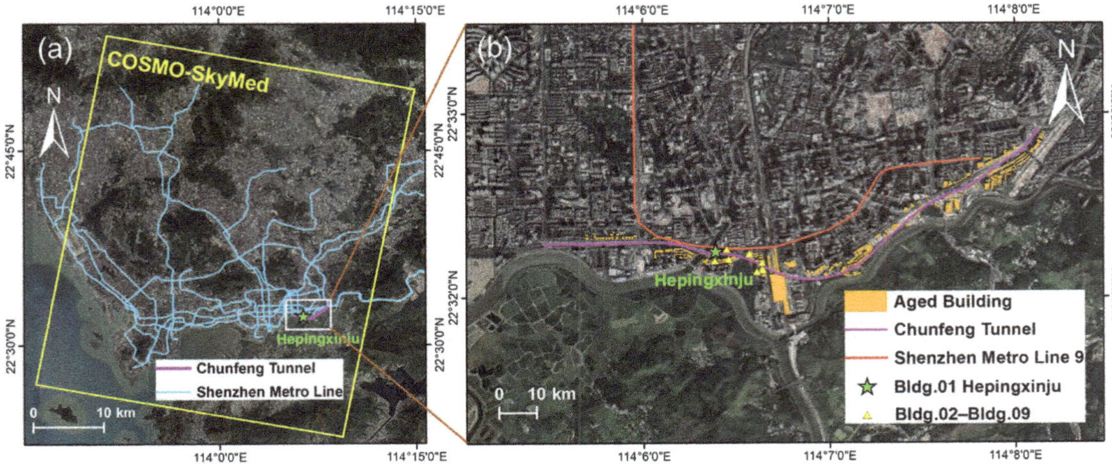

Figure 3. Test site of the study. (**a**) Overview; the yellow line region represents the spatial coverage of COSMO-SkyMed. (**b**) Enhanced view of the region shown in (**a**) by the white polygon.

Table 1. Basic information of the tested aging buildings.

Building No.	Service Status	Year of Completion
Bldg.01 (Hepingxinju)	Inclined in 2019; demolished in 2019	1990
Bldg.02	Vacant in 2019; demolished in 2020	1989
Bldg.03	In use	1991
Bldg.04	In use	1995
Bldg.05	In use	2000
Bldg.06	In use	1982
Bldg.07	In use	1982
Bldg.08	In use	1999
Bldg.09	In use	1988

3.1.2. Hepingxinju

Hepingxinju (Bldg.01 of the tested buildings) was constructed in June 1989 and was completed in January 1990; it has been in service for more than 30 years. It is about 50 m long from east to west, and 20 m wide from north to south. The underground foundations of the building are built on a trunk canal, which is the main drainage channel in the low-lying areas of the central urban area of Luohu District. Referring to the geology condition, there is a thick mud layer under the building, and the sand layer is unevenly distributed beneath the mud layer. The settlement and inclination incident of Hepingxinju occurred on 28 August 2019. After that, an investigation of the incident was gradually carried out.

3.1.3. Tunneling Works

There are two tunneling projects located around Hepingxinju, which potentially threaten to the safety condition of the building at various periods.

One of these is the Shenzhen Metro Line 9. It passes through Hepingxinju in the Luren section, on which construction started in 2014 and finished at the end of 2016. The right line of the tunnel in the Luren section runs through the northeast corner of the building. The horizontal distance between the tunnel vault and the bottom of the immersed pipe pile of Hepingxinju is 1.1 m, and the vertical distance is 3.0 m, as shown in Figure 4b.

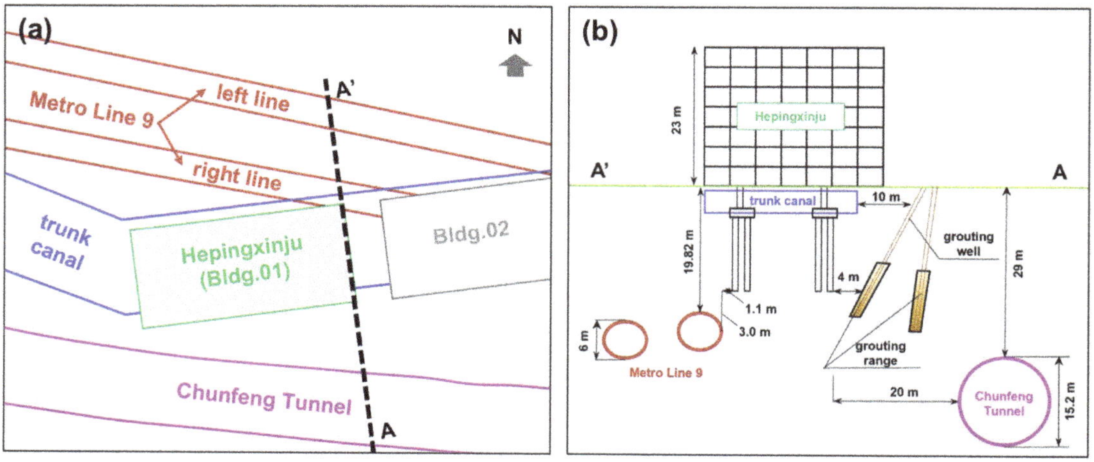

Figure 4. Spatial relationship between Hepingxinju and tunneling works. (**a**) Top view; (**b**) look-up view of section A'A given in (**a**).

The other one is Chunfeng Tunnel. This passes through the old urban area, with complex engineering geological conditions. The urban area locating above Chunfeng Tunnel is shown by the optical image in Figure 3b, where the purple solid line is the central line of the tunnel, and the orange polygons are 150 aging buildings located in the 100 m buffer zone along the tunnel central line. These aging buildings have been in service for over 20 years. The foundation forms are mostly natural foundation and small-diameter friction piles, and the above-ground structures are masonry and bottom frames, which have weak resistance to nonuniform deformation. On the corresponding ground surface, public facilities are densely covered, including the Shangbu overpass and Luohu Railway Station. Chunfeng Tunnel passes through this area from the southern side of Hepingxinju (shown in Figure 4a). The horizontal and vertical distances between the tunnel and the building are about 20 m and 29 m, respectively, as shown in Figure 4b.

3.2. Data

3.2.1. SAR Data

In total, 147 scenes of COSMO-SkyMed images obtained from 2013 to 2022 were used in our study. The whole dataset was processed by three groups by dividing from November 2016 and August 2019, since single processing can hardly preserve high coherence during nine years. These three groups were all acquired in descending orbit with 3 × 3 spatial resolution and HH polarization. The satellite observes the test site with a frequency of two times per month on average. The coverage of the COSMO-SkyMed acquisition is shown by the yellow polygon in Figure 3a, which covers most of the central and western parts of Shenzhen. The basic information of the three SAR datasets is given in Table 2.

Table 2. Basic information of the COSMO-SkyMed SAR datasets.

COSMO SkyMed dataset I Temporal domain: 2013–2016					
No.	**Date (yy-mm-dd)**	**No.**	**Date (yy-mm-dd)**	**No.**	**Date (yy-mm-dd)**
1	2013-10-16	17	2014-11-20	33	2015-10-10
2	2013-11-17	18	2014-11-24	34	2015-11-07
3	2013-12-07	19	2014-12-10	35	2015-11-23
4	2014-01-08	20	2014-12-26	36	2016-01-14
5	2014-01-24	21	2015-01-23	37	2016-03-02
6	2014-02-09	22	2015-02-08	38	2016-03-18
7	2014-03-13	23	2015-02-28	39	2016-06-06
8	2014-03-25	24	2015-03-12	40	2016-07-12
9	2014-04-10	25	2015-03-28	41	2016-07-24
10	2014-05-28	26	2015-04-29	42	2016-08-05
11	2014-06-17	27	2015-05-31	43	2016-08-25
12	2014-06-29	28	2015-06-20	44	2016-09-26
13	2014-07-19	29	2015-07-06	45	2016-10-12
14	2014-08-04	30	2015-07-22	46	2016-10-28
15	2014-09-17	31	2015-08-07	47	2016-11-29
16	2014-10-03	32	2015-09-08		/
COSMO SkyMed dataset II Temporal domain: 2016–2019					
No.	**Date (yy-mm-dd)**	**No.**	**Date (yy-mm-dd)**	**No.**	**Date (yy-mm-dd)**
1	2016-11-29	16	2017-10-15	31	2018-10-18
2	2017-01-16	17	2017-10-31	32	2018-11-03
3	2017-02-17	18	2017-11-13	33	2018-12-01
4	2017-04-02	19	2017-11-20	34	2019-01-06
5	2017-04-18	20	2017-12-14	35	2019-02-07
6	2017-04-19	21	2018-02-04	36	2019-03-11
7	2017-04-22	22	2018-03-24	37	2019-03-27
8	2017-06-21	23	2018-04-09	38	2019-04-12
9	2017-07-07	24	2018-04-25	39	2019-05-10
10	2017-07-27	25	2018-05-11	40	2019-06-10
11	2017-08-28	26	2018-06-12	41	2019-06-26
12	2017-09-10	27	2018-07-11	42	2019-07-12
13	2017-09-26	28	2018-08-31	43	2019-07-28
14	2017-09-29	29	2018-09-13	44	2019-08-14
15	2017-10-12	30	2018-10-02	45	2019-08-29
COSMO SkyMed dataset III Temporal domain: 2019–2022					
No.	**Date (yy-mm-dd)**	**No.**	**Date (yy-mm-dd)**	**No.**	**Date (yy-mm-dd)**
1	2019-08-29	20	2020-10-18	39	2021-11-06
2	2019-09-27	21	2020-11-03	40	2021-11-22
3	2019-10-09	22	2020-11-19	41	2021-12-09
4	2019-10-25	23	2020-12-05	42	2021-12-24
5	2019-11-01	24	2020-12-21	43	2022-01-10
6	2020-01-13	25	2021-01-06	44	2022-01-25
7	2020-02-05	26	2021-01-22	45	2022-02-23
8	2020-02-21	27	2021-02-08	46	2022-03-14
9	2020-03-24	28	2021-02-23	47	2022-04-24
10	2020-04-09	29	2021-03-11	48	2022-05-17
11	2020-04-25	30	2021-04-28	49	2022-06-02
12	2020-05-11	31	2021-05-30	50	2022-06-18
13	2020-06-12	32	2021-06-15	51	2022-07-05
14	2020-06-28	33	2021-07-17	52	2022-08-30
15	2020-07-14	34	2021-08-02	53	2022-09-22
16	2020-07-30	35	2021-08-18	54	2022-11-25
17	2020-08-15	36	2021-09-04	55	2022-12-12
18	2020-09-16	37	2021-09-28		/
19	2020-10-11	38	2021-10-30		

3.2.2. In Situ Observations

To validate the reliability of time-series InSAR processing, data collected by in situ static level were employed for cross-comparison with satellite-derived subsidence. In our study, 34 static level points installed on five buildings were collected. Table 3 shows the number of points; Figure 5 gives the static level layout of each building. Generally, the No.1 point on each building is the reference of the static level. The static level points were installed on other adjacent aging buildings along Chunfeng Tunnel after the inclination incident of Hepingxinju; data were collected after September 2020, and could only be prepared with SAR dataset III. To verify the proposed NSI, grades by manual inspection of each building were employed here; these were collected by carrying out in situ investigations in 2017, following the local standard [32]. In addition, this study used the footprint vector data of the aging buildings along the tunnel to extract PSs clusters belonging to each building (see the orange polygon proposed in Figure 3b).

Table 3. Basic information of the ground truth of the tested aging buildings.

Building No.	In Situ Monitoring (No. of the Points)	Grade by Manual Investigation
Bldg.01 (Hepingxinju)	N/A	Unknown
Bldg.02	N/A	Unknown
Bldg.03	Static level (6)	B
Bldg.04	Static level (6)	A
Bldg.05	Static level (12)	A
Bldg.06	Static level (6)	C
Bldg.07	Static level (4)	C
Bldg.08	N/A	B
Bldg.09	N/A	B

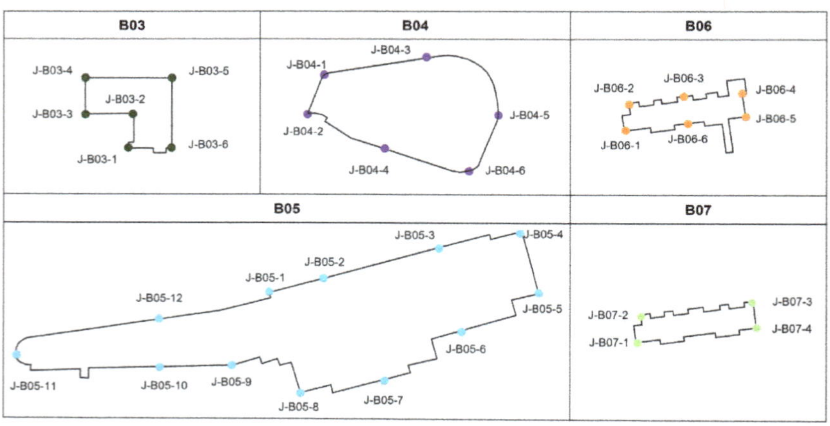

Figure 5. Layout of static level on Bldg.03–Bldg.07.

4. Results and Analysis

4.1. Monitoring Result

The vertical deformation rates derived by time-series InSAR from COSMO-SkyMed datasets are given in Figure 6. PSs within the 500 m buffer zone of Chunfeng Tunnel have been retained, where the red points represent a subsidence rate of less than −8 mm/year; the blue points represent an uplift rate of larger than 8 mm/year; and the green points represent the deformation rate ranging from −4 mm/year to 4 mm/year, which can be considered stable on the surface. In the period of 2013 to 2016, a stable pattern with deformation rate ranging from −10.98 mm/year to 9.78 mm/year was recognized along the centerline of the tunnel. From 2016 to 2019, an uneven deformation pattern was exhibited by PSs ranging from −15.91 mm/year to 12.20 mm/year. Subsidence mainly occurred to the western side when the cut-and-cover section was constructed here. During the third period, the overall pattern stabilized, with the deformation rate ranging from −11.40 mm/year to 9.34 mm/year.

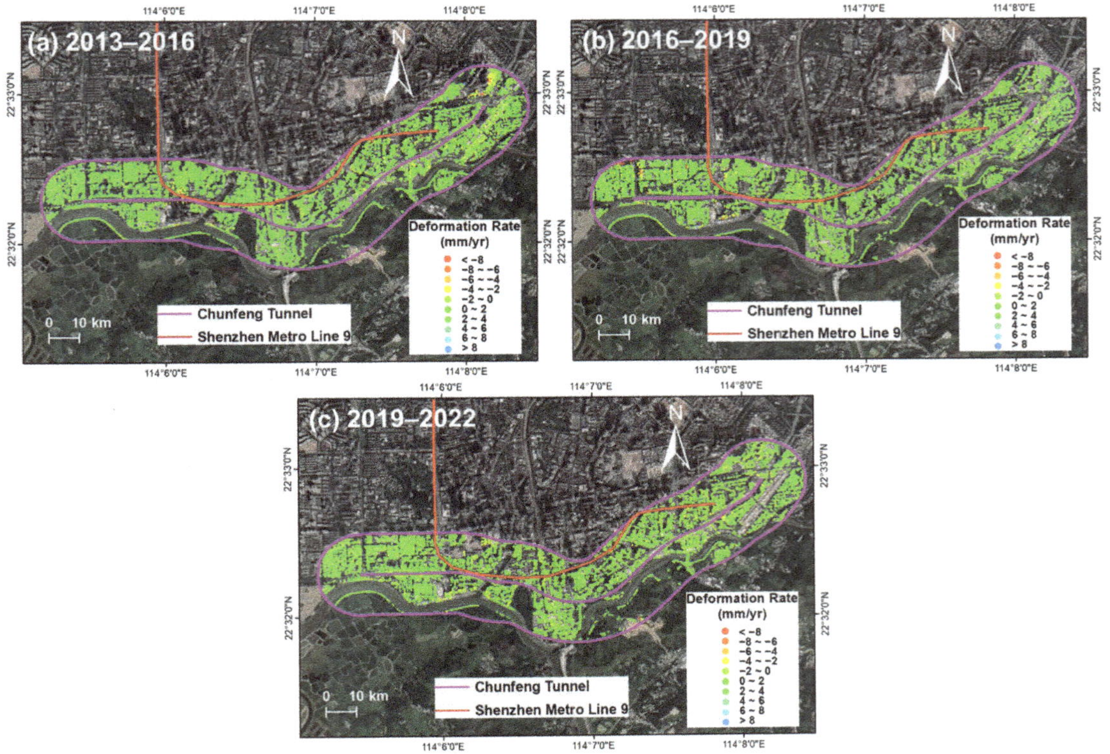

Figure 6. Vertical deformation rate maps of Chunfeng Tunnel. (**a**) PSs from dataset I (2013–2016); (**b**) PSs from dataset II (2016–2019); (**c**) PSs from dataset III (2019–2022).

The time-series InSAR monitoring results were cross-validated by static level data in the five tested buildings. The sensing period of the static level was from October 2020 to September 2021; therefore, validation was conducted on the PSs generated from dataset III. As described in Section 2.1.2, due to the side view of SAR, PSs could only be generated on specific sides of the building; only part of the points of static level can be taken advantage of. By double difference illustrated in Section 2.1.2, spatio-temporal aligned results from two techniques are generated and compared in ten locations, as listed in Table 4. The mean error and root mean square error of the measured results were ±1.97 mm and ±2.2 mm, respectively. The evaluation results indicate that time-series InSAR monitoring shows preferable consistence with in situ measurement.

Table 4. Error evaluation between time-series InSAR and static level.

No.	J-B03-03	J-B03-4	J-B03-6	J-B04-4	J-B04-5
Δ_i (mm)	1.29	−0.98	−1.55	3.46	3.07
No.	J-B04-6	J-B05-10	J-B06-5	J-B06-6	J-B07-4
Δ_i (mm)	3.49	−0.57	0.05	1.89	−1.11
$\overline{\Delta} = \pm 1.97$ mm; $m = \pm 2.2$ mm					

Focusing on Hepingxinju, Figure 7a,c display the PSs generated that belong to the polygon vectors of Hepingxinju as well as its adjacent building. Although the aging Hepingxinju building finally inclined, precursor information cannot be obtained by only determining from the deformation velocity. The deformation rate varied from −4.39 mm/year to 3.14 mm/year during 2013 to 2016, and from −0.74 mm/year to 3.24 mm/year during 2016 to 2019, neither of which denoted significant risky conditions of the two buildings.

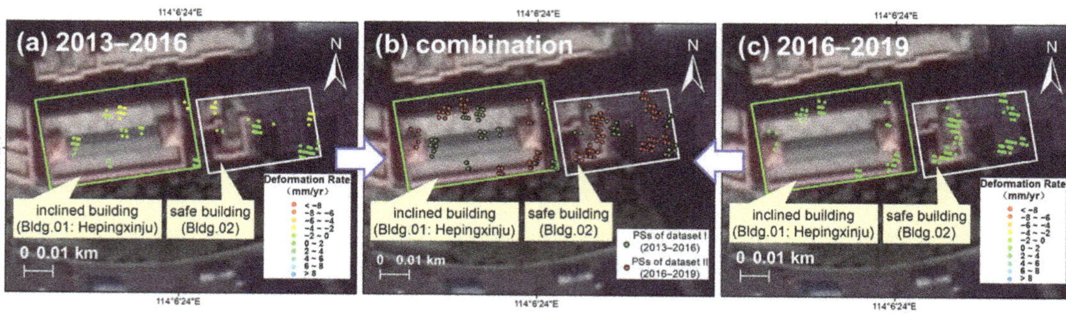

Figure 7. Vertical deformation rate maps of Bldg.01 (Hepingxinju) and its adjacent Bldg.02. (**a**) Results from dataset I (2013–2016); (**b**) combination of PSs acquired from 2013 to 2019; (**c**) results from dataset II (2016–2019).

4.2. *Risk Analysis of Bldg.01–02*

4.2.1. NSI Analysis

Hepingxinju and its adjacent building, which are marked as Bldg.01 and Bldg.02, respectively, were first analyzed and compared using InSAR NSI. Since Bldg.01 had been inclined and damaged in August 2019, its adjacent Bldg.02, which shared very similar above-ground and underground environment, was kept unoccupied and until finally being demolished in 2020, even though no obvious uneven subsidence occurred. Therefore, no PSs belonging to these two buildings were generated from the processing of dataset III. Additionally, the NSI developed in 2.2 could be calculated from 2013 to August 2019 for these two buildings.

Figure 8 presents the calculation results, showing the time-series curves of the PS point clouds of the two buildings. Figure 8a–c were derived from the settlement data of the inclined building Hepingxinju, and Figure 8d–f show the comparison curves calculated from the normal building settlement data in the same period. The curves were calculated at each time point using screened PSs. Compared with existing analysis methods of selecting single or multiple points as representatives, calculation results from the whole point clouds indicating the settlement plane and the inclination angle may better reflect the objective conditions of the buildings.

By comparison, it is easy to notice that the curves of the cumulative maximum uplift and settlement in the first and second rows have larger fluctuations and higher frequencies than the curves in the third row, whereas the nonuniform settlement curves in the third row are more stable in numerical values. Comparing the overall trends in the left and right columns, the curves of the normal building on the right show a certain degree of global linear trend in the three indices, while the three indices of the inclined building on the left stabilize in the middle part and start climbing at the end of the curves. The acceleration rate of the first line on the left is significantly weaker compared with the upward trend of the third line on the left at the end of the curve.

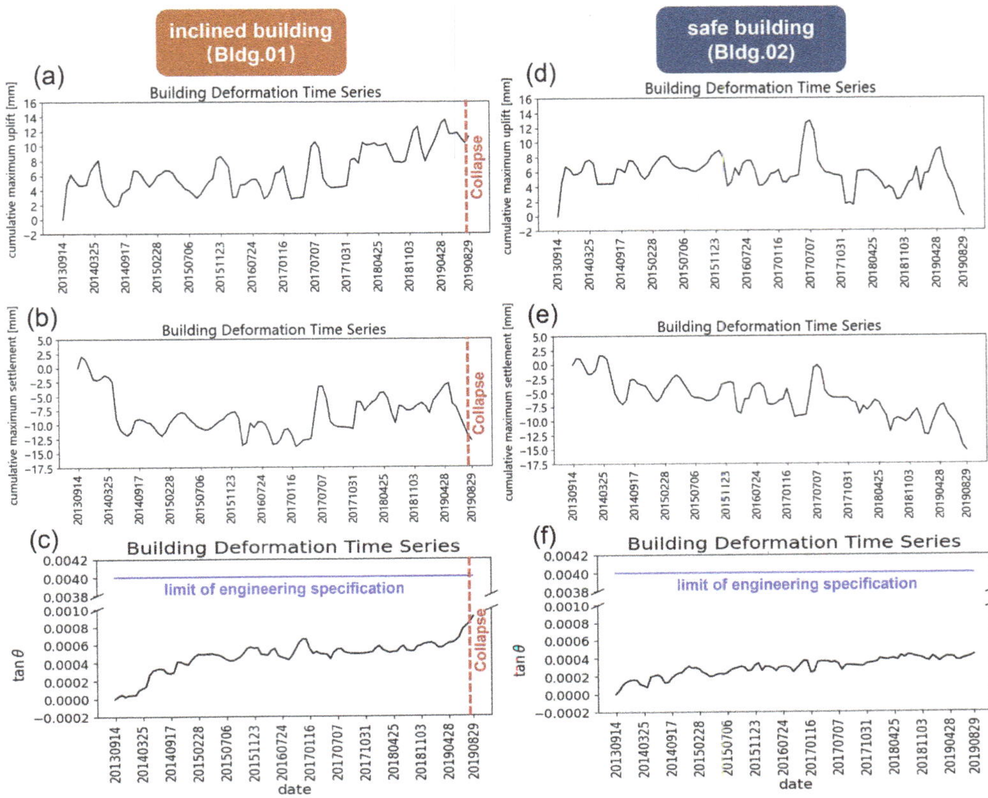

Figure 8. Time-series of the PSs of the two buildings: (**a–c**) cumulative maximum uplift, cumulative maximum settlement, and $\tan\theta$ of the inclined Hepingxinju (Bldg.01); (**d–f**) above three parameters of the adjacent safe building (Bldg.02). The red dashed lines in (**a**)–(**c**) represent the collapse date (28 August 2019) of the Bldg.01. Additionally, the blue lines in (**c**) and (**f**) denote the limit of engineering specification of technical standard, the maximum $\tan(\theta)$ of which should be less than 0.004.

4.2.2. Trend Analysis

In order to further compare the differences in each settlement index between inclined buildings and normal buildings and exclude the influence of random noise in the indices on the building risk distinguishment, this study used the open-source third-party function library PolyTrend to perform trend analysis and remove the noise of the time series signal. PolyTrend has been applied and verified in many fields of remote sensing as an effective trend fitting method which uses the least-square principle to fit time series data according to a group of models, including the cubic polynomial, quadratic polynomial, and linear equation. Then, it uses the t-Distribution Statistical Hypothesis Test to compare the coefficients of the highest-order terms obtained by fitting each model with a value of zero. It selects the effective model according to statistical significance, and retains the highest-order model as the final fitting result.

Considering that the first part of the time series data was the initial construction stage, which was quite different from the subsequent observation data and had a weaker correlation with the mechanism behind the settlement and inclination incident, this study fitted the time series data of one and a half years, one year, and half a year before the settlement and inclination incident to present the long-term, medium-term, and short-term trend curves, respectively.

As shown in Figure 9, the left-hand column is the fitting curves of the settlement index of the inclined Hepingxinju, and the right-hand side is the curves of the normal building for comparison. The top line of the graph represents the fitting curve of the accumulated maximum settlement, while the bottom line of the graph represents the fitting curve of the inclination angle, respectively. The black line represents the original time series data, and the blue, orange, and green lines represent the long-term, medium-term, and short-term fitting trends, respectively.

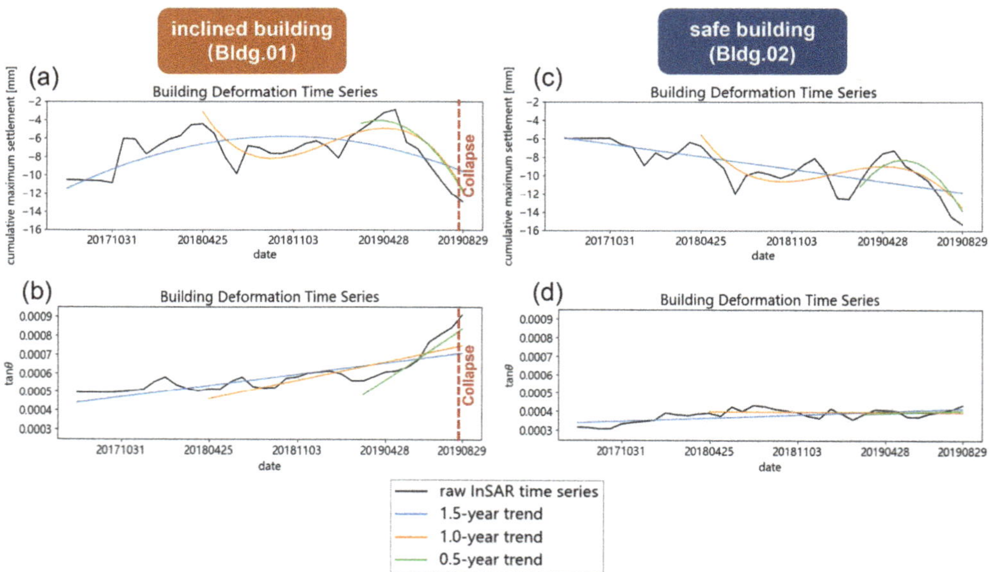

Figure 9. Fitting curves of the InSAR time series: (**a**,**b**) cumulative maximum settlement and tan θ of the inclined Hepingxinju (Bldg.01); (**c**,**d**) above two parameters of the adjacent normal building (Bldg.02).

It is easy to identify that the cumulative sedimentation indices in the first row represent a long-term linear trend. As the time interval shortens, the trend fitting results become cubic and quadratic, respectively. This variation lies in the fact that the original cumulative settlement index has strong volatility in the medium and short term, resulting in the model used for trend analysis needing to increase its complexity to fit the local fluctuations of the data. When using this index to analyze the risk of a building, it is necessary to design sophisticated determination rules to describe this model's complexity.

However, because short-term data have a stronger correlation with the current building risk status, this has a greater impact on the discrimination results. However, in the first row, the short-term trend curves of accumulated settlements show a rapid decline in accumulated settlements before the settlement and inclination incidents. Usually, a decrease in cumulative settlement represents a decrease in the risk of building safety. Therefore, it is impossible to give timely warning to the settlement and inclination incident only based on short-term trends in cumulative settlement.

Compared with the first row, the settlement inclination represented by the second row shows a clear linear trend in the long-term, medium-term, and short-term trends in the inclined building on the left, and the slopes of the three straight lines change significantly, with a clear acceleration trend. Based on this index, it is easy to determine that the risk of the Bldg.01 (Hepingxinju) is increasing, which is consistent with the fact that the data reflect the imminent inclined trend. It is also worth noting that, as has been marked in Figure 7c, even though Hepingxinju finally collapsed, and the InSAR NSI retrospective analysis showed strong indication of its risky condition, the calculated $\tan\theta$ had a maximum value of 0.0009, which was still significantly less than the threshold of 0.004, given by the engineering specifications.

From the trend analysis in the second row on the right, which represents the condition of Bldg.02, the three trend curves almost overlap with each other. This shows that the NSI changed very little for a long time before the collapse of the adjacent Hepingxinju. According to the index, it is easy to determine that Bldg.02 is in a stable state, which is consistent with the fact that the data on the right reflect the safe status of the building.

Comparing the graphs in the first row and the second row, the time series shows obvious slope changes in the inclined Hepingxinju, whereas the index shows strong stability in the case of Bldg.02. Due to the high degree of discrimination displayed by the settlement inclination index in the two samples, efficient building safety risk analysis can be carried out by setting a reasonable threshold for this index.

4.2.3. Cause Analysis of the Incident

We also calculated the spatial orientation of the nonuniform settlement plane. The results showed that the settlement plane sank towards the northeast with an azimuth of 29 degrees with respect to the north orientation, as shown in Figure 10.

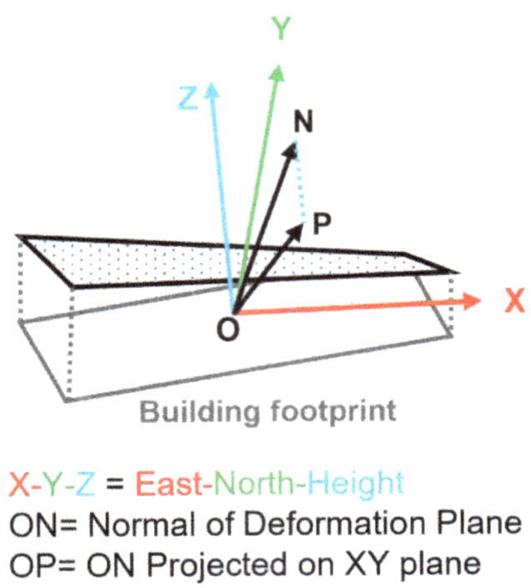

Figure 10. A schematic description of the spatial orientation of the settlement plane for the inclined building. OXYZ represents the East–North–Height coordinate reference frame. ON is the normal of the settlement plane, and OP is its projection on the ground plane. The spatial orientation of the settlement plane is described in this frame by the normal vector, ON, with respect to axes OY and OZ. The angle between vector ON and OZ measures the inclination of the settlement plane as proposed in this study by the $\tan\theta$. The angle between vector ON and OY describes the largest descending direction inside the settlement plane.

According to the field investigation and analysis, it was found that the construction and the operation of Metro Line 9 were continuously disturbing the aging building at the northeast corner and its surrounding surface, resulting in a subsidence trend. Before the incident on 28 August 2019, the shield has not started tunneling, whilst grouting works has been implemented on 25 June 2019 at the southeast part of the building to prevent potential deformation caused by tunneling. The minimum horizontal distance between the grouting well to the building is only about four meters. The grouting works give the building an upward force on the southeast corner, which was opposite to the influence of Metro Line 9 on the northeast corner (see Figure 4b). The surrounding two underground works induced uneven deformation of the building. In addition, the concealed culvert caused corrosion and deterioration of the main stressed component. Consequently, the nonuniform settlement of the pile foundation cap was intensified; the northeast side caps of the building were separated from the foundation due to the large settlement. In this case, internal force was redistributed because the foundation bearing capacity of southwest was higher than others, and the southwest columns bore a larger superstructure weight. Then, as the pressure of the beam and column damage on the south side of axes 10 and 11 gradually increased, the column eventually exhibited compression-controlled failure; the east–west main beam also occurred shearing-controlled failure. Finally, the column and the east–west girder on the south side of axis 10 and axis 11 were damaging from south to north, and the overall settlement of the eastern side structure was inclined to the western residual part. The directions of inclination and collapse were highly consistent with InSAR NSI analysis, from the general comparison of Figures 10 and 11.

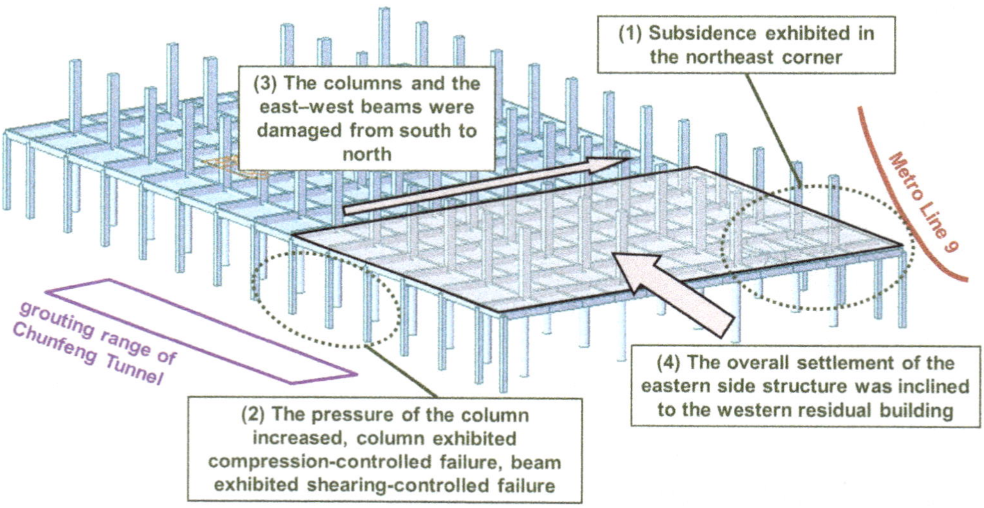

Figure 11. The mechanism of the settlement and inclination of Hepingxinju according to the investigation.

4.3. Risk Analysis of Bldg.03–09

On the basis of the analysis of Bldg.01–02, seven aging buildings, marked as Bldg.03–09 along Chunfeng Tunnel, were introduced to further verify the effectiveness of the proposed NSI. As described in Section 3.2.2, the grades of each building were determined by following local standards. The standard defines the grades as follows. Grade A buildings can continue to be used or can be used after the necessary treatment of damage. Grade B buildings should be carefully observed, with damage properly addressed. When abnormal situations occur, structure testing is mandatory. Both these grades of building should be inspected every ten years and every five years, respectively. Grade C buildings require measures to be taken immediately, including structural tests, reinforcement, keeping the building unoccupied, or even demolition. Among the seven samples we collected, Bldg.06–07 were grade C, which we defined as positive samples; the other five buildings were grade A and B, which we defined as negative samples. The grades were specified in 2017, denoting the safety conditions of corresponding buildings at that time; NSI analysis was performed from 2013 to 2016, comparing between the grades.

Figure 12 depicts the nonuniform settlement curve of the seven buildings. Positive samples and negative samples exhibit significant differences in the variation in NSI. From Figure 12a, the tangent value of the inclination angle reached 0.0009 at the grade C Bldg.06, which was equivalent to the value of Hepingxinju (0.0009 before collapse). Additionally, the other grade C building (Bldg.07 shown in Figure 12b) had a maximum value of 0.0003. Even though this is much lower than that of Bldg.06, the time series also showed a value exceeding 0.0002 (marked with a purple dashed line in Figure 12) in four periods, which almost accounted for half of the temporal domain. Among the negative samples, the values of Bldg.03, 08, 09, and 04 were generally lower than 0.0002 (see Figure 12c–f). Additionally, Bldg.05 showed almost flat trends with values consistently lower than 0.0001, which coincided well with the safe conditions of grade A.

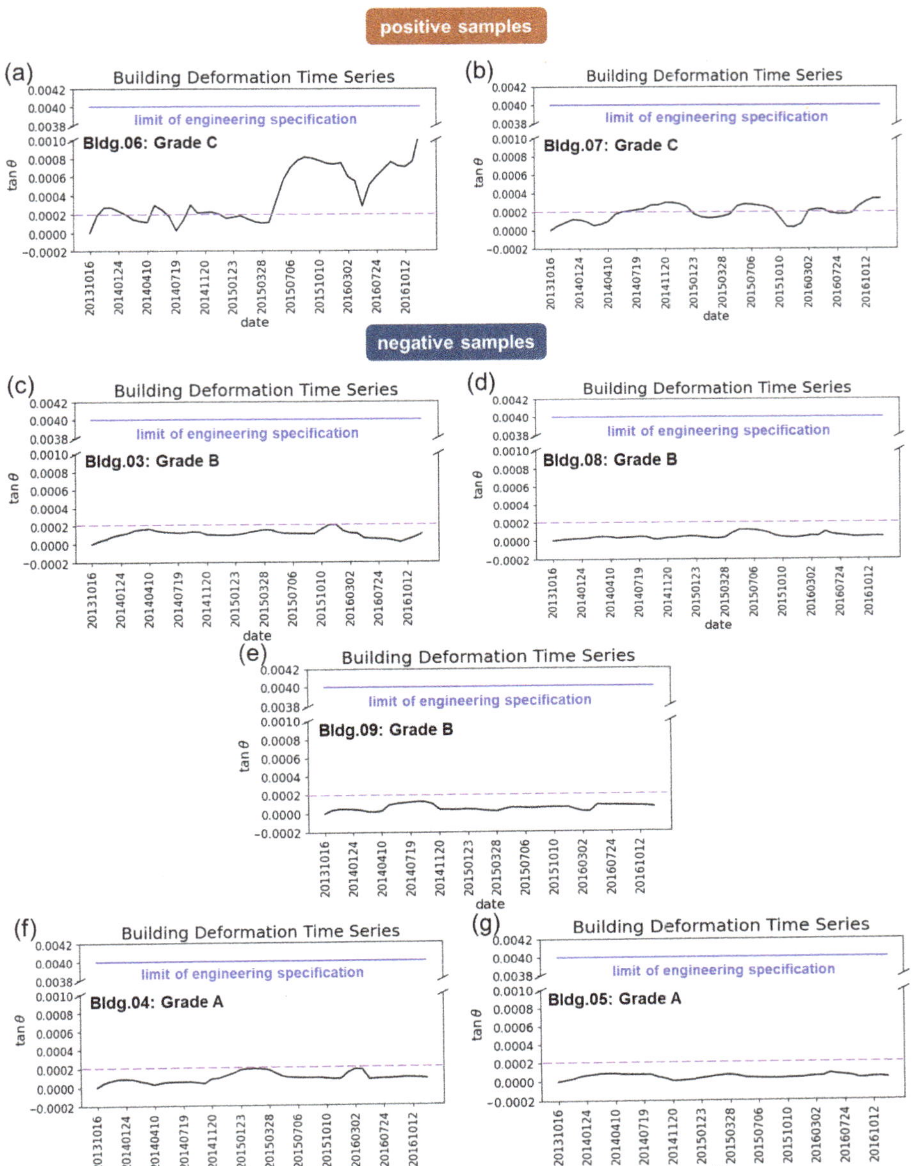

Figure 12. Nonuniform settlement curves of the tested buildings: (**a**,**b**) positive samples including Bldg.06–07; (**c**–**g**) negative samples including Bldg.03, 08, 09, 04, and 05.

5. Discussion

In our study, we propose the NSI as an evaluation method of time-series InSAR. Compared with existing risk assessment methods, we suggest that the strength of the NSI is building-oriented, which may influence long-term structural health monitoring. Given that using too large a time series dataset for PSInSAR processing will result in a lack of PSs due to signal decorrelation, the available SAR data were divided into several continuous batches to perform time-series InSAR processing separately. Then, the calculated PSs were spliced together to form a complete long time series. In general, the PSs obtained by separate calculations did not coincide completely in space, which may have caused data mismatching as well as failure in generating long time series for the single PS. In our method, the full cluster of PSs was used to simulate the plane, which characterizes the status of the building rather than a single point at each temporal batch. In this way, the mismatching of PSs during different temporal batches has little influence on the proposed method. Moreover, the focus is shifted from monitoring each single point on a building to a quantitative index related to each building.

However, the proposed NSI still has limitations that need to be improved in future studies. First and foremost, the setting of a threshold is critical to risk assessments of building clusters. From a data-driven perspective, accurate determination of the threshold depends on sufficient samples, especially the proportion of positive samples to the overall samples, which is commonly unavailable. In our study, based on limited positive samples, we may preliminarily suggest that a value of 0.0009 indicates the risk of uneven subsidence in buildings. A more rigorous threshold could be given by quantitative and systematical comparison between space- and ground-based monitoring. From a mechanism-driven perspective, structure types, usages, foundations, geological conditions, and external disturbances should be taken into consideration. It is impossible to apply a set of fixed thresholds to assess all individual buildings in the area. For example, reaching values of 0.0009 during temporal evolution, Hepingxinju collapsed, and Bldg.09 remained standing, since these two buildings varied not only in location, but in many mechanical aspects as well. Therefore, the accurate index threshold still needs to be determined through the analysis of many samples in different scenarios.

Second, fluctuations exist in nonuniform settlement curves. Clusters of PSs corresponding to the top of the building were utilized to generate the NSI, with the thermal expansion component not being removed. We suggest that trend analysis can be an effective way to follow the overall temporal evolution in NSI, especially the short-term increase in the index that indicates the unsafety condition of a building.

Third, the requirement of NSI is crucial. Ideally, PSs identical in height should be evenly distributed on a building to enable correct estimation of the deformation plane. However, these requirements are hard to meet due to the side-looking geometry of satellite SAR sensors. We omitted buildings where fewer than 5 points were acquired, and applied the SVD-based least-square method to mitigate the effect of a degraded plane model. At the same time, the accuracy of PS geolocations and heights should be taken into account, because they both have strong impact on point extraction for individual buildings. In this study, we inflated the building footprint with a buffer of 2 m to compensate for the geolocation error of PSs, and set an empirical threshold of 10 m to filter the height of the PSs on each building roof. Additionally, these empirical parameters need to be adjusted for specific SAR data processing.

Last, the applicability of the method is still limited. The method developed in our study was tested on existing multistory buildings, particularly aging structures. Considering high-rise buildings, rare PSs can be used due to the limited extent of building footprints. In this situation, other indexes that characterize the safety conditions of buildings should also be introduced, such as the inclined condition generated by PSs on the facades.

6. Conclusions

This study developed a Nonuniform Settlement Index as a subsequent evaluation method of time-series InSAR monitoring. The NSI calculated the inclination angle and generated a 3D settlement plane for performing building risk assessments. Compared with screening by thresholds of the deformation rate and the cumulative settlement of specific points, it provides a more intuitive evaluation of buildings using complete spatio-temporal information of the building's PSs. This new method was first applied to an aging building, Hepingxinju, which had inclined and subsequently collapsed on 28 August 2019 due to tunneling works and culvert erosion; Hepingxinju was assessed using X-band COSMO-SkyMed images. The Nonuniform Settlement Index of Hepingxinju PSs showed significant risk characteristics compared with an adjacent safe building. The settlement plane sank towards the northeast, with an azimuth of 29 degrees with respect to the north orientation, which is highly consistent with the conclusions of the investigation performed by the government into the incident. Further verification of the method on eight aging buildings demonstrated the positive effectiveness of the method. We suggest that such a methodology can be applied as a subsequent analyzing tool of time-series InSAR, which also has promising prospects in the risk management of building clusters over wide coverage.

Author Contributions: Y.L. (Yuzhou Liu): conceptualization, visualization, writing—original draft and editing. W.C.: algorithm development, data analysis, writing—original draft. Z.S.: resources, methodology, writing—original draft. Q.Y.: supervision, project administration, methodology. T.C.: data processing, validation, writing—original draft. L.T.: writing—review and editing. R.Z.: investigation, writing-editing. Y.L. (Yuke Liu): investigation, in situ data analysis. All authors have read and agreed to the published version of the manuscript.

Funding: This research was financially supported by the National Key Research and Development Program (grant no.: 2022YFC3801203-1-1).

Data Availability Statement: Not applicable.

Conflicts of Interest: The authors declare no conflict of interest.

References

1. Martín, G.; Hooper, A.; Wright, T.J.; Selvakumaran, S. Blind Source Separation for MT-InSAR Analysis With Structural Health Monitoring Applications. *IEEE J. Sel. Top. Appl. Earth Obs. Remote Sens.* **2022**, *15*, 7605–7618. [CrossRef]
2. Rosen, P.A.; Hensley, S.; Joughin, I.R.; Li, F.K.; Madsen, S.N.; Rodríguez, E.; Goldstein, R.M. Synthetic aperture radar interferometry. *Proc. IEEE* **2000**, *88*, 333–382. [CrossRef]
3. Huang, M.-H.; Fielding, E.J.; Liang, C.; Milillo, P.; Bekaert, D.; Dreger, D.; Salzer, J. Coseismic deformation and triggered landslides of the 2016 Mw 6.2 Amatrice earthquake in Italy. *Geophys. Res. Lett.* **2017**, *44*, 1266–1274. [CrossRef]
4. Jung, H.S.; Hong, S.M. Mapping three-dimensional surface deformation caused by the 2010 Haiti earthquake using advanced satellite radar interferometry. *PLoS ONE* **2017**, *12*, e0188286. [CrossRef] [PubMed]
5. Zhu, M.; Chen, F.; Zhou, W.; Lin, H.; Parcharidis, I.; Luo, J. Two-Dimensional InSAR Monitoring of the Co- and Post-Seismic Ground Deformation of the 2021 Mw 5.9 Arkalochori (Greece) Earthquake and Its Impact on the Deformations of the Heraklion City Wall Relic. *Remote Sens.* **2022**, *14*, 5212. [CrossRef]
6. Zebker, H.A.; Rosen, P.A.; Hensley, S. Atmospheric effects in interferometric synthetic aperture radar surface deformation and topographic maps. *J. Geophys. Res.* **1997**, *102*, 7547–7563. [CrossRef]
7. Zebker, H.A.; Villasenor, J.D. Decorrelation in interferometric radar echoes. *IEEE Trans. Geosci. Remote Sens.* **1992**, *30*, 950–959. [CrossRef]
8. Ferretti, A.; Prati, C.; Rocca, F. Nonlinear subsidence rate estimation using permanent scatterers in differential SAR interferometry. *IEEE Trans. Geosci. Remote Sens.* **2000**, *38*, 2202–2212. [CrossRef]
9. Ferretti, A.; Prati, C.; Rocca, F. Permanent scatterers in SAR interferometry. *IEEE Trans. Geosci. Remote Sens.* **2001**, *39*, 8–20. [CrossRef]
10. Hooper, A.; Segall, P.; Zebker, H. Persistent scatterer interferometric synthetic aperture radar for crustal deformation analysis, with application to Volcán Alcedo, Galápagos. *J. Geophys. Res. Solid Earth* **2007**, *112*, B7. [CrossRef]
11. Lanari, R.; Mora, O.; Manunta, M.; Mallorquí, J.J.; Berardino, P.; Sansosti, E. A small-baseline approach for investigating deformations on full-resolution differential SAR interferograms. *IEEE Trans. Geosci. Remote Sens.* **2004**, *42*, 1377–1386. [CrossRef]

12. Samsonov, S.V.; d'Oreye, N.F. Multidimensional Small Baseline Subset (MSBAS) for Two-Dimensional Deformation Analysis: Case Study Mexico City. *Can. J. Remote Sens.* **2017**, *43*, 318–329. [CrossRef]
13. Werner, C.L.; Wegmüller, U.; Strozzi, T.; Wiesmann, A. Interferometric point target analysis for deformation mapping. In *IGARSS 2003. 2003 IEEE International Geoscience and Remote Sensing Symposium. Proceedings (IEEE Cat. No.03CH37477)*; IEEE: Piscataway, NJ, USA, 2003; Volume 7, pp. 4362–4364.
14. Costantini, M.; Falco, S.; Malvarosa, F.; Minati, F.; Trillo, F. Method of persistent scatterer pairs (PSP) and high resolution SAR interferometry. In *2009 IEEE International Geoscience and Remote Sensing Symposium*; IEEE: Piscataway, NJ, USA, 2009; Volume 3, pp. III-904–III-907.
15. Zhang, L.; Lu, Z.; Ding, X.; Jung, H.-S.; Feng, G.; Lee, C.-W. Mapping ground surface deformation using temporarily coherent point SAR interferometry: Application to Los Angeles Basin. *Remote Sens. Environ.* **2012**, *117*, 429–439. [CrossRef]
16. Devanthéry, N.; Crosetto, M.; Monserrat, O.; Cuevas-González, M.; Crippa, B. An Approach to Persistent Scatterer Interferometry. *Remote Sens.* **2014**, *6*, 6662–6679. [CrossRef]
17. Blasco, J.M.D.; Foumelis, M.; Stewart, C.; Hooper, A.J. Measuring Urban Subsidence in the Rome Metropolitan Area (Italy) with Sentinel-1 SNAP-StaMPS Persistent Scatterer Interferometry. *Remote Sens.* **2019**, *11*, 129. [CrossRef]
18. Ferretti, A.; Bianchi, M.; Novali, F.; Tamburini, A.; Rucci, A. Volcanic Deformation Mapping using PSInSARTM: Piton de la Fournaise, Stromboli and Vulcano test sites for the Globvolcano project. In *2008 Second Workshop on Use of Remote Sensing Techniques for Monitoring Volcanoes and Seismogenic Areas*; IEEE: Piscataway, NJ, USA, 2008; pp. 1–5.
19. Parcharidis, I.S.; Kokkalas, S.; Fountoulis, I.; Foumelis, M. Detection and Monitoring of Active Faults in Urban Environments: Time Series Interferometry on the Cities of Patras and Pyrgos (Peloponnese, Greece). *Remote Sens.* **2009**, *1*, 676–696. [CrossRef]
20. Yastika, P.E.; Shimizu, N.; Verbovšek, T. A Case Study on Landslide Displacement Monitoring by SBAS DInSAR in the Vipava River Valley, Slovenia. In Proceedings of the 5th ISRM Young Scholars' Symposium on Rock Mechanics and International Symposium on Rock Engineering for Innovative Future, Okinawa, Japan, 1–4 December 2019.
21. Karamvasis, K.; Karathanassi, V. Performance Analysis of Open Source Time Series InSAR Methods for Deformation Monitoring over a Broader Mining Region. *Remote Sens.* **2020**, *12*, 1380. [CrossRef]
22. Osmanoglu, B.; Dixon, T.H.; Wdowinski, S.; Cabral-Cano, E.; Jiang, Y. Mexico City subsidence observed with persistent scatterer InSAR. *Int. J. Appl. Earth Obs. Geoinf.* **2011**, *13*, 1–12. [CrossRef]
23. Dai, K.; Liu, G.; Li, Z.; Ma, D.; Wang, X.; Zhang, B.; Tang, J.; Li, G. Monitoring Highway Stability in Permafrost Regions with X-band Temporary Scatterers Stacking InSAR. *Sensors* **2018**, *18*, 1876. [CrossRef] [PubMed]
24. Qin, X.; Liao, M.; Zhang, L.; Yang, M. Structural health and stability assessment of high-speed railways via thermal dilation mapping with time-series InSAR analysis. *IEEE J. Sel. Top. Appl. Earth Obs. Remote Sens.* **2017**, *10*, 2999–3010. [CrossRef]
25. Ma, P.; Lin, H. Robust detection of single and double persistent scatterers in urban built environments. *IEEE Trans. Geosci. Remote Sens.* **2015**, *54*, 2124–2139. [CrossRef]
26. Qin, X.; Li, Q.; Ding, X.; Xie, L.; Wang, C.; Liao, M.; Zhang, L.; Zhang, B.; Xiong, S. A structure knowledge-synthetic aperture radar interferometry integration method for high-precision deformation monitoring and risk identification of sea-crossing bridges. *Int. J. Appl. Earth Obs. Geoinf.* **2021**, *103*, 102476. [CrossRef]
27. Qin, X.; Zhang, L.; Yang, M.; Luo, H.; Liao, M.; Ding, X. Mapping surface deformation and thermal dilation of arch bridges by structure-driven multi-temporal DInSAR analysis. *Remote Sens. Environ.* **2018**, *216*, 71–90. [CrossRef]
28. Jiang, L.; Lin, H. Integrated analysis of SAR interferometric and geological data for investigating long-term reclamation settlement of Chek Lap Kok Airport, Hong Kong. *Eng. Geol.* **2010**, *110*, 77–92. [CrossRef]
29. Ma, P.; Wang, W.; Zhang, B.; Wang, J.; Shi, G.; Huang, G.; Chen, F.; Jiang, L.; Lin, H. Remotely sensing large-and small-scale ground subsidence: A case study of the Guangdong–Hong Kong–Macao Greater Bay Area of China. *Remote Sens. Environ.* **2019**, *232*, 111282. [CrossRef]
30. Ma, P.; Liu, Y.; Wang, W.; Lin, H. Optimization of PSInSAR networks with application to TomoSAR for full detection of single and double persistent scatterers. *Remote Sens. Lett.* **2019**, *10*, 717–725. [CrossRef]
31. Huber, P.J. Robust Estimation of a Location Parameter. *Ann. Math. Stat.* **1964**, *35*, 73–101. [CrossRef]
32. Municipality, H.A.C.B.O.S. Notice of Housing and Construction Bureau of Shenzhen Municipality on Issuing the "Methods for Investigation of Potential Safety Hazard of Existing Buildings in Shenzhen". Available online: http://zjj.sz.gov.cn/csml/zcfg/xxgk/zcfg_1/zcfg/jsgcgl/content/post_7625382.html (accessed on 24 May 2023).

remote sensing

MDPI

Article

Spatial Distribution Analysis of Landslide Deformations and Land-Use Changes in the Three Gorges Reservoir Area by Using Interferometric and Polarimetric SAR

Jun Hu [1,2], Yana Yu [1], Rong Gui [1,2,*], Wanji Zheng [1] and Aoqing Guo [1]

[1] School of Geosciences and Info-Physics, Central South University, Changsha 410083, China
[2] Hunan Geological Disaster Monitoring, Early Warning and Emergency Rescue Engineering Technology Research Center, Changsha 410004, China
* Correspondence: ronggui@csu.edu.cn

Abstract: Landslides are geological events that frequently cause major disasters. Research on landslides is essential, but current studies mostly use historical landslide data and do not reflect dynamic, real-time research results. In this study, landslide deformations and land-use changes were used to analyze the landslide distribution in Fengjie County and Wushan County in the Three Gorges Reservoir Area (TGRA) by using interferometric and polarimetric SAR. In this study, the mean annual rate of landslide deformations was obtained using the small baseline subset interferometric synthetic aperture radar (SBAS-InSAR) for the ALOS-2 (2014–2019) data. Land-use changes were based on the 2007 and 2017 land-use results from dual-polarization ALOS-1 and ALOS-2 data, respectively. To address the problem of classification accuracy reduction caused by geometric distortion in mountainous areas, we first used texture maps and pseudocolor maps synthesized with dual-polarization intensity maps to perform classification with random forest (RF), and then we used coherence and slope maps to run the K-Means algorithm (KMA). We named this the secondary classification method. It is an improvement on the single classification method, exhibiting a 94% classification accuracy, especially in rugged areas. Combined with land-use changes, GIS spatial analysis was used to analyze the spatial distribution of landslides, and it was found that the landslide rate was significantly correlated with the type after change, with a correlation coefficient of 0.7. In addition, land-use types associated with human activities, such as cultivated vegetation, were more likely to cause landslide deformation, which can be used to guide local land-use planning.

Keywords: dual-polarization SAR classification; machine learning; land-use changes; SBAS-InSAR; landslide spatial distribution

1. Introduction

From 1949 to 2010, China experienced 20,000 landslide and debris-flow disasters each year, causing more than 1000 casualties, affecting more than 900,000 people, and causing direct economic losses of RMB 2–6 billion. The Three Gorges Reservoir Area is one of the areas that is most prone to landslide disasters in China. This seriously affects the socio-economic development of the reservoir area and causes incalculable economic and human losses. Research on landslides currently focuses on landslide hazard assessment [1–4], forecasting and early warning [5,6], etc., mainly to minimize losses by predicting the occurrence of landslides in advance. However, because landslides often occur in areas with complex environments and dense forests, there are still major difficulties in identifying hidden hazards using remote sensing methods. As a result, more than 70% of landslide disasters that have occurred have not been predicted in advance [7]. Even when landslides can be accurately predicted, property such as fields and buildings in the disaster area will suffer damage. Therefore, it is of great importance to effectively reduce the losses from landslide disasters by understanding the distribution law of landslides and slowing down or preventing the occurrence of landslides at the source.

InSAR technology has developed rapidly in recent years. Time series InSAR techniques such as PS-InSAR [8], SBAS-InSAR [9] and SqueeSAR [10] have achieved good results in monitoring cities, mining areas and landslide areas [11,12]. When time-series InSAR technology was combined with land-use data to study the deformation in urban areas, plains, peatlands, flooded areas, and other areas, it was found that the average deformation rates corresponding to different land-use categories differed in the same study area [13,14], and that the type of land use is an important factor in deformation [15,16]. However, in deformation rate prediction using land-use types, the prediction results obtained after adding historical land-use data are more accurate [17], demonstrating that the influence of historical land use on the local deformation rate cannot be ignored. Changes in land use in urban areas are mainly reflected in changing building loads due to accelerated urban development [18]. The location of the main subsidence areas in Wuhan's urban areas changed after 2010, gradually moving into areas near new metro lines [19]. In addition, at different spatial scales, the Moran index shows that there is always a significant correlation between urbanization indicators and subsidence [20]. Thus, results concerning the flood inundation area and subsidence rates obtained using historical land-use predictions have realistic value and can guide the future planning of urban areas to reduce human casualties and economic losses caused by disasters [21–23]. The joint analysis of land use type/change and surface deformation rate provides a new solution for the prevention and control of surface deformation, and also brings new ideas to the study of the spatial distribution of landslide deformation.

The formation of landslides is influenced by a variety of internal and external factors [24,25], such as distance from water systems, faults, slopes, slope aspects, undulations, elevations, rainfall, human activities, etc. Among them, the intensity of human activities is the only controllable factor that can be used as the core when studying the spatial distribution of landslide deformation.

Currently, an increasing amount of machine learning and deep learning algorithms are being applied to classification, and the improved performance of these algorithms is improving classification accuracy. However, as compared with the problem of classification accuracy differences caused by different classification methods, the problem of accuracy degradation caused by a lack of training samples appears to be more serious [26]. Multispectral remote sensing images are widely used for land classification due to their high spatial resolution [27], but they are susceptible to cloud occlusion, which can lead to missing information and a failure to achieve effective classification. Synthetic aperture radar (SAR) has become an important resource for land use classification due to its ability to penetrate clouds and rain. The SAR's multipolarization channel provides more adequate information for classification in many regions, such as urban areas, humid tropical areas, and forest areas, and achieves a high classification accuracy [28–32]. However, as a result of the side-look imaging method of SAR, geometric distortion tends to occur in areas with rough terrain, and the intensity information caused by overlapping or shadowing is confused with other land types, resulting in misclassification problems.

In this study, land use changes are used as a characterization of the intensity of human activities; we first combined land use changes and landslide deformation to analyze the spatial distribution using interferometric and polarimetric SAR. On the basis of the dual-polarization of ALOS-1 (2007) and ALOS-2 (2014–2019) data, we adopted a secondary classification method, that is, the random forest (RF) was used for the first classification and then the K-Means algorithm (KMA) was performed. We effectively reduced the classification error caused by geometric distortion and improved the accuracy of land-use classification results of Wushan County and Fengjie County in 2007 and 2017. Combined with the landslide rates obtained using SBAS-InSAR technology, the relationship between land-use changes and landslide deformations was quantitatively evaluated using spatial analysis method.

2. Methods

This chapter introduces the estimation of landslide rates using SBAS-InSAR technology, the secondary classification method based on machine learning algorithms, and the analysis of the landslide spatial distribution with land use. The main flow of our method is shown in Figure 1.

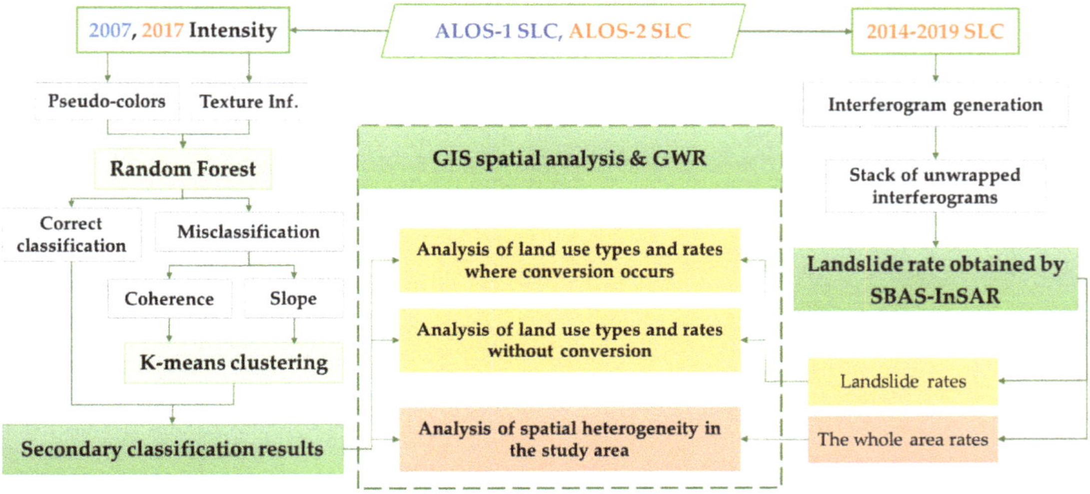

Figure 1. General flow chart.

2.1. SBAS-InSAR Technology

SBAS-InSAR technology is a time-series technique that was proposed in 2002 [9]. Its basic principle is to select appropriate spatial and temporal baselines to form differential interference pairs to create multiple small baseline subsets. This can improve image exploitation and reduce the effects of spatial-temporal decorrelation.

In this study, HH polarization data from the ALOS-2 satellite were selected to implement SBAS-InSAR technology using GAMMA software-64-18.04. First, we set appropriate threshold of spatial-temporal baseline to generate interference pairs to attenuate the decorrelation noise. Second, we simulated the terrain-related phases according to the Copernicus DEM. Then, the coherence threshold was set and all pixels above the threshold were retained to complete the phase unwrapping using the minimum cost flow (MCF) method. In addition, we used DEM to calculate the height-dependent atmospheric phase delay. Finally, the linear rate of ground points from 2014 to 2019 was obtained using the singular value decomposition (SVD).

2.2. The Secondary Classification Method and Accuracy Assessment

2.2.1. Secondary Classification with Dual-Polarization SAR Data

There are five types of land use in the Fengjie and Wushan areas: forest, water, cropland, cultivated vegetation and buildings. Of these, the cultivated vegetation types are mainly fruit trees such as navel oranges and plums, and the cropland are rice, corn and cotton. Although both are highly affected by human activities, there are differences in their growing conditions, such as terrain and slope. Figure 2 shows comparisons of the pseudocolor image and the optical images of the five types.

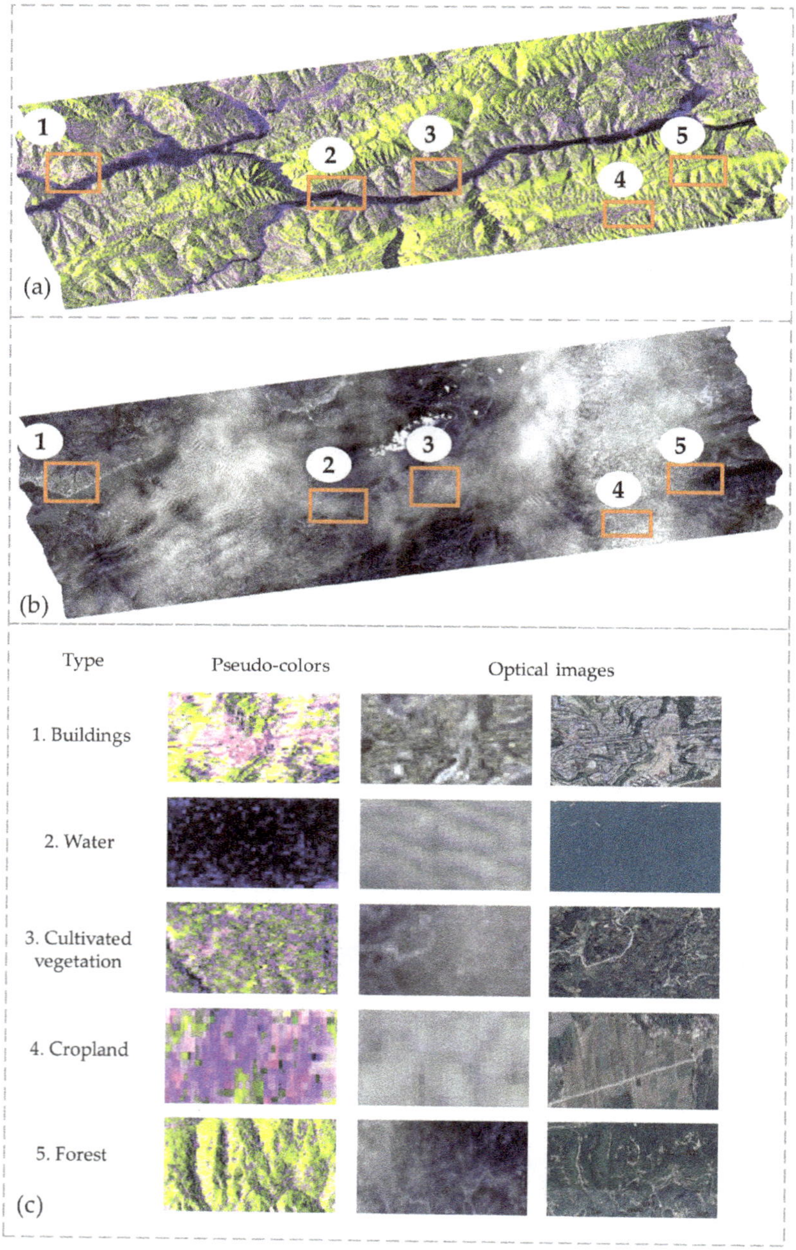

Figure 2. Comparison of pseudocolor and optical maps of five land-use types. (**a**) The pseudocolor map from 2017. (**b**) The Landsat8 optical map from 2017, provided by the Geospatial Data Cloud site, Computer Network Information Center, Chinese Academy of Sciences (http://www.gscloud.cn, accessed on 23 October 2022). (**c**) The optical and pseudocolor maps representation of the five regions in (**a**,**b**).

It can be seen that some optical images are largely covered by clouds, making it difficult to distinguish features. SAR images are susceptible to geometric distortion, and errors will occur when used for classification. Therefore, we proposed a secondary classification method to solve this problem. One scene of single look complex (SLC) images from the same season (July and August) in both 2007 and in 2017 was selected, with two types of polarization, i.e., HH and HV, which comprised the original data source for the secondary classification. This method mainly uses the RF algorithm and KMA to complete the first and second classification steps, respectively, and then synthesize the two results to obtain the final classification results. The secondary classification process is shown in Figure 1.

The random forest algorithm was used in the first classification process. It is a typical supervised learning algorithm, i.e., an integrated algorithm based on a decision tree. Its "random" nature is reflected in two ways: first, there is put-back sampling from the original set of samples; second, there is put-back sampling from the original features and then the optimal features are selected among them. The subset of samples and features form a decision tree, and multiple decision trees form a "forest" in which all trees are integrated to vote on the classification results. The category with the highest number of votes is then output as the result [33]. The advantage of this is that it can handle multiple input variables and produce a high accuracy rate for multiple input elements.

The second classification process was performed using the K-means algorithm, which is an unsupervised learning algorithm. The principle is to randomly select K objects as initial cluster centers, calculate the distance between each object and each cluster center, and assign each object to the cluster center closest to it. The cluster centers and the objects assigned to them form a cluster. The method can combine classes based on distance without sampling, but it allows only one input quantity [34].

The secondary classification method was adopted to extract two classes when serious confusion occurred in the first classification result, and select the input quantity that had high discriminative power for these two classes to perform K-means clustering after achieving the RF. The essence of this method is to simplify the multiclassification task into a two-classification task, so that it can still maintain a high classification accuracy when there is a large number of categories.

The secondary classification method has four kinds of characteristic data, which are pseudo-color map, texture map, coherence map and slope map. Among them, the pseudo-color map is synthesized from dual-polarization SAR images, and the discrimination of different land use types can be improved by displaying different colors. Texture information and coherence maps are derived from HH polarimetric SAR images, and slope maps are calculated from DEM.

2.2.2. Accuracy Evaluation Index

Overall accuracy (OA) is a commonly used accuracy evaluation index. If there are two types of features A and B in a region, the actual A and the classification result A is denoted as TP, the actual A but the classification result B is denoted as FN, the actual B and the classification result B is denoted as TN, and the actual B but the classification result A is denoted as FP; then, the OA is calculated as follows [28]:

$$\mathrm{OA} = \frac{\mathrm{TP} + \mathrm{TN}}{\mathrm{TP} + \mathrm{TN} + \mathrm{FP} + \mathrm{FN}} \quad (1)$$

Another evaluation index is the Kappa coefficient, which is obtained on the basis of overall accuracy. It can be expressed as:

$$\mathrm{K} = \frac{\mathrm{OA} - \mathrm{P}}{1 - \mathrm{P}} \quad (2)$$

among them, the expression of P is:

$$\mathrm{P} = \frac{(\mathrm{TP} + \mathrm{FN}) \times (\mathrm{TP} + \mathrm{FP}) + (\mathrm{FN} + \mathrm{TN}) \times (\mathrm{FP} + \mathrm{TN})}{(\mathrm{TP} + \mathrm{TN} + \mathrm{FP} + \mathrm{FN})^2} \quad (3)$$

2.3. Spatial Analysis

2.3.1. Data Preprocessing for Spatial Analysis

Using the secondary classification method, the land-use results for 2007 and 2017 were obtained by inputting the ALOS-1 and ALOS-2 data, respectively. Then, using the ArcGIS 10.2 software, both land-use results were resampled to the same spatial resolution as the average landslide rates of ALOS-2. On the basis of the landslide rates in the study area, the typical landslide areas were vectorized, and the land-use and landslide rates corresponding to the typical landslide areas were separately extracted to perform the following analysis.

First, for the typical landslide areas, the land use in 2017 was overlaid with the average rates to analyze the relationship between the landslide deformations and land-use types. Second, for the typical landslide areas, land-use changes from 2007 to 2017 were overlaid with the average rates to obtain the influence of land-use changes on the landslide deformations. Finally, a spatial heterogeneity analysis was performed using the geographically weighted regression (GWR) for the landslide rates over the whole study area with influence factors, such as slope, aspect, elevation, undulation, land-use type, and distance from the water system.

2.3.2. Spatial Analysis Method

(1) Overlay analysis. Overlay analysis is a very important spatial analysis technique in GIS (the geographic information system). It refers to the process of generating new data under the same spatial reference system through a series of set operations on two data (Figure 3). The aim is to analyze the relationship between the spatial characteristics and properties of spatial objects that have some correlation in terms of spatial location.

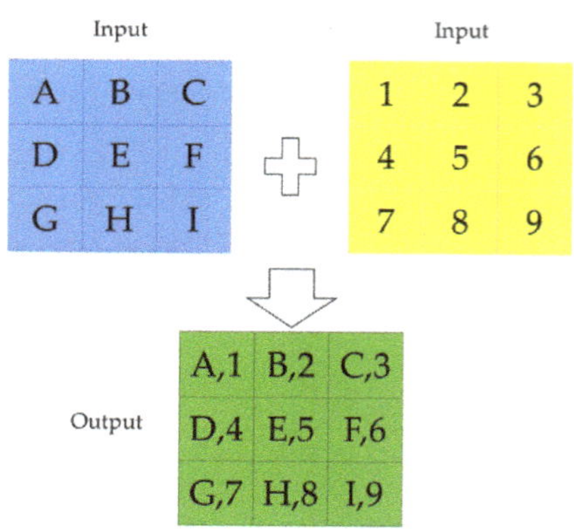

Figure 3. Overlay analysis schematic (image reference: https://desktop.arcgis.com/zh-cn/arcmap, accessed on 16 March 2023).

(2) Transfer matrix. The land use transfer matrix [17] is an application of the Markov model in land-use change, which not only quantitatively represents the changes between land-use types, but also reveals the transfer rates between different land-use types. In addition, it can be obtained via the overlay analysis method using ArcGIS. The matrix calculation formula is as follows:

$$\text{Area Percentage} = \frac{A_i}{W} \times 100\% \tag{4}$$

where A_i is the area corresponding to each type of change and W is the total area of the study area.

(3) Geographically weighted regression model. Traditional regression analysis was developed based on the stability of the relationship between the independent variable and

the dependent variable in a given area. Only a unique spatial coefficient could be obtained with the following mathematical expression:

$$y = \beta_0 + \beta_1 x_1 + \beta_2 x_2 + \ldots \beta_p x_n + \varepsilon \tag{5}$$

where y is the dependent variable, $x_{1,2,\ldots n}$ is the explanatory variable (independent variable), $\beta_{1,2,\ldots p}$ is the coefficient of each explanatory variable, and ε is the random error.

In reality, performances will always differ depending on the spatial location, i.e., spatial heterogeneity. The GWR model [35] is a local regression analysis method that can obtain the respective spatial coefficients at each spatial location, thereby preserving the spatial heterogeneity of the data and expressing the relationship between the independent and dependent variables more accurately than traditional methods. Its mathematical expression is as follows:

$$y_i = \beta_0(u_i, v_i) + \sum_{k=1}^{p} \beta_k(u_i, v_i) x_k + \varepsilon_i \tag{6}$$

where i is the sampling point serial number, (u_i, v_i) is the geographic coordinate of sampling point i, $\beta_k(u_i v_i)$ is the coefficient of the kth explanatory variable at sampling point i, and ε_i is the random error at sampling point i.

3. Study Area and Data

3.1. Overview of the Study Area

The Fengjie and Wushan districts are located in the eastern part of Chongqing, in the hinterland of the TGRA. The study area is bounded by east longitudes 109°25′30″ and 109°55′58″ and north latitudes 30°58′29″ and 31°5′25″, with the Yangtze River running east to west, a well-developed water system, and numerous river networks and reservoirs. The area is crisscrossed by ravines, and has an undulating terrain with the Yangtze River as the axis of symmetry. In addition, it has a gradually increasing elevation on both sides of the river, tectonic development, and a complex geological background. It has a humid subtropical monsoon climate with four distinct seasons, abundant rainfall, and sufficient sunshine. The rugged terrain and complex geographical environment have led to serious geological disasters in the region, resulting in significant losses each year.

By 2020, there were 2 roads, 11 cities, and 13 townships in Wushan County and 4 roads, 18 cities, and 11 townships in Fengjie County, with a population of 462,400 and 744,800, respectively. The area is rich in tourism resources, and with the completion and opening of the Yuyi Expressway, the level of economic development has gradually improved.

3.2. Data

One single-look complex (SLC) image from the ALOS-1 satellite in 2007 was acquired for both Fengjie and Wushan counties. In addition, 11 SLC images from the ALOS-2 satellite were acquired for the period 2014–2019. The SAR data bands used are all L-band and the polarization methods were HH and HV (see Table 1). From the SLC thumbnails, it can be seen that the HH or HV image alone could not be used to discriminate land use, so it was necessary to combine data from these two channels for classification. A download of Copernicus DEM (30 m spatial resolution) [36] data was used as the basis for topographic phase removal and geocoding.

Two existing land-use classification sets were collected, namely, the Sentinel-2 satellite classification dataset published by ESRI [37] and the annual Chinese land-cover dataset (CLCD) obtained from Landsat data published by Wuhan University [38], with resolutions of 10 m and 30 m, respectively.

Table 1. Data of ALOS-1 and ALOS-2.

Sensor	Date	Counts	SLC Thumbnails		Resolution (m)	Coverage
			HH	HV		
ALOS-1	2007	1			9 (range) × 3 (azimuth)	Fengjie County
	2007	1				Wushan County
ALOS-2	2014–2019	11	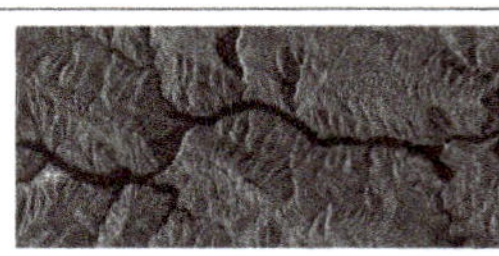	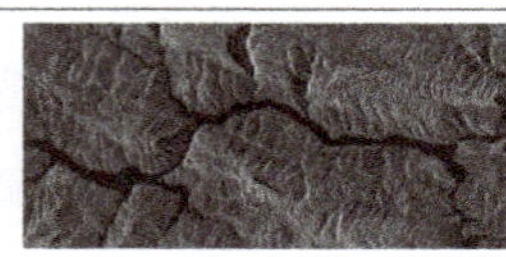	4 (range) × 3 (azimuth)	Fengjie and Wushan County

4. Results

4.1. SBAS-InSAR to Monitor Landslide Deformation Rates

We first obtained 22 interference pairs from 11 SLC by setting the temporal baseline to 400 days and the spatial baseline to 300 m. To obtain an accurate solution, we selected all pixels with a coherence value greater than 0.32. Figure 4 depicts the landslide rates in the study area from 2014 to 2019, which were derived by SBAS-InSAR and ranged from −9 to 9 cm/year. Despite the temporal span of the study, most of the pixels exhibited no deformation, indicating stable geological condition. However, representative landslide areas were found to be distributed along the Yangtze River, with a maximum deformation rate of 9 cm/year. Figure 4 (right) highlights prominent landslide features that can be used for analyzing the spatial distribution of landslides. These results provide valuable insights into the landslide patterns in this region, contributing to our understanding of the dynamics of landslide-prone areas.

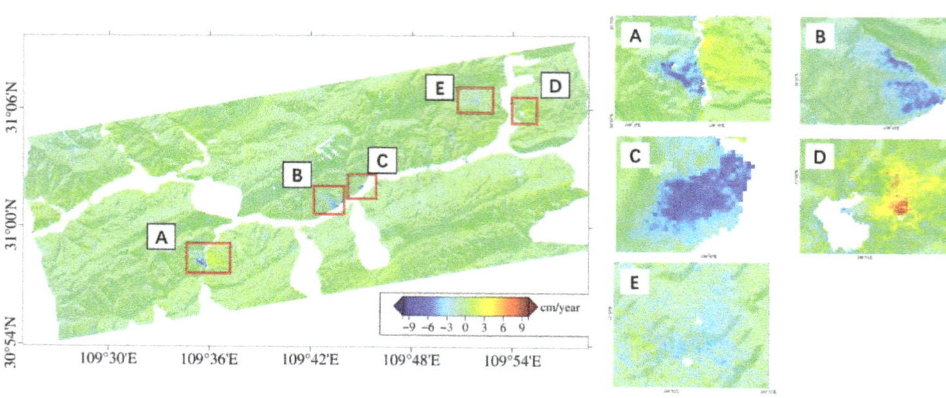

Figure 4. SBAS-InSAR average rate results. (**A–E**) show the deformation details of the main landslides.

4.2. Secondary Classification Results and Accuracy Assessment

Figure 5a,c,e, and Figure 5b,d,f show the data sources of the secondary classification method for the ALOS-1 and ALOS-2 data, respectively. There were two input data sources for the first classification, the pseudocolor map shown in Figure 5a,b, and the texture map shown in Figure 5c,d. Figure 5e,f and Figure 5g show the coherence and slope maps used for the second classification, respectively. The 2007 and 2017 land-use results were obtained from the secondary classification using these data sources (Figure 6).

Two validation areas and three comparison methods were selected for the secondary classification experiments. The first validation area contains five land-use types, mainly forested and rugged terrain. The second validation area contains only three land-use types, forest, and water, and mostly consists of buildings and flat terrain. Figure 7a,b and Figure 7g,h show the pseudocolor map coverage and validation samples, respectively. Figure 7c,i show the results of the secondary classification method performed for the two validation regions, respectively, with an overall accuracy of 94.44% and 95.52% and Kappa coefficient of 91.59% and 92.29%, and the confusion matrix as shown in Table 2.

Comparison Method 1: Only the first classification was performed and only the pseudocolor map was input. The results for the first and second validation areas are shown in Figure 7d,j, respectively, with overall accuracies of 82.29% and 87.38%, and Kappa coefficients of 74.72% and 78.14%. The classification results show that most of the areas could be well distinguished using the pseudocolor map alone, but some of the forest types were misclassified as building types due to the severe geometric distortion in the mountainous areas. Thus, more input information was needed to distinguish between them.

Comparison Method 2: All four types of data sources were input for the first classification, and no second classification was performed. When more data sources were input, the overall accuracy greatly improved in flat areas, reaching 96.02% (Figure 7k). However, the accuracy did not significantly improve in rough areas, reaching only 86.12% (Figure 7e). There were also large differences in their Kappa coefficients, 93.02% and 80.33%, respectively (Table 2).

Comparison Method 3: The classification correction step using coherence was removed from the secondary classification framework. This comparison method achieved the lowest overall accuracy of all experiments in both validation areas, i.e., 78.97% and 87.04%, respectively (Figure 7f,l). The Kappa coefficients are also inaccurate.

The above comparison methods show that, for flat areas, adding data sources can effectively improve the classification accuracy, but not well in all types. The secondary classification method can be used to mitigate the effect of geometric distortion with coherence, showing good accuracies in both rugged and flat areas.

The CLCD and ESRI datasets selected for the rugged areas are shown in Figure 8a,b and Figure 8c,d, respectively. The results of the ESRI datasets (Figure 8d) show that forests and buildings were misclassified in the rugged areas, and cropland was not subdivided in the CLCD results (Figure 8b). Therefore, the land-use data used in this study were the results of the secondary classification process.

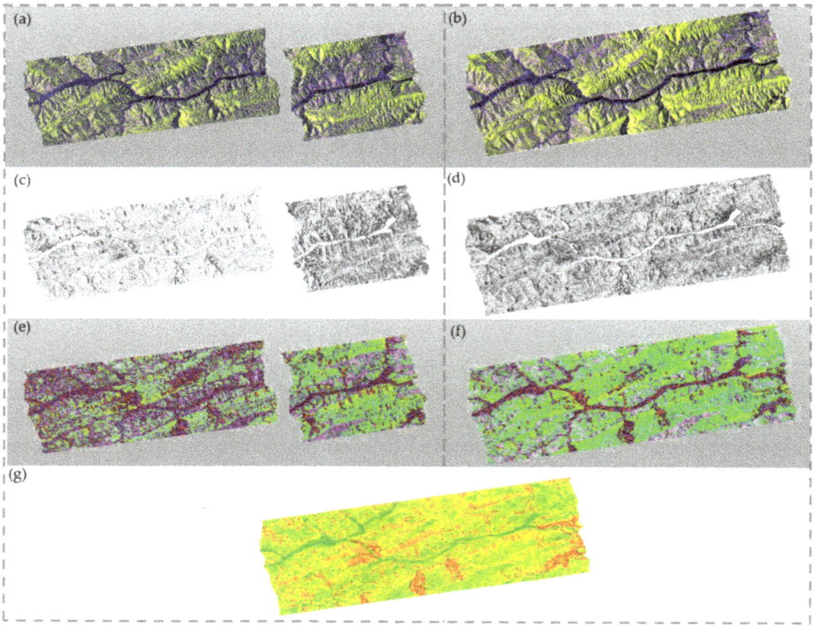

Figure 5. Input data source for ALOS-1 and ALOS-2 classification using the secondary classification method. (**a**,**c**,**e**) and (**b**,**d**,**f**) the data sources for ALOS-1 and ALOS-2 classification, respectively. (**a**,**b**) Pseudocolors maps; (**c**,**d**) texture maps; (**e**,**f**) coherence maps; (**g**) the slope map.

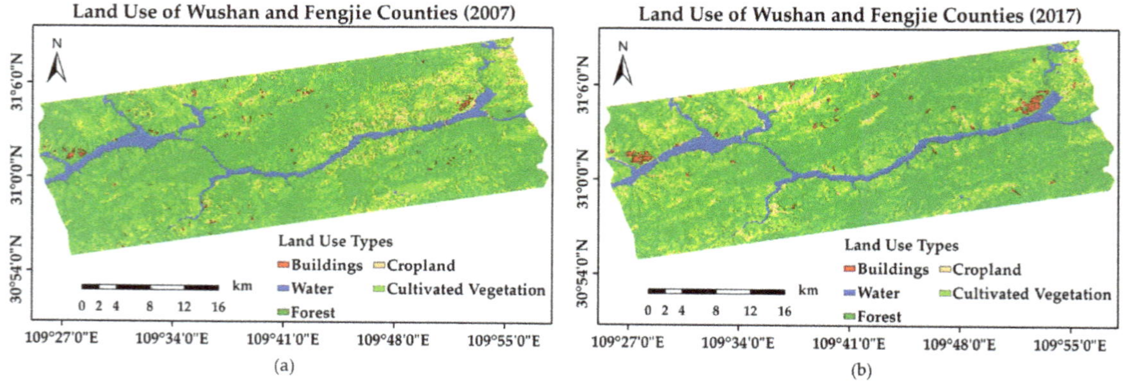

Figure 6. Land use in Wushan and Fengjie counties in 2007 and 2017. (**a**) The result from 2007; (**b**) the result from 2017.

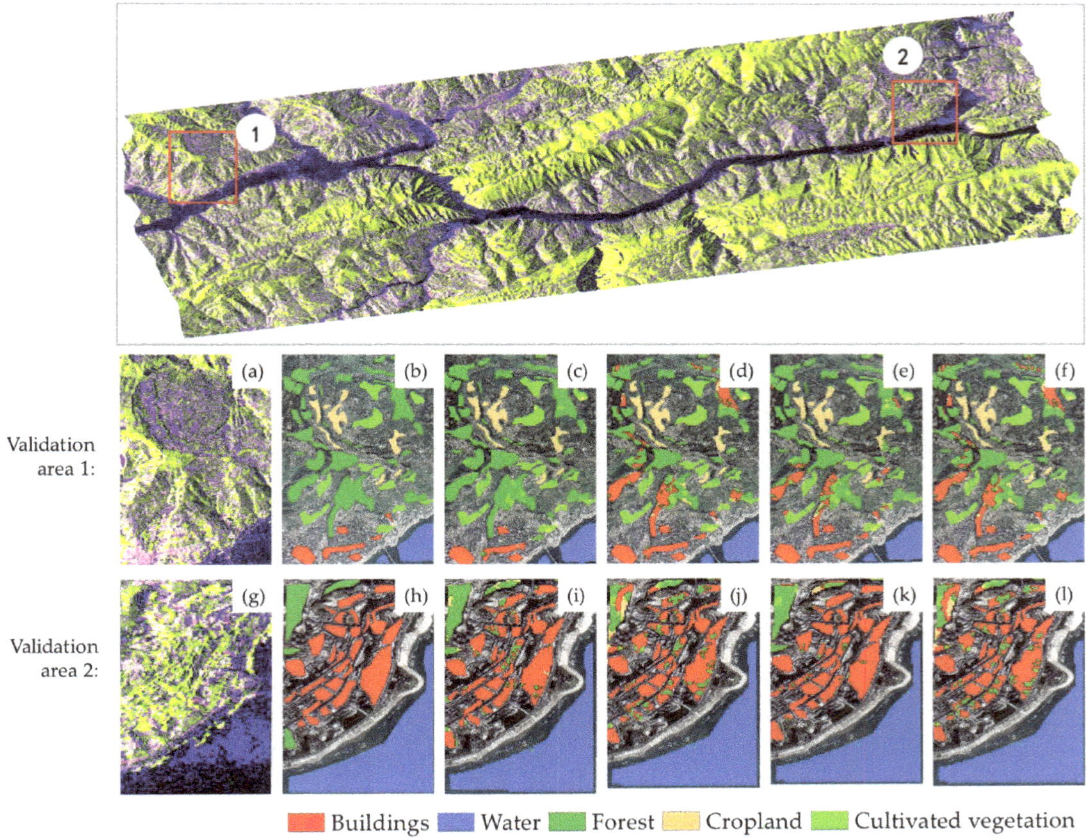

Figure 7. Validation of land-use classification results in 2017. (**a–f**) and (**g–l**) the results of the first and second validation areas, respectively. (**a**,**g**) The pseudocolor map display; (**b**,**h**) the validation sample; (**c**,**i**) the results of the secondary classification method; (**d**,**j**) the results of the comparison method 1; (**e**,**k**) the results of the comparison method 2; (**f**,**l**) the results of the comparison method 3.

Table 2. Confusion matrix for the classification results.

Name	Method	Classification Accuracy of Each Type(%)					OA (%)	Kappa (%)
		Buildings	Forest	Water	Cropland	Cultivated Vegetation		
Validation Area 1	Comparison Method 1	89.63	76.03	100.00	84.70	83.70	82.29	74.72
	Comparison Method 2	99.67	78.88	100.00	91.16	88.58	86.12	80.33
	Comparison Method 3	96.57	64.56	99.94	96.88	89.32	78.97	71.50
	Secondary Classification	**84.45**	**95.80**	**99.94**	**98.07**	**89.00**	**94.44**	**91.59**

Table 2. *Cont.*

Name	Method	Classification Accuracy of Each Type(%)					OA (%)	Kappa (%)
		Buildings	Forest	Water	Cropland	Cultivated Vegetation		
Validation Area 2	Comparison Method 1	81.35	40.18	99.92	——	——	87.38	78.14
	Comparison Method 2	97.21	70.44	99.92	——	——	96.02	93.02
	Comparison Method 3	81.74	35.33	99.92	——	——	87.04	77.46
	Secondary Classification	**90.62**	**89.83**	**99.96**	——	——	**95.52**	**92.29**

The bold in the table are the results of the method proposed in this paper.

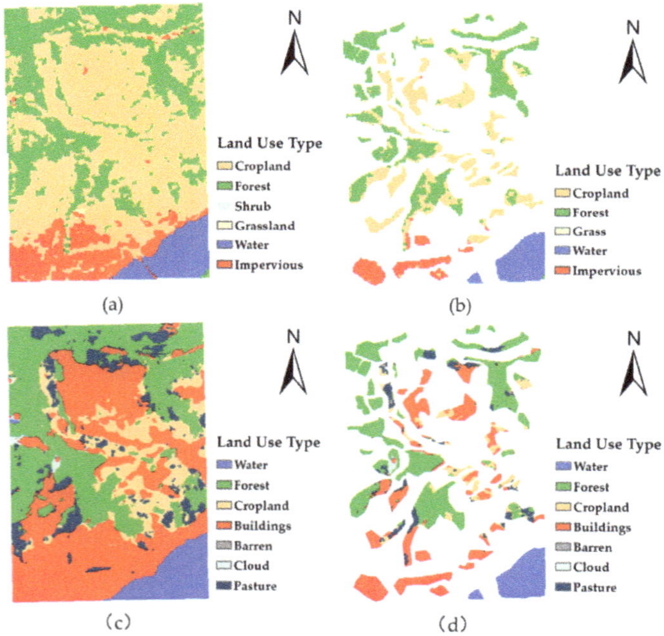

Figure 8. CLCD and ESRI dataset results for rugged regions. (**a**,**b**) The CLCD results; (**c**,**d**) the ESRI results. (**b**,**d**) Are the samples of (**a**,**b**), which are the same as in the first validation area.

4.3. Land-Use Changes from 2007 to 2017

On the basis of the 2007 and 2017 land-use results, GIS spatial analysis was used to derive land-use changes from 2007 to 2017 (Figure 9). This method of first classifying and then calculating the change can directly show the type of change, making it easier to understand. Figure 9 (right) shows the land use changes in the five landslide areas marked in Figure 4.

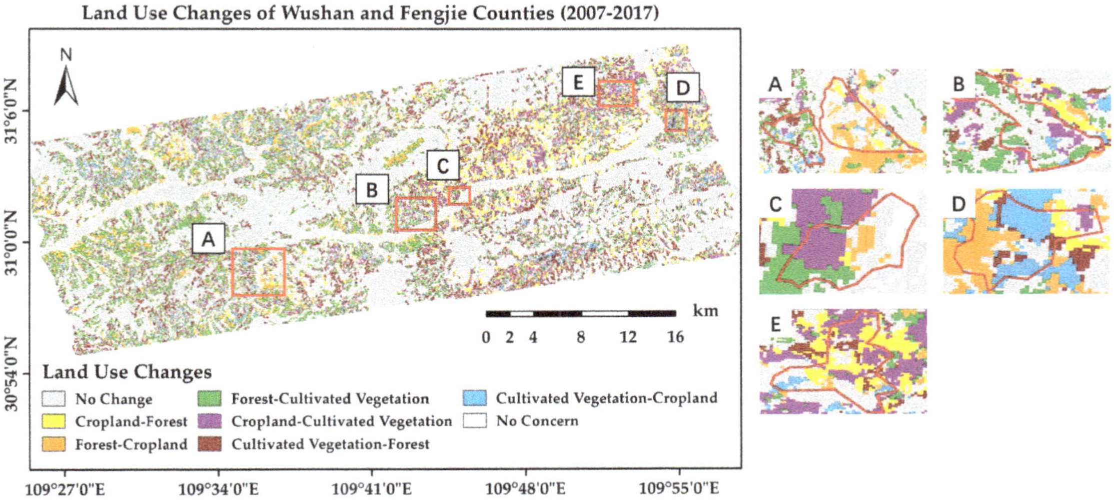

Figure 9. Land-use changes from 2007 to 2017. (**A–E**) show the land use changes of the main landslides.

In Figure 4, the rates in the A-D are large, while those in E are relatively small. From the type changes in Figure 9, it can be seen that the rates are not directly related to the type change or not. There is a large area of unchanged type in B, but the landslide deformation rate reaches 9 cm/year. Area E has a large number of change types, but the rates are relatively small.

Transfer matrixes for the study area and typical landslide areas were constructed according to the results of land-use change (Tables 3 and 4, respectively).

During this decade, the main land type in the study area was forest, covering almost 70% of the land, and more than three-quarters of the forest area was in stable condition. The major land-use changes in both the study area and the typical landslide areas were between forest, cropland, and cultivated vegetation, but the area composition of these three types differed greatly. For the whole area (Table 3), the area of forest was absolutely dominant, whereas in the typical landslide areas (Table 4), the area percentage of the three land types did not differ significantly. The area of cultivated vegetation was higher in typical landslide areas than for the whole area, indicating that the intensity of the influence of human activity was greater in the landslide areas.

Table 3. Land-use transfer matrix for the whole area from 2007–2017. The area is color-coded from green (small) to red (large).

2007	2017					
	Buildings	Water	Forest	Cropland	Cultivated Vegetation	Total
Buildings	0.15	0.01	0.17	0.04	0.01	0.39
Water	0.00	4.88	0.17	0.13	0.04	5.23
Forest	0.41	0.83	53.65	3.99	9.46	68.33
Cropland	0.13	0.10	3.42	3.11	2.67	9.43
Cultivated Vegetation	0.05	0.02	6.65	2.29	7.61	16.62
Total	0.74	5.85	64.06	9.55	19.79	100.00

Table 4. Land-use transfer matrix for the typical landslide areas from 2007 to 2017. The area is color-coded from green (small) to red (large).

2007	2017					
	Buildings	**Water**	**Forest**	**Cropland**	**Cultivated Vegetation**	**Total**
Buildings	0.00	0.00	0.74	0.29	0.00	1.03
Water	0.00	1.86	0.26	0.19	0.13	2.45
Forest	0.00	0.97	11.18	12.32	9.64	34.11
Cropland	0.00	0.36	7.49	17.99	7.87	33.72
Cultivated Vegetation	0.00	0.00	4.34	5.76	18.59	28.70
Total	0.00	3.20	24.02	36.55	36.24	100.00

4.4. GIS Spatial Analysis with Landslide Deformations and Land-Use Changes

4.4.1. For Typical Landslide Areas with No Change in Land Use from 2007 to 2017

In practical production, it is difficult to determine normality of data, so when comparing the differences between the means of several independent datasets, nonparametric test methods are generally used. The K–W test (Kruskal-Wallis test) can compare the differences between more than two independent datasets. The null hypothesis is that all data distributions are the same and there is no difference.

Forest, cropland and cultivated vegetation account for more than 90% of the total landslide area, so this paper only considered these three main types and the conversion between the three, and did not consider information on other types. All pixel points in typical landslide areas with no change in land-use type between 2007 and 2017 were extracted, and the mean rates corresponding to these points were overlaid and analyzed. The K–W test was used to test the nonparametric test of the overlay analysis results. The results are shown in Table 5, with a p-value of 0.000 *** and a significance level of 1%. The null hypothesis was rejected, i.e., there were significant differences between the landslide deformation rates corresponding to different land use types. The conclusion showed that in the landslide area, different land use types had different effects on the landslide rate, i.e., human intensity had different effects on landslide deformation. When the intensity of human activities was higher, the resulting landslide rate was significantly higher than in other areas.

Table 5. Significance analysis of the corresponding rates of land-use types in landslide areas.

Analysis Items	**Variables**	**Sample Size**	**Mean Velocity (cm/year)**	**Statistics**	***p*-Value**	**Effect Amount**
Velocity	Cultivated Vegetation	1308	**3.47**	1362.433	**0.000 *****	0.019
	Forest	572	**1.35**			
	Cropland	1322	**1.54**			
	Total	3202	-			

*** represents 1% significance levels, respectively. Those in bold in the table were mentioned in this paper.

The average rates of the three types were calculated separately, and it was found that the rate of cultivated vegetation (3.47 cm/year) was significantly higher than that of the other two types (forest: 1.35 cm/year and cropland: 1.54 cm/year). It showed that for the landslide area, if the land use type does not change, the cultivated vegetation type has a promoting effect on the landslide deformation, while the other two types have relatively little promoting effect on the landslide. The different facilitating effects of these three types on the landslide rate are related to the intensity of human activities they bear, which has important implications for future land use planning.

4.4.2. For Typical Landslide Areas with Land-Use Changes from 2007 to 2017

The pixels of land-use changes in typical landslide areas and the corresponding landslide rates were extracted. Then, the two were used to perform an overlay analysis to obtain the data in Table 6.

Table 6. Correlation between land-use changes and landslide deformation rates.

Type 1	Type 2	Type 1 Rate	Type 2 Rate	2017 Rate
Forest	Cropland	1.35	1.54	1.58
Forest	Cultivated Vegetation	1.35	3.47	3.36
Cropland	Forest	1.54	1.35	1.59
Cropland	Cultivated Vegetation	1.54	3.47	2.73
Cultivated Vegetation	Forest	3.47	1.35	2.79
Cultivated Vegetation	Cropland	3.47	1.54	2.30
Correlation Coefficient		0.15	**0.70**	1.00

Type 1 denotes the type before the change; type 2 denotes the type after the change; type 1 rate denotes the average rate corresponding to type 1; type 2 rate denotes the average rate corresponding to type 2. 2017 rate shows the average rate after the changes in the area. And the bold in the table was our concern.

During the period 2007–2017, there were six land-use changes. The correlation coefficient between the actual rates after the changes and the other rates was calculated, and it was found that the actual landslide rates in the changed area were significantly influenced by the land-use type after change, with a correlation coefficient of 0.7. If the land use change was of a type that can promote landslide deformation, the deformation rate would increase, and if the land use change was of a type that slows down the deformation rate, the deformation rate would have a downward trend. This is a good illustration of the effect of land use changes on the landslide deformation rates. Therefore, in order to achieve the purpose of slowing down and preventing landslide deformation from the perspective of land use planning, it is necessary to fully consider whether land use change has a promoting effect on landslide deformation.

4.4.3. For the Typical Landslide Areas from 2007 to 2017

On the basis of the contents of the previous two subsections, all types of changes that occurred in typical landslide areas (including changes from forest to forest in the same type) were organized, as shown in Table 7. It was found that, regardless of the type of change, the maximum landslide rate occurred in areas after changes to cultivated vegetation. This indicates that the change type has a significant influence on the landslide rate.

Table 7. Land-use change in landslide areas. The area is color-coded from green (small) to red (large).

Velocity (cm/year)		Type after Change		
		Forest	**Cropland**	**Cultivated Vegetation**
Type before Change	Forest	1.35	1.58	3.36
	Cropland	1.59	1.54	2.73
	Cultivated Vegetation	2.79	2.30	3.47
	Mean	1.91	1.81	3.19

From the analysis of typical landslide areas, the cultivated vegetation area, which is a land-use type that is heavily influenced by human activities, was shown to be more prone to landslides. When the land-use type changed from cultivated vegetation to forest and cropland, the landslide rates decreased more significantly, but they remained higher than the rates observed after other changes to forest land and cropland. This indicates that the landslide rates are not only influenced by the land type after change, but also by the land type before change. It can be seen that, although changing the land-use type is effective to slow down the occurrence of landslides, the historical land-use type still has a certain influence for a short period of time. Therefore, when selecting sites for populated areas, such as areas for construction, both the current land-use type and the historical type should be considered in order to avoid landslide disasters.

4.5. Spatial Heterogeneity Analysis with GWR

On the basis of typical landslide areas, we found that the landslide rate was higher in cultivated vegetation areas; however, from the perspective of land-use type for the whole area, cultivated vegetation areas did not all experience landslide phenomena. This is due to spatial heterogeneity, i.e., different spatial locations are affected by the same factors, but react differently. In reality, the occurrence of landslides is not only influenced by land-use change. It is, also influenced by factors such as elevation, undulation, distance from the water system, aspect, and slope (Figures 10a–d and 5, respectively).

GWR was used to analyze the spatial heterogeneity of the study area, and the overall process is shown in Figure 11. Firstly, the ArcGIS 10.2 software was used to create a raster network for the study area, with a total of 31,344 raster points being obtained. Then, the elevation, undulation, land-use change, distance from the water system, slope, aspect, and landslide rate data were extracted according to the grid points, which were used as the input for GWR. Finally, the output from the GWR software was visualized in ArcGIS (Figure 12).

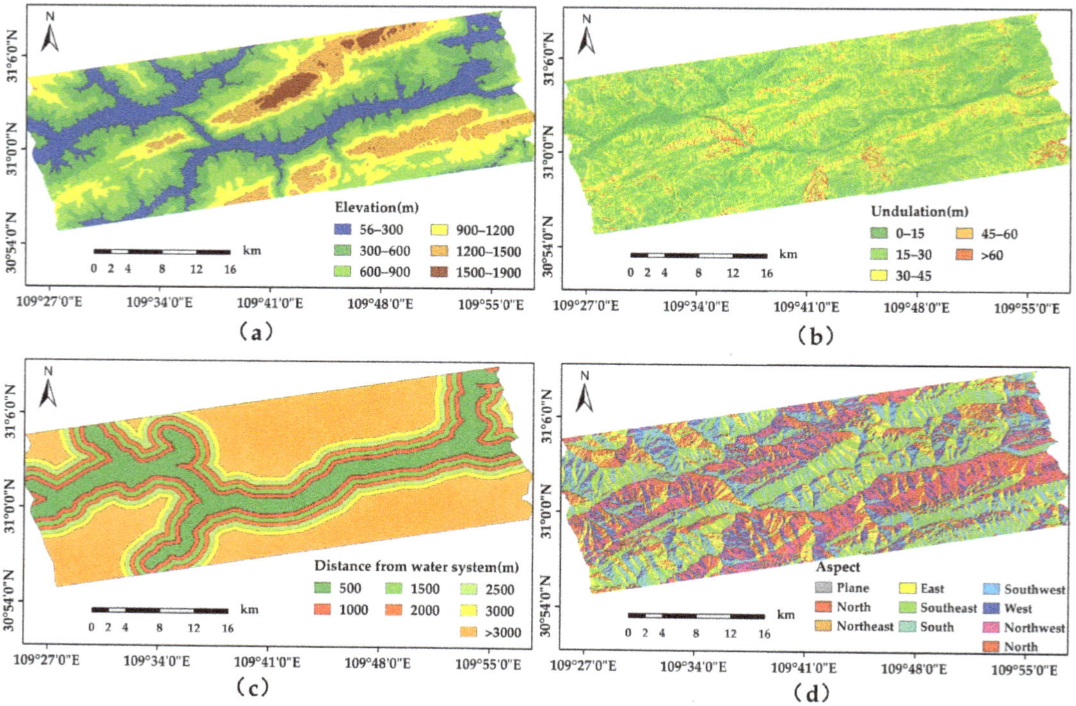

Figure 10. Landslide impact factors. (**a**) Elevation; (**b**) undulation; (**c**) distance from the water system; (**d**) aspect.

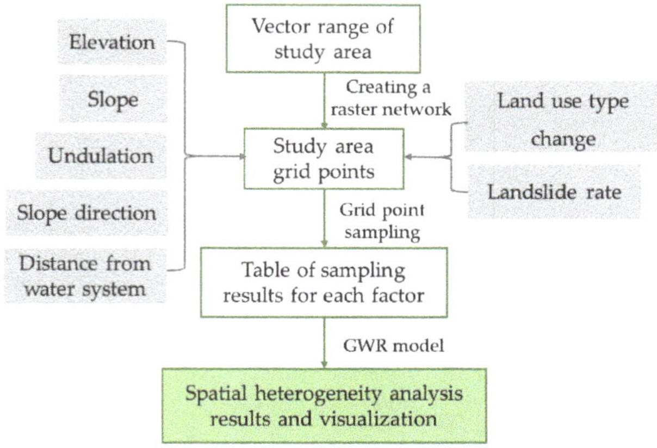

Figure 11. Flow chart of the spatial heterogeneity analysis using the GWR model.

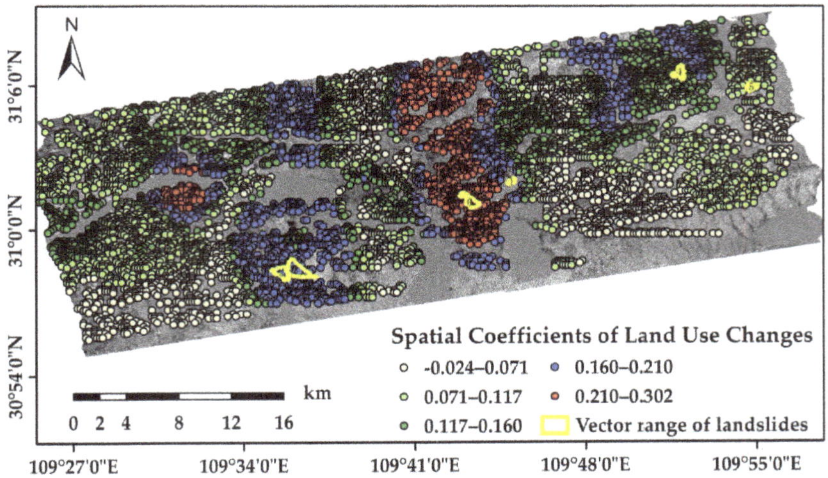

Figure 12. Results of the spatial heterogeneity analysis.

Figure 12 shows the influence of land use change on the landslide rate at different spatial locations, in which the base map is the deformation rate. The yellow irregular area is the landslide area, and the blue and red circles represent the influence of the landslide rate, which is in the range of (0.160, 0.210) and (0.210, 0.302), respectively. It can be seen that the landslide vector range has a high degree of overlap with the blue and red circles. This indicates that in the landslide area, the landslide deformation rate is more affected by land use change than in other areas.

Land use type/change had an effect on landslide deformation rate, but it was not the only factor in landslide occurrence. It is only when the slope meets the geological environment that the effect of land use on landslides becomes apparent. Therefore, not all areas heavily influenced by human activities will have landslide deformation, reflecting the spatial heterogeneity of landslide distribution.

After analyzing the laws of typical landslide areas and the whole study area, it was concluded that land-use change has an important impact on landslide occurrence, which can be used to provide guidance for local land-use planning. However, when land use planning was used to slow down or prevent the occurrence of landslides, it was necessary not only to consider the type of land use and its effect on deformation, but also to judge whether it has the basic conditions for landslides according to the geographical environment. This paper combined the analysis of spatial heterogeneity theory, which can avoid the blind reduction or increase of certain types in planning, resulting in the instability of the local ecological environment.

5. Discussion

5.1. Landslide Rates Monitored by SBAS-InSAR

SBAS-InSAR technology is a time-series observation technology that enables large-scale, high-precision measurements. It can be used to monitor landslides, earthquakes, urban areas, etc., providing a scientific basis for scientific disaster prevention and post-disaster reconstruction [39]. In this work, only 11 images from the ALOS-2 satellite were available between 2014 and 2019. Considering the stability of results, we set the spatial baseline at 300 m and the temporal baseline at 400 days. With these thresholds, 22 interferograms were generated that retained good coherence. By setting the coherence threshold to 0.32, the landslide rates in Fengjie and Wushan counties were obtained, in a range from −9 to 9 cm/year.

The area under study is stable, with only five significant landslides in the region. These landslides develop close to the water and cover a large area, so when they collapse they not only cause local damage but also affect the area upstream. Therefore, it is worth exploring the mechanisms that affect their development.

5.2. Land-Use Classification with the Secondary Classification Method

ALOS-1 and ALOS-2 both have two channels, i.e., HH and HV, which can provide more information than single-polarization, which aids in distinguishing different land use types. Using these two types of SAR data, the land-use results of the region in 2007 and 2017 were obtained using the secondary classification method, with the classification accuracy reaching 94%. The secondary classification method was performed by first using RF and then KMA with the dual-polarization SAR data. This addressed the problem of distortion. In addition, it produced a higher accuracy than the other methods, which only perform single classification, especially in rugged areas.

Thereafter, land-use changes from 2007 to 2017 (Figure 9) were obtained from the land-use information from 2007 and 2017. The types of land-use changes were directly obtained by classifying and then calculating the change types, which avoid the labeling of a large number of change types. The majority of land-use types in the region were in a stable state, and changes between three land types, i.e., forest, cropland, and cultivated vegetation, were our focus.

The combination of RF and KMA exhibited a good performance in the classification of rugged areas, which demonstrates that it can be used to convert complex classification problems into binary classification problems.

5.3. Relationship between Landslide Deformation Rates and Land-Use Changes

Previous studies analyzed the relationship between deformation rates and land-use changes in urban areas, peatlands, and other areas [13–20]. They concluded that land-use changes have an impact on the deformation rates. At present, the majority of research on landslide areas uses historical landslide data to evaluate and analyze the hazards and risks, with the use of real-time landslide monitoring being limited. However, it is necessary to incorporate time-series InSAR technology into the field of landslide monitoring. To the best of our knowledge, this study is the first to analyze the spatial distribution by linking landslide deformation rates from SBAS-InSAR with land-use changes.

First, we analyzed five typical landslide areas. After an overlay analysis of land-use changes and landslide rates, it was found that landslide rates were significantly related to the rates of the change types for a short period of time (with a correlation coefficient of 0.7), but they were not only influenced by the change type. First, no matter whether the change was from forest, cropland, or cultivated vegetation, as long as the change type was to cultivated vegetation, the landslide rate in the corresponding area was greater than the rate of other change types. Second, when the rate of the change type was smaller than that of the before-change type, the landslide rate in the corresponding area reduced to some extent; however, this reduction was still affected by the before-change type.

Thereafter, we used the GWR model to ensure spatial heterogeneity over the whole area. The results showed that slope, aspect, elevation, undulation, land-use changes, distance from the water system, etc., had different effects on the landslide rate in different geographical locations. In the study area, land-use change had a significant effect on the landslide rate, and the affected area coincided with the landslide area monitored by SBAS-InSAR, which further confirmed the conclusion proposed in this paper that land-use change affects landslide distribution.

However, there are still some limitations in this study. First, the lack of dual-polarization SAR data is not conducive to the analysis of long-term land use changes. Second, the combination of random forest and K-means clustering is not suitable for all regions due to algorithmic limitations.

In the future, more and more SAR satellite missions will be successfully launched, providing more polarimetric SAR data for long-term research. Machine learning algorithms with higher accuracy and applicability will also be applied to mountain classification. This will complement the research in this paper.

6. Conclusions

From the perspective of landslide mitigation and prevention, this paper combined polarimetric SAR and InSAR for the first time to complete the study of the spatial distribution of landslide deformation. To solve the problem that dual-polarization SAR images are easily affected by geometric distortion, this paper proposed a secondary classification method that first performed random forest classification and then K-means clustering, and the accuracy was greatly improved. Using spatial analysis methods, the landslide deformation rates and land use data were combined for analysis, and finally the following findings were obtained:

1. Land use classification in rugged areas cannot improve accuracy just by increasing feature data.
2. It was possible to complete the classification by simplifying the multi-classification task into a binary classification task, and the classification accuracy obtained was higher and more reliable than that of only one classification.
3. The land use types strongly influenced by the intensity of human activities can promote landslide deformation, such as cultivated vegetation.
4. The landslide deformation rates were affected not only by the current land use type, but also by the historical land use type.
5. Landslides were influenced by various internal and external factors. It was only when the geological conditions of landslides were met that the effects of land use and land use changes became apparent.

This paper comprehensively analyzed the spatial distribution of landslide deformation from both local and overall perspectives, which can provide a reasonable basis for local land use planning to slow down and inhibit the occurrence of landslides.

Author Contributions: Conceptualization, J.H., Y.Y. and R.G.; methodology, J.H. and Y.Y.; software, J.H.; validation, J.H., Y.Y. and R.G.; formal analysis, J.H. and Y.Y.; investigation, W.Z. and A.G.; resources, J.H., R.G. and W.Z.; data curation, J.H. and Y.Y.; writing—original draft preparation, J.H., Y.Y. and R.G.; writing—review and editing, all authors; visualization, J.H. and Y.Y.; supervision, J.H. and R.G.; project administration, J.H. and R.G.; funding acquisition, J.H. All authors have read and agreed to the published version of the manuscript.

Funding: This work was supported by the National Natural Science Foundation of China under Grant 42030112 and 42201432, and the Science and Technology Innovation Program of Hunan Province under Grant 2022RC2042.

Data Availability Statement: The data presented in this study are available on request from the corresponding author.

Acknowledgments: The ALOS-1 data are made freely available by the European Space Agency and distributed and archived by the Alaska Satellite Facility (https://search.asf.alaska.edu/#/?dataset=ALOS, accessed on 20 June 2022).

Conflicts of Interest: The authors declare no conflict of interest.

References

1. Dai, F.; Lee, C.F.; Ngai, Y.Y. Landslide risk assessment and management: An overview. *Eng. Geol.* **2002**, *64*, 65–87. [CrossRef]
2. Zhao, F.; Meng, X.; Zhang, Y.; Chen, G.; Su, X.; Yue, D. Landslide susceptibility mapping of karakorum highway combined with the application of SBAS-InSAR technology. *Sensors* **2019**, *19*, 2685. [CrossRef]
3. Reichenbach, P.; Busca, C.; Mondini, A.; Rossi, M. The influence of land use change on landslide susceptibility zonation: The Briga catchment test site (Messina, Italy). *Environ. Manag.* **2014**, *54*, 1372–1384. [CrossRef] [PubMed]
4. Huang, Y.; Zhao, L. Review on landslide susceptibility mapping using support vector machines. *Catena* **2018**, *165*, 520–529. [CrossRef]
5. Tang, M.; Xu, K. Study on spatio-temporal evolution law and early warning and prediction of landslide. *J. Rock Mech. Eng.* **2008**, *27*, 1104–1112. [CrossRef]
6. Luo, S.; Sarabandi, K.; Tong, L.; Pierce, L. Landslide prediction using soil moisture estimation derived from polarimetric Radarsat-2 data and SRTM. In *2016 IEEE International Geoscience and Remote Sensing Symposium (IGARSS)*; IEEE: New York, NY, USA, 2016; pp. 5386–5389.
7. Qiang, X.; LU, H.; Weile, L.; Xiujun, D.; Chen, G. Types of Potential Landslide and Corresponding Identification Technologies. *Geomat. Inf. Sci. Wuhan Univ.* **2022**, *47*, 11. [CrossRef]
8. Ferretti, A.; Prati, C.; Rocca, F. Permanent scatterers in SAR interferometry. *IEEE Trans. Geosci. Remote Sens.* **2001**, *39*, 8–20. [CrossRef]
9. Berardino, P.; Fornaro, G.; Lanari, R.; Sansosti, E. A new algorithm for surface deformation monitoring based on small baseline differential SAR interferograms. *IEEE* **2002**, *40*, 2375–2383. [CrossRef]
10. Ferretti, A.; Fumagalli, A.; Novali, F.; Prati, C.; Rocca, F.; Rucci, A. A new algorithm for processing interferometric data-stacks: SqueeSAR. *IEEE Trans. Geosci. Remote Sens.* **2011**, *49*, 3460–3470. [CrossRef]
11. Guo, H.; Yi, B.; Yao, Q.; Gao, P.; Li, H.; Sun, J.; Zhong, C. Identification of Landslides in Mountainous Area with the Combination of SBAS-InSAR and Yolo Model. *Sensors* **2022**, *22*, 6235. [CrossRef]
12. Yao, J.; Yao, X.; Liu, X. Landslide Detection and Mapping Based on SBAS-InSAR and PS-InSAR: A Case Study in Gongjue County, Tibet, China. *Remote Sens.* **2022**, *14*, 4728. [CrossRef]
13. Umarhadi, D.A.; Widyatmanti, W.; Kumar, P.; Yunus, A.P.; Khedher, K.M.; Kharrazi, A.; Avtar, R. Tropical peat subsidence rates are related to decadal LULC changes: Insights from InSAR analysis. *Sci. Total Environ.* **2022**, *816*, 151561. [CrossRef]
14. Wang, F.; Ding, Q.; Zhang, L.; Wang, M.; Wang, Q. Analysis of Land Surface Deformation in Chagan Lake Region Using TCPInSAR. *Sustainability* **2019**, *11*, 5090. [CrossRef]
15. Gebremichael, E.; Sultan, M.; Becker, R.; El Bastawesy, M.; Cherif, O.; Emil, M. Assessing Land Deformation and Sea Encroachment in the Nile Delta: A Radar Interferometric and Inundation Modeling Approach. *J. Geophys. Res. Solid Earth* **2018**, *123*, 3208–3224. [CrossRef]
16. Chaofan, Z.; Huili, G.; Beibei, C.; Jiwei, L.; Mingliang, G.; Feng, Z.; Wenfeng, C.; Yue, L. InSAR Time-Series Analysis of Land Subsidence under Different Land Use Types in the Eastern Beijing Plain, China. *Remote Sens.* **2017**, *9*, 380. [CrossRef]
17. Minderhoud, P.; Coumou, L.; Erban, L.E.; Middelkoop, H.; Stouthamer, E.; Addink, E.A. The relation between land use and subsidence in the Vietnamese Mekong delta. *Sci. Total Environ.* **2018**, *634*, 715–726. [CrossRef]
18. Abidin, H.Z.; Andreas, H.; Gumilar, I.; Fukuda, Y.; Pohan, Y.E.; Deguchi, T. Land subsidence of Jakarta (Indonesia) and its relation with urban development. *Nat. Hazards* **2011**, *59*, 1753–1771. [CrossRef]
19. Han, Y.; Zou, J.; Lu, Z.; Qu, F.; Kang, Y.; Li, J. Ground deformation of wuhan, china, revealed by multi-temporal insar analysis. *Remote Sens.* **2020**, *12*, 3788. [CrossRef]
20. Wang, Z.; Liu, Y.; Zhang, Y.; Liu, Y.; Wang, B.; Zhang, G. Spatially Varying Relationships between Land Subsidence and Urbanization: A Case Study in Wuhan, China. *Remote Sens.* **2022**, *14*, 291. [CrossRef]
21. Maraun, D.; Knevels, R.; Mishra, A.N.; Truhetz, H.; Bevacqua, E.; Proske, H.; Zappa, G.; Brenning, A.; Petschko, H.; Schaffer, A.; et al. A severe landslide event in the Alpine foreland under possible future climate and land-use changes. *Commun. Earth Environ.* **2022**, *3*, 87. [CrossRef]
22. Idham, R.M.; Kure, S.; Januriyadi, N.F.; Farid, M.; Udo, K.; Kazama, S.; Koshimura, S. Future projection of flood inundation considering land-use changes and land subsidence in Jakarta, Indonesia. *Hydrol. Res. Lett.* **2017**, *11*, 99–105. [CrossRef]
23. Zhuo, G.; Dai, K.; Huang, H.; Li, S.; Shi, X.; Feng, Y.; Li, T.; Dong, X.; Deng, J. Evaluating Potential Ground Subsidence Geo-Hazard of Xiamen Xiang'an New Airport on Reclaimed Land by SAR Interferometry. *Sustainability* **2020**, *12*, 6991. [CrossRef]
24. Fell, R.; Corominas, J.; Bonnard, C.; Cascini, L.; Leroi, E.; Savage, W.Z. Guidelines for landslide susceptibility, hazard and risk zoning for land use planning. *Eng. Geol.* **2008**, *102*, 85–98. [CrossRef]

25. Dou, J.; Yamagishi, H.; Pourghasemi, H.R.; Yunus, A.P.; Song, X.; Xu, Y.; Zhu, Z. An integrated artificial neural network model for the landslide susceptibility assessment of Osado Island, Japan. *Nat. Hazards* **2015**, *78*, 1749–1776. [CrossRef]
26. Li, C.; Wang, J.; Wang, L.; Hu, L.; Gong, P. Comparison of Classification Algorithms and Training Sample Sizes in Urban Land Classification with Landsat Thematic Mapper Imagery. *Remote Sens.* **2013**, *6*, 964. [CrossRef]
27. Karalas, K.; Tsagkatakis, G.; Zervakis, M.; Tsakalides, P. Land Classification Using Remotely Sensed Data: Going Multilabel. *IEEE Trans. Geosci. Remote Sens.* **2016**, *54*, 3548–3563. [CrossRef]
28. Merchant, M.A.; Obadia, M.; Brisco, B.; DeVries, B.; Berg, A. Applying Machine Learning and Time-Series Analysis on Sentinel-1A SAR/InSAR for Characterizing Arctic Tundra Hydro-Ecological Conditions. *Remote Sens.* **2022**, *14*, 1123. [CrossRef]
29. Gao, W.; Yang, J.; Ma, W. Land Cover Classification for Polarimetric SAR Images Based on Mixture Models. *Remote Sens.* **2014**, *6*, 3770–3790. [CrossRef]
30. Salehi, M.; Sahebi, M.R.; Maghsoudi, Y. Improving the Accuracy of Urban Land Cover Classification Using Radarsat-2 PolSAR Data. *IEEE J. Sel. Top. Appl. Earth Obs. Remote Sens.* **2014**, *7*, 1394–1401. [CrossRef]
31. Alberga, V. A study of land cover classification using polarimetric SAR parameters. *Int. J. Remote Sens.* **2007**, *28*, 3851–3870. [CrossRef]
32. Qi, Z.; Yeh, G.O.; Xia, L.; Zheng, L. A novel algorithm for land use and land cover classification using RADARSAT-2 polarimetric SAR data. *Remote Sens. Environ.* **2012**, *118*, 21–39. [CrossRef]
33. Breiman, L. Random forests. *Mach. Learn.* **2001**, *45*, 5–32. [CrossRef]
34. Macqueen, J. Some methods for classification and analysis of multivariate observations. In *Proceedings of the Fifth Berkeley Symposium on Mathematical Statistics and Probability, Volume 1: Statistics*; University of California Press: Berkeley, CA, USA, 1967.
35. Fotheringham, A.S.; Brunsdon, C. Local Forms of Spatial Analysis. *Geogr. Anal.* **1999**, *31*, 340–358. [CrossRef]
36. European Space Agency, Sinergise. *Copernicus Global Digital Elevation Model*; OpenTopography: La Jolla, CA, USA, 2021. [CrossRef]
37. Karra, K.; Kontgis, C.; Statman-Weil, Z.; Mazzariello, J.C.; Mathis, M.; Brumby, S.P. Global land use/land cover with Sentinel 2 and deep learning. In Proceedings of the 2021 IEEE International Geoscience and Remote Sensing Symposium IGARSS, Brussels, Belgium, 11–16 July 2021; pp. 4704–4707.
38. Yang, J.; Huang, X. The 30 m annual land cover dataset and its dynamics in China from 1990 to 2019. *Earth Syst. Sci. Data* **2021**, *13*, 3907–3925. [CrossRef]
39. Zhu, J.; Li, Z.; Hu, J. Research progress and methods of InSAR for deformation monitoring. *Acta Geod. Cartogr. Sin.* **2017**, *46*, 1717. [CrossRef]

remote sensing

MDPI

Article

Joint Estimation of Ground Displacement and Atmospheric Model Parameters in Ground-Based Radar

Yan Zhu, Bing Xu *, Zhiwei Li , Jie Li, Jingxin Hou and Wenxiang Mao

School of Geosciences and Info-Physics, Central South University, Changsha 410083, China; yanzhu@csu.edu.cn (Y.Z.); zwli@csu.edu.cn (Z.L.); lijcsu@csu.edu.cn (J.L.); houjingxin@csu.edu.cn (J.H.); wenxiangmao@csu.edu.cn (W.M.)

* Correspondence: xubing@csu.edu.cn

Abstract: Atmospheric delay is the primary error in ground-based synthetic aperture radar (GBSAR). The existing compensation methods include the external meteorological data correction method, the polynomial fitting method, and the persistent scatterers SAR interferometry (PSInSAR) calibration method. Combining the polynomial fitting and the persistent scatterers targets is the most popular method of GBSAR atmospheric delay compensation. However, the displacement component of the coherent target is always ignored in the atmospheric delay compensation, which is unpractical. A joint estimation method of ground displacement and atmospheric model parameters is developed in this paper. The displacement component is determined by the spatial and temporal features of the objects. The atmospheric delay component is regarded as a systematic error represented by a quadratic polynomial related to distance. The result is resolved by the least-square method. Compared to the existing method, the root-mean-square error (RMSE) of the proposed method had a significant improvement in the validation experiment. In the real in situ experiment, the time series obtained by the GBSAR had a similar trend to that acquired by the Global Positioning System (GPS) receiver. It is indicated that the proposed method can lead to a better deformation estimation by taking the deformation component into account in the atmospheric compensation.

Keywords: GBSAR; atmospheric delay; displacement estimation; spatial and temporal features; bridge vibration monitoring

1. Introduction

GBSAR has been applied to monitor the deformation in various scenarios, including dams [1], bridges [2], and slopes [3,4]. The atmospheric delay is composed of tropospheric delay and ionospheric delay in the process of spaceborne interferometry SAR [5]. The spatial–temporal variation feature of tropospheric delay is the biggest challenge in spaceborne InSAR. Atmospheric delay is an important factor affecting GBSAR deformation monitoring, as with spaceborne SAR [6]. Up to now, there are primarily three methods for the atmospheric delay phase compensation: the correction method by external meteorological data [7], the polynomial fitting method [8–10], and the correction method by time-series InSAR [11,12].

The observation instrument and the targets are located under the troposphere, which is the reason that the atmospheric delay contains only tropospheric delay in the ground-based InSAR. The correction method by external meteorological data is the most direct. However, there are unavoidable observation errors in external meteorological data. The sampling frequency of GBSAR is often inconsistent with the sampling frequency of meteorological data. Also, it is difficult to install meteorological observation instruments in the observation area. Therefore, the correction result by this method has uncertainty.

The polynomial fitting method is a common method. Under the assumption of spatial homogeneity for the atmosphere in the small scenarios, the atmospheric phase screen is fitted by a polynomial function. A function of the tropospheric delay phase is established for the interferometric phase on the stable point targets, and the atmospheric parameters are obtained by polynomial fitting. Compared to the correction method by external meteorological data, this method prevents the correction results from external errors and reduces uncertainty.

The correction method by time-series InSAR builds the relationship between the time-series interferometric phase and deformation phase, and obtains the linear deformation velocity by the least-square (LS) method. Then, the non-linear deformation contribution and the atmospheric phase contribution are separated from the residual phase by filtering, based on their different inherent spatio-temporal features in the frequency domain. The external meteorological data are unnecessary for this method. It depends on practical experience to choose the filtering algorithm and determine the window size, and it is assumed that the magnitude of deformation is significantly greater than that of atmospheric delay. This is inappropriate for high-frequency deformation monitoring by GBSAR.

So far, it is popular to compensate for the atmospheric delay phase by combining the polynomial fitting method and the correction method by time-series InSAR, which breaks through the limitation of external meteorological data and reduces the practical experiences. Most of the existing research assumes that the coherent point targets hold still and the interferometric phase consists of only atmospheric delay, which is not rigorous. To overcome this shortcoming, a joint estimation method of ground displacement and atmospheric model parameters is proposed in this paper. In Section 2, the joint estimation method is described in detail. This method establishes the function model and stomatic model between the interferometric phase and the deformation phase and atmospheric model parameters, and obtains the parameters by the LS method. In Section 3, the proposed method is validated. The estimation results of the proposed method are compared with other methods. The proposed method is applied to an in situ experiment on the Sanchaji Bridge in Changsha in Section 4. In Section 5, the necessity of the additional systematic parameters is discussed. The results obtained by different methods in the first experiment are compared and discussed, and the time series acquired by GBSAR and the GPS are also compared. Finally, the conclusion is presented in Section 6.

2. Method Development for Joint Estimation of Ground Displacement and Atmospheric Model Parameters

2.1. Phase Model of Ground-Based Radar

GBSAR has three scanning modes: linear scanning mode, arc scanning mode, and rotation scanning mode [6]. The equipment obtains two acquisitions, φ_1 and φ_2, respectively at the moment t_1 and t_2 for a target on the ground. The single acquisition consists of the contributions of the geometric distance phase and the scattering phase [13]:

$$\varphi_1 = 2\frac{2\pi}{\lambda}R + \varphi_{scatt-1} \tag{1}$$

$$\varphi_2 = 2\frac{2\pi}{\lambda}(R + \Delta R) + \varphi_{scatt-2} \tag{2}$$

where R is the geometric distance between the GBSAR and the target, ΔR is the path difference during the acquisitions, and $\varphi_{scatt-1}$ and $\varphi_{scatt-2}$ are the contributions of the scattering phase. It is necessary to co-register the master and the slave images before interferometry because of the different incident angles during the two acquisitions. In this paper, we fix the scanning angle to monitor an area continuously, so it is unnecessary to do co-registration. The interferometric phase is expressed as:

$$\Delta\varphi = -\frac{4\pi}{\lambda}\Delta R + (\varphi_{scatt-1} - \varphi_{scatt-2}) + 2n\cdot\pi \quad n = 0, \pm1, \pm2\cdots \tag{3}$$

where n is the integer ambiguity.

The path difference results from the atmospheric delay, the displacement in the line-of-sight (LOS) direction, the geometric phase error, and the noise. Because of the fixed scanning angle, the geometric phase error can be ignored in this paper. Here, the interferometric phase is expressed as:

$$\Delta\varphi = \varphi_{defo} + (\varphi_{atm,2} - \varphi_{atm,1}) + \varphi_{noise} + 2n \cdot \pi \tag{4}$$

where φ_{defo} is the deformation phase during the different acquisitions in the LOS direction, $\varphi_{atm,2} - \varphi_{atm,1}$ is the difference between the atmospheric delay phases, and φ_{noise} is the noise phase composed of different scattering phases and noise contribution and the integer phase.

2.2. Atmospheric Phase Modeling for Ground-Based Radar

The propagation of microwaves in the atmosphere will be affected by the refraction of the atmosphere. Its speed is slower than that in the vacuum due to the index of refraction. The index of refraction is defined as $n = c_0/c$, where c_0 is the speed of the electromagnetic wave in a vacuum and c is the speed in the atmosphere. The relation between the refractivity index N and the index of refraction n is expressed as:

$$N = (n-1) \times 10^6 \tag{5}$$

The atmospheric refractive index is a million times the difference between the index of refraction and 1. The observation instrument and the targets are located under the troposphere. The refractivity index in the troposphere is a function of temperature T (in Kelvin), relative humidity H (in percentage), and pressure P (in millibars). The atmospheric delay is composed of contributions of atmospheric dry delay and wet delay, which is expressed as [14,15]:

$$\begin{aligned} N &= N(T,H,P) \\ &= N_{dry} + N_{wet} \\ &= \tfrac{77.6}{T} p_d + \left(77.6 + \tfrac{3.73\times10^5}{T}\right)\tfrac{e}{T} \end{aligned} \tag{6}$$

where p_d is the partial pressure of dry gases (in millibars), e is the partial pressure of water vapor in millibars, and the relation between them is $P = p_d + e$. The partial pressure of water vapor is the product of relative humidity H and standard saturation vapor pressure e_s. There are many methods to calculate standard saturation vapor pressure, and the Magnus-Tetens function [16] is applied here:

$$e = He_s = H \cdot 6.11 exp\left[\frac{17.27(T-237.16)}{T-35.86}\right] \tag{7}$$

There are two meteorological devices installed at the approximate height on the ground. Two data sets are acquired respectively from 0:00 h on 28 September 2022 to 14:40 h on 29 September 2022, and from 0:00 h on 15 October 2022 to 13:56 h on 16 October 2022. The dry and wet components of the refractivity index are shown in Figures 1 and 2. It is obvious that the magnitude of N_{dry} is greater than that of N_{wet}. N_{dry} fluctuates more gently than N_{wet} in the time domain. It is assumed that N is more sensitive to N_{wet}.

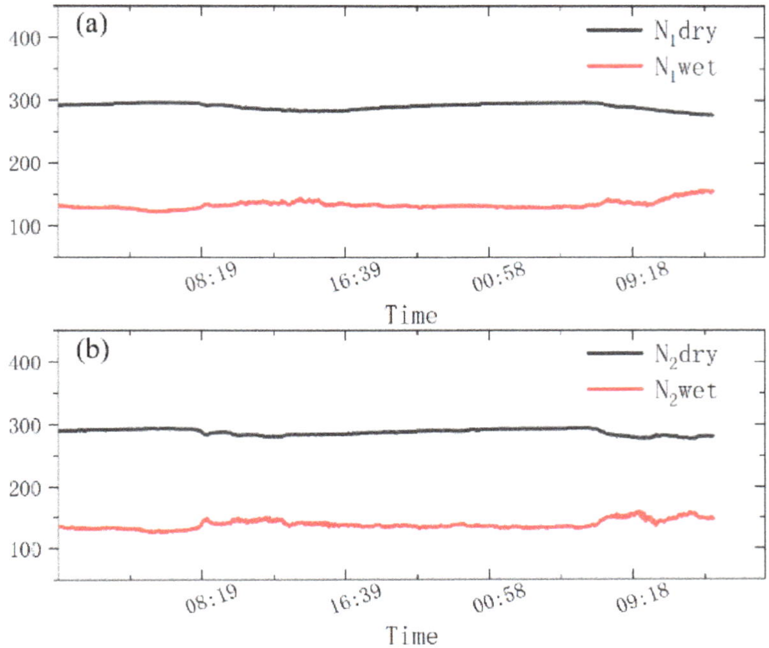

Figure 1. The dry and wet components of the refractivity index from 0:00 h on 28 September 2022 to 14:40 h on 29 September 2022. (**a**) The refractivity index of P_1. (**b**) The refractivity index of P_2.

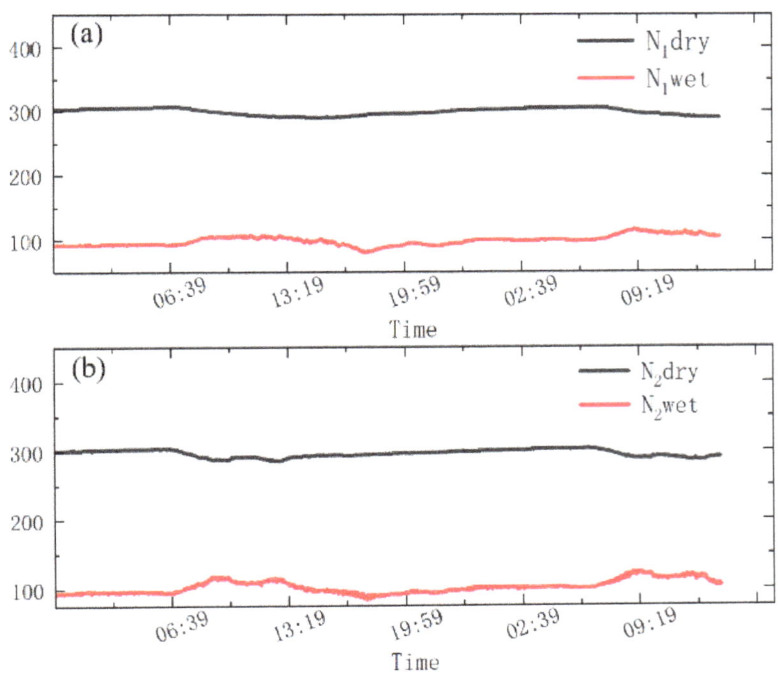

Figure 2. The dry and wet components of the refractivity index from 0:00 h on 15 October 2022 to 13:56 h on 16 October 2022. (**a**) The refractivity index of P_1. (**b**) The refractivity index of P_2.

The atmospheric phase contribution at one acquisition is the function of the refractivity index:

$$\varphi_{atm,p}(t) = 10^{-6}.\frac{4\pi}{\lambda}\int_{0}^{L} N(T,H,P)dl \tag{8}$$

where L is the distance between the GBSAR and the target.

It is demonstrated that the atmospheric phase has spatial homogeneity at a short distance and in a small area [1], so the atmosphere has a similar impact on the targets at the same distance. Therefore, (8) is adapted to:

$$\varphi_{atm,p}(t) = 10^{-6}.\frac{4\pi}{\lambda}\cdot l_p \cdot N(t) \tag{9}$$

The atmospheric delay component in the interferometric phase between time t_1 and t_2 on the target P at the distance l_p is expressed as:

$$\begin{aligned}\Delta\varphi_{atm,p}(t_1,t_2) &= \varphi_{atm,p}(t_2) - \varphi_{atm,p}(t_1) \\ &= 10^{-6}.\tfrac{4\pi}{\lambda}\cdot l_p\cdot(N(t_2) - N(t_1)) \\ &= 10^{-6}.\tfrac{4\pi}{\lambda}\cdot l_p\cdot\Delta N\end{aligned} \tag{10}$$

The atmospheric refractivity index is in inverse proportion to height. Usually, the horizontal variations of N can be neglected, and the troposphere can be regarded as a quasi-homogeneous spherically layered medium [17]. Therefore, the primary variation of N is vertical, and N increases as the height is decreased, which means that the tropospheric delay is greater near the ground surface. The tropospheric-delay relationship can be modeled using an exponential function [18] as:

$$N = N_S exp\left(-\frac{h}{H}\right) \tag{11}$$

where N_S is the average value of refractivity at the Earth's surface, H is the height scale of the standard atmosphere, and h is the height above the Earth's surface. For convenience, the refractivity index can be approximated by the first two terms of the Taylor series at $h = 0$:

$$N = a_0 + a_1 h \tag{12}$$

We can replace the refractivity index N in Equation (10) with Equation (12); h is the height difference between the GBSAR and a target. The relationship between the distance l in the LOS direction and the height difference h can be expressed as $h = l\sin\theta$, where θ is the angle between the LOS and the horizontal line:

$$\begin{aligned}\varphi_{atm,p}(t) &= 10^{-6}.\tfrac{4\pi}{\lambda}\int_{0}^{L}(a_0(t) + a_1(t)h)dl \\ &= 10^{-6}.\tfrac{4\pi}{\lambda}\int_{0}^{L}(a_0(t) + a_1(t)l\sin\theta)dl \\ &= 10^{-6}.\tfrac{4\pi}{\lambda}\cdot\left(a_0(t)\cdot l + \tfrac{1}{2}a_1(t)\sin\theta l^2\right)\end{aligned} \tag{13}$$

Let

$$a = 10^{-6}\cdot a_0(t) \tag{14}$$

$$b = 10^{-6}.\frac{1}{2}a_1(t)\sin\theta \tag{15}$$

The observation phase consists of the deformation phase, atmospheric delay phase, and noise:

$$\varphi = \varphi_{defo} + \frac{4\pi}{\lambda}\left(al_p + bl_p^2\right) + \varphi_{noise} \tag{16}$$

2.3. Function and Stochastic Model for Joint Estimation of Displacement and Atmosphere

On the assumption of atmospheric spatial homogeneity at a short distance and in a small area, the function and stochastic mode for joint estimation of displacement and atmospheric parameters on the coherent targets are established.

Using the dispersion index to select permanent scatterers, which was proposed by Ferretti [19], is one of the most popular methods up to now. The dispersion index D_A is a measure of phase stability:

$$D_A = \frac{\sigma_A}{\mu_A} \tag{17}$$

where μ_A and σ_A are the mean and the standard deviation of the amplitude. Small values of D_A are good estimates of the phase dispersion, which means that there is a domain scatterer in the pixel.

Generally, the deformation of a target is a function of time:

$$\varphi_{defo} = f(t|a_r) \tag{18}$$

where t is the acquisition moment, and $a_r(r = 1,2,3\ldots,\tau)$ stands for τ coefficients in the deformation model. In this paper, the periodic model is selected to simulate the deformation phase:

$$\varphi_{defo} = \frac{4\pi}{\lambda}(c_1 cos2\pi t + c_2 sin2\pi t) \tag{19}$$

where c_1 and c_2 are the coefficients. The function can be expressed in the matrix form, $\varphi_{defo} = \boldsymbol{qv}$, where $\boldsymbol{q}$ is the coefficient vector, and $\boldsymbol{v}$ represents the unknown parameters:

$$\boldsymbol{q} = [cos2\pi t, sin2\pi t] \tag{20}$$

$$\boldsymbol{v} = [c_1, c_2]^T \tag{21}$$

For the kth interferogram, its master and slave images are acquired at t_m and t_s. The deformation phase at the point P can be derived as:

$$\varphi^P_{defo,k} = \frac{4\pi}{\lambda}(\boldsymbol{q_m} - \boldsymbol{q_s})\boldsymbol{v^P} \tag{22}$$

Atmospheric delay is spatially homogeneous but independent at every acquisition. The atmospheric phase can be regarded as a systematical error in the time series. Therefore, the atmospheric phase at one acquisition can be expressed as a quadratic polynomial:

$$\varphi^P_{atm} = \frac{4\pi}{\lambda}\left(al^P + bl^{P2}\right) \tag{23}$$

Let

$$\boldsymbol{m} = \left[l^P, l^{P2}\right] \tag{24}$$

$$\boldsymbol{r} = [a, b]^T \tag{25}$$

where $\boldsymbol{m}$ is the coefficient matrix, and $\boldsymbol{r}$ is the unknown polynomial parameter matrix. Then, Equation (23) is adapted to:

$$\varphi^P_{atm} = \frac{4\pi}{\lambda}\boldsymbol{m^P r} \tag{26}$$

The atmospheric delay difference $\Delta\varphi^P_{atm,k}$ at the target P can be derived as:

$$\Delta\varphi^P_{atm,k} = \frac{4\pi}{\lambda}\boldsymbol{m^P}(\boldsymbol{r_m} - \boldsymbol{r_s}) \tag{27}$$

There are S PS targets in the scenario, $p_1, p_2, \cdots, p_S$ with the distance $l_1, l_2, \cdots, l_S$ from the GBSAR, and Q acquisitions are captured. The triangulation network is recommended to combine the acquisitions to obtain M interferometric phase, which coubld be referred to Appendix A. The phase connects to the subsequent two phases in chronological order just like Figure A1. Then, $M \times S$ observation equations are derived for all the targets:

$$\boldsymbol{\Phi} = \boldsymbol{AX} + \boldsymbol{BY} + \boldsymbol{\varepsilon} \tag{28}$$

where $\boldsymbol{\Phi}$ is the interferometric phase vector; $\boldsymbol{A}$ is the coefficient matrix for the unknown parameters vector of the deformation model; $\boldsymbol{X}$ is the unknown parameters vector including $\boldsymbol{v}$; $\boldsymbol{B}$ is the coefficient matrix of the additional systematic parameters vector; $\boldsymbol{Y}$ is the unknown additional systematic parameters vector including $\boldsymbol{r}$; $\boldsymbol{\varepsilon}$ is the noise vector consisting of different scattering phases and noise contributions.

The stochastic model is expressed as:

$$\boldsymbol{D} = \sigma_0^2 \boldsymbol{P}^{-1} \tag{29}$$

where $\boldsymbol{D}$ is the covariance matrix, σ_0^2 is the variance of unit weight, and $\boldsymbol{P}$ is the weight matrix of the observations which is derived from the coherence value generally. The variance of unit weight is expressed as:

$$\sigma_0^2 = \frac{\boldsymbol{V}^T \boldsymbol{P} \boldsymbol{V}}{n - t} \tag{30}$$

where $\boldsymbol{V}$ is the error vector, which is the difference between the observed interferometric phase vector and the estimated interferometric phase vector. $\boldsymbol{V}$ is derived from:

$$\boldsymbol{V} = \boldsymbol{\Phi} - \left(\boldsymbol{A}\widehat{\boldsymbol{X}} + \boldsymbol{B}\widehat{\boldsymbol{Y}} \right) \tag{31}$$

2.4. Joint Estimation of Ground Displacement and Atmospheric Model Parameters

According to the principle of LS, we get:

$$\begin{bmatrix} \boldsymbol{A}^T\boldsymbol{PA} & \boldsymbol{A}^T\boldsymbol{PB} \\ \boldsymbol{B}^T\boldsymbol{PA} & \boldsymbol{B}^T\boldsymbol{PB} \end{bmatrix} \begin{bmatrix} \widehat{\boldsymbol{X}} \\ \widehat{\boldsymbol{Y}} \end{bmatrix} = \begin{bmatrix} \boldsymbol{A}^T\boldsymbol{Pf} \\ \boldsymbol{B}^T\boldsymbol{Pf} \end{bmatrix} \tag{32}$$

where

$$-\boldsymbol{f} = \boldsymbol{AX}^0 + \boldsymbol{BY}^0 - \boldsymbol{\Phi} \tag{33}$$

In general, the approximate value of $\boldsymbol{X}^0$ and $\boldsymbol{Y}^0$ can be set as a zero vector.

Let $\boldsymbol{N}_{XX} = \boldsymbol{A}^T\boldsymbol{PA}, \boldsymbol{N}_{XY} = \boldsymbol{A}^T\boldsymbol{PB}, \boldsymbol{N}_{YX} = \boldsymbol{B}^T\boldsymbol{PA}, \boldsymbol{N}_{YY} = \boldsymbol{B}^T\boldsymbol{PB}, = \boldsymbol{N}_{YY} - \boldsymbol{N}_{YX}\boldsymbol{N}_{XX}^{-1}\boldsymbol{N}_{XY}$, then we get the solution:

$$\begin{bmatrix} \widehat{\boldsymbol{X}} \\ \widehat{\boldsymbol{Y}} \end{bmatrix} = \begin{bmatrix} \boldsymbol{N}_{XX}^{-1} + \boldsymbol{N}_{XX}^{-1}\boldsymbol{N}_{XY}\boldsymbol{J}^{-1}\boldsymbol{N}_{YX}\boldsymbol{N}_{XX}^{-1} & -\boldsymbol{N}_{XX}^{-1}\boldsymbol{N}_{XY}\boldsymbol{J}^{-1} \\ -\boldsymbol{J}^{-1}\boldsymbol{N}_{YX}\boldsymbol{N}_{XX}^{-1} & \boldsymbol{J}^{-1} \end{bmatrix} \begin{bmatrix} \boldsymbol{A}^T\boldsymbol{Pf} \\ \boldsymbol{B}^T\boldsymbol{Pf} \end{bmatrix} \tag{34}$$

So far, the estimation of displacement and atmospheric model parameters can be realized.

It should be noted that the weight matrix of the observations $\boldsymbol{P}$ can be determined by the coherence, and the coherence value $|\widehat{\gamma}|$ can be derived by:

$$|\widehat{\gamma}| = \left| \frac{\sum_{i=1}^{j} Z_{i,m} \cdot Z_{i,s}^*}{\sqrt{\sum_{i=1}^{j} |Z_{i,m}| \cdot \sum_{i=1}^{j} |Z_{i,s}|}} \right| \tag{35}$$

where $Z_{i,m}$ and $Z_{i,s}$ are the complex values of two different SAR images at the ith pixel, * stands for complex conjugate multiplication, and j is the window size to estimate the coherence.

3. Validation of the Developed Method

To validate the above algorithm, an in situ experiment was implemented near a hill behind the Zhongda Group in the Yuelu District in Changsha, China. Four corner reflectors were installed in the scenario. As Figure 3 shows, two of them were installed on the top of an office building, and the others were installed on the hill. At the same time, a meteorological device was installed on the office building and another one was installed around the corner reflectors on the hill, which collected meteorological data, including temperature, pressure, and relative humidity.

Figure 3. The spatial location of the four reflectors. (**a**) the overall observation view, (**b**) the position of the four reflectors.

The ground-based radar is a real aperture radar that was developed by the Zhongda Group. The data set was collected between 18:09:01 h on 15 October and 14:21:17 h on 16 October. We collected a frame once in 0.108 s and acquired 432,284 frames in total. The bandwidth was 600 Hz, the sampling rate was 24.3 GHz, and the wavelength was 12.3 mm. The distances were respectively 62.19 m, 69.00 m, 328.79 m, and 358.52 m for the four reflectors P_1, P_2, P_3, and P_4. The temperature at the top of the building and on the slope was different. Therefore, the four reflectors were separated at different sites and different distances.

The atmospheric delay time series of the four reflectors are shown in Figure 4 based on the collected meteorological data. The first meteorological device provided data for P_1 and P_2, and the collecting time covered that of the radar. The second device provided data for P_3 and P_4, but the collecting time did not cover that of the radar completely.

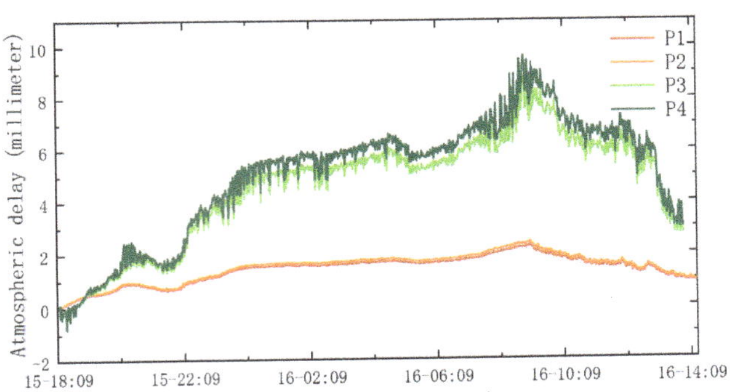

Figure 4. The atmospheric delay for the four reflectors P_1, P_2, P_3, and P_4 calculated from the meteorological data.

The proposed algorithm was applied to the time series data of the four reflectors acquired by the ground-based radar. The results are shown in Figure 5, where the blue line is the original observed displacement data, the red line is the atmospheric delay, the yellow line is the displacement fitting line, and the dark line represents the difference value between the original observed displacement data and the atmospheric delay. The mean value, standard deviation (SD), and the RMSE of every time series of the four reflectors are shown in Table 1.

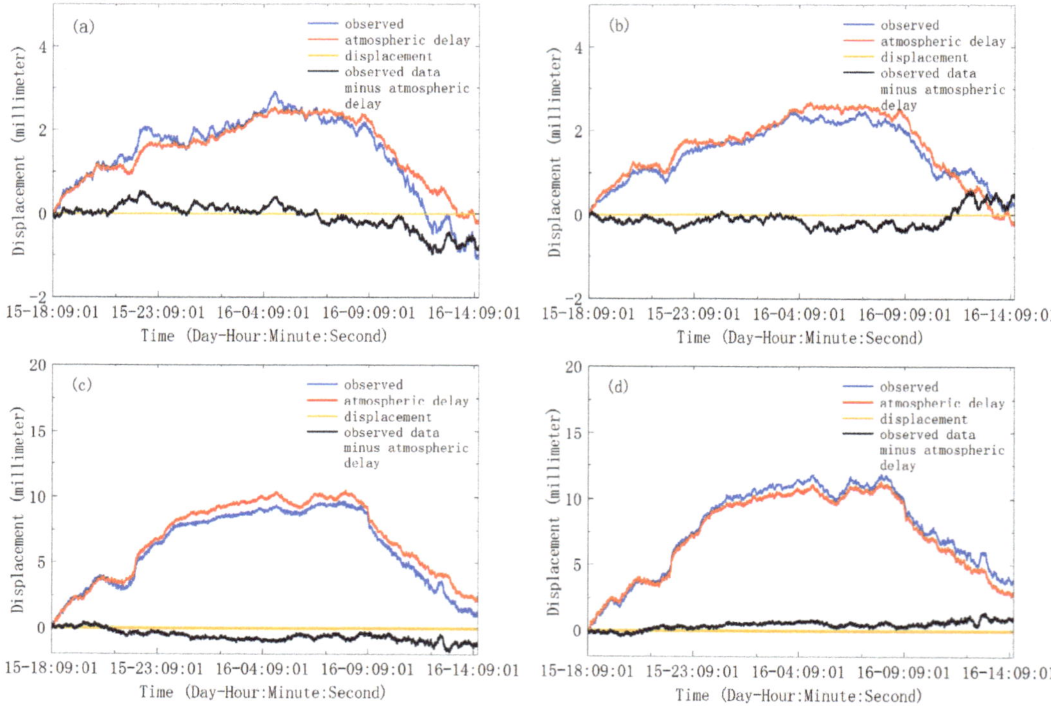

Figure 5. The displacement time series obtained by the proposed method for the four reflectors P_1, P_2, P_3, and P_4 respectively in (**a**–**d**). The blue line is the original observed displacement data, the red line is the atmospheric delay, the yellow line is the displacement fitting line, and the dark line represents the difference between the original observed displacement data and the atmospheric delay.

Table 1. The mean value, SD, and RMSE of the time series of the four reflectors. (All values in the table are expressed in millimeters).

	P_1	P_2	P_3	P_4
Mean	−0.07	−0.11	−0.61	0.42
SD	0.32	0.21	0.40	0.34
RMSE	0.33	0.24	0.73	0.54

4. Application of the Developed Method for Monitoring Bridge Displacement

Another experimental observation of the long-span Sanchaji Bridge, which is located in northern Changsha and connects the Yuelu District with the Kaifu District, was implemented. In this experiment, the GAMMA Portable Radar Interferometer II (GPRI-II), which was developed by GAMMA Remote Sensing and Consulting AG, was deployed under the bridge on its western upstream sides at a sampling frequency of 2000 Hz. To validate the monitoring capability of GPRI-II, a GPS receiver developed by Trimble Inc at a sampling frequency of 50 Hz was mounted on the balustrade to observe the vibration of the bridge synchronously. The real-time kinematic (RTK) solution mode was applied to monitor the vibration. The basic parameters of the GPRI-II are shown in Table 2.

Table 2. The basic parameters of the GPRI-II.

Parameter	Value
Radar type	Frequency-modulated continuous wave (FMCW)
Antenna type	Slotted waveguide
Frequency range	17.1–17.3 GHz (Ku-band)
Bandwidth	200 MHz
Frequency accuracy	<100 Hz
Maximum sampling frequency	4000 Hz
Measurement range	50–10,000 m
Azimuth beamwidth	0.385 deg (−3 dB)
Elevation beamwidth	35 deg (−3 dB)
Range sample spacing	0.75 m
Range resolution	0.95 m (−3 dB)
Azimuth resolution	6.8 m at 1 km (−3 dB)
Displacement accuracy	<1 mm at 1 km
Time reference	UTC

The data were collected in the fixed scanning mode without angular rotation. The data at every sample were called a frame and recorded in a row in Figure 6c, and the time series of every pixel was arranged in a column. The interferometric phase starting at 10:31:07 h and lasting 45 s are shown in Figure 6c. As illustrated in Figure 7, the Sanchaji Bridge is a suspension bridge. The GPS receiver was installed in the middle of the bridge, and the GPRI-II was placed on the west bank.

Figure 6. (**a**) Monitoring the bridge vibration by GPRI-II. (**b**) Mounting the GPS receiver on the bridge balustrade. (**c**) The interferometric result acquired at 10:31:07 h.

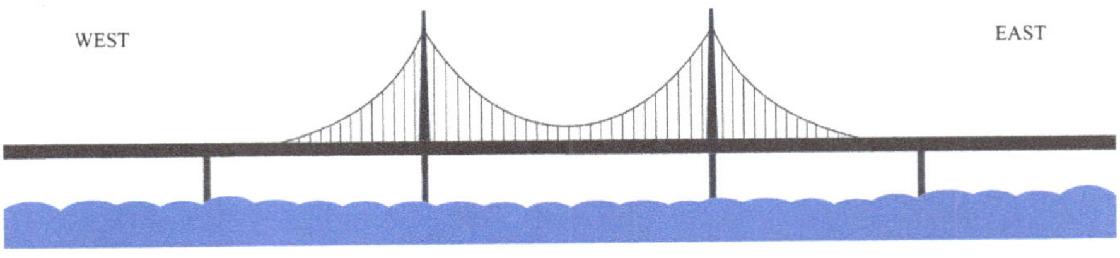

Figure 7. Sketch of the Sanchaji Bridge.

According to geometry, the 935th pixel from left to right in the frame was linked to the GPS receiver in space. We employed the data recorded by the GPS receiver installed on the top of GPRI-II, as well as the distance of every pixel recorded by the GBSAR, and measured the vertical height between the bridge and the GBSAR. Then, the geographic coordinates of every pixel in the images can be solved. The pixels around it, whose index was 926, 927, 928, 929, 930, 931, 933, 934, 936, 939, 940, 941, 942, 943, were selected as the permanent scatterers with D_A less than 0.25. The function model was established for these point targets. These 15 pixels join together with each other to form a segment of the bridge in space. Unlike the prior experiment, the deformation model was updated considering the spatial feature of displacement:

$$\varphi_{defo} = \frac{4\pi}{\lambda}(c_1 cos2\pi t + c_2 sin2\pi t) \times c_3 x \tag{36}$$

where x is the coordinate in space.

The solution at the 935th pixel is shown in Figure 8, where the blue line represents the observed vibration of the bridge, the red line represents the atmospheric delay, the yellow line represents the vibration fitting line, and the dark line represents the difference value between the original observed displacement data and the atmospheric delay. It is noted that the vibration is transformed from the LOS to the vertical direction.

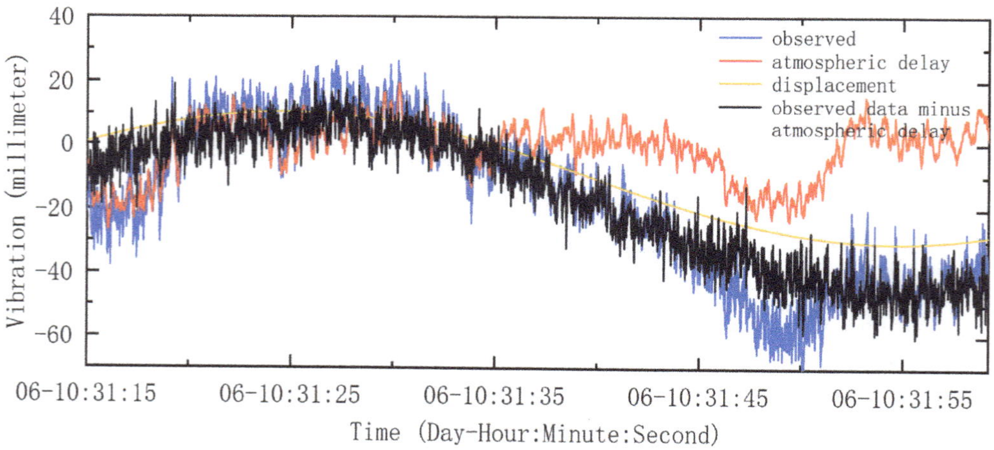

Figure 8. The solution at the 935th pixel. The blue line represents the observed vibration of the bridge, the red line represents the atmospheric delay, the yellow line represents the vibration fitting line, and the dark line represents the difference value between the original observed displacement data and the atmospheric delay.

The vibration of the 15 pixels acquired by the GBSAR is shown in Figure 9. As in Figure 8, the vibration is the difference between the observed data and the estimated atmospheric delay. Because the range spacing is 0.75 m, the 15 pixels are spread at the corresponding distances. The amplitude of the vibration time series ranged from −60 mm to 20 mm relative to the starting time. There were some pixels masked among the samples because of their high D_A values. However, from Figure 9, we can see this segment of the bridge had a feature from up to down in general during observation time.

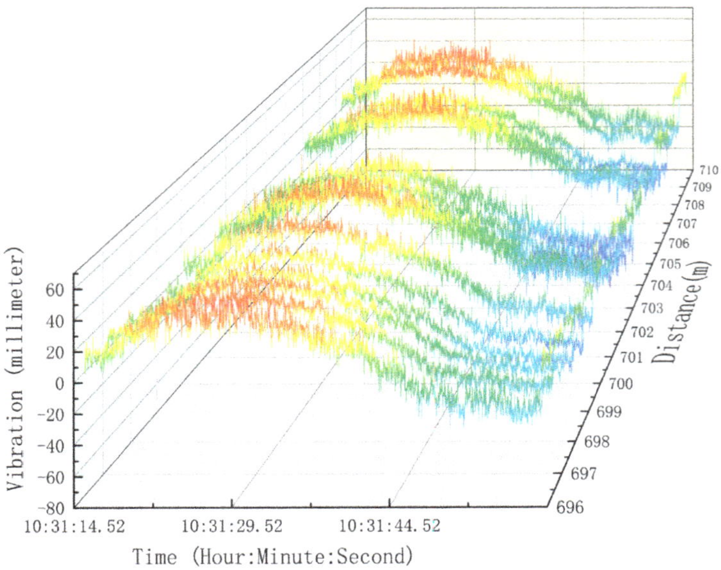

Figure 9. The vibration of the 15 pixels acquired by the GBSAR.

5. Discussion

5.1. Significance of Incorporating the System Parameters

The atmospheric component in the function model is regarded as a systematic error. A quadratic polynomial with two coefficients describes the atmospheric delay. The two coefficients are called systematic parameters in the function model and are solved by the LS method. The additional system parameters change the original model, i.e., $\boldsymbol{\Phi} = \boldsymbol{AX} + \boldsymbol{\varepsilon}$. Therefore, we need to consider whether these additional parameters are necessary or not. Here, it is necessary to do significance testing for the systematic parameters. If the testing result is significant, the parameters should be reserved.

The null and alternate hypotheses are stated: H_0: $\widehat{\boldsymbol{Y}} = 0$, H_1: $\widehat{\boldsymbol{Y}} \neq 0$; the F test statistic formula is given below:

$$F = \frac{\widehat{\boldsymbol{Y}}^T \boldsymbol{J}^{-1} \widehat{\boldsymbol{Y}} / m}{\boldsymbol{V}^T \boldsymbol{PV} / n-t} = \widehat{\boldsymbol{Y}}^T \boldsymbol{J}^{-1} \widehat{\boldsymbol{Y}} / \widehat{\delta}_0^2 m \sim F(m, n-t) \tag{37}$$

where $\widehat{\boldsymbol{Y}}$ is the solved value of the system parameters vector, $\boldsymbol{J}$ is the variance–covariance matrix of the system parameters vector, $\boldsymbol{V}$ is the error vector that is the difference between the observed value and the estimated value, $\boldsymbol{P}$ is the weighting matrix of the observed vector that is expressed by the coherence of the master and the slave images, $\widehat{\delta}_0^2$ is the variance of unit weight, m is the first degree of freedom, $n-t$ is the second degree of freedom, m is the rank of $\boldsymbol{B}$, n is the number of the observed values, and t is the number of systematic parameters.

Given a significance level α, if

$$F > F_{1-\alpha}(m, n-t) \tag{38}$$

the null hypothesis is rejected.

As for the first experiment, at the significance level $\alpha = 0.05$, the first degree of freedom is 4324, and the second degree of freedom is 17,276, then $F_{0.95}(4324, 17276) = 1.0401$. $F = 4.9550 > 1.0401$. Therefore, the null hypothesis is rejected, and the alternate is accepted.

For the second experiment, at the significance level $\alpha = 0.05$, the first degree of freedom is 4500, the second degree of freedom is 67,425, and $F_{0.95}(4500, 67425) = 1.0361$. $F = 3.0990 > 1.0361$. Thus, the null hypothesis is rejected, and the alternate is accepted.

Therefore, we believe that the system parameters should be considered in the function model. It is indicated that the original function model which only contains the unknown deformation parameters is inappropriate.

On the other hand, according to the meteorological data, the atmospheric disturbance caused a measuring error of approximately 10 mm about 330 m away in Figure 4. We can see that the humidity presents the strongest fluctuations in one day compared to the pressure and the temperature in Figure 10, and the humidity is the primary reason for the atmospheric disturbance which results in the variation of the refractive index. This is the practical reason for the additional systematic parameters in the function model.

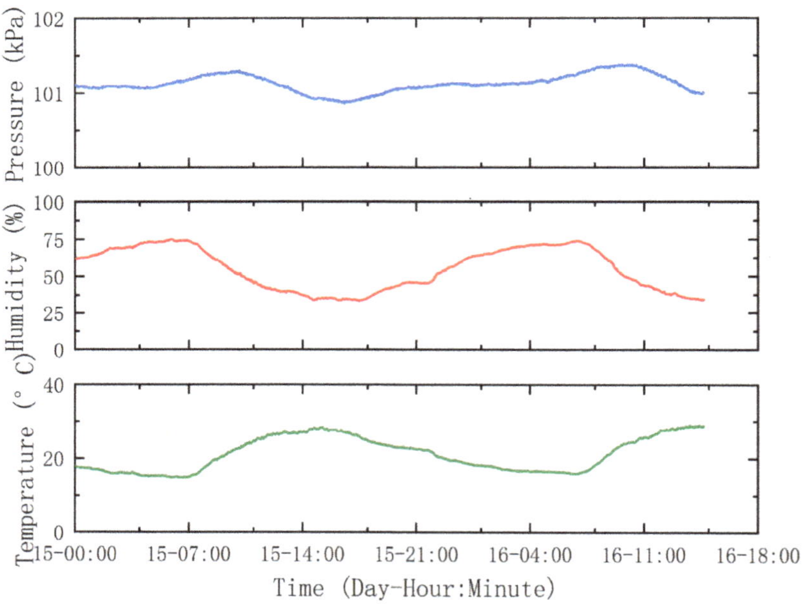

Figure 10. The time series of pressure, humidity, and temperature at a meteorological data collector from 15 October 2022 to 16 October 2022.

5.2. Comparisons of Atmospheric Delay Calculated by Different Methods

The atmospheric delay was calculated by the meteorological data, polynomial fitting, and the proposed methods. Before the comparison, the atmospheric delay calculated based on the meteorological data was interpolated because of its lower sampling rate. As with the polynomial fitting method, the nearest and the farthest reflectors were chosen as the stable reference points. The four reflectors P_1, P_2, P_3, and P_4 are located at distances of 65.19, 69.00, 328.79, and 358.52 m.

The time series obtained by the meteorological data are shown in Figure 11. The red line represents the atmospheric delay. We can see that the atmospheric delay is proportional to the range distance. As mentioned before, the wet partial component of tropospheric delay is the primary component. Therefore, the atmospheric delay climbed to the summit in the morning. We can see that the displacement after the atmospheric compensation of P_1 and P_2 is smaller than that of P_3 and P_4, as with the observed displacement. Because the reflectors stood still during the observation, the displacement of the targets should have been zero or around zero in a tiny interval. It seems that the external meteorological data cannot satisfy the accuracy requirements.

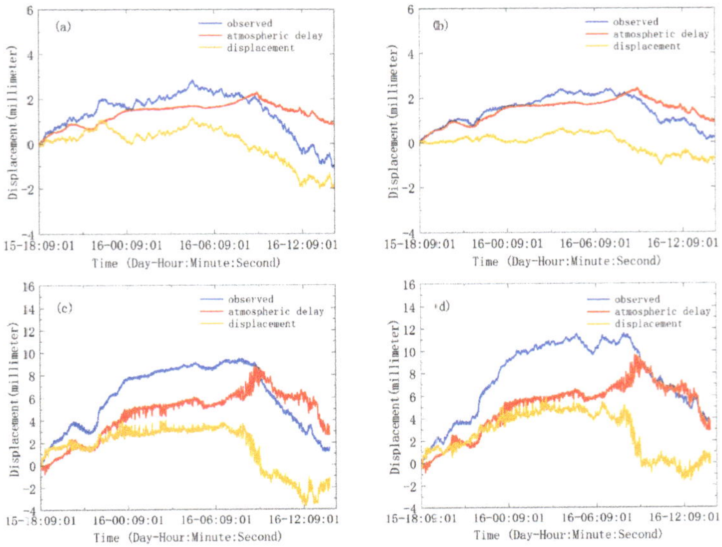

Figure 11. The time series obtained by the meteorological data of four reflectors (**a**) P_1, (**b**) P_2, (**c**) P_3, and (**d**) P_4.

The result obtained by the polynomial fitting method is shown in Figure 12. A quadratic polynomial relative to distance, Equation (23), is employed based on the spatial homogeneity of the atmosphere in a small area. The reflectors P_1 and P_4 were selected as the reference points. We can see that the atmospheric delay is fitted well for P_2 and P_3. The displacement in Figure 12 is similar to the difference value between the original observed displacement data and the atmospheric delay in Figure 5. However, the time series around the end of the observation is more stable by the proposed method.

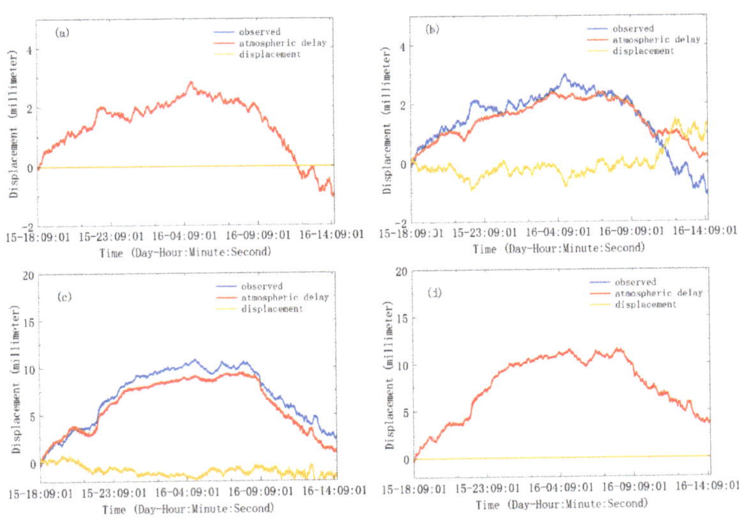

Figure 12. The time series obtained by the polynomial fitting method of four reflectors (**a**) P_1, (**b**) P_2, (**c**) P_3, and (**d**) P_4.

We compared the difference value between the original observed displacement data and the atmospheric delay by the proposed method with the displacement obtained after the atmospheric compensation by the external meteorological data correction method and polynomial fitting method. The mean and SD were calculated to evaluate the precision of the estimation of displacement. The RMSE between them and the zero array was also calculated. The zero array was regarded as the actual value because the reflectors were stable.

The comparison results are shown in Table 3. The reflectors P_1 and P_4 were selected as the reference points; therefore, the SD and RMSE obtained by the polynomial fitting method are zero. We can see that the SD and RMSE for all points by the proposed method are significantly improved compared to those of the other two methods.

Table 3. Statistical results of the four reflectors. (All values in the table are expressed in millimeters).

	P_1 [1]			P_2			P_3			P_4 [2]		
	M1 [3]	**M2** [4]	**M3** [5]	**M1**	**M2**	**M3**	**M1**	**M2**	**M3**	**M1**	**M2**	**M3**
Mean	0.03	0.00	−0.07	0.00	−0.03	−0.11	1.53	−0.89	−0.61	2.61	0.00	0.42
SD	0.80	0.00	0.32	0.42	0.49	0.21	2.00	0.60	0.40	1.99	0.00	0.34
RMSE	0.80	0.00	0.33	0.42	0.49	0.24	2.52	1.08	0.73	3.28	0.00	0.54

[1,2] the reflectors P_1 and P_4 were selected as the reference points in the polynomial fitting method. [3] the external meteorological data correction method. [4] the polynomial fitting method. [5] the proposed method.

For reflector P_1, the SD and RMSE by the proposed method are respectively improved by 60.00% and 58.75% compared to that by the external meteorological data correction method.

For reflector P_2, the SD and RMSE by the proposed method are respectively improved by 50.00% and 42.86% compared to that by the external meteorological data correction method. The SD and RMSE by the proposed method are respectively improved by 33.33% and 32.41% compared to that by the polynomial fitting method.

For reflector P_3, the SD and RMSE by the proposed method are respectively improved by 80.00% and 71.03% compared to that by the external meteorological data correction method. The SD and RMSE by the proposed method are respectively improved by 57.14% and 51.02% compared to that by the polynomial fitting method.

For reflector P_4, the SD and RMSE by the proposed method are respectively improved by 82.91% and 83.54% compared to that by the external meteorological data correction method.

5.3. Comparisons between the Vibration Time Series Acquired by the GPS and GBSAR

In the real in situ experiment, we applied the proposed method to the time series acquired by GBSAR. A set of pixels around the GPS receiver are selected to resolve the function model. The solution at the 935th pixel is shown in Figure 13. In the time domain, the displacement fitting line shows the periodic feature of the bridge vibration.

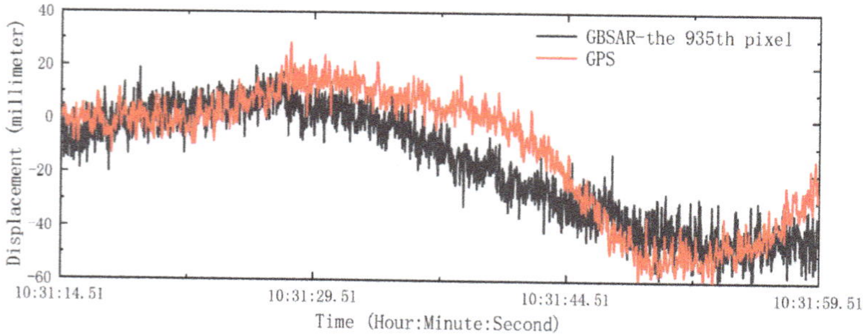

Figure 13. Comparison of the result of GBSAR at the 935th pixel and the time series acquired by the GPS receiver.

The difference value of the observed data and the atmospheric delay is shown in Figure 13 with the comparison with the time series acquired by the GPS receiver. The sampling frequency of GBSAR is 200 Hz, and the sampling frequency of GPS is 50 Hz. Therefore, the GBSAR result was sampled every four frames. The RMSE of the time series relative to that acquired by GPS is 12.19 mm. From the results, we can see that they have a familiar trend from up to down relative to the first time stamp. The vibration results from the coupling of various excitation of the cars, trucks, and wind. The excitation of the trucks is the primary reason for the trend in Figure 13. However, there are two differences at the beginning and end of the curves between the two time series in Figure 13. It is thought that the position-matching error is the primary reason. We used the position data acquired from the GPS receiver set on the top of GPRI-II, and the range measured by the antenna to locate the pixel corresponding to the GPS receiver on the bridge. It was unavoidable that the positioning and ranging were affected during the observation. Moreover, the GPS receiver was mounted on the balustrade, but the bottom of the bridge was actually observed. The structure and the components of the bridge are too complicated to be regarded as a rigid body in this comparison. Therefore, corner reflectors are recommended when jointly monitoring the vibration of a bridge by GPS and GBSAR. The reflectors improve the visual quality of targets in the SAR image, enhancing the difference or feature of the target object.

The vibration of a segment of the bridge around the 935th pixel is shown in Figure 14. A set of pixels were collected to jointly estimate the vibration and atmospheric model parameters. After interpolation in space, we modeled the temporal and spatial variation of a segment of the bridge about 10 m (the range resolution of GPRI-II is 0.75 m). The atmospheric delay in the LOS direction, vibration fitting result, and the difference between the observed data and the atmospheric delay are shown in sequence.

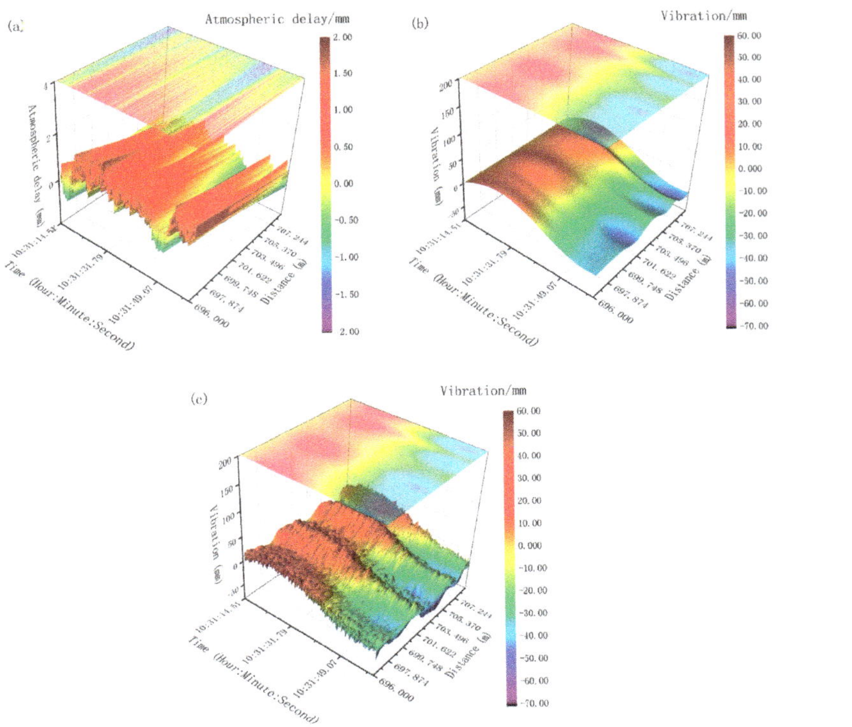

Figure 14. Temporal and spatial variation of a segment of the bridge. (**a**) The atmospheric delay in the LOS direction, (**b**) the vibration fitting result, and (**c**) the difference between the observed data and the atmospheric delay.

The atmospheric delay was chaotic in the time domain but consecutive in space. The patterns of atmospheric delay of every unit were different, but they had a common feature of up-to-down. Compared to the vibration fitting, the atmospheric delay was a smaller partial component of the observed data, but it changed rapidly. As we stated before, a displacement model considering the spatial and temporal features was applied. Although the vibration magnitude was different for every unit in the space, we can see that this segment of the bridge had a unified variation. The difference between the observed data and the atmospheric delay reserved more details. It was assumed that the load was the main reason for the vibration and the wind vibration was the secondary reason.

6. Conclusions

A method of joint estimation of ground displacement and atmospheric model parameters for GBSAR is proposed in the paper. This method has better precision compared to the external meteorological data correction method, and is operated more flexibly than the polynomial fitting method. This method considers both the spatial and temporal features of the displacement and the spatial feature of the atmospheric delay. We implemented a validation experiment to prove the capacity of joint estimation of the proposed method for stable artificial targets. We also applied the developed method to monitor the vibration of a bridge along the GPS receiver. These results show that:

(1) Additional systematic parameters are necessary for the functional model according to the hypothesis testing and the practical test. It is indicated that the original function model which only contains the unknown deformation parameters is inappropriate.
(2) The proposed method is a significant improvement compared to the external meteorological data correction method and the polynomial fitting method. The external meteorological data correction method is the worst among the three methods.
(3) The proposed method can split the atmospheric delay and displacement, and enhance the capacity of the monitoring bridge with the GBSAR device. It is suggested that reflectors are recommended when the device is employed to monitor the vibration of structures. An appropriate displacement model should be selected based on the displacement features of the structures.

Author Contributions: Conceptualization, B.X. and Y.Z.; methodology, Y.Z.; software, Y.Z. and J.L.; writing—original draft preparation, Y.Z.; writing—review and editing, J.H. and W.M.; funding acquisition, Z.L. All authors have read and agreed to the published version of the manuscript.

Funding: The research was partly funded by the National Science Fund for Distinguished Young Scholars, grant number No. 41925016, and the Fundamental Research Funds for the Central Universities of Central South University, grant number No. 2020zzts191.

Data Availability Statement: The data is not publicly available due to privacy.

Acknowledgments: The authors would like to thank Zhongda Group for the support of the GBSAR data and the meteorological data.

Conflicts of Interest: The authors declare no conflict of interest.

Appendix A

Given that there are N images in chronological order, let the single-look complex (SLC) phase be $\phi_1, \phi_2 \cdots, \phi_N$ at time $t_1, t_2 \cdots, t_N$. We can get M interferometric pairs $\Delta\phi_1, \Delta\phi_2 \cdots, \Delta\phi_M$, and the number of interferometric pairs M satisfies the inequality (we have implicitly assumed that N is odd):

$$\frac{N+1}{2} \leq M \leq N\left(\frac{N+1}{2}\right)$$

As for the triangulation network, every frame will connect to the following frames in chronological order. In this paper, we use the 2-connection triangulation network as shown in Figure A1.

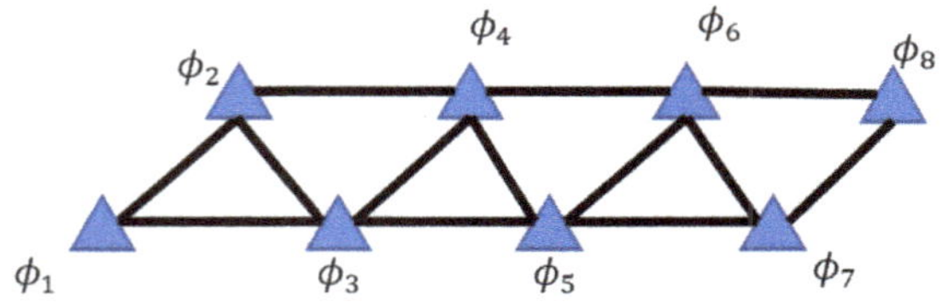

Figure A1. The 2-connection triangulation network. $\phi_1, \phi_2 \cdots, \phi_8$ are the SLC phase acquired at time $t_1, t_2 \cdots, t_N$.

References

1. Tarchi, D.; Rudolf, H.; Luzi, G.; Chiarantini, L.; Coppo, P.; Sieber, A.J. SAR Interferometry for Structural Changes Detect ion a Demonstration Test on a Dam. In Proceedings of the IGARSS, Hamburg, Germany, 28 June–2 July 1999; pp. 1522–1524.
2. Zhang, B.; Ding, X.; Werner, C.; Tan, K.; Zhang, B.; Jiang, M.; Zhao, J.; Xu, Y. Dynamic displacement monitoring of long-span bridges with a microwave radar interferometer. *ISPRS J. Photogramm. Remote Sens.* **2018**, *138*, 252–264. [CrossRef]
3. Tarchi, D.; Casagli, N.; Fanti, R.; Leva, D.D.; Luzi, G.; Pasuto, A.; Pieraccini, M.; Silvano, S. Landslide monitoring by using ground-based SAR interferometry: An example of application to the Tessina landslide in Italy. *Eng. Geol.* **2003**, *68*, 15–30. [CrossRef]
4. Luzi, G.; Pieraccini, M.; Mecatti, D.; Noferini, L.; Macaluso, G.; Galgaro, A.; Atzeni, C. Advances in ground-based microwave interferometry for landslide survey: A case study. *Int. J. Remote Sens.* **2006**, *27*, 2331–2350. [CrossRef]
5. Li, Z.; Cao, Y.; Wei, J.; Duan, M.; Wu, L.; Hou, J.; Zhu, J. Time-series InSAR ground deformation monitoring: Atmospheric delay modeling and estimating. *Earth-Sci. Rev.* **2019**, *192*, 258–284. [CrossRef]
6. Monserrat, O.; Crosetto, M.; Luzi, G. A review of ground-based SAR interferometry for deformation measurement. *ISPRS J. Photogramm. Remote Sens.* **2014**, *93*, 40–48. [CrossRef]
7. Owerko, T.; Kuras, P.; Ortyl, Ł. Atmospheric Correction Thresholds for Ground-Based Radar Interferometry Deformation Monitoring Estimated Using Time Series Analyses. *Remote Sens.* **2020**, *12*, 2236. [CrossRef]
8. Noferini, L.; Pieraccini, M.; Mecatti, D.; Luzi, G.; Atzeni, C.; Tamburini, A.; Broccolato, M. Permanent scatterers analysis for atmospheric correction in ground-based SAR interferometry. *IEEE Trans. Geosci. Remote Sens.* **2005**, *43*, 1459–1471. [CrossRef]
9. Iglesias, R.; Fabregas, X.; Aguasca, A.; Mallorqui, J.J.; Lopez-Martinez, C.; Gili, J.A.; Corominas, J. Atmospheric Phase Screen Compensation in Ground-Based SAR With a Multiple-Regression Model Over Mountainous Regions. *IEEE Trans. Geosci. Remote Sens.* **2014**, *52*, 2436–2449. [CrossRef]
10. Pipia, L.; Fabregas, X.; Aguasca, A.; Lopez-Martinez, C. Atmospheric Artifact Compensation in Ground-Based DInSAR Applications. *IEEE Geosci. Remote Sens. Lett.* **2008**, *5*, 88–92. [CrossRef]
11. Qiu, Z.; Ma, Y.; Guo, X. Atmospheric phase screen correction in ground-based SAR with PS technique. *SpringerPlus* **2016**, *5*, 1594. [CrossRef] [PubMed]
12. Jianping, Y.; Zhiwei, Q.; Xueqin, W.; Shun, Y. Atmospheric phase correction using permanent scatterers in ground-based radar interferometry. *J. Appl. Remote Sens.* **2016**, *10*, 046013. [CrossRef]
13. Hanssen, R.F. Radar system theory and interferometric processing. In *Radar Interferometry: Data Interpretation and Error Analysis*; Hanssen, R.F., Ed.; Springer: Dordrecht, The Netherlands, 2001; pp. 9–60.
14. Thayer, G.D. An improved equation for the radio refractive index of air. *Radio Sci.* **1974**, *9*, 803–807. [CrossRef]
15. Liebe, H.J. Modeling attenuation and phase of radio waves in air at frequencies below 1000 GHz. *Radio Sci.* **1981**, *16*, 1183–1199. [CrossRef]
16. Murray, J. On the computation of saturated vapour pressure. *J. Appl. Meteorol.* **1967**, *6*, 203–204. [CrossRef]
17. Blaunstein, N.; Christodoulou, C.G. (Eds.) Effects of the Troposphere on Radio Propagation. In *Radio Propagation and Adaptive Antennas for Wireless Communication Networks*; Wiley: Hoboken, NJ, USA, 2014; pp. 536–590.
18. Radiocommunication Study Group 3. *Effects of Tropospheric Refraction on Radiowave Propagation*, 9th ed.; International Telecommunication Union: Genevam Switzerland, 2017; pp. 1–15.
19. Ferretti, A.; Prati, C.; Rocca, F. Permanent scatterers in SAR interferometry. *IEEE Trans. Geosci. Remote Sens.* **2001**, *39*, 8–20. [CrossRef]

remote sensing

MDPI

Article

Ground Deformation Monitoring over Xinjiang Coal Fire Area by an Adaptive ERA5-Corrected Stacking-InSAR Method

Yuxuan Zhang [1,2], Yunjia Wang [1,2,*], Wenqi Huo [1,2], Feng Zhao [1,2], Zhongbo Hu [3], Teng Wang [1,2], Rui Song [1,2], Jinglong Liu [4], Leixin Zhang [1,2], José Fernández [3], Joaquin Escayo [3], Fei Cao [5] and Jun Yan [5]

[1] Key Laboratory of Land Environment and Disaster Monitoring, MNR, China University of Mining and Technology (CUMT), Xuzhou 221116, China; zhangyx99@cumt.edu.cn (Y.Z.); huowenqi@cumt.edu.cn (W.H.); feng.zhao@cumt.edu.cn (F.Z.); wteng_611@cumt.edu.cn (T.W.); rui_song@cumt.edu.cn (R.S.); zhangleix1028@cumt.edu.cn (L.Z.)

[2] School of Environment Science and Spatial Informatics, China University of Mining and Technology (CUMT), Xuzhou 221116, China

[3] Instituto de Geociencias (IGEO), CSIC-UCM, 7, 28040 Madrid, Spain; zhongbo.hu@csic.es (Z.H.); jft@mat.ucm.es (J.F.); jescayo@ucm.es (J.E.)

[4] CommSensLab, Department of Signal Theory and Communications, Universitat Politecnica de Catalunya (UPC), 08034 Barcelona, Spain; jinglong.liu@cumt.edu.cn

[5] Xinjiang Uygur Autonomous Region Mine Safety Service and Guarantee Center, Urumqi 830063, China; figo6507804@163.com (F.C.); yanjun3183@163.com (J.Y.)

* Correspondence: wyj4139@cumt.edu.cn

Abstract: Underground coal fire is a global geological disaster that causes the loss of resources as well as environmental pollution. Xinjiang, China, is one of the regions suffering from serious underground coal fires. The accurate monitoring of underground coal fires is critical for management and extinguishment, and many remote sensing-based approaches have been developed for monitoring over large areas. Among them, the multi-temporal interferometric synthetic aperture radar (MT-InSAR) techniques have been recently employed for underground coal fires-related ground deformation monitoring. However, MT-InSAR involves a relatively high computational cost, especially when the monitoring area is large. We propose to use a more cost-efficient Stacking-InSAR technique to monitor ground deformation over underground coal fire areas in this study. Considering the effects of atmosphere on Stacking-InSAR, an ERA5 data-based estimation model is employed to mitigate the atmospheric phase of interferograms before stacking. Thus, an adaptive ERA5-Corrected Stacking-InSAR method is proposed in this study, and it is tested over the Fukang coal fire area in Xinjiang, China. Based on original and corrected interferograms, four groups of ground deformation results were obtained, and the possible coal fire areas were identified. In this paper, the ERA5 atmospheric delay products based on the estimation model along the LOS direction (D-LOS) effectively mitigate the atmospheric phase. The accuracy of ground deformation monitoring over a coal fire area has been improved by the proposed method choosing interferograms adaptively for stacking. The proposed Adaptive ERA5-Corrected Stacking-InSAR method can be used for efficient ground deformation monitoring over large coal fire areas.

Keywords: coal fire detection; atmospheric correction; Stacking-InSAR; ground deformation

1. Introduction

Underground coal fire combustion has caused serious resource loss in many countries [1–4]. Coals burning underground change the ground environment to different degrees, causing ground high temperature anomalies, ground deformation, land destruction and other ecological environmental disturbances [5–7]. Xinjiang, China, is one of the regions suffering from serious underground coal fires due to the extremely dry climate, special geological conditions and large mining activities [8–10]. The accurate monitoring of underground coal fires is critical for management and extinguishment. At present, the methods used to detect coal fires mainly include geophysical exploration, geochemical exploration [11,12], thermal exploration, drilling exploration and remote sensing techniques [13–16]. The first four types can accurately detect coal fires in small areas but are unsuitable for multi-time synchronous identification and monitoring in large coal fire areas. Fortunately, remote sensing techniques can efficiently identify the range of coal fires in large areas by extracting and analyzing the land surface temperature anomalies, ground deformation and collapse, which makes up for the shortcomings of these detection methods [17–20].

Based on land surface temperature (LST), the thermal infrared remote sensing technique can be used to extract the surface thermal anomaly by a certain threshold determination method, so as to identify coal fire regions [21–24]. However, there are many low specific heat capacity substances on the surface of mining areas, and the surface temperature is greatly affected by the seasons. Additionally, the resolution of a thermal infrared image is low. These factors are likely to cause misidentification of some coal fire areas.

Thanks to the large-width imaging of SAR satellites and the sensitivity of radar signal to the deformation phase, differential interferometric synthetic aperture radar (D-InSAR) is an effective technique for ground deformation monitoring over large areas. However, D-InSAR is easily affected by the phase decoherence caused by system noise, orbit error and other noise sources. Therefore, multi-temporal InSAR (MT-InSAR) techniques, such as PS-InSAR [25], SBAS-InSAR [26] methods, have been proposed, which use time-series SAR images covering the same area to form interferometric pairs of different spatio-temporal baselines, to then separate the errors effectively based on redundancy observation. Therefore, MT-InSAR has been developed into a useful tool for monitoring ground deformation and has been applied in earthquakes [27], volcanoes [28], glacier movement [29], landslide [30], mining activity [31] and so on. In recent years, scholars have used this technique to monitor deformation caused by coal fires [32–35].

PS-InSAR and SBAS-InSAR techniques obtain ground deformation on coherent points. These techniques are based on permanent scatterers (PSs) for deformation monitoring, while in some regions with few strong scatters, the monitoring results will be unreliable due to the insufficient spatial density of monitoring points. The DS-InSAR technique [36] can improve the drawback, which is used to monitor the deformation of non-urban areas through distributed scatterers (DSs) obtained by homogeneous pixel identification and distributed phase optimization. Meanwhile, recently, the polarimetric information of SAR images has been employed to improve interferograms' phase qualities, thus enhancing the density of ground deformation monitoring pixels [37–39]. The above time-series InSAR methods come with a relatively high computational cost, especially when the monitoring area is large. In contrast, the Stacking-InSAR, which linearly stacks the unwrapped interferograms and weights them by a relatively simple mathematical model, can efficiently and rapidly obtain accurate deformation results. It has great potential in monitoring coal fire-related ground deformation over large regions.

The atmospheric delay is caused by the difference of the atmospheric signal in the SAR image at different imaging times due to the influence of the propagating medium. The atmospheric delay includes ionospheric delay and tropospheric delay. For short wavelength SAR data, the tropospheric delay is more common in the atmospheric delay error [40–43]. Therefore, most of the current atmospheric correction studies are focused on tropospheric delay [41], including turbulence and vertical stratification. The turbulence part is independent of topography and mainly affected by atmospheric turbulence. The vertical stratification part is related to topographic relief, and the effect is more visible in mountainous areas. Coal fires in Xinjiang are often located in mountainous regions with serious atmospheric phase delays. Atmospheric delay cannot be accurately eliminated by temporal–spatial filtering based on the statistical characteristics of the tropospheric delay in space and time. The linear model of Stacking-InSAR may correct the differential phase for atmospheric contributions, but at the same time it will likely mask ground deformation signals correlated with topography [44]. Accordingly, it may not accurately divide the coal fire range based on the obtained ground deformation results. Therefore, the tropospheric error should be corrected based on the external atmospheric data [45].

Atmospheric delay (mainly tropospheric delay) correction methods based on external atmospheric data include GPS data, surface meteorological data and global weather forecast models [46–48]. The common approach of calculating tropospheric delay using global weather forecasting models is to integrate zenith delay first and then convert it to LOS (line-of-sight). However, the atmosphere is a dynamic and complex system. In the region of uneven atmospheric distribution, the atmospheric delay phase in the zenith distance direction is divided by an angle factor to convert to LOS (Zenithal-LOS, Z-LOS), which could produce a large error. Therefore, a precise atmospheric phase delay estimation model along the LOS direction (D-LOS) has been proposed [48–50]. The high-precision atmospheric phase delay results based on this model have been verified in many regions [51,52]. It is expected to be useful for the accurate extraction of ground deformation over spontaneous coal fire areas.

To this end, an Adaptive ERA5-Corrected Stacking-InSAR method is proposed in this study. In this method, the ERA5 atmospheric phase delay product generated by an accurate model based on the D-LOS direction is used, and the interferograms with better phase quality after correction are adaptively selected for stacking. It has been applied to monitor ground deformation of coal fires over the Fukang coal fire area in Xinjiang, China. Firstly, precise atmospheric phase delay products were obtained based on ERA5 reanalysis data, and 57 small baseline interferograms were generated using Sentinel-1 data. Then, the atmospheric phase term in the interferogram was removed by using ERA5 data, and the quality of the original interferogram and the corrected interferogram was compared and analyzed. Finally, based on original and corrected interferograms, ground deformation results were obtained by adaptively choosing the interferograms with better quality for stacking, and the possible coal fire areas were identified.

This paper is organized as follows. Section 2 introduces the study area and datasets. Section 3 gives the details of the methods used in this study. In Section 4, the results are described and analyzed. In Section 5, the accuracy and validity of the results are discussed. Section 6 provides the conclusion.

2. Study Area and Datasets

2.1. Study Area

As shown in Figure 1, the Fukang coalfield, the study area selected in this paper, is located in the north-central part of the Xinjiang Uygur Autonomous Region, China, at the northern foot of Bogda and the southern part of Junggar Basin. The geomorphic features of the region can be divided into three units from south to north: southern mountainous area, central plain and northern desert. The height varies greatly and the average altitude is high. The temperature difference between day and night is in the tens of degrees range. This belongs to a typical continental arid climate in the medium temperate zone. The coal in this region is of good quality, low metamorphism and high calorific value. Moreover, the unique climate conditions and important mining activities aggravate the weathering and rupture of coal outcrops and surrounding rocks. This leads to the surface collapse and prominent coal fire problems [9].

2.2. Datasets

2.2.1. ERA5 Dataset

The ERA5 dataset comprises the fifth-generation atmospheric reanalysis of global climate provided by the European Center for Medium-Range Weather Forecasts (ECMWF). It combines model data with observations from around the world into a globally complete and consistent dataset. The dataset provides hour-by-hour observations of atmospheric, land and ocean climate variables, spanning from 1979 to near real-time [53,54]. The ERA5 dataset has a higher resolution in time and space than the ERA-Interim dataset, with a horizontal resolution of 31 km per hour. Moreover, the ERA5 dataset has a shorter temporal sampling than Generic Atmospheric Correction Online Service for InSAR (GACOS) [55]. The higher temporal resolution reduces the acquisition error between SAR data and meteorological data. It is worth noting that although the spatial scale of the study area in this paper is slightly smaller than the spatial resolution of ERA5, we will obtain more accurate atmospheric parameters through interpolation. The selection of the scope of the study area is to some extent a priority, so we sample the ERA5 atmospheric delay products to a smaller spatial scale according to the study area. The effect of tropospheric noise related to topography on smaller spatial scales can be reduced in certain case. Accordingly, the ERA5 data with the closest acquisition time to SAR images have been selected in this study.

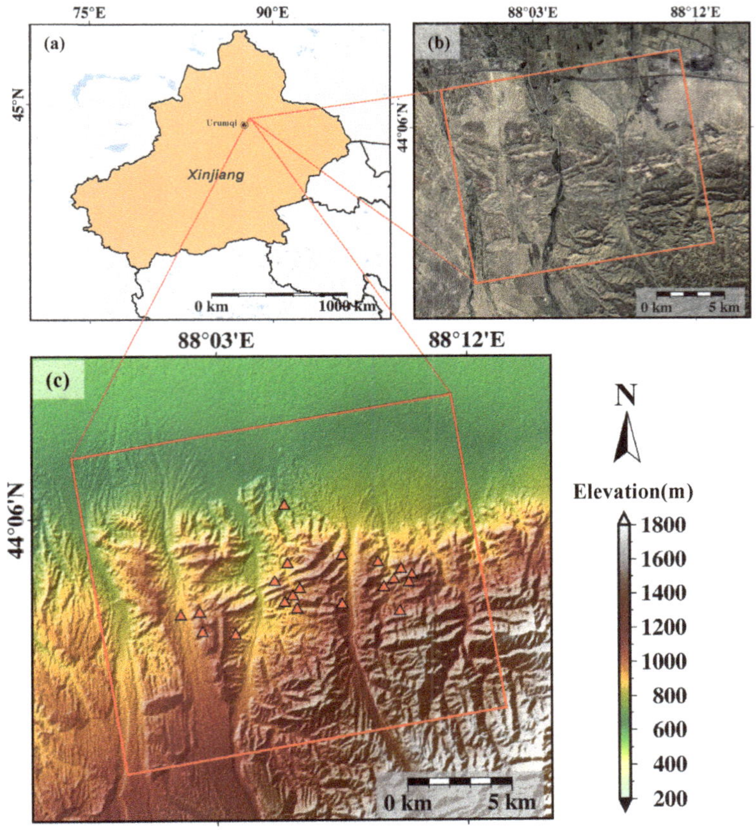

Figure 1. Sketch map of the study area. (**a**) Shows the geographical location of study area, (**b**) is optical image and (**c**) is DEM over the study area derived from SRTM data. The red box indicates the detection range of ground deformation in (**b**,**c**). The red triangles in (**c**) represent the detected coal fire points.

2.2.2. Sentinel-1 Dataset

This study used Sentinel-1A data provided by the European Space Agency (ESA). It is a C-band satellite with a 12-day revisit period. The standard acquisition mode of Sentinel-1, Interferometric Wide (IW), provides a ground resolution of about 5 m × 20 m (Range × Azimuth) with a footprint of 250 kilometers width. The Sentinel-1A satellite provides high-quality data with a low revisit time and global coverage that are freely available to use for ground deformation monitoring over a wide range of areas. In this study, 23 images from 3 May 2019 to 9 May 2020 were selected. A 30 meter resolution DEM, derived from the Shuttle Radar Topography Mission (SRTM) data, was used to remove the topographic contribution to the phase in the differential interferometric processing chain. Based on the SBAS-InSAR technique, 57 small baseline interferograms were obtained, and their spatio-temporal baseline distributions are shown in Figure 2.

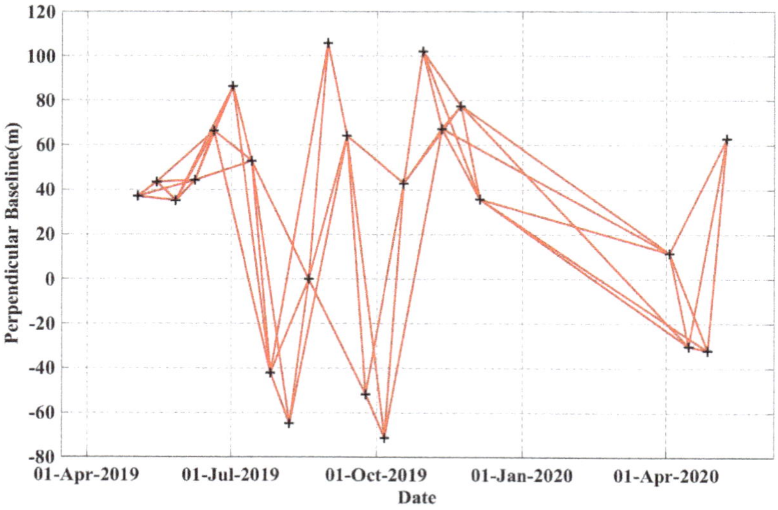

Figure 2. Temporal and perpendicular baseline distribution of the acquisitions used in this study. Plus symbols represent the acquisitions and red lines denote the interferometric pairs used to form interferograms. The perpendicular baseline was set to be within 150 m, and the maximum temporal baseline was 144 days.

3. Methods

3.1. Direction-LOS (D-LOS) Phase Delay Calculation

Variations of temperature, pressure and humidity in the troposphere make the atmospheric refractive index N not constant, which includes the dry component N_{dry} and the wet component N_{wet}. The delay of the atmosphere to the radar signal can be expressed as the atmospheric refractive index N [56]:

$$N(T,P,e) = k_1\frac{P}{T} + k_2\frac{e}{T} + k_3\frac{e}{T^2} = N_{dry} + N_{wet} \tag{1}$$

where T is the temperature, P is the partial pressure of dry air, e is the partial pressure of water vapor , k_1=0.776 KPa^{-1}, k_2=0.716 KPa^{-1} and k_3=3.75e3 K^{2}Pa^{-1}.

For a specific position between h_1 and h_2, the atmospheric phase delay term is

$$\begin{aligned}\varphi_{atm} &= \frac{-4\pi}{\lambda}10^{-6}\int_{h_1}^{h_2}[N_{dry}(\vec{h}) + N_{wet}(\vec{h})]d\vec{h} \\ &= \frac{-4\pi}{\lambda}10^{-6}\int_{h_{ground}}^{h_{sat}}[N_{dry}(\vec{h}) + N_{wet}(\vec{h})]d\vec{h}\end{aligned} \tag{2}$$

where λ is the radar wavelength. For an orbital SAR image, h_2 will be the location of the satellite when the image was acquired, h_{sat}, and h_1 will be the ground location of the pixel for which the atmospheric artifacts are calculated, h_{ground}. For the interferogram, the differential atmospheric delay $\Delta\varphi_{atm}$ is the difference between the atmospheric delay at two acquisition times. Unlike the phase delay obtained by integrating along the zenith direction and then transforming to the LOS direction, a more accurate phase delay can be obtained by integrating along the LOS direction directly through the above equation. Therefore, this method is denoted as D-LOS [49]. The steps are as follows:

a. Determination of the sampling locations along the LOS path.

The LOS vector, $\overrightarrow{LOS}$, is calculated from the Cartesian coordinates of the ground point and the satellite,

$$\overrightarrow{LOS} = \vec{\gamma}_{sat} - \vec{\gamma}_{ground} \tag{3}$$

The direction vector, $\mu_{\hat{LOS}}$, which describes the LOS direction, is calculated from the unit vector,

$$\mu_{\hat{LOS}} = \frac{\overrightarrow{LOS}}{\left\|\overrightarrow{LOS}\right\|} = [\hat{\mu_x}, \hat{\mu_y}, \hat{\mu_z}] \tag{4}$$

Once the direction vector is determined, the coordinates of any point on the LOS path can be obtained:

$$\left.\begin{array}{l} P_{ix} = G_x + (\Delta LOS \cdot i)\hat{\mu_x} \\ P_{iy} = G_y + (\Delta LOS \cdot i)\hat{\mu_y} \\ P_{iz} = G_z + (\Delta LOS \cdot i)\hat{\mu_z} \end{array}\right\} \tag{5}$$

where the required sampling data are based on the available global atmospheric model data resolution. In general, the LOS spatial sampling resolution is set to 200 m for efficient calculation without loss of reliability [50].

b. Interpolation of atmospheric parameters.

After obtaining the position of any point in the LOS direction according to Equation (5), the atmospheric parameters at these positions could be obtained from the existing global atmospheric model data. For the ERA5 data used in this paper, raster sampling values are 37 pressure levels at altitude and 31 km horizontally. To obtain more accurate spatial sampling values of atmospheric state parameters at the desired location, cubic spline and bilinear interpolation are employed for interpolating the vertical and horizontal directions, respectively. It should be noted that the atmospheric parameters are consistent with the datum for DEM data in the case of vertical interpolation.

3.2. Stacking-InSAR

The Stacking-InSAR, namely interferogram stacking, is a kind of InSAR time-series technique. In 1998, the Stacking-InSAR technique was first proposed by Sandwell and applied to the post-earthquake deformation analysis of the Landers earthquake area [57]. Subsequently, many researchers used it to monitor ground deformation of large magnitudes, such as earthquake [58], landslide [59–62] and volcanoes [44]. It assumes that the ground deformation in the study area is linear in the Stacking-InSAR technique. To improve the signal-to-noise ratio (SNR) in the stacked phase and reduce the influence of noise, the unwrapped phases of a series of interferograms are stacked and average weighted. Its model can be simply expressed as Equation (6):

$$V_{mean} = \frac{\lambda}{4\pi} \cdot \frac{\sum_{i=1}^{N} \varphi_i \Delta T_i}{\sum_{i=1}^{N} \Delta T_i^2} \tag{6}$$

where V_{mean} is the annual average deformation rate in the LOS direction; φ_i is the unwrapped phase of the interferogram and ΔT is the time baseline corresponding to the interferogram. N is the number of stacked interferograms. The standard deviation of the average deformation rate can be expressed as Equation (7):

$$std(V_{mean}) = \sqrt{\frac{1}{n} \cdot \frac{\sum_{i=1}^{n} \left(\Delta T_i^2 \cdot \left(\frac{\varphi_i}{T_i} - V_{mean}\right)^2\right)}{\sum_{i=1}^{n} \Delta T_i^2}} \tag{7}$$

3.3. An Adaptive ERA5-Corrected Stacking-InSAR

As shown in Figure 3, an adaptive ERA5-Corrected Stacking-InSAR method is proposed in this paper. Its main steps include:

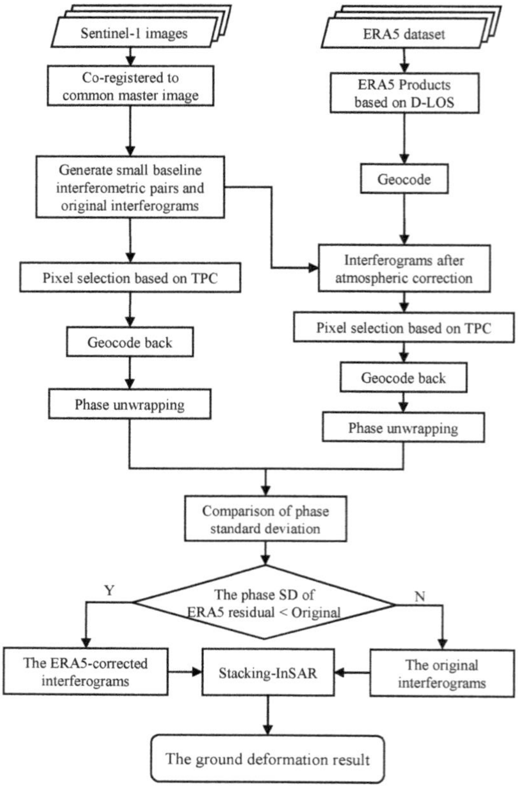

Figure 3. Data processing flowchart of adaptive ERA5-Corrected Stacking-InSAR.

(1) In order to ensure the quality of the interferograms and reduce the influence of spatio-temporal incoherence as much as possible, the small baseline principle is used to generate interferometric pairs;

(2) According to Equations (2)–(5), an ERA5 atmospheric delay product based on D-LOS model is generated;

(3) The atmospheric delay product in the radar coordinate system after geocoding is removed from the original interferogram to obtain the atmospheric corrected interferogram;

(4) To ensure the precision and reliability of the unwrapped results, the temporal phase coherence (TPC) index is used to select pixels with high interferometric phase quality [63]. Its basic principle is shown in Equation (8):

$$\gamma_{TPC} = \frac{1}{M}\left|\sum_{i=1}^{M} e^{j\cdot\psi_{noise,i}}\right| \quad (8)$$

where M is the number of interferograms and $\psi_{noise,i}$ is the noise phase corresponding to the first interferogram. The larger the TPC, the higher the pixel's quality;

(5) The interferogram phase is unwrapped on the coherent pixels selected by the TPC index;

(6) The quality of the interferograms is compared and evaluated by standard deviation (SD) of the unwrapped phase;

(7) The interferograms with lower phase SD than the original interferogram and the high-quality original interferograms (generally lower than the average phase SD) are selected for stacking. The ground deformation result of the study area is obtained.

4. Results and Analysis

4.1. Atmospheric Correction Results and Analysis

Figure 4 shows a part of the atmospheric delay products, namely atmospheric phase screen (APS) estimated using ERA5 based on the D-LOS model. It can be found that the phase of atmospheric delay is different in different periods. Furthermore, the distribution of atmospheric delay is related to the topography of the study area. The APS using ERA5 based on the D-LOS model is removed from the original interferogram to obtain the interferogram after atmospheric correction.

In order to ensure the precision and reliability of the results, a value of 0.8 for the temporal coherence estimator is used as the threshold to select pixels with high interferometric phase quality. The standard deviation (SD) of the unwrapped phase is selected as the evaluation index of interferogram quality.

As shown in Table 1, to evaluate atmospheric correction performance on the study area, statistical analysis is carried out to all 57 interferograms by comparing their SD. Furthermore, the overall change is shown in Figure 5. The light green bar represents correction percentage. The positive value represents the decrease in SD, which can be considered as a good atmospheric correction effect. The phase SD of most interferograms decreases after atmospheric correction. The largest reduction is 63.72% of the 20190608–20190620 interferogram pair. The average phase SD of the interferograms after atmospheric correction is 13.6% lower than that of the original interferograms. Therefore, it can be concluded that the D-LOS atmospheric phase correction method using ERA5 data has a good correction effect in this study area.

Table 1. Statistics using D-LOS mitigation model for 57 interferograms in study area. Correction percentage is calculated by the following equation: (Original−Residual)/Original.

ifg.	Reference	Secondary	Phase SD		Correction Percentage/%
			Original	ERA5 Residual	
1	03 May 2019	15 May 2019	0.7197	0.819	−13.80
2	03 May 2019	27 May 2019	1.0875	0.8687	20.12
3	03 May 2019	08 June 2019	1.5488	0.9662	37.62
4	15 May 2019	27 May 2019	0.9027	0.7415	17.86
5	15 May 2019	08 June 2019	1.6538	1.0448	36.82
6	15 May 2019	20 June 2019	1.4149	1.2141	14.19
7	27 May 2019	08 June 2019	2.1456	1.0152	52.69
8	27 May 2019	20 June 2019	0.9351	1.1429	−22.22
9	27 May 2019	02 July 2019	1.6791	1.4598	13.06
10	08 June 2019	20 June 2019	2.7458	0.9963	63.72
…	…	…	…	…	…
17	02 July 2019	26 July 2019	1.8197	1.3066	28.20
…	…	…	…	…	…
21	26 July 2019	07 August 2019	1.6325	1.5131	7.32
…	…	…	…	…	…
33	24 September 2019	06 October 2019	0.6633	1.0748	−62.04
…	…	…	…	…	…
52	03 April 2020	15 April 2020	1.8175	0.7095	60.96
53	03 April 2020	27 April 2020	0.7391	1.3078	−76.94
54	03 April 2020	09 May 2020	0.7281	0.9989	−37.20
55	15 April 2020	27 April 2020	2.0743	1.483	28.50
56	15 April 2020	09 May 2020	2.1282	1.2939	39.20
57	27 April 2020	09 May 2020	0.6743	0.896	−32.87
Mean			1.4305	1.2359	13.60

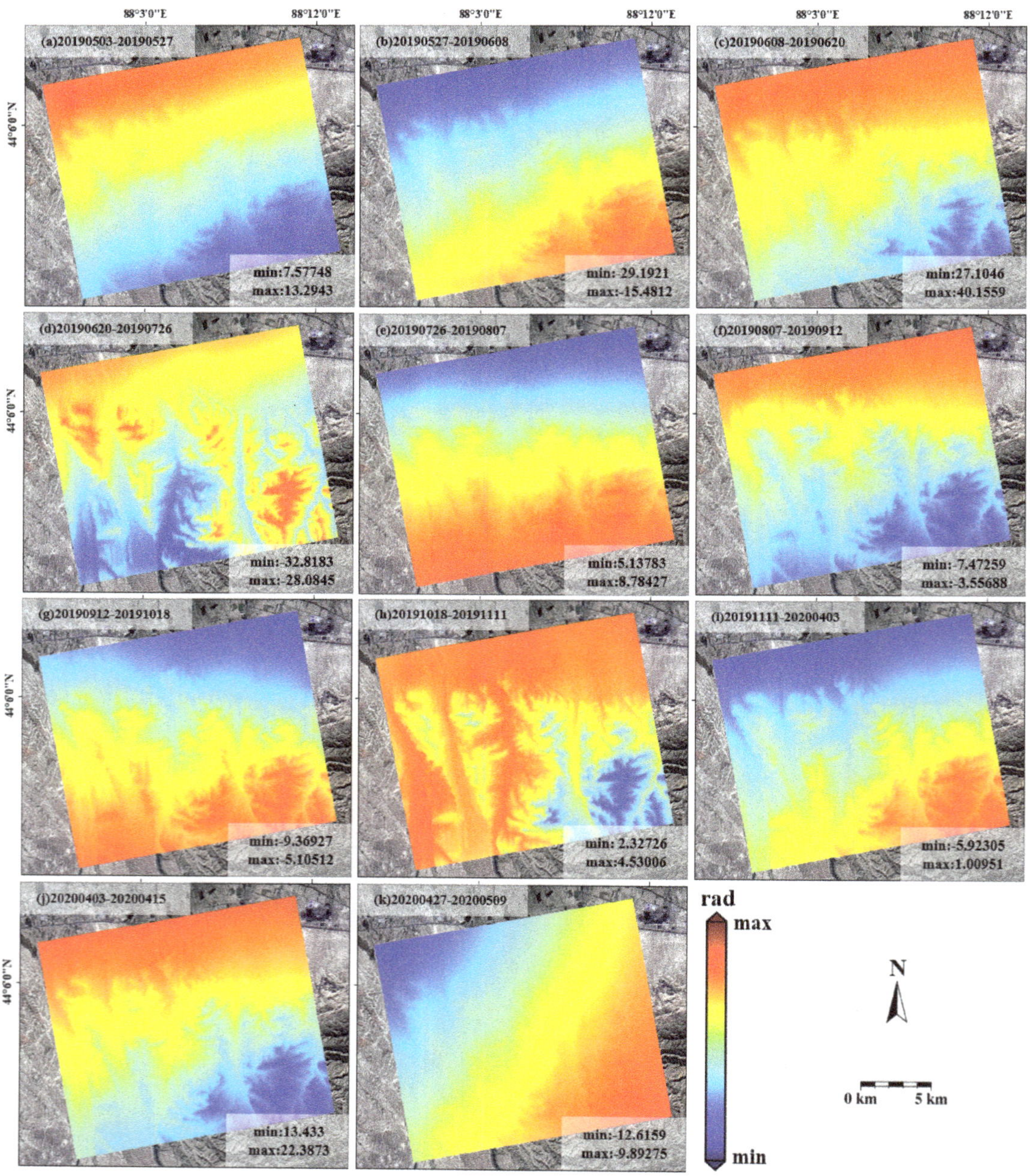

Figure 4. Atmospheric phase screen (APS) estimated by D-LOS model using ERA5. (**a–k**) Shows the estimation of APS by D-LOS model for some interferograms showing the maximum and minimum values obtained.

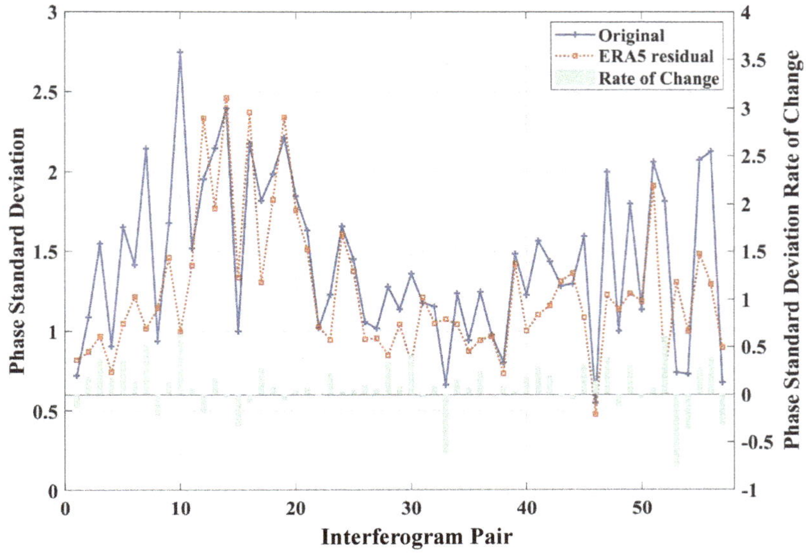

Figure 5. Phase standard deviation of original interferogram and ERA5 residual interferogram. The light green bar represents the Original−Residual/Original rate of phase standard deviation change. The positive value represents the decrease in standard deviation.

As shown in Figure 6a–h, four groups of interferogram results with reduced phase SD after correction are selected for comparison. Figure 6a,c,e,g are the original unwrapped results of the interferograms 20190527–20190608, 20190608–20190620, 20190726–20190807 and 20200403–20200415, respectively. The short temporal and perpendicular baseline preclude deformation and DEM phase errors. Therefore, the phase component can be considered as atmospheric artifacts in the original interferograms. The distribution of phase values shown in the figure has a certain tendency. The phase SD of these four interferograms is 2.1456, 2.7458, 1.6325 and 1.8175, respectively. Figure 6b,d,f,h are the residual unwrapped phases of the corresponding interferograms after atmospheric correction. It can be seen that the trend characteristics in the unwrapped results are significantly reduced, and the phase SD is reduced to 1.0152, 0.9963, 1.5131 and 0.7095, respectively.

Figure 6 shows that the original phase unwrapped value has a certain trend. At the same time, it can be seen from Figure 4 that the vertical stratification part of tropospheric delay has a strong correlation with topography. This correlation is more visible when looking at the phase-elevation scatter plots in Figure 7. It is evident that the slope of the fitting line between the unwrapped phase and the terrain is significantly reduced after removing APS predicted by the D-LOS model using ERA5. The tropospheric delay related to elevation is effectively weakened. However, although the 20190726–20190807 interferogram shown in Figure 7e,f has improved, the effect is not evident. The correlation between tropospheric delay and topography is weak. Most of the atmospheric delay here may come from the turbulent part unrelated to topography.

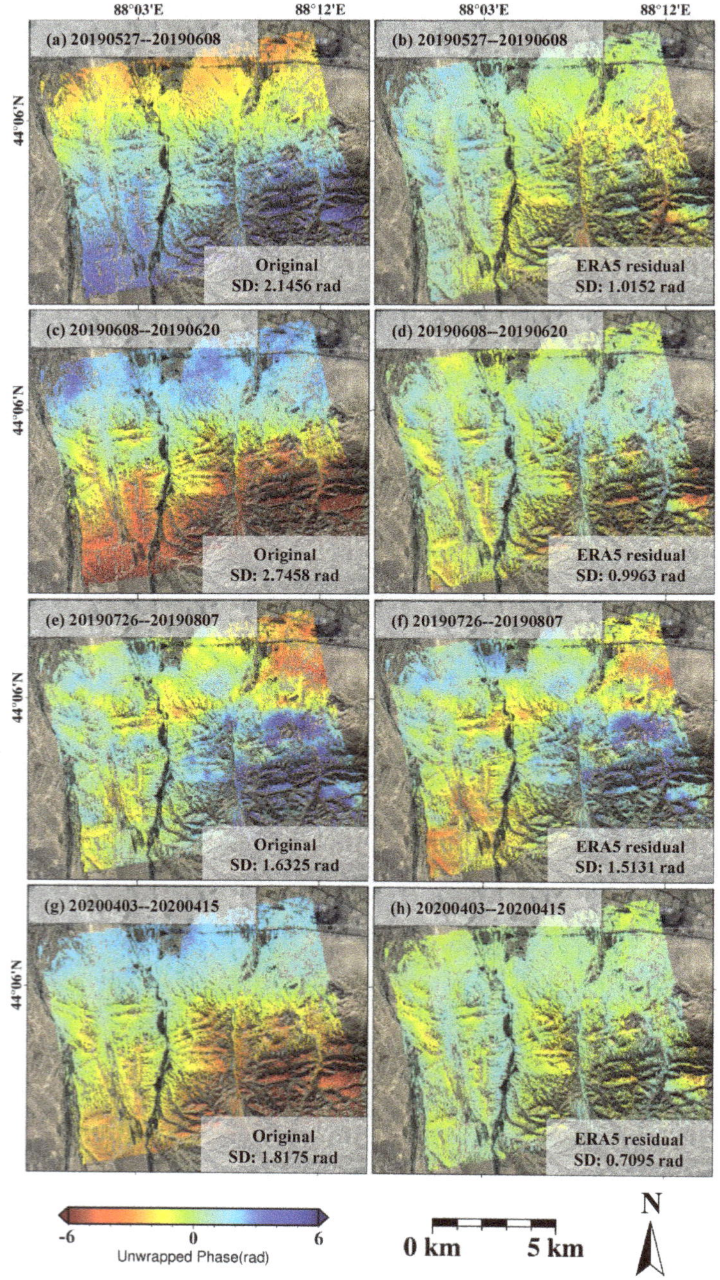

Figure 6. Phase comparison between original interferograms and ERA5 residual interferograms after TPC selection. (**a**,**c**,**e**,**g**) represents the original interferogram of 20190527–20190608, 20190608–20190620, 20190726–20190807 and 20200403–20200415, respectively. (**b**,**d**,**f**,**h**) represents the interferogram with residual phase after atmospheric correction of corresponding time, respectively.

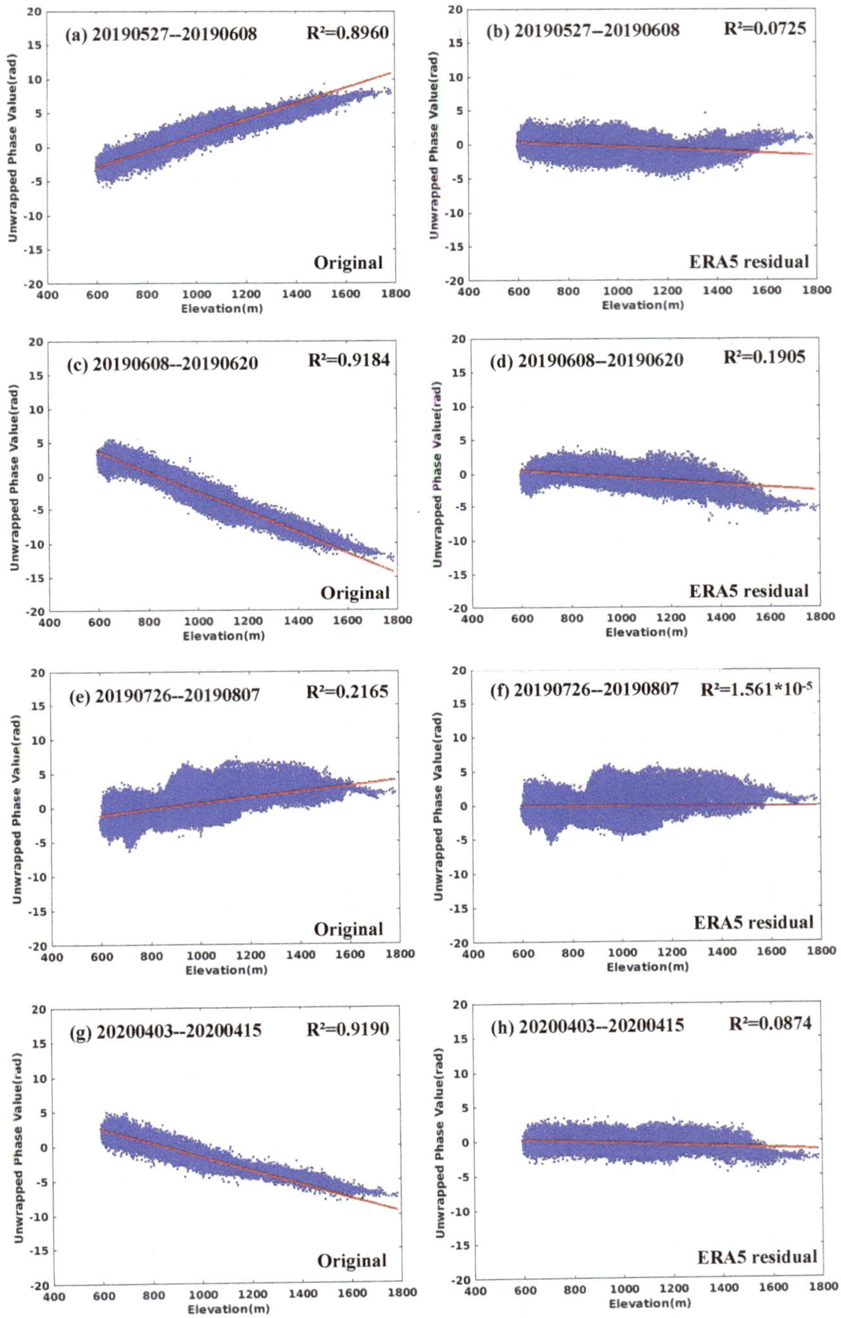

Figure 7. Unwrapped phase-elevation scatter plots for original phase and ERA5 residual phase. (**a**,**c**,**e**,**g**) represents the original phase-elevation of 20190527–20190608, 20190608–20190620, 20190726–20190807 and 20200403–20200415, respectively. (**b**,**d**,**f**,**h**) represents the residual phase-elevation of corresponding time, respectively.

According to Table 1, the phase SD of some interferograms increases after removing APS predicted by the D-LOS model using ERA5. As shown in Figure 8, the unwrapped phase of the interferogram 20190924–20191006 with increased phase SD after correction was selected for demonstration. Figure 8a,c shows the original and residual phase, respectively, of the interferogram 20190924–20191006. Figure 8b,d shows the distribution relationship between the corresponding phase and the elevation. It can be seen that the unwrapped phase of the original interferogram is small, and that the correlation between the phase shown in the scatter plot and the elevation is weak. In addition, from Table 1, among the 17 interferograms with increased phase SD after atmospheric correction, the original unwrapped phase SD of 14 interferograms is lesser than the average value of the original unwrapped phase SD. The phase SD of the three other interferograms increased after correction. It can be inferred that these 17 interferograms are less affected by the atmosphere, and the quality of the original interferograms is better.

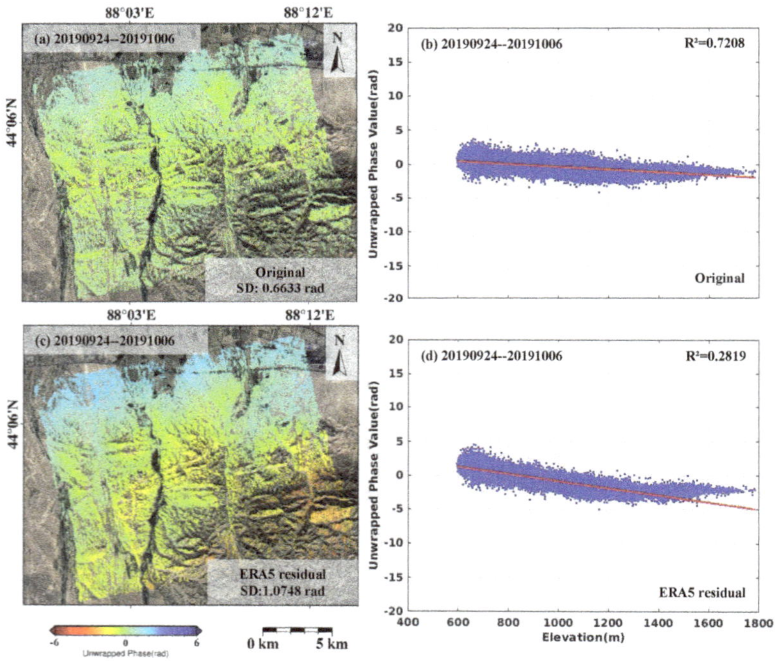

Figure 8. (**a**,**c**) show the original and residual phase, respectively, of the interferogram 20190924–20191006. (**b**,**d**) show the distribution relationship between the corresponding phase and elevation, respectively.

4.2. Deformation Monitoring Result and Analysis

In this paper, 57 original interferograms were first used for Stacking-InSAR (referred to as Original Stacking-InSAR) to obtain the average deformation velocity in the LOS direction of the study area, as shown in Figure 9a. Negative LOS values indicate movement away from the satellite, while positive values indicate movement toward the satellite. The red triangle in the figure represents the location of the coal fire point, and the area circled by the black box is the main coal fire deformation area. It can be seen that there is visible deformation around most coal fire points, while the deformation trend around some coal fire points is not significant. A large area of abnormal deformation is shown in the red box in the southeastern part of the study area, which is magnified as shown in Figure 9e. According to Figure 1c, there is a mountainous area with a high altitude. Therefore, it is highly likely to be affected by the atmosphere. The topography-related tropospheric delay exists in the interferograms in this region, which leads to the anomaly of the average velocity.

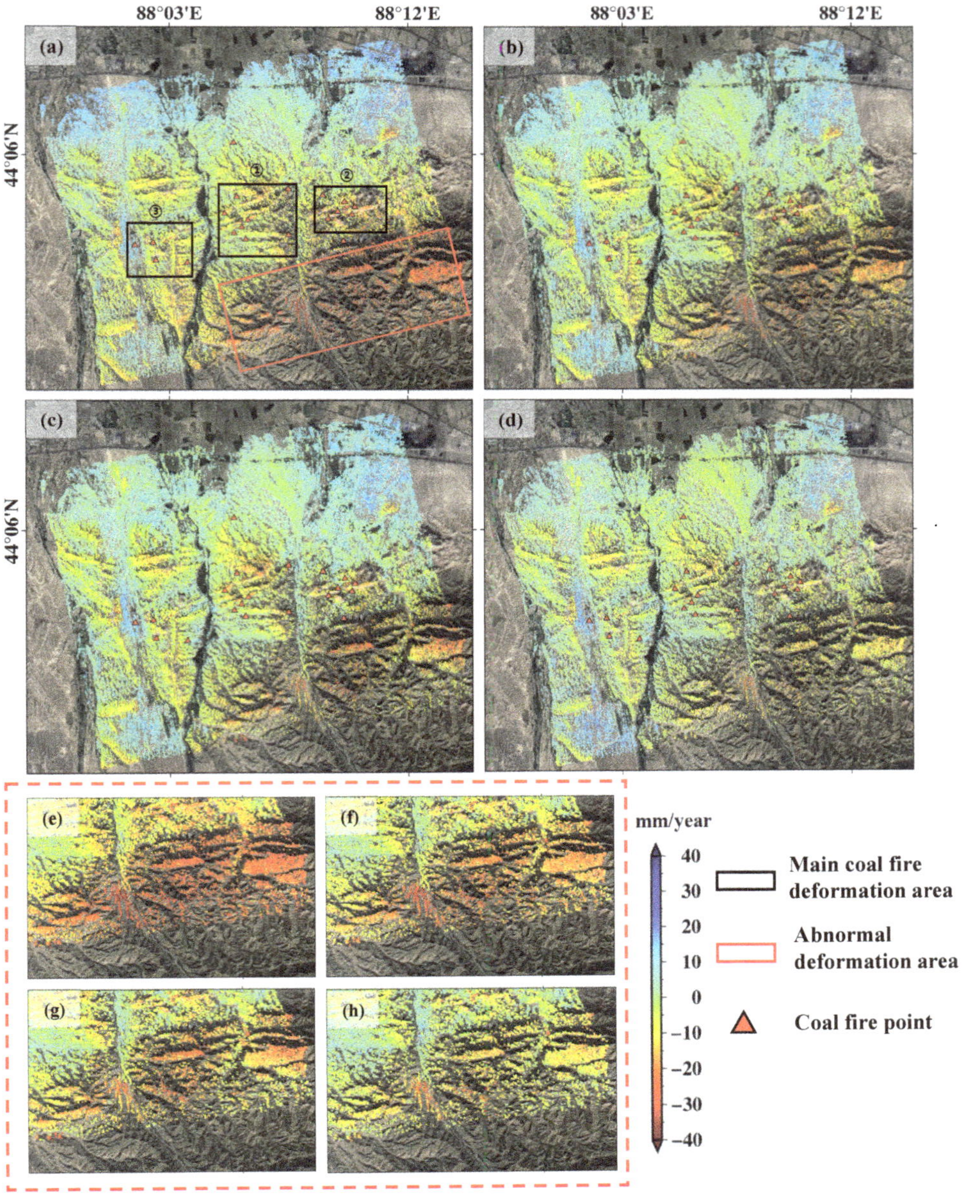

Figure 9. Deformation monitoring results. (**a**–**d**) are the deformation monitoring results of Original Stacking-InSAR, Original ERA5-Corrected Stacking-InSAR, Effective ERA5-Corrected Stacking-InSAR and Adaptive ERA5-Corrected Stacking-InSAR, respectively. (**e**–**h**) are the areas in the red boxes of (**a**) corresponding to the magnification of the results of (**a**–**d**). The black boxes in (**a**) indicate the three main coal fire deformation areas over the study area.

Subsequently, the atmospheric products estimated from the D-LOS model of the ERA5 dataset obtained above were removed from the 57 original interferograms. The ERA5-Corrected Stacking-InSAR method was used to calculate the average deformation velocity (referred to as Original ERA5-Corrected Stacking-InSAR). The result is shown in Figure 9b. As can be seen from the deformation velocity map, the deformation range of the main coal fire in the middle of the study area practically does not change. However, the abnormal deformation value of the red box in the southeast direction (as shown in Figure 9f) decreases significantly. Then, 40 interferograms with reduced SD of the unwrapped phase after atmospheric correction were selected for stacking (referred to as Effective ERA5-Corrected Stacking-InSAR). The average deformation velocity map obtained is shown in Figure 9c. Similarly, the abnormal deformation (magnified as shown in Figure 9g) in the red box range described above is further reduced. This indicates that the above atmospheric products have achieved good results in correcting the interferogram in the study area. The phase quality of the stacked interferogram determines the accuracy of the Stacking-InSAR processing results.

Finally, 40 interferograms with reduced SD of unwrapped phase after atmospheric correction and 17 original interferograms with increased SD of phase after atmospheric correction that are not seriously affected by the atmosphere were stacked for Stacking-InSAR calculation (referred to as Adaptive ERA5-Corrected Stacking-InSAR). The obtained average deformation result is shown in Figure 9d. It can be clearly seen that the abnormal deformation value in the red box range obtained by Effective ERA5-Corrected Stacking-InSAR (Figure 9g) is reduced more significantly (magnified as shown in Figure 9h). Consequently, this confirms that, as expected, the more interferograms with better quality, the more precise and reliable the deformation results obtained by Stacking-InSAR.

5. Discussion

5.1. Internal Accuracy

The standard deviation of average deformation velocity is a direct evaluation index of the quality of time-series InSAR results, which represents the separation degree of deformation phase and residual phase. The smaller standard deviation of the average deformation velocity, the smaller residual phase in the deformation velocity and the higher theoretical accuracy of the deformation estimation results [64].

Figure 10a–d shows the standard deviation of the average velocity of the Original Stacking-InSAR result, Original ERA5-Corrected Stacking-InSAR result, Effective ERA5-Corrected Stacking-InSAR result and Adaptive ERA5-Corrected Stacking-InSAR result, respectively. The above results are amplified by Figure 10e–h in the area circled by the red box in (a). The overall standard deviation of all high coherence point targets is distributed between 0 and 5 mm/year, and the monitoring results are relatively reliable. In addition, the standard deviation of high coherent pixels in Figure 10e is further reduced in Figure 10f–h, which is consistent with the corrected change in deformation anomalies in Section 4.2.

5.2. Comparison with GACOS-Corrected Stacking-InSAR Results

The Generic Atmospheric Correction Online Service (GACOS) atmospheric delay products, which are based on numerical weather models, are the highest-resolution atmospheric model of ECMWF. By using the iterative tropospheric decomposition interpolation model, the stratified and turbulent components are separated, and the high-resolution zenith total delay (ZTD) is generated [55,65,66]. In recent studies, the GACOS atmospheric delay products have been applied in Stacking-InSAR to obtain the ground deformation [62].

As mentioned in Sections 2 and 3, the ERA5 dataset has a shorter sampling time. At the same time, a realistic integration strategy along the LOS direction (D-LOS) has been used for estimating atmospheric artifacts. Therefore, the ground deformation result and standard deviation of the LOS velocity result base on GACOS-Corrected Stacking-InSAR were acquired (Figure 11).

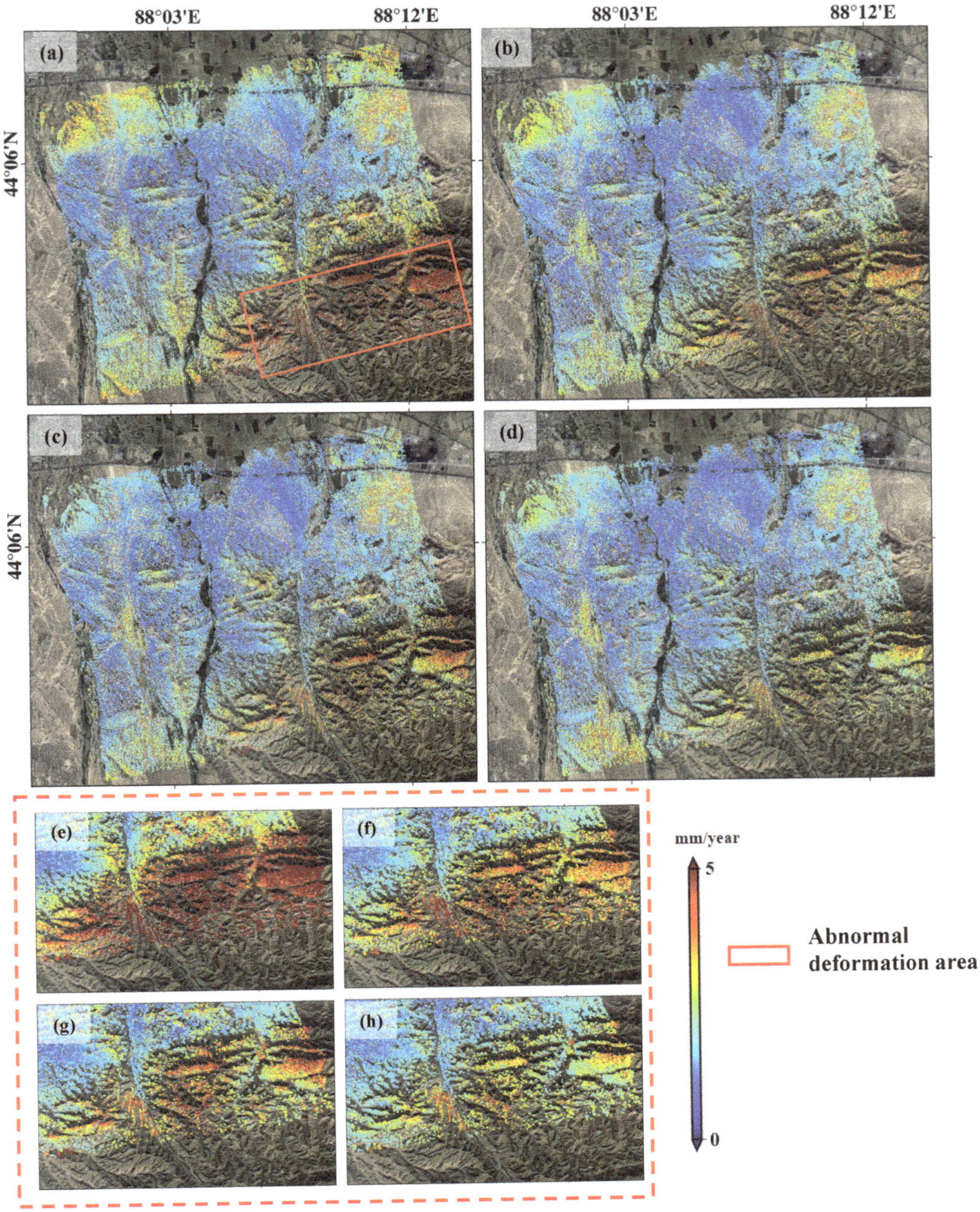

Figure 10. Standard deviation of the LOS velocity. (**a**–**d**) are the results of Original Stacking-InSAR, Original ERA5-Corrected Stacking-InSAR, Effective ERA5-Corrected Stacking-InSAR and adaptive ERA5-Corrected Stacking-InSAR, respectively. (**e**–**h**) are the areas in the red boxes of (**a**) corresponding to the magnification of the results of (**a**–**d**).

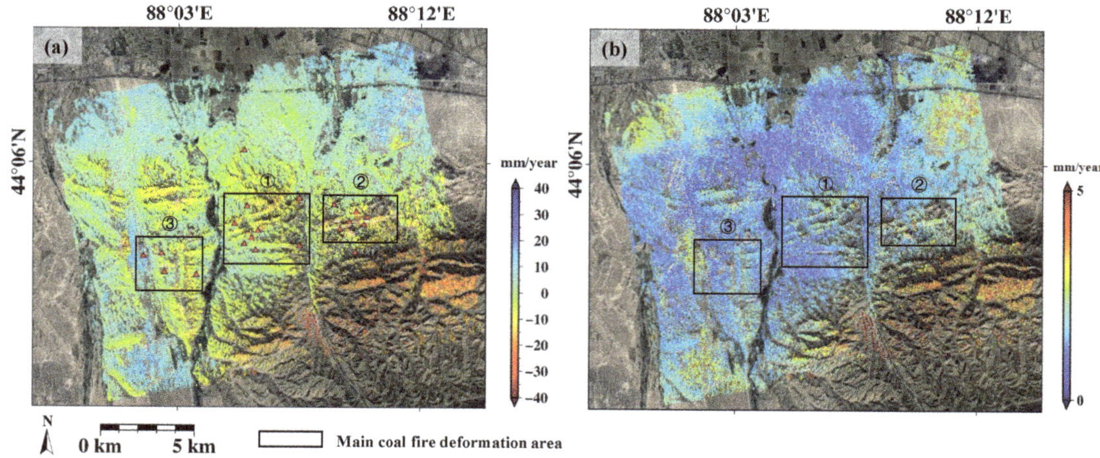

Figure 11. The results of GACOS-Corrected Stacking-InSAR. (**a**) is deformation monitoring result and (**b**) is standard deviation of the LOS velocity. The black boxes in (**a**) indicate the three main coal fire deformation areas over the study area.

It can be seen from Figure 11 that, compared with Original Stacking-InSAR, ground deformation errors caused by atmospheric delay are effectively alleviated by atmospheric correction. However, compared with the result of proposed Adaptive ERA5-Corrected stacking-InSAR, the abnormal deformation value in the southeast toward the mountain area is more visible in the result of GACOS-Corrected stacking-InSAR. In order to further verify the performance of the proposed adaptive ERA5-Corrected Stacking-InSAR, the mean values of standard deviations of the LOS velocity in the three main coal fire deformation areas in Figure 11 are calculated, respectively, (Table 2). As shown in Table 2, after atmospheric correction, the standard deviation of LOS velocity in the three main coal fire areas decreases compared with the Original Stacking-InSAR. The mean values of standard deviations of the adaptive ERA5-Corrected stacking-InSAR method in the three main coal fire deformation areas are minimal, so the deformation result in the coal fire area obtained by the proposed method has a better performance relative to the study area.

Table 2. Statistics on the mean values of standard deviations in the three main coal fire deformation areas.

		Deformation Area ①	Deformation Area ②	Deformation Area ③
Original Stacking-InSAR		2.0764	1.8943	2.9254
ERA5-Corrected Stacking-InSAR	Original ERA5-Corrected	1.5697	1.4391	1.8363
	Effective ERA5-Corrected	2.0869	1.7874	2.1903
	Adaptive ERA5-Corrected	1.5101	1.4220	1.6294
GACOS-Corrected Stacking-InSAR		1.5214	1.4407	1.8645

5.3. *Coal Fire Related Ground Deformation Anomalies Identification*

In Section 4.2 above, four groups of deformation results in the study area were obtained. Kriging interpolation was performed. The mean value minus standard deviation of the four groups of interpolated raster images was used as the threshold to recognize the deformation anomalies. As shown in Figure 12, the red area is the deformation anomalies, and the black triangles show the detected coal fire points. Figure 12a–d shows the deformation anomalies identified by Original Stacking-InSAR result, Original ERA5-Corrected Stacking-InSAR result, Original ERA5-Corrected Stacking-InSAR result and Adaptive ERA5-Corrected Stacking-InSAR result, respectively. With the improvement of Stacking-InSAR results, the deformation abnormal areas obtained by the southeastern division of the study area decrease. The coincidence with the detected coal fire points gradually increase. Many deformation studies [67] in mining areas show that ground cracks generally appear in places with large curvatures, but not in places with maximum deformation. Normally, coal fire points are marked near ground cracks. Thus, the location of coal fire point and deformation anomaly area is not highly consistent.

According to the mine data obtained, the mining scope in the fire area can reach several hundred meters. In this paper, we generated a 400-meter buffer at the location of the coal fire points and intersected it with the deformation anomaly area shown in Figure 12. The effect of ERA5-Corrected Stacking-InSAR results on the monitoring of ground deformation in the coal fire area were evaluated by the size of the overlapping area. As shown in Table 3, the area of abnormal deformation zones divided by the above four results and the overlapping area with the coal fire point buffer zone are counted. The ratio of coincidence area to area of abnormal deformation was used to evaluate the results. The results in the table show that the effective deformation area divided by the Original Stacking-InSAR result accounted for 2.96%; while the counterparts for the Original ERA5-Corrected Stacking-InSAR, Effective ERA5-Corrected Stacking-InSAR and Adaptive ERA5-Corrected Stacking-InSAR are 3.01%, 4.19% and 4.33%, respectively. Compared with the effective deformation area divided by the Original Stacking-InSAR result, the effective area identified by the other three methods increased by 1.6%, 41.5% and 46.3%, respectively.

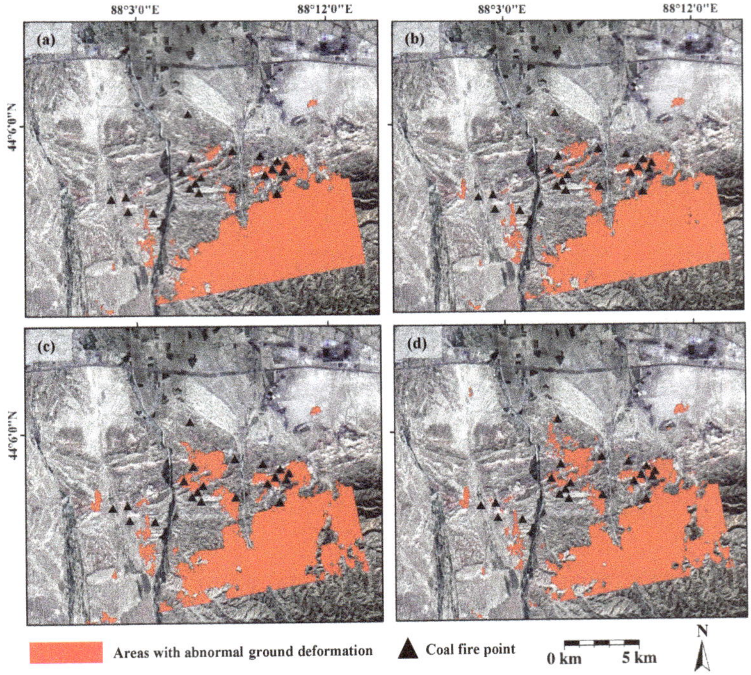

Figure 12. Areas with abnormal ground deformation. (**a–d**) are the divided results of Original Stacking-InSAR, Original ERA5-Corrected Stacking-InSAR, Effective ERA5-Corrected Stacking-InSAR and adaptive ERA5-Corrected Stacking-InSAR, respectively.

Based on the optical image and the local geographical characteristics of the study area, it is inferred that the abnormal deformation in the southeastern part of the study area toward the mountainous area may be the result of the mountain erosion caused by the water flow of melting snow. In the follow-up research work, we will combine more surface information, such as temperature, to further accurately identify the coal fire area.

Given these points, the deformation result based on the proposed adaptive ERA5-corrected Stacking-InSAR is beneficial to accurately monitor the ground deformation range over large-scale coal fire areas rapidly and at a low cost. At the same time, it was further proved that the quality and quantity of stacking interferometric pairs would have a certain impact on the Stacking-InSAR results. The higher the quality and quantity of the interferometric pair, the more precise and reliable the deformation velocity result obtained by Stacking-InSAR.

Table 3. Statistics on the effectiveness of Stacking-InSAR results in identifying fire areas.

		Area of Abnormal Deformation/m²	**Coincidence Area/m²**	**Validity/%**
Original Stacking-InSAR		61,182,730.54	1,810,926.175	2.96
ERA5-Corrected Stacking-InSAR	Original ERA5-Corrected	60,468,157.06	1,819,869.388	3.01 (1.6)
	Effective ERA5-Corrected	59,531,085.59	2,493,108.873	4.19 (41.5)
	Adaptive ERA5-Corrected	55,993,651.4	2,424,075.254	4.33 (46.3)

6. Conclusions

To improve the monitoring efficiency of large-scale coal fire ground deformation, an Adaptive ERA5-Corrected Stacking-InSAR method is proposed to monitor the ground deformation over the Fukang coal fire area of Xinjiang in this study.

After atmospheric correction, the unwrapped standard deviations (SDs) of 40 interferograms are reduced, and the topography-related unwrapped phase terms are visibly decreased. Specifically, the average phase SD of the corrected interferograms is reduced by 13.6% compared with that of the original ones. This indicates that the ERA5 atmospheric product obtained by the D-LOS model can effectively remove the atmospheric delay in the study area. The ground deformation result and standard deviation of the LOS velocity result based on GACOS-Corrected Stacking-InSAR are also acquired, and the results show that the proposed Adaptive ERA5-Corrected Stacking-InSAR method has a better and more reliable performance.

By stacking the interferograms with different phase standard deviation, four ground deformation results are obtained. Based on the detected coal fire points, the four obtained ground deformation results are evaluated. Compared with the Original Stacking-InSAR, the effective area identified by Original ERA5-Corrected Stacking-InSAR, Effective ERA5-Corrected Stacking-InSAR and the proposed adaptive ERA5-Corrected Stacking-InSAR, is increased by 1.6%, 41.5% and 46.3%, respectively. The proposed adaptive ERA5-Corrected Stacking-InSAR method presents the best performance.

In this paper, the ERA5 atmospheric delay product generated based on the D-LOS model is used to remove atmospheric delay in mountainous areas. By comparing the interferogram quality before and after correction, an adaptive method that selects interferograms with better phase quality for Stacking-InSAR deformation estimation is proposed. The proposed adaptive ERA5-Corrected Stacking-InSAR can efficiently retrieve ground deformation over underground coal fire areas with mountains. However, it is difficult to accurately identify underground coal fire areas only relying on the ground deformation anomaly. The proposed adaptive ERA5-Corrected Stacking-InSAR algorithm should be combined with other techniques to more effectively delineate and identify underground coal fire areas.

Author Contributions: Conceptualization: Y.Z., Y.W., W.H., F.Z. and Z.H.; methodology: Y.Z., F.Z., Z.H. and T.W.; formal analysis: Y.Z.; investigation: Y.W., R.S., F.C. and J.Y.; resources: Z.H. and W.H.; data curation: R.S. and L.Z.; writing—original draft preparation: Y.Z.; writing—review and editing: Y.W., F.Z., Z.H., J.L., T.W., J.F., J.E. and L.Z.; visualization: Y.Z.; supervision: Y.W. All authors have read and agreed to the published version of the manuscript.

Funding: This research was supported in part by the National Natural Science Foundation of China (Grant No.41874044 and Grant No. 42004011), in part by project G2HOTSPOTS (PID2021-122142OB-I00) from the MCIN /AEI /10.13039 /501100011033 /FEDER, UE and in part by China Postdoctoral Science Foundation (Grant No. 2020M671646). At the same time, the research was also funded by the Construction Program of Space-Air-Ground-Well Cooperative Awareness Spatial Information Project (B20046) and National Key R&D Program of China (Grant No. 2022YFE0102600).

Data Availability Statement: Not applicable.

Acknowledgments: We thank the ESA and USGS for providing Sentinel-1 SLC data and SRTM elevation data used in this study. Further thanks to ECMWF for providing meteorological data. We also want to thank Xinjiang Coal Fire Geology Bureau, China, for providing the coal fire survey data.

Conflicts of Interest: The authors declare no conflict of interest.

References

1. Tan, Y. Disaster and control of spontaneous combustion in coal field, China. *Meitiandizhi Kantan* **2000**, *28*, 8–10.
2. Rosema, A.; Guan, H.; Veld, H. Simulation of spontaneous combustion, to study the causes of coal fires in the Rujigou Basin. *Fuel* **2001**, *80*, 7–16. [CrossRef]
3. Deng, J.; Ge, S.; Qi, H.; Zhou, F.; Shi, B. Underground coal fire emission of spontaneous combustion, Sandaoba coalfield in Xinjiang, China: Investigation and analysis. *Sci. Total Environ.* **2021**, *777*, 146080. [CrossRef] [PubMed]
4. Qi, X.; Wang, D.; Xin, H.; Zhong, X. Environmental Hazards of Coal Fire and Their Prevention in China. *Environ. Eng. Manag. J. (EEMJ)* **2013**, *12*, 1915–1919. [CrossRef]
5. Jianjun, W.; Weiguo, J.; Xiaochen, L.; Lei, G.; Jiahong, L. Innovative Technologies for Exploration, Monitoring and Extinction of Underground Coal Fires. *J. China Coal Soc.* **2009**, *34*, 1669–1674.
6. Stracher, G.B. Coal fires burning around the world: A global catastrophe. *Int. J. Coal Geol.* **2004**, *1*, 1–152. [CrossRef]
7. Zhou, B.; Wu, J.; Wang, J.; Wu, Y. Surface-based radon detection to identify spontaneous combustion areas in small abandoned coal mine gobs: Case study of a small coal mine in China. *Process Saf. Environ. Prot.* **2018**, *119*, 223–232. [CrossRef]
8. Xueqing, Z.; Yu, Z.; Mingda, Y.; Xiaofei, L.; Tian, W.; Sherong, H. Damages and Cellenge for Governing of Coalfield Fires in Xinjiang. *China Min. Mag.* **2014**, *23*, 93–96.
9. Tan, B.; Zhang, F.; Zhang, Q.; Wei, H.; Shao, Z. Firefighting of subsurface coal fires with comprehensive techniques for detection and control: A case study of the Fukang coal fire in the Xinjiang region of China. *Environ. Sci. Pollut. Res.* **2019**, *26*, 29570–29584. [CrossRef]
10. Shao, Z.; Jia, X.; Zhong, X.; Wang, D.; Wei, J.; Wang, Y.; Chen, L. Detection, extinguishing, and monitoring of a coal fire in Xinjiang, China. *Environ. Sci. Pollut. Res.* **2018**, *25*, 26603–26616. [CrossRef]
11. Xie, J.; Xue, S.; Cheng, W.; Wang, G. Early detection of spontaneous combustion of coal in underground coal mines with development of an ethylene enriching system. *Int. J. Coal Geol.* **2011**, *85*, 123–127. [CrossRef]
12. Singh, A.K.; Singh, R.; Singh, M.P.; Chandra, H.; Shukla, N. Mine fire gas indices and their application to Indian underground coal mine fires. *Int. J. Coal Geol.* **2007**, *69*, 192–204. [CrossRef]
13. Zhang, J.; Wagner, W.; Prakash, A.; Mehl, H.; Voigt, S. Detecting coal fires using remote sensing techniques. *Int. J. Remote Sens.* **2004**, *25*, 3193–3220. [CrossRef]
14. Riyas, M.J.; Syed, T.H.; Kumar, H.; Kuenzer, C. Detecting and Analyzing the Evolution of Subsidence Due to Coal Fires in Jharia Coalfield, India Using Sentinel-1 SAR Data. *Remote Sens.* **2021**, *13*, 1521. [CrossRef]
15. Yuan, G.; Wang, Y.; Zhao, F.; Wang, T.; Zhang, L.; Hao, M.; Yan, S.; Dang, L.; Peng, B. Accuracy assessment and scale effect investigation of UAV thermography for underground coal fire surface temperature monitoring. *Int. J. Appl. Earth Obs. Geoinf.* **2021**, *102*, 102426. [CrossRef]
16. Liu, J.; Wang, Y.; Yan, S.; Zhao, F.; Li, Y.; Dang, L.; Liu, X.; Shao, Y.; Peng, B. Underground coal fire detection and monitoring based on Landsat-8 and Sentinel-1 data sets in Miquan fire area, XinJiang. *Remote Sens.* **2021**, *13*, 1141. [CrossRef]
17. Wang, Y.; Yuan, G.; Wang, T.; Liu, J.; Zhao, F.; Feng, H.; Dang, L.; Peng, K.; Zhang, L. *Research on Multi-Source Remote Sensing Detection of Concealed Fire Sources in Coalfields*; Geomatics and Information Science of Wuhan University: Wuhan, China, 2022; pp. 1651–1661.
18. Huo, H.; Jiang, X.; Song, X.; Li, Z.L.; Ni, Z.; Gao, C. Detection of coal fire dynamics and propagation direction from multi-temporal nighttime Landsat SWIR and TIR data: A case study on the Rujigou coalfield, Northwest (NW) China. *Remote Sens.* **2014**, *6*, 1234–1259. [CrossRef]

19. Yan, S.; Shi, K.; Li, Y.; Liu, J.; Zhao, H. Integration of satellite remote sensing data in underground coal fire detection: A case study of the Fukang region, Xinjiang, China. *Front. Earth Sci.* **2020**, *14*, 1–12. [CrossRef]
20. Wang, T.; Wang, Y.; Zhao, F.; Feng, H.; Liu, J.; Zhang, L.; Zhang, N.; Yuan, G.; Wang, D. A spatio-temporal temperature-based thresholding algorithm for underground coal fire detection with satellite thermal infrared and radar remote sensing. *Int. J. Appl. Earth Obs. Geoinf.* **2022**, *110*, 102805. [CrossRef]
21. Mansor, S.B.; Cracknell, A.P.; Shilin, B.; Gornyi, V. Monitoring of underground coal fires using thermal infrared data. *Int. J. Remote Sens.* **1994**, *15*, 1675–1685. [CrossRef]
22. Kuenzer, C.; Zhang, J.; Jing, L.; Huadong, G.; Dech, S. Thermal infrared remote sensing of surface and underground coal fires. In *Thermal Infrared Remote Sensing: Sensors, Methods, Applications*; Springer: Berlin/Heidelberg, Germany, 2013; pp. 429–451.
23. Shao, Z.; Li, Y.; Deng, R.; Wang, D.; Zhong, X. Three-dimensional-imaging thermal surfaces of coal fires based on UAV thermal infrared data. *Int. J. Remote Sens.* **2021**, *42*, 672–692. [CrossRef]
24. Gao, Y.; Hao, M.; Wang, Y.; Dang, L.; Guo, Y. Multi-scale coal fire detection based on an improved active contour model from Landsat-8 Satellite and UAV images. *ISPRS Int. J. Geo-Inf.* **2021**, *10*, 449. [CrossRef]
25. Ferretti, A.; Prati, C.; Rocca, F. Permanent scatterers in SAR interferometry. *IEEE Trans. Geosci. Remote Sens.* **2001**, *39*, 8–20. [CrossRef]
26. Berardino, P.; Fornaro, G.; Lanari, R.; Sansosti, E. A new algorithm for surface deformation monitoring based on small baseline differential SAR interferograms. *IEEE Trans. Geosci. Remote Sens.* **2002**, *40*, 2375–2383. [CrossRef]
27. Polcari, M.; Montuori, A.; Bignami, C.; Moro, M.; Stramondo, S.; Tolomei, C. Using multi-band InSAR data for detecting local deformation phenomena induced by the 2016–2017 Central Italy seismic sequence. *Remote Sens. Environ.* **2017**, *201*, 234–242. [CrossRef]
28. Camacho, A.G.; Fernández, J.; Samsonov, S.V.; Tiampo, K.F.; Palano, M. 3D multi-source model of elastic volcanic ground deformation. *Earth Planet. Sci. Lett.* **2020**, *547*, 116445. [CrossRef]
29. Zhang, X.; Feng, M.; Zhang, H.; Wang, C.; Tang, Y.; Xu, J.; Yan, D.; Wang, C. Detecting Rock Glacier Displacement in the Central Himalayas Using Multi-Temporal InSAR. *Remote Sens.* **2021**, *13*, 4738. [CrossRef]
30. Zhao, F.; Mallorqui, J.J.; Iglesias, R.; Gili, J.A.; Corominas, J. Landslide monitoring using multi-temporal SAR interferometry with advanced persistent scatterers identification methods and super high-spatial resolution TerraSAR-X images. *Remote Sens.* **2018**, *10*, 921. [CrossRef]
31. Escayo, J.; Marzan, I.; Martí, D.; Tornos, F.; Farci, A.; Schimmel, M.; Carbonell, R.; Fernández, J. Radar Interferometry as a Monitoring Tool for an Active Mining Area Using Sentinel-1 C-Band Data, Case Study of Riotinto Mine. *Remote Sens.* **2022**, *14*, 3061. [CrossRef]
32. Jiang, L.; Lin, H.; Ma, J.; Kong, B.; Wang, Y. Potential of small-baseline SAR interferometry for monitoring land subsidence related to underground coal fires: Wuda (Northern China) case study. *Remote Sens. Environ.* **2011**, *115*, 257–268. [CrossRef]
33. Liu, J.; Wang, Y.; Li, Y.; Dang, L.; Liu, X.; Zhao, H.; Yan, S. Underground coal fires identification and monitoring using time-series InSAR with persistent and distributed scatterers: A case study of Miquan coal fire zone in Xinjiang, China. *IEEE Access* **2019**, *7*, 164492–164506. [CrossRef]
34. Kai, P. Research on Surface Deformation Monitoring Using DS-InSAR in Fukang Coal fire Area, Xinjiang. Master's Thesis, China University of Mining and Technology, Beijing, China, 2021.
35. Chatterjee, R.; Thapa, S.; Singh, K.; Varunakumar, G.; Raju, E. Detecting, mapping and monitoring of land subsidence in Jharia Coalfield, Jharkhand, India by spaceborne differential interferometric SAR, GPS and precision levelling techniques. *J. Earth Syst. Sci.* **2015**, *124*, 1359–1376. [CrossRef]
36. Ferretti, A.; Fumagalli, A.; Novali, F.; Prati, C.; Rocca, F.; Rucci, A. A new algorithm for processing interferometric data-stacks: SqueeSAR. *IEEE Trans. Geosci. Remote Sens.* **2011**, *49*, 3460–3470. [CrossRef]
37. Zhao, F.; Mallorqui, J.J. SMF-POLOPT: An adaptive multitemporal pol (DIn) SAR filtering and phase optimization algorithm for PSI applications. *IEEE Trans. Geosci. Remote Sens.* **2019**, *57*, 7135–7147. [CrossRef]
38. Zhao, F.; Mallorqui, J.J. Coherency matrix decomposition-based polarimetric persistent scatterer interferometry. *IEEE Trans. Geosci. Remote Sens.* **2019**, *57*, 7819–7831. [CrossRef]
39. Zhao, F.; Wang, T.; Zhang, L.; Feng, H.; Yan, S.; Fan, H.; Xu, D.; Wang, Y. Polarimetric Persistent Scatterer Interferometry for Ground Deformation Monitoring with VV-VH Sentinel-1 Data. *Remote Sens.* **2022**, *14*, 309. [CrossRef]
40. Yu, C.; Li, Z.; Penna, N.T. Interferometric synthetic aperture radar atmospheric correction using a GPS-based iterative tropospheric decomposition model. *Remote Sens. Environ.* **2018**, *204*, 109–121. [CrossRef]
41. Bekaert, D.; Walters, R.; Wright, T.; Hooper, A.; Parker, D. Statistical comparison of InSAR tropospheric correction techniques. *Remote Sens. Environ.* **2015**, *170*, 40–47. [CrossRef]
42. Shamshiri, R.; Motagh, M.; Nahavandchi, H.; Haghighi, M.H.; Hoseini, M. Improving tropospheric corrections on large-scale Sentinel-1 interferograms using a machine learning approach for integration with GNSS-derived zenith total delay (ZTD). *Remote Sens. Environ.* **2020**, *239*, 111608. [CrossRef]
43. Dong, J.; Zhang, L.; Liao, M.; Gong, J. Improved correction of seasonal tropospheric delay in InSAR observations for landslide deformation monitoring. *Remote Sens. Environ.* **2019**, *233*, 111370. [CrossRef]
44. González, P.J.; Tiampo, K.F.; Camacho, A.G.; Fernández, J. *Shallow Flank Deformation at Cumbre Vieja Volcano (Canary Islands): Implications on the Stability of Steep-Sided Volcano Flanks at Oceanic Islands*; Elsevier: Amsterdam, The Netherlands, 2010.

45. Carmon, N.; Berk, A.; Bohn, N.; Brodrick, P.G.; Kalashnikova, O.; Nguyen, H.; Thompson, D.R.; Turmon, M. Unified Topographic and Atmospheric Correction for Remote Imaging Spectroscopy. *Front. Remote Sens.* **2022**, *3*, 916155. [CrossRef]
46. Jolivet, R.; Agram, P.S.; Lin, N.Y.; Simons, M.; Doin, M.P.; Peltzer, G.; Li, Z. Improving InSAR geodesy using global atmospheric models. *J. Geophys. Res. Solid Earth* **2014**, *119*, 2324–2341. [CrossRef]
47. Jolivet, R.; Grandin, R.; Lasserre, C.; Doin, M.P.; Peltzer, G. Systematic InSAR tropospheric phase delay corrections from global meteorological reanalysis data. *Geophys. Res. Lett.* **2011**, *38*. [CrossRef]
48. Hu, Z.; Mallorqui, J.J. A direct method to estimate atmospheric phase delay for InSAR with global atmospheric models. In Proceedings of the IGARSS 2018-2018 IEEE International Geoscience and Remote Sensing Symposium, Valencia, Spain, 22–27 July 2018; IEEE: New York, NY, USA, 2018; pp. 2196–2199.
49. Hu, Z. *Atmospheric Artifacts Correction for InSAR Using Empirical Model and nUmerical Weather Prediction Models*; Universitat Politècnica de Catalunya: Barcelona, Spain, 2019.
50. Hu, Z.; Mallorquí, J.J. An accurate method to correct atmospheric phase delay for insar with the era5 global atmospheric model. *Remote Sens.* **2019**, *11*, 1969. [CrossRef]
51. Fernández, J.; Escayo, J.; Hu, Z.; Camacho, A.G.; Samsonov, S.V.; Prieto, J.F.; Tiampo, K.F.; Palano, M.; Mallorquí, J.J.; Ancochea, E. Detection of volcanic unrest onset in La Palma, Canary Islands, evolution and implications. *Sci. Rep.* **2021**, *11*, 2540. [CrossRef]
52. Fernández, J.; Escayo, J.; Camacho, A.G.; Palano, M.; Prieto, J.F.; Hu, Z.; Samsonov, S.V.; Tiampo, K.F.; Ancochea, E. Shallow magmatic intrusion evolution below La Palma before and during the 2021 eruption. *Sci. Rep.* **2022**, *12*, 20257. [CrossRef]
53. Hersbach, H. The ERA5 Atmospheric Reanalysis. In Proceedings of the AGU fall Meeting Abstracts, Francisco, CA, USA, 12–16 December 2016; Volume 2016, p. NG33D–01.
54. Hersbach, H.; Bell, B.; Berrisford, P.; Hirahara, S.; Horányi, A., Muñoz-Sabater, J.; Nicolas, J.; Peubey, C.; Radu, R.; Schepers, D.; et al. The ERA5 global reanalysis. *Q. J. R. Meteorol. Soc.* **2020**, *146*, 1999–2049. [CrossRef]
55. Xiao, R.; Yu, C.; Li, Z.; He, X. Statistical assessment metrics for InSAR atmospheric correction: Applications to generic atmospheric correction online service for InSAR (GACOS) in Eastern China. *Int. J. Appl. Earth Obs. Geoinf.* **2021**, *96*, 102289. [CrossRef]
56. Smith, E.K.; Weintraub, S. The constants in the equation for atmospheric refractive index at radio frequencies. *Proc. IRE* **1953**, *41*, 1035–1037. [CrossRef]
57. Sandwell, D.T.; Price, E.J. Phase gradient approach to stacking interferograms. *J. Geophys. Res. Solid Earth* **1998**, *103*, 30183–30204. [CrossRef]
58. Li, Z. Locating the Small 1999 Frenchman Flat, Nevada Earthquake with InSAR Stacking. *J. Geod. Geoinf. Sci.* **2022**, *5*, 39.
59. Zhang, L.; Dai, K.; Deng, J.; Ge, D.; Liang, R.; Li, W.; Xu, Q. Identifying potential landslides by stacking-InSAR in southwestern China and its performance comparison with SBAS-InSAR. *Remote Sens.* **2021**, *13*, 3662. [CrossRef]
60. Kang, Y.; Zhao, C.; Zhang, Q.; Lu, Z.; Li, B. Application of InSAR techniques to an analysis of the Guanling landslide. *Remote Sens.* **2017**, *9*, 1046. [CrossRef]
61. Xu, Y.; Li, T.; Tang, X.; Zhang, X.; Fan, H.; Wang, Y. Research on the Applicability of DInSAR, Stacking-InSAR and SBAS-InSAR for Mining Region Subsidence Detection in the Datong Coalfield. *Remote Sens.* **2022**, *14*, 3314. [CrossRef]
62. Xiao, R.; Yu, C.; Li, Z.; Song, C.; He, X. General Survey of Large-scale Land Subsidence by GACOS-Corrected InSAR Stacking: Case Study in North China Plain. *Proc. Int. Assoc. Hydrol. Sci.* **2020**, *382*, 213–218. [CrossRef]
63. Zhao, F.; Mallorqui, J.J. A temporal phase coherence estimation algorithm and its application on DInSAR pixel selection. *IEEE Trans. Geosci. Remote Sens.* **2019**, *57*, 8350–8361. [CrossRef]
64. Ge, D. *Research on the Key Techniques of SAR Interferometry for Reg ional Land Subsidence Monitoring*; China University of Geosciences Beijing: Beijing, China, 2013.
65. Murray, K.D.; Bekaert, D.P.; Lohman, R.B. Tropospheric corrections for InSAR: Statistical assessments and applications to the Central United States and Mexico. *Remote Sens. Environ.* **2019**, *232*, 111326. [CrossRef]
66. Wang, Q.; Yu, W.; Xu, B.; Wei, G. Assessing the use of GACOS products for SBAS-INSAR deformation monitoring: A case in Southern California. *Sensors* **2019**, *19*, 3894. [CrossRef]
67. Yang, J. Study on Mining Subsidence Law of Whole Basin in Shilawusu Mine Based on InSAR Technology. Master's Thesis, China University of Mining and Technology, Beijing, China, 2021.

remote sensing

MDPI

Article

Coseismic Rupture Behaviors of the January and March 2022 $M_W > 5.5$ Hala Lake Earthquakes, NE Tibet, Constrained by InSAR Observations

Jiuyuan Yang [1], Caijun Xu [1,2,3,*] and Yangmao Wen [1,2]

1 School of Geodesy and Geomatics, Wuhan University, Wuhan 430079, China
2 Key Laboratory of Geospace Environment and Geodesy, Ministry of Education, Wuhan University, Wuhan 430079, China
3 Hubei Luojia Laboratory, Wuhan 430079, China
* Correspondence: cjxu@sgg.whu.edu.cn

Abstract: On 23 January and 25 March 2022, two $M_W > 5.5$ Hala Lake earthquakes characterized by right-lateral strike-slip faulting occurred around the Elashan Fault in Northeastern Tibet, marking the two largest events since the 1927 M_W 6.2 Hala Lake earthquake. Since no surface rupture related to the two earthquakes has been reported, the seismogenic faults and coseismic rupture behaviors of the two events are still unknown. The occurrence of the two events provides a rare opportunity to gain insight into the seismogenic structure and rupture behavior of the less studied region, further helping us accurately evaluate the regional seismic hazard. Here, we first exploit Interferometric synthetic aperture radar (InSAR) data to obtain the coseismic deformation associated with the two earthquakes and then invert for the fault geometry and detailed coseismic slip of the two events. Coseismic modeling reveals that the January and March 2022 earthquakes ruptured two buried west-dipping moderate-angle and high-angle right-lateral strike-slip faults, respectively. Most of the slip of the January event occurred at depths from 1.7–7.6 km, while the majority of the slip associated with the March event occurred at depths from 2.5–10 km, which may have been restricted by the intersections between the January and March Hala Lake seismogenic faults. By a comprehensive analysis of the coseismic inversions, stress changes, and early postseismic signal, we suggest that the significant fault dip difference (~30°), highlighting a fault segmentation, stops the rupture propagation from one fault segment to another and that fluid migration may encourage the restart of the rupture of the later event, which requires further investigation. Moreover, Coulomb stress modeling shows stress loading on the eastern segment of the Daxueshan–Shule Fault and the northern segment of the Elashan fault, which we should pay more attention to.

Keywords: Hala Lake earthquake; InSAR; coseismic deformation; buried strike-slip fault; coulomb stress

1. Introduction

On 23 January 2022 (UTC Time 2:21), an M_W 5.6 shallow earthquake, which was followed by one $M_S > 3.0$ aftershock, occurred ~13 km northwest of the Hala Lake in Qinghai Province, China (Figure 1). On 25 March 2022 (UTC Time 16:21), a much larger shallow earthquake with M_W 5.7—marking the largest event around the Hala Lake for the last 95 years—occurred ~7 km northwest of the January 2022 Hala Lake event (Figure 1). After the March 2022 earthquake, a total of 11 $M_S > 3.0$ aftershocks was recorded in the following 45 days from 25 March to 12 May 2022. As the epicenters of the two Hala Lake earthquakes were located in No Man's Land, the events caused no casualties. The focal mechanism solutions from the Global Centroid Moment Tensor (GCMT; https://www.globalcmt.org/, accessed on 1 January 2023) and the United States Geological Survey (USGS; https://www.usgs.gov/, accessed on 1 January 2023) (Tables 1 and 2) reveal that the January and March 2022 Hala Lake earthquakes activated two nearly NS-striking moderate-angle and high-angle right-lateral strike-slip faults, respectively. The occurrence of the January and March 2022 events offers an important opportunity to improve our knowledge of the seismogenic structure of the regional active fault with modern datasets (e.g., InSAR). So far, no related geodetic studies about the two Hala Lake earthquakes have been published. The detailed InSAR study of the two events can contribute to a deeper understanding of the regional seismogenic mechanism and tectonic deformation. Moreover, a coinstantaneous multi-fault rupture in a single earthquake often results in a higher hazard than that induced by the delayed rupture of multiple faults in an earthquake doublet or a seismic sequence, which spans a long period of days to months [1,2]. Studying the delayed rupture (about two months apart) between the two Hala Lake events can also enhance our understanding of the controlling factors for the kinematic evolution of rupture during an earthquake doublet or a seismic sequence, which will help us accurately evaluate the regional seismic hazard.

Table 1. Source parameters of the 23 January 2022 M_W 5.6 Hala Lake earthquake.

Model	Lon/°	Lat/°	Strike/°	Dip/°	Rake/°	Length/km	Depth/km	Slip/m	M_W
USGS	97.34	38.46	171	60	−168	-	10	-	5.6
GCMT	97.39	38.52	169	74	−173	-	18.4	-	5.6
U-S-model	$97.37^{+0.24\text{km}}_{-0.24\text{km}}$	$38.46^{+0.43\text{km}}_{-0.43\text{km}}$	$172.42^{+4.3}_{-4.3}$	$61.8^{+2.3}_{-2.3}$	-175.1^{+4}_{-4}	$7.4^{+0.28}_{-0.28}$	$1.9^{+0.15}_{-0.15}$	$0.15^{+0.02}_{-0.02}$	5.53

Notes: U–S model represents the uniform slip model. The location (longitude and latitude) of the uniform slip model indicates the center of up-dip surface projection of the rupture fault plane. Depth shows the midpoint of the upper boundary of the uniform fault plane.

Table 2. Source parameters of the 25 March 2022 M_W 5.7 Hala Lake earthquake.

Model	Lon/°	Lat/°	Strike/°	Dip/°	Rake/°	Length/km	Depth/km	Slip/m	M_W
USGS	97.29	38.54	352	90	172	-	10	-	5.7
GCMT	97.34	38.54	173	87	−174	-	21.1	-	5.8
U-S-model	$97.34^{+0.18\text{km}}_{-0.18\text{km}}$	$38.50^{+0.25\text{km}}_{-0.25\text{km}}$	$176^{+2.2}_{-2.2}$	87 (Fixed)	$-165^{+4.1}_{-4.1}$	$5.3^{+0.6}_{-0.6}$	$2.5^{+0.3}_{-0.3}$	$0.35^{+0.08}_{-0.08}$	5.71

Notes: All the abbreviations and symbols in Table 2 are the same as those in Table 1, but for the March 2022 Hala Lake earthquake.

InSAR data, characterized by high precision and high resolution [3,4], have been widely applied to investigate crustal deformation caused by the seismic cycle [5–8] since its successful use to the 1992 Mw 7.3 Landers earthquake [4]. As the first two seismic events detected by InSAR in the Hala Lake area, it is meaningful to derive the interferometric phase associated with the Hala Lake earthquakes so as to gain insight into the regional seismogenic stucture and seismic hazard. In this study, we first make use of Sentinel-1 SAR data to image the coseismic surface displacements of the January and March 2022 Hala Lake earthquakes. Then, we utilize the coseismic observations to invert for the fault geometry and detailed coseismic slip of the two earthquakes. Subsequently, we explore the effect of the January 2022 M_W 6.7 Menyuan earthquake on the two Hala Lake earthquakes and analyze the possible causes for the termination and restart of the slip during the two similar magnitudes and temporally separated Hala Lake earthquakes. Lastly, the influence of the coseismic coulomb stress changes caused by the two Hala Lake events on the surrounding faults is calculated in order to assess the regional seismic hazards.

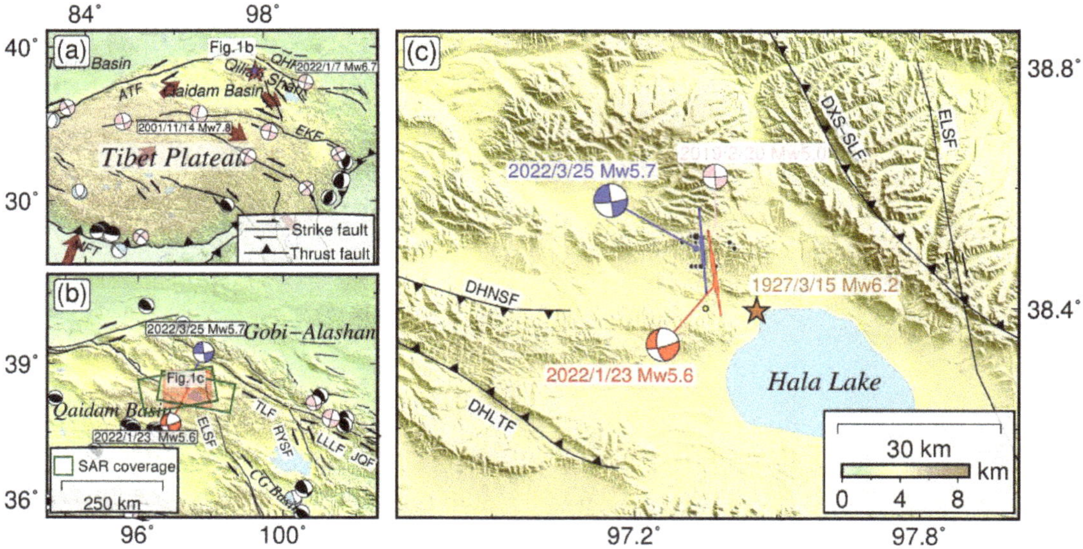

Figure 1. (**a**) Tectonic background of Tibet plateau. Large dark red arrows show the plate motion [9]. ATF: Altyn Tagh fault; EKF: East Kunlun fault; MFT: Main frontal thrust; QHF: Qilian-Haiyuan fault; Red and blue stars represent the epicenters of the January and March 2022 Hala Lake earthquakes, respectively. (**b**) Tectonic map of the NE Tibet. TLF: Tuolaishan fault; JQF: Jinqianghe fault; LLLF: Lenglongling fault; ELSF: Elashan fault; RYSF: Riyueshan fault; CG basin: Chaka-Gonghe basin. (**c**) Tectonic setting around the two 2022 Hala Lake earthquakes. Thin red and blue lines indicate the coseismic fault traces of the January and March 2022 Hala Lake earthquakes, respectively, from the slip distribution models, while the thick red and blue lines superimposed on the thin lines depict the coseismic fault traces of the January and March events, respectively, from the uniform slip models. Yellow circle represents the $M_S > 3.0$ aftershock after the January 2022 event, whereas black circles are $M_S > 3.0$ aftershocks occurred between 26 March and 13 May 2022. All aftershocks are acquired from the China Earthquake Networks Center (CENC; https://www.cenc.ac.cn/, accessed on 1 January 2023). DHLTF: Dahaletenghe fault; DHNSF: Danghenanshan fault; DXS-SLF: Daxueshan-shule fault. Faults are acquired from Institute of Geology, China Earthquake Administration (https://www.eq-igl.ac.cn/, accessed on 1 January 2023). Black, pink, and light-blue beach balls denote the focal mechanisms of historical thrust, strike-slip and normal earthquakes, respectively, from GCMT (Thereinto, beach balls in (**a**,**b**) represent $M_W > 6.5$ and $M_W > 5.5$ earthquakes, respectively, while those in Figure 1c indicate $M_W > 5.0$ earthquake).

2. Tectonic Background

As the forefront of the northward expansion of the Tibet plateau moves towards the interior continent, the northeast margin of the Tibet Plateau characterized by strong tectonic activity has been suffering from the intensive shearing deformation since Late Quaternary due to the continuing collision between the Indian and Eurasian plates, thus developing many prominent strike-slip faults such as the nearly E-W-trending left-lateral strike-slip East Kunlun fault (EKLF), the Qilian–Haiyuan fault (QHF), the NW–SE-trending right-lateral strike-slip Elashan fault (ELSF) and Riyueshan fault (RYSF) ([10–12]; Figure 1a,b). These strike-slip faults are considered to play an important role in regulating the eastward motion of Tibet plateau relative to the Gobi–Alashan block (GAB) and to have frequent seismic activity (e.g., [13]). However, compared with that the 2001 M_W 7.8 Kokoxili and 2022 M_W 6.7 Menyuan earthquakes ruptured the large sinistral strike-slip EKLF and QHF, respectively ([14,15]; Figure 1a), the lack of recent $M_W > 5.5$ moderate-to-large earthquakes occurred in the secondary dextral strike-slip faults such as the ELSF and RYSF (Figure 1b), which hinders our understanding of the regional tectonic environment. As the tectonically active boundary between the Qaidam basin and Chaka–Gonghe basin, the ELSF consisting of several discontinuous subparallel NW–SE-trending right-stepping or left-stepping "en echelon" strike-slip fault segments have a length of ~200 km ([16]; Figure 1b). Its northern segment is especially considered to be characterized by some horsetail splay faults [17], which may be associated with the seismogenic faults of the January and March 2022 Hala Lake events. As the two largest earthquakes since the 1927 M_W 6.2 Hala Lake earthquake (Figure 1c), the two 2022 Hala Lake earthquakes occurred around the northern segment of the ELSF, presenting a rare chance to gain insight into the regional tectonic deformation and seismogenic structure.

3. InSAR Observations

Benefitting from the short revisit period of Sentinel-1A satellite, we derive a rare chance to study the 2022 Hala Lake seismic sequence separately. Aiming at acquiring the coseismic deformation associated with the January and March 2022 Hala Lake earthquakes, we use the two-pass differential SAR interferometry method [18] to process six pairs of Sentinel-1 Single Look Complex SAR images (Tables 3–5) with a multi-looking factor of 2 by 10 along the azimuth and range directions on the basis of the Gamma software [19]. A 30 m digital elevation model and a power spectrum filter [20] are exploited to exclude the topographic contributions and filter the phase, respectively. Finally, we use the branch cut method [21] to unwrap the interferograms and further geocoded them to the WGS84 geographic coordinates. These things considered, in order to eliminate both the topography-correlated atmospheric delays and residual orbital errors, a linear function between the error phase, location, and elevation is estimated by the virtue of coseismic observations far from the major deformation area [22]. The continuous deformation fringe pattern of the coseismic interferograms (Figure 2a–d) implies that the coseismic rupture of the two earthquakes doesn't propagate to the surface. For the January 2022 Hala Lake earthquake, the ascending coseismic interferograms (Figure 2a) show two major lobe deformation areas with the southwest quadrant moving away from the satellite and the northwest quadrant moving towards the satellite, whereas the descending coseismic interferograms (Figure 2b) reveal three prominent lobe deformation areas with the southwest quadrant moving away from the satellite and the northwest and southeast quadrants moving towards the satellite. Such asymmetric deformation patterns exhibited in the ascending and descending interferograms (Figure 2a,b) indicate a predominantly dextral strike-slip motion. In addition, the deformation magnitude in the west is much larger than that in the east in the two interferograms, indicating a west-dipping seismogenic fault. For the March 2022 Hala Lake earthquake, the overall deformation pattern shown in the ascending and descending interferograms (Figure 2c,d) is generally similar to that of the January 2022 Hala Lake earthquake (Figure 2a,b). In particular, the deformation magnitude in the east is much larger than that in the west in the descending interferogram (Figure 2d), which is contrary to that in the ascending interferogram (Figure 2c), implying a nearly sub-vertical fault. Hence, taking into consideration the above descriptions, we suggest that one west-dipping and one nearly sub-vertical buried right-lateral strike-slip faults may be activated during the January and March 2022 Hala Lake earthquakes, respectively. The ranges of line-of-sight (LOS) displacements in the two ascending interferograms are −1.9 to 1.9 cm for the 23 January event (Figure 2e) and −3.0 to 1.2 cm for the 25 March event (Figure 2g), respectively, while the ranges of LOS displacements in the two descending interferograms are −1.2 to 0.7 cm for the 23 January event (Figure 2f) and −1.4 to 2.9 cm for the 25 March event (Figure 2h), respectively. In addition, we also acquired the coseismic interferograms associated with both the 23 January and 25 March events. The overall deformation exhibited in the ascending and descending interferograms (Figure 2m,o) is generally similar to that of any single Hala Lake event (Figure 2a–d) but has a more complex and larger deformation (Figure 2e–h,n,p). It should be noted that we do not use the total coseismic deformation to the geodetic inversion because solving for the geometries of multiple faults simultaneously will result in trade-offs between fault parameters during the inversion [23]. Finally, to preliminarily assess the early postseismic deformation associated with the 23 January event, five Sentinel-1A ascending images spanning the time period from 27 January 2022 to 16 March 2022, and five descending images spanning the time period from 1 February 2022 to 21 March 2022, are also analyzed (Table 6). We processed all interferometric pairs in the same way as the coseismic interferogram and apply the MintPy package to process the following InSAR time series on the basis of the small baseline method [24–26]. Our preliminary postseismic displacement (Figure 3) highlights that the cumulative early postseismic is limited and can be ignored.

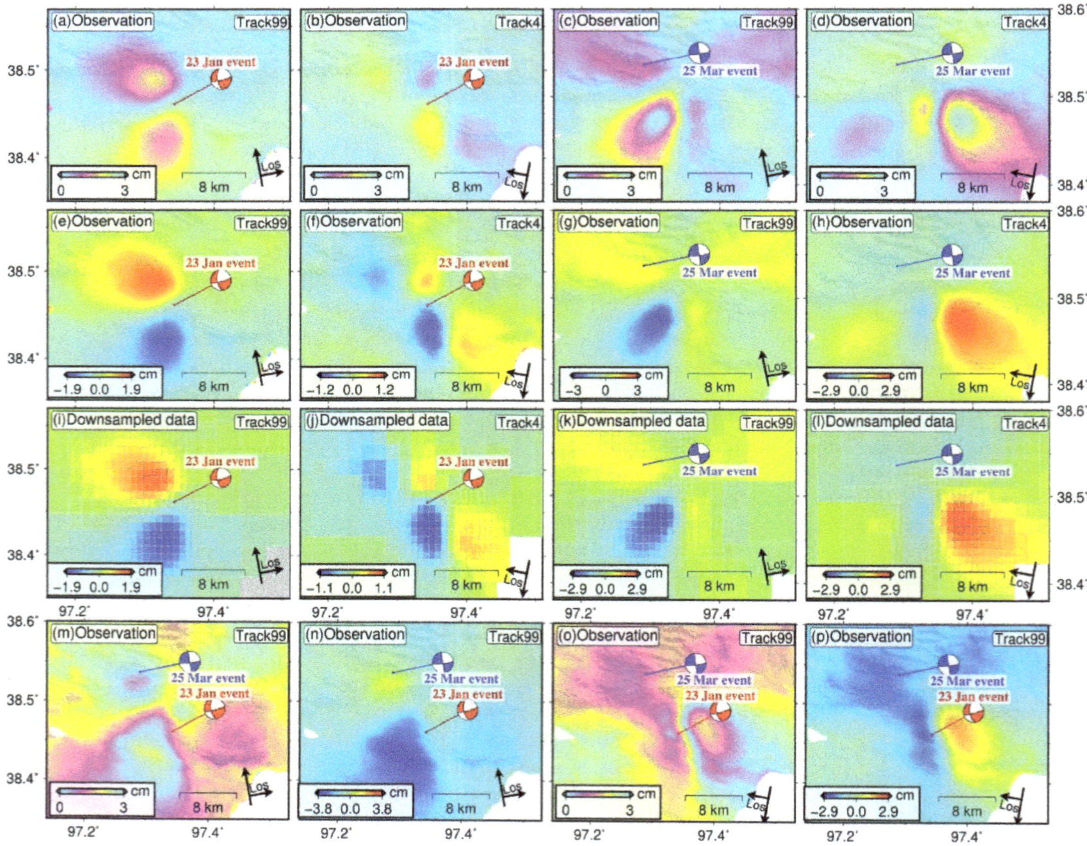

Figure 2. (**a**,**b**) are ascending and descending coseismic interferograms, respectively, covering the 23 January 2022 Hala Lake earthquake. (**e**,**f**) are corresponding coseismic displacements. (**i**,**j**) are corresponding down-sampled LOS displacement. (**c**,**d**) are ascending and descending coseismic interferograms, respectively, covering the 25 March 2022 Hala Lake earthquake. (**g**,**h**) are corresponding coseismic displacements. (**k**,**l**) are corresponding down-sampled LOS displacements. (**m**) is ascending coseismic interferograms covering the 23 January and 25 March 2022 Hala Lake earthquakes. (**n**) is corresponding coseismic displacements. (**o**) is descending coseismic interferograms covering the 23 January and 25 March 2022 Hala Lake earthquakes. (**p**) is corresponding coseismic displacements.

Table 3. Details of SAR data used for coseismic deformation of the 23 January 2022 M_W 5.6 Hala Lake earthquake.

Satellite	Track	Reference Date	Repeat Date	Perp. B (m)	Inc. Angle	Azi. Angle
Sentinel-1A	T99A	15 January 2022	27 January 2022	−13.1	36.9	−10.3
Sentinel-1A	T4D	8 January 2022	1 February 2022	15.7	36.9	−169.7

Notes: Perp. B denotes the perpendicular baseline. Inc. Angle and Azi. Angle represent the incidence and azimuth angles, respectively.

Table 4. Details of SAR data used for coseismic deformation of the 25 March 2022 M_W 5.7 Hala Lake earthquake.

Satellite	Track	Reference Date	Repeat Date	Perp. B (m)	Inc. Angle	Azi. Angle
Sentinel-1A	T99A	16 March 2022	28 March 2022	−96.6	36.9	−10.3
Sentinel-1A	T4D	21 March 2022	2 April 2022	51.2	36.9	−169.7

Notes: All the abbreviations in Table 4 are the same as those in Table 3, but for the March 2022 Hala Lake earthquake.

Table 5. Details of SAR data used for the total coseismic deformation of the 23 January and 25 March 2022 $M_W > 5.5$ Hala Lake earthquakes.

Satellite	Track	Reference Date	Repeat Date	Perp. B (m)	Inc. Angle	Azi. Angle
Sentinel-1A	T99A	15 January 2022	28 March 2022	−86.9	36.9	−10.3
Sentinel-1A	T4D	8 January 2022	2 April 2022	80.2	36.9	−169.7

Notes: All the abbreviations in Table 5 are the same as those in Table 3, but for both the 23 January and 25 March 2022 $M_W > 5.5$ Hala Lake earthquakes.

Table 6. Details of SAR data used for postseismic deformation of the 23 January 2022 M_W 5.6 Hala Lake earthquake.

Satellite	Track	Reference Date	Date Due	No. of Images	Used Interferograms
Sentinel-1A	T99A	27 January 2022	16 March 2022	5	10
Sentinel-1A	T4D	1 February 2022	21 March 2022	5	10

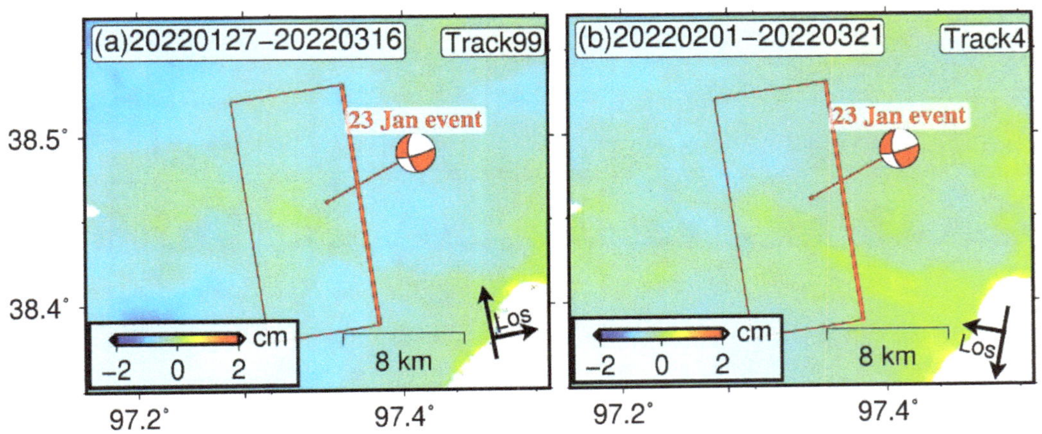

Figure 3. (**a**,**b**) are the ascending and descending postseismic cumulative deformation maps of the 23 January 2022 Hala Lake earthquake, respectively. Red rectangular box represents the rupture fault plane from the coseismic slip distribution model of the January 2022 event. The solid red line shows the fault surface trace.

4. Geodetic Modelling

To gain an insight into the source characteristics, we exploit the resolution-based resampling method [27] to downsample the coseismic LOS deformation related to the 23 January and 25 March 2022 Menyuan earthquakes (Figure 2i–l) and further invert for slip on the rectangular dislocation, assuming a homogeneous, elastic, and isotropic half-space [28]. At first, we perform a non-linear inversion to hunt for the optimal fault geometrical parameters by means of the multi-peak particle swarm optimization algorithm [29] and then estimate the uncertainty of each obtained fault parameter through Monte Carlo inversions [30] of 100 datasets perturbed with random noise (Figures 4 and 5). Subsequently, we extend the derived fault planes responsible for the two earthquakes along strike and dip directions, respectively, and carry out a linear inversion to resolve the variable slip distribution on the enlarged fault plane subdivided into subpatches of 1 by 1 km. In addition, we added a befitting smoothing factor to the linear inversion by examining the trade-off curve between the RMS and roughness (Figure 6) in order to avoid the abrupt slip variations and further utilize the one-dimensional grid search method to optimize the fault dip during the coseismic slip distribution inversion (Figure 7).

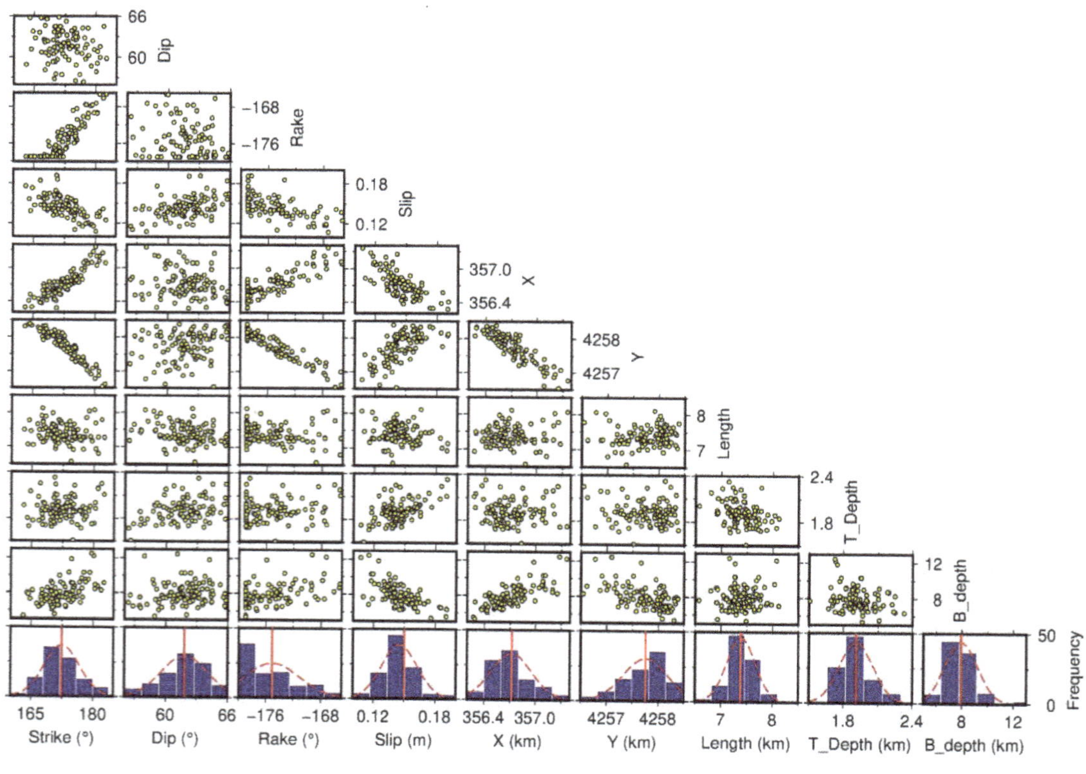

Figure 4. Fault geometry parameters for the uniform fault plane of the January 2022 Hala Lake earthquake from the Monte-Carlo analysis. B_depth: the midpoint of the bottom boundary of the uniform fault plane; T_depth: the midpoint of the upper boundary of the uniform fault plane; Histograms show the distribution of the optimal solutions of fault geometry parameters during the 100 inversions. The solid red line represents the optimal value.

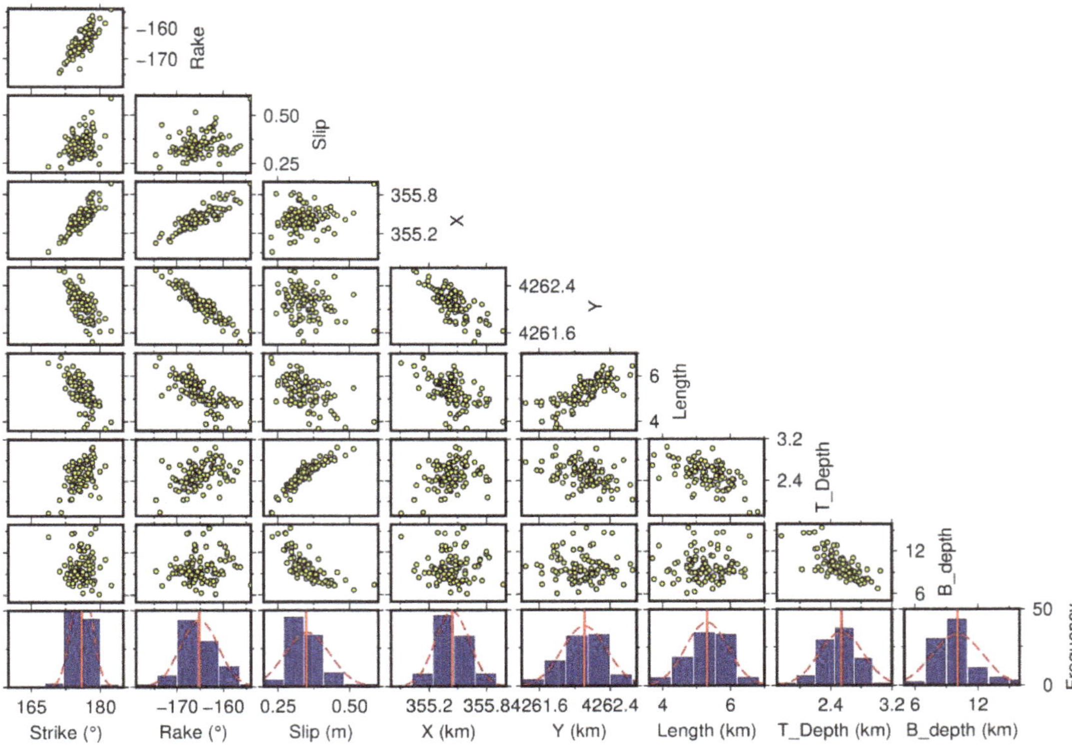

Figure 5. All the symbols in Figure 5 are the same as those in Figure 4, but for the uniform fault model of the March 2022 Hala Lake earthquake.

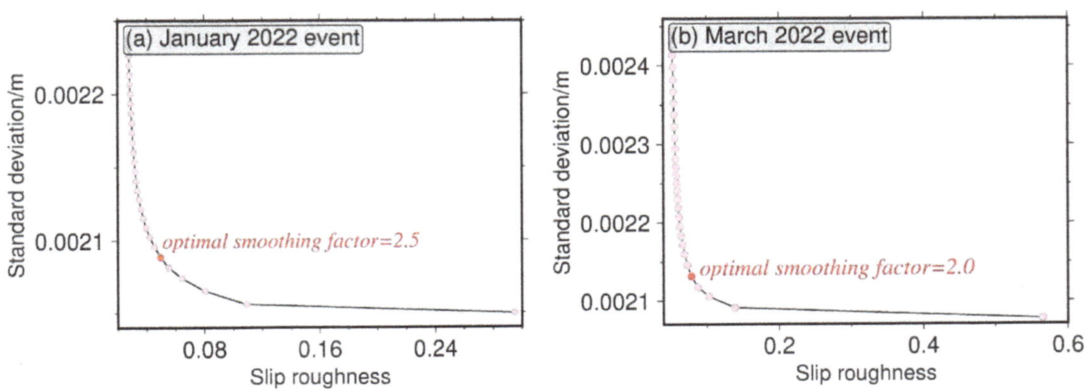

Figure 6. Trade-off curve of the standard deviation of data versus the slip roughness. Red circle denotes the selected smoothing factor, which is used to the coseismic slip distribution inversion.

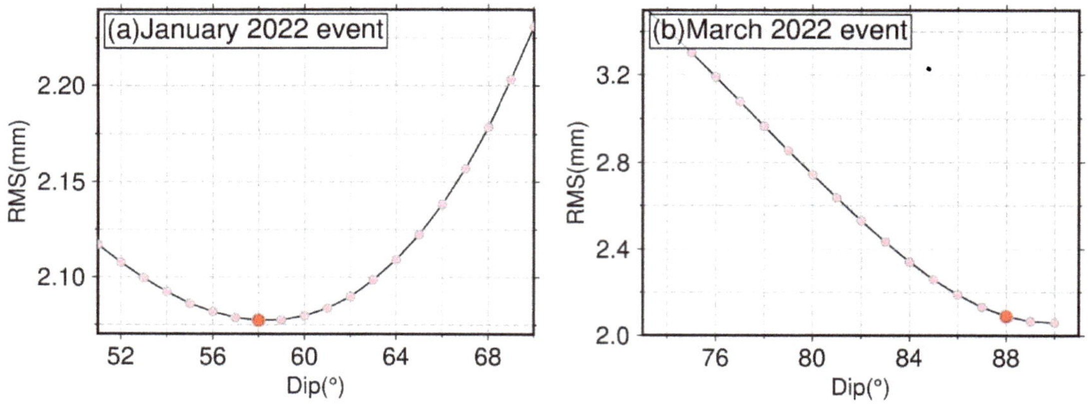

Figure 7. Trade-off curve between the RMS and the dip of the rupture fault segment. Red circle indicates the optimal fault dip used in the coseismic slip distribution inversion. In (**b**), the RMS decreases rapidly with increasing dip but no longer decreases significantly when dip reaches 88°, so we regard the 88° as the optimal fault dip.

4.1. The 23 January 2022 Hala Lake Earthquake

According to the detailed analysis of the coseismic interferograms (Figure 2a,b) in Section 2, we believe the west-dipping dextral strike-slip fault to be the causative fault responsible for the January 2022 Hala Lake earthquake and then set a search interval for the fault geometrical parameters. The rake and strike are constrained between −225° and −135°, and 135° and 225°, respectively, while the other fault geometrical parameters are unconstrained. (For example, the search range for the dip is set to 0°~90°). The best-fitting solutions for each fault geometrical parameter shown in Table 1 and Figure 4 reveal an SSE-striking strike-slip fault with a minor normal slip during the Hala Lake earthquake. The uniform coseismic slip of up to ~0.15 m extends from a depth of 7.9 km up to 1.9 km on a ~7.4 km-long and ~6.3 km-wide rupture fault (Table 1 and Figure 4). As a whole, the fault parameters are well-resolved with small uncertainties (Table 1). For example, the fault location (X and Y) has an uncertainty of less than 500 m while the strike, dip, and rake have an uncertainty of less than 4.3°. Moreover, the uniform slip model can reproduce the observed ascending and descending coseismic deformations (Figure 8). The corresponding slip distribution model (Figure 9a–c) shows that the rupture fault is dominated by nearly pure dextral strike-slip faulting, and that most slips are concentrated at a depth from 1.7–7.6 km, with the maximum slip of about 0.21 m at a depth of 3.8 km, suggesting a buried event. The location of the epicenter relative to the inverted slip distribution implies that the coseismic rupture mainly propagates northward unilaterally. The seismic moment generated by the coseismic slip distribution model is ~2.4×10^{17} Nm, corresponding to M_W 5.6. Compared with the modeled interferograms by the uniform slip model (Figure 8), the detected ascending and descending coseismic deformations can be better explained (Figure 10) with the rms of ~2.5 and 1.4 mm, respectively.

4.2. The 25 March 2022 Hala Lake Earthquake

On the basis of the coseismic interferogram described in Section 2, we consider the seismogenic fault to be a sub-vertical right-lateral strike-slip fault. Initially, we constrain the rake between −225° and −135°, while other source parameters are not restricted. However, after several nonlinear inversions, the dip always reaches its maximum limit of 90°. Hence, we fix the dip to be 87° according to the reported focal mechanism solutions from GCMT (Table 2) and run the inversion again. The optimal uniform slip model (Table 2 and Figure 5) reveals 0.35 m of coseismic slip on a 5.3 km-long and 7.2 km-wide rupture fault and generally fits the observed ascending and descending coseismic deformations (Figure 11).

Furthermore, the fault parameters are well-resolved with small uncertainties (Table 2). For instance, the fault location (X and Y) has an uncertainty of less than 300 m while the strike and rake have an uncertainty of less than 4.1°. The corresponding slip distribution model (Figure 9a,b,d) indicates that the rupture fault is characterized by dextral strike-slip faulting with a slight normal-slip component, and that the majority of the slip is limited at depths between 2.5 and 10 km, with the peak slip of about 0.47 m at a depth of 5.5 km. The location of the epicenter relative to the inverted slip distribution indicates that the coseismic rupture mainly propagates southward unilaterally. Interestingly, the coseismic slip of the March 2022 event terminates just before the junction of the two seismogenic faults responsible for the January and March earthquakes at depths of ~2.5 km (Figure 9e). We suggest that the intersection of the moderate-angle seismogenic fault of the January 2022 event with the high-angle seismogenic fault of the March 2022 event may restrict the slip extent in the March 2022 event to deep depths of <~2.5 km (Figure 9e; e.g., [2]). The seismic moment yielded by the best-fitting slip distribution model is ~4.4×10^{17} Nm, equal to M_W 5.7. In contrast to the modeled interferograms by the uniform slip model (Figure 11), the best-fitting slip distribution reproduces the observed ascending and descending coseismic deformations better with the rms of ~2.3 and 1.8 mm, respectively (Figure 12).

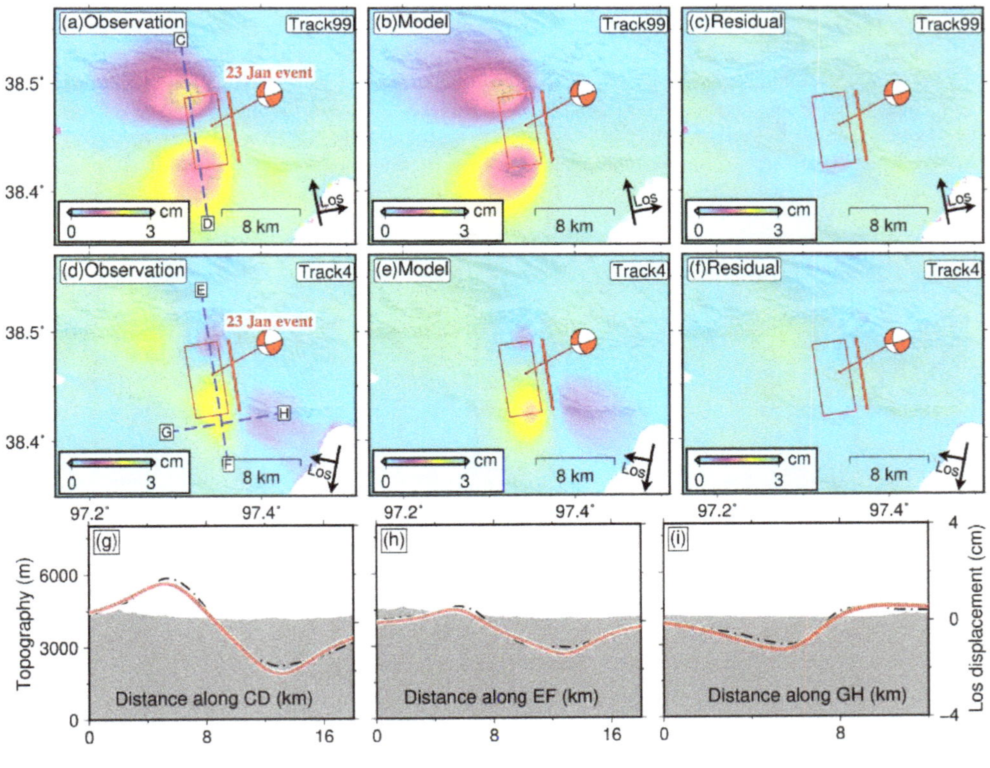

Figure 8. (**a**,**d**) are the ascending and descending coseismic interferograms, respectively, covering the 23 January 2022 Hala Lake earthquake. (**b**,**e**) are the modeled interferograms using the uniform slip model of the January 2022 event. (**c**,**f**) are corresponding residuals. The thick red line and thin red box indicate the surface projection of the seismogenic fault and rupture fault plane, respectively, from the uniform slip model of the January 2022 event. (**g**–**i**) are LOS displacements along Profiles CD, EF and GH, respectively. The dashed black line depicts the observed LOS displacement, while the red circles represent the modeled LOS displacement.

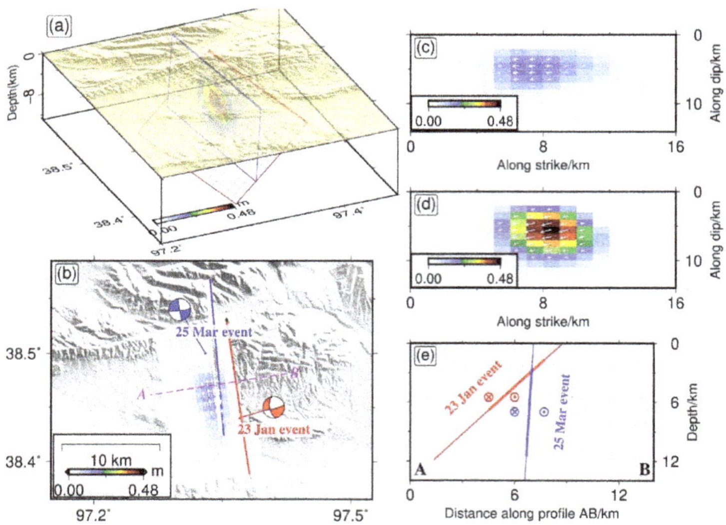

Figure 9. (**a**) Three-dimensional view of the coseismic slip distribution models of the January and March 2022 Hala Lake earthquakes. (**b**) Two-dimensional views of the coseismic slip distribution models of the January and March 2022 Hala Lake earthquakes. (**c**,**d**) show coseismic slip distributions of the January and March 2022 Hala Lake events along the strike and dip directions, respectively. (**e**) Fault substructures along the profile AB. Thin red and blue lines indicate the rupture fault planes of the two Hala Lake events, respectively, and the thick red and blue lines denote the major slip area.

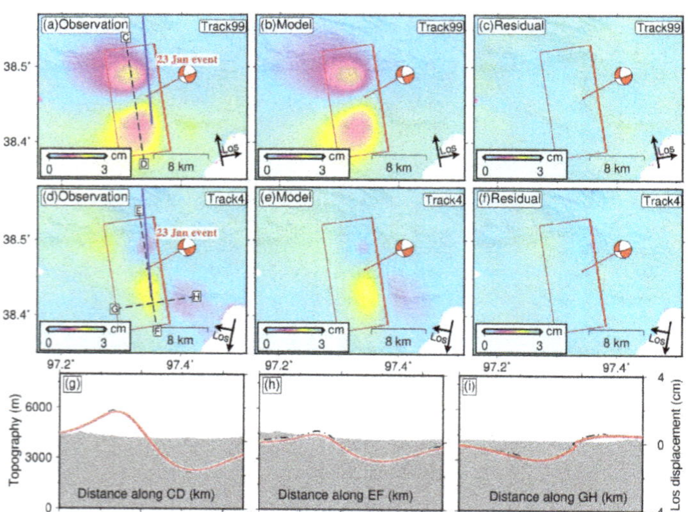

Figure 10. (**a**,**d**) are the ascending and descending coseismic interferograms, respectively, covering the 23 January 2022 Hala Lake earthquake. (**b**,**e**) are the modeled interferograms using the coseismic slip distribution models of the January 2022 event. (**c**,**f**) are corresponding residuals. The thick red line and thin red box indicate the surface projection of the seismogenic fault and rupture fault plane, respectively, from the coseismic slip distribution model of the January 2022 event. (**g**–**i**) are LOS displacements along Profiles CD, EF and GH, respectively. The dashed black line depicts the observed LOS displacement, while the red circles represent the modeled LOS displacement.

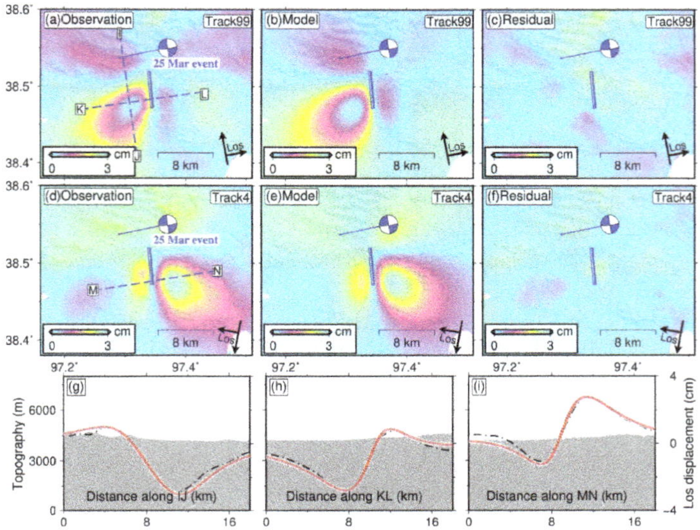

Figure 11. (**a**,**d**) are ascending and descending coseismic interferograms, respectively, covering the 25 March 2022 Hala Lake earthquake. (**b**,**e**) are modeled interferograms using the uniform slip model of the March 2022 event. (**c**,**f**) are corresponding residuals. The thick blue line and thin blue box indicate the surface projection of seismogenic fault and rupture fault plane, respectively, from the uniform slip model of the March 2022 event. (**g**–**i**) are LOS displacements along the profile IJ, KL and MN, respectively. The dashed black line depicts the observed LOS displacement, while the red circles represent the modeled LOS displacement.

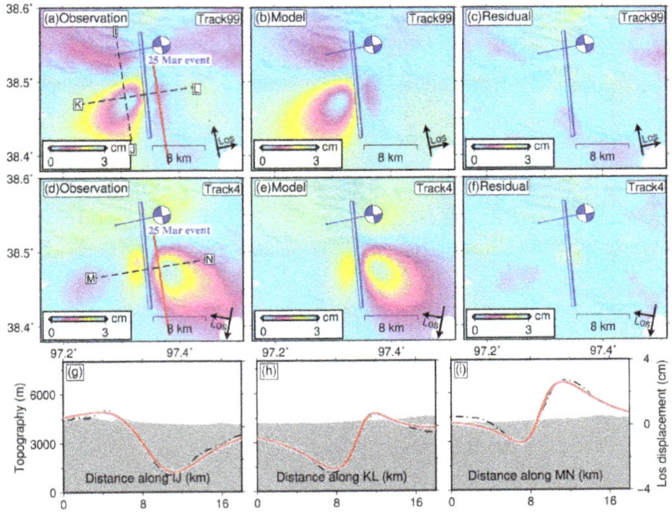

Figure 12. (**a**,**d**) are ascending and descending coseismic interferograms, respectively, covering the 25 March 2022 Hala Lake earthquake. (**b**,**e**) are modeled interferograms using the coseismic slip distribution model of the March 2022 event. (**c**,**f**) are corresponding residuals. The thick blue line and thin blue box indicate the surface projection of seismogenic fault and rupture fault plane, respectively, from the coseismic slip distribution model of the March 2022 event. (**g**–**i**) are LOS displacements along the profile IJ, KL and MN, respectively. The dashed black line depicts the observed LOS displacement, while the red circles represent the modeled LOS displacement.

5. Discussion

5.1. Relationship between the 7 January 2022 M_W 6.7 Menyuan Earthquake and the January and March 2022 M_W > 5.5 Hala Lake Earthquakes

A coseismic slip during a large earthquake can change the stress status of the nearby faults, thus resulting in the advance or delay of the future seismic events [31–33]. Considering that the 7 January 2022 M_W 6.7 Menyuan earthquake occurred ~350 km southeast of the two Hala Lake earthquakes and only 16 days before the first Hala Lake event (Figure 1a), we utilize the coulomb failure stress (CFS) Formula (1) [34] to calculate the coseismic CFS changes due to the 2022 Menyuan event at the maximum slip area of the two Hala Lake events with a common friction coefficient of 0.4 (e.g., [33]).

$$CFS = \Delta\tau - \mu'\Delta\sigma \quad (1)$$

Thereinto, μ' represents the effective friction coefficient, whereas $\Delta\tau$ and $\Delta\sigma$ indicate the shear stress and normal stress changes, respectively [34].

Furthermore, it should be noted that the positive stress value usually encourages a rupture, while a negative one often prohibits a rupture. The previously published coseismic slip distribution model of the 2022 Menyuan earthquake, which can be openly obtained from the Zenodo (https://zenodo.org/record/6816540#.YsuwwciVVbl, accessed on 1 January 2023), is exploited as the source model, while the focal mechanism solutions of the two Hala Lake events (Tables 1 and 2) are regarded as the receiver mechanism. Finally, the open psgrn/pscmp program [35] is used to carry out the stress perturbation calculations. The derived CFS results (Figure 13) show a negligible stress change of ~0 Bar on the rupture area of the two Hala Lake earthquakes, implying that the occurrence of the 2022 Menyuan earthquake had a limited effect on promoting the occurrence of the two Hala Lake events.

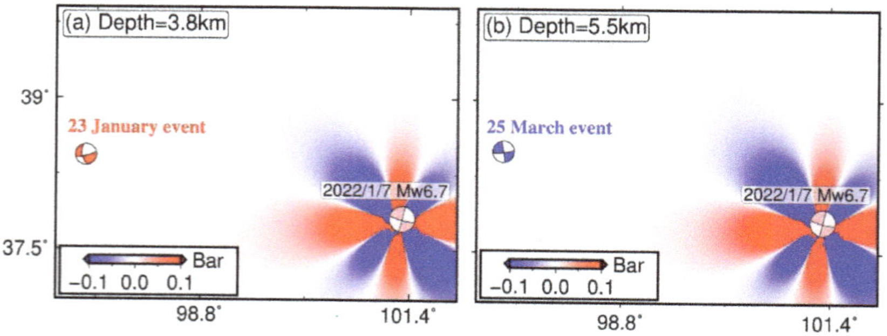

Figure 13. (**a**) Coseismic CFS changes at a depth of 3.8 km induced by the 2022 Menyuan earthquake. The focal mechanism solutions of the 23 January 2022 Hala Lake earthquake (Table 1) are set as the receiver mechanism. The depth of 3.8 km, where the maximum slip is located, is set as the calculated depth. (**b**) Coseismic CFS changes at a depth of 5.5 km induced by the 2022 Menyuan earthquake. The focal mechanism solutions of the 25 March 2022 Hala Lake earthquake (Table 2) are set as the receiver mechanism. The depth of 5.5 km, where the maximum slip occurs, is chosen as the calculated depth.

5.2. Possible Causes for The Stop-Start Rupture of the Two Hala Lake Events

Geometric complexities consisting of fault segmentation, intersection, stepovers, and bends are thought as a barrier to rupture propagation, thus halting an instantaneous multi-fault rupture in one large earthquake (e.g., [1,36]). Our preliminary geodetic observation reveals a complex two-fault delayed failure during the two 2022 Hala Lake earthquakes that span a long period of about two months. Further InSAR modeling shows that, although the strike (a difference of ~4°) and location (a difference of ~2 km) of the two seismogenic faults are basically the same, their dip angles exhibit a quite difference (~30°) from each other (Figures 7 and 9b). This significant discrepancy in fault geometry implies an obvious fault segmentation that is capable of stopping the rupture propagation from one fault segment to another (e.g., [37]). For example, the 2018 Lombok earthquake sequence is considered as a failed multi-segment large earthquake mainly because the distinct dip and strike differences in fault geometry control the rupture termination in each event [38]. Similarly, we highlight that the prominent fault dip difference between the two Hala Lake events may prevent two simultaneous ruptures in a single large earthquake. The static stress transfer is generally known as the major cause for the rupture reinitiation of an earthquake doublet or seismic sequence (e.g., [39–41]). To assess this hypothesis, we quantify the effect of the coseismic coulomb failure stress (CFS) changes induced by the January 2022 Hala Lake earthquake (source fault) on the March 2022 Hala Lake earthquake (receiver fault) with a common friction coefficient of 0.4 (e.g., [33]). Our result (Figure 14) reveals a negative stress value of up to ~ -1.1 bar at the main slip area of the March 2022 Hala Lake event, which does not support the hypothesis that coseismic CFS played a crucial role in promoting the rupture reinitiation of the later Hala Lake earthquake. As another triggering mechanism, the afterslip propagation may be an important cause for promoting the restart of the slip of the later earthquake because the cumulative CFS due to postseismic afterslips may further encourage failure [1,2,42]. However, we find that no significant postseismic signals are detected during the period from 23 January to 25 March 2022 (Figure 3), indicating a limited afterslip magnitude. In addition, fluid migration following the large earthquake is also considered to be capable of encouraging rupture reinitiation since the arrival of the underground fluids are able to increase pore-pressure and thus unclamp the critically stressed fault to allow its movement [43]. We suggest that a detailed mapped subsurface fault networks in the epicentral area needs to be investigated for analyzing the channel of fluid diffusion, thus verifying the role of fluid migration in the two 2022 Hala Lake earthquakes (e.g., [2]). In particular, the roughly two months' delay between the two Hala Lake events may be also determined by the fluid migration, which will need to be verified in the future investigation by collecting relocated aftershock data (e.g., [2]).

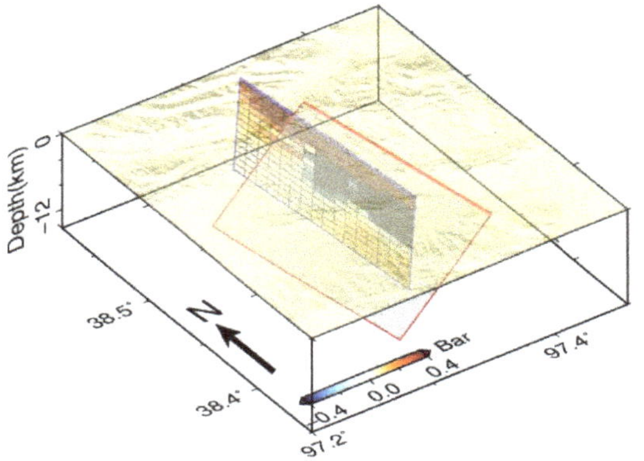

Figure 14. Coseismic CFS changes along the rupture fault of the 25 March 2022 Hala Lake earthquake induced by the 23 January 2022 Hala Lake earthquake. Red and blue rectangular frames are the rupture fault planes from the coseismic slip distribution model of the January and March 2022 events, respectively.

5.3. Regional Seismic Hazards Assessment

As the two largest earthquakes around Hala Lake since the 15 March 1927 M_W 6.2 earthquake (Figure 1c), the 2022 M_W 5.6 and M_W 5.7 Hala Lake earthquakes, which ruptured closely in space, make more sense in the aspect of assessing the regional seismic risk. In order to investigate the effect of the two Hala Lake earthquakes on the regional seismicity, we calculated the static CFS changes at the depth of 10 km where the most aftershocks are located. The result (Figure 15a,b) reveals that ~58% of aftershocks are concentrated in the regions of positive CFS of >0.1 Bar (an earthquake triggering threshold [44]), indicating that the statics CFS is not the unique triggering mechanism for aftershocks. However, it is worth noting that only M_S > 3.0 aftershocks have been collected and that the aftershock distribution is not the result of relocated aftershock sequences, which requires further research on the trigger mechanisms of aftershocks. To explore the impact of the two events on the surrounding faults, we utilize coseismic slip distributions of these two earthquakes (source fault) to calculate the CFS changes along the mapped faults (receiver fault). According to the known surface trace, a strike-variable fault plane composed of many discrete sub-patches with a size of 2 km by 2 km, is constructed with the purpose to obtain detailed stress distribution along the entire subsurface fault structure e.g., [8]. In detail, we first divide the mapped fault traces into small segments of a fixed length of 2 km along the strike direction and then extend the width of the fault plane to 16 km along the down-dip direction by applying a constant value of dip e.g., [45]. Moreover, we set a pure dip-slip mechanism (a rake of 90°) for the known DHLTF, DHNSF and DXS-SLF with a constant dip of 45° and a pure dextral strike-slip mechanism (a rake of 180°) for the mapped ELSF with a steep dip of 90° as the receiver mechanism. The acquired total CFS changes (Figure 15e) due to the 23 January and 25 March 2022 Hala Lake earthquakes (Figure 15c,d) exhibiting stress unloading on the eastern segment of the DHLTF and DHNSF (a stress value of up to ~−0.03 bar and −0.014 bar, respectively), the western segment of the DXS-SLF (maximum ~−0.044 bar), and the southern segment of the ELSF (up to ~−0.025 bar). In addition, given that the eastern segment of the DXS-SLF and the northern segment of the ELSF reveal stress loading (Figure 15e), we should pay more attention to these fault segments.

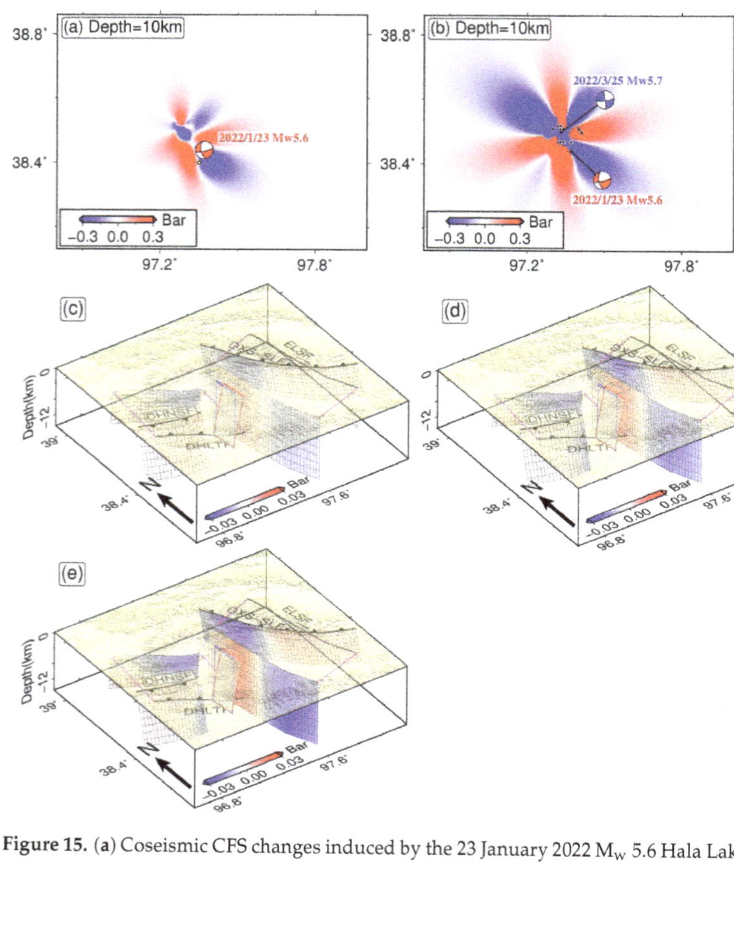

Figure 15. (**a**) Coseismic CFS changes induced by the 23 January 2022 M_w 5.6 Hala Lake earthquake

at a depth of 10 km. The focal mechanism solutions (Table 1) of the January event are set as the receiver mechanism. (**b**) Coseismic CFS changes caused by the 23 January and 25 March 2022 $M_W > 5.5$ Hala Lake earthquakes at a depth of 10 km. The focal mechanism solutions (Table 2) of the March event are regarded as the receiver mechanism. (**c**) Coseismic CFS changes along the known DHLTF, DHNSF, ELSF and DXS-SLF induced by the January 2022 Hala Lake event. (**d**) Coseismic CFS changes along the known DHLTF, DHNSF, ELSF and DXS-SLF due to the March 2022 Hala Lake event. (**e**) Coseismic CFS changes along the known DHLTF, DHNSF, ELSF, and DXS-SLF caused by both the January and March 2022 Hala Lake events. The red and blue rectangular boxes represent the rupture fault planes from the coseismic slip distribution models of the January and March 2022 Hala Lake events, respectively. The magenta lines in Figure (**c**–**e**) show where the fault planes have moved.

6. Conclusions

We investigate the coseismic rupture behaviors of the January and March 2022 Hala Lake earthquakes on the basis of the coseismic InSAR observations. The two Hala Lake events ruptured two unmapped west-dipping, left-stepping dextral strike-slip faults with a dip of 58° and 88°, respectively. Most of the slip of the January event is confined to depths from 1.7–7.6 km with the maximum slip of ~0.21 m at a depth of 3.8 km while the majority of slip of the March event is limited at depths between 2.5 and 10 km, with the peak slip of ~0.47 m at a depth of 5.5 km. According to the in-depth analysis of the possible causes for the stop-start rupture of the two Hala Lake earthquakes, we propose that fault segmentation plays a key role in impeding the rupture propagation, thus resulting in a two-fault delayed rupture, and that fluid migration may promote the slip reinitiation of the later Hala Lake event, which requires further analysis. Additionally, we should note the eastern segment of the DXS-SLF and the northern segment of the ELSF due to the state of stress loading.

Author Contributions: Conceptualization, J.Y. and C.X.; methodology, J.Y.; software, J.Y.; validation, J.Y., C.X. and Y.W.; formal analysis, J.Y.; investigation, J.Y.; resources, J.Y.; data curation, J.Y.; writing—original draft preparation, J.Y. and C.X.; writing—review and editing, J.Y., C.X. and Y.W; visualization, J.Y.; supervision, C.X.; project administration, C.X.; funding acquisition, C.X. All authors have read and agreed to the published version of the manuscript.

Funding: This research was funded by the National Natural Science Foundation of China (Nos. 42074007, 41721003, 42130101 and 41974004).

Data Availability Statement: The original Sentinel-1 images are downloaded from the European Space Agency (https://scihub.copernicus.eu/dhus/#/home, accessed on 1 January 2023). The coseismic slip distribution model of the 7 January 2022 M_W 6.7 Menyuan earthquake is openly available from Zenodo (https://zenodo.org/record/6816540#.YsuwwciVVbl, accessed on 1 January 2023).

Conflicts of Interest: The authors declare no conflict of interest.

References

1. Yang, J.; Xu, C.; Wen, Y.; Xu, G. Complex coseismic and postseismic faulting during the 2021 northern Thessaly (Greece) earthquake sequence illuminated by InSAR observations. *Geophys. Res. Lett.* **2022**, *49*, e2022GL098545. [CrossRef]
2. Walters, R.J.; Gregory, L.C.; Wedmore, L.N.; Craig, T.J.; McCaffrey, K.; Wilkinson, M.; Chen, J.; Li, Z.; Elliott, J.R.; Goodall, H.; et al. Dual control of fault intersections on stop-start rupture in the 2016 Central Italy seismic sequence. *Earth Planet. Sci. Lett.* **2018**, *500*, 1–14. [CrossRef]
3. Elliott, J.R.; Walters, R.J.; Wright, T.J. The role of space-based observation in understanding and responding to active tectonics and earthquakes. *Nat. Commun.* **2016**, *7*, 13844. [CrossRef]
4. Massonnet, D.; Rossi, M.; Carmona, C.; Adragna, F.; Peltzer, G.; Feigl, K.; Rabaute, T. The displacement field of the Landers earthquake mapped by radar interferometry. *Nature* **1993**, *364*, 138–142. [CrossRef]
5. Cakir, Z.; Akoglu, A.M. Synthetic aperture radar interferometry observations of the $M = 6.0$ Orta earthquake of 6 June 2000 (NW Turkey): Reactivation of a listric fault. *Geochem. Geophys. Geosyst.* **2008**, *9*, Q08009. [CrossRef]
6. Yang, J.; Xu, C.; Wang, S.; Wang, X. Sentinel-1 observation of 2019 Mw 5.7 Acıpayam earthquake: A blind normal-faulting event in the Acipayam basin, southwestern Turkey. *J. Geodyn.* **2020**, *135*, 101707. [CrossRef]

7. Yang, J.; Xu, C.; Wen, Y. The 2019 Mw 5.9 Torkaman chay earthquake in Bozgush mountain, NW Iran: A buried strike-slip event related to the sinistral Shalgun-Yelimsi fault revealed by InSAR. *J. Geodyn.* **2020**, *141*, 101798. [CrossRef]
8. Yang, J.; Xu, C.; Wen, Y.; Xu, G. The July 2020 M w 6.3 Nima Earthquake, Central Tibet: A Shallow Normal-Faulting Event Rupturing in a Stepover Zone. *Seismol. Res. Lett.* **2022**, *93*, 45–55. [CrossRef]
9. Xu, X.W.; Tan, X.B.; Yu, G.H.; Wu, G.D.; Fang, W.; Chen, J.B.; Song, H.P.; Shen, J. Normal-and oblique-slip of the 2008 Yutian earthquake: Evidence for eastward block motion, northern Tibetan Plateau. *Tectonophysics* **2013**, *584*, 152–165. [CrossRef]
10. Yuan, D.Y.; Champagnac, J.D.; Ge, W.P.; Molnar, P.; Zhang, P.Z.; Zheng, W.J.; Zhang, H.P.; Liu, X.W. Late Quaternary right-lateral slip rates of faults adjacent to the lake Qinghai, northeastern margin of the Tibetan Plateau. *Bulletin* **2011**, *123*, 2016–2030. [CrossRef]
11. Zheng, W.J.; Zhang, P.Z.; He, W.G.; Yuan, D.Y.; Shao, Y.X.; Zheng, D.W.; Ge, W.P.; Wei, M. Transformation of displacement between strike-slip and crustal shortening in the northern margin of the Tibetan Plateau: Evidence from decadal GPS measurements and late Quaternary slip rates on faults. *Tectonophysics* **2013**, *584*, 267–280. [CrossRef]
12. Jian, H.Z.; Wang, L.F.; Ren, Z.K.; Gong, W.Y.; LI, Y.C.; LIU, J.R. Present-day slip rate and interseismic fault coupling along the Elashan fault using GPS. *Chin. J. Geophys.* **2020**, *63*, 1127–1142.
13. Pan, Z.; Yun, Z.; Shao, Z. Contemporary crustal deformation of Northeast Tibet from geodetic investigations and a comparison between the seismic and geodetic moment release rates. *Phys. Earth Planet. Inter.* **2020**, *304*, 106489. [CrossRef]
14. Wen, Y.; Li, Z.; Xu, C.; Ryder, I.; Bürgmann, R. Postseismic motion after the 2001 MW 7.8 Kokoxili earthquake in Tibet observed by InSAR time series. *J. Geophys. Res. Solid Earth* **2012**, *117*, B08405. [CrossRef]
15. Li, Y.; Jiang, W.; Li, Y.; Shen, W.; He, Z.; Li, B.; Li, Q.; Jiao, Q.; Tian, Y. Coseismic Rupture Model and Tectonic Implications of the January 7 2022, Menyuan Mw 6.6 Earthquake Constraints from InSAR Observations and Field Investigation. *Remote Sens.* **2022**, *14*, 2111. [CrossRef]
16. Gan, C.; Ming, A.; Wenjun, Z.; Haiyun, B.; Jinrui, L.; Yipeng, Z.; Weipeng, G.; Dongli, Z.; Rong, H. Nonrigid Bookshelf Kinematics of Northeastern Tibet: Constrains from Fault Slip Rates around the Qinghai Lake and Chaka-Gonghe Basins. *Lithosphere* **2021**, *2021*, 4115729. [CrossRef]
17. Cheng, F.; Zuza, A.V.; Haproff, P.J.; Wu, C.; Neudorf, C.; Chang, H.; Li, X.; Li, B. Accommodation of India–Asia convergence via strike-slip faulting and block rotation in the Qilian Shan fold–thrust belt, northern margin of the Tibetan Plateau. *J. Geol. Soc.* **2021**, *178*, jgs2020-20. [CrossRef]
18. Werner, C.; Wegmüller, U.; Strozzi, T.; Wiesmann, A. Gamma SAR and interferometric processing software. In Proceedings of the ERS-ENVISAT Symposium, Gothenburg, Sweden, 16–20 October 2000; Volume 1620, p. 1620.
19. Wegnüller, U.; Werner, C.; Strozzi, T.; Wiesmann, A.; Frey, O.; Santoro, M. Sentinel-1 support in the GAMMA software. *Procedia Comput. Sci.* **2016**, *100*, 1305–1312. [CrossRef]
20. Goldstein, R.M.; Werner, C.L. Radar interferogram filtering for geophysical applications. *Geophys. Res. Lett.* **1998**, *25*, 4035–4038. [CrossRef]
21. Goldstein, R.M.; Zebker, H.A.; Werner, C.L. Satellite radar interferometry: Two-dimensional phase unwrapping. *Radio Sci.* **1998**, *23*, 713–720. [CrossRef]
22. Cavalié, O.; Doin, M.P.; Lasserre, C.; Briole, P. Ground motion measurement in the Lake Mead area, Nevada, by differential synthetic aperture radar interferometry time series analysis: Probing the lithosphere rheological structure. *J. Geophys. Res. Solid Earth* **2007**, *112*, B03403. [CrossRef]
23. Funning, G.J.; Parsons, B.; Wright, T.J.; Jackson, J.A.; Fielding, E.J. Surface displacements and source parameters of the 2003 Bam (Iran) earthquake from Envisat advanced synthetic aperture radar imagery. *J. Geophys. Res. Solid Earth* **2005**, *110*, B09406. [CrossRef]
24. Zhang, Y.; Fattahi, H.; Amelung, F. Small baseline InSAR time series analysis: Unwrapping error correction and noise reduction. *Comput. Geosci.* **2019**, *133*, 104331.
25. Fattahi, H.; Amelung, F. DEM error correction in InSAR time series. *IEEE Trans. Geosci. Rem. Sens.* **2013**, *51*, 4249–4259. [CrossRef]
26. Fattahi, H.; Amelung, F. InSAR observations of strain accumulation and fault creep along the Chaman Fault system, Pakistan and Afghanistan. *Geophys. Res. Lett.* **2016**, *43*, 8399–8406. [CrossRef]
27. Lohman, R.B.; Simons, M. Some thoughts on the use of InSAR data to constrain models of surface deformation: Noise structure and data downsampling. *Geochem. Geophys. Geosystems* **2005**, *6*, Q01007. [CrossRef]
28. Okada, Y. Surface deformation due to shear and tensile faults in a half-space. *Bull. Seismol. Soc. Am.* **1985**, *75*, 1135–1154. [CrossRef]
29. Feng, W.; Li, Z.; Elliott, J.R.; Fukushima, Y.; Hoey, T.; Singleton, A.; Cook, R.; Xu, Z.H. The 2011 MW 6.8 Burma earthquake: Fault constraints provided by multiple SAR techniques. *Geophys. J. Int.* **2013**, *195*, 650–660. [CrossRef]
30. Parsons, B.; Wright, T.; Rowe, P.; Andrews, J.; Jackson, J.; Walker, R.; Khatib, M.; Tablebian, M.; Bergman, E.; Engdahl, E.R. The 1994 Sefidabeh (eastern Iran) earthquakes revisited: New evidence from satellite radar interferometry and carbonate dating about the growth of an active fold above a blind thrust fault. *Geophys. J. Int.* **2006**, *164*, 202–217. [CrossRef]
31. Symithe, S.J.; Calais, E.; Haase, J.S.; Freed, A.M.; Douilly, R. Coseismic slip distribution of the 2010 M 7.0 Haiti earthquake and resulting stress changes on regional faults. *Bull. Seismol. Soc. Am.* **2013**, *103*, 2326–2343. [CrossRef]
32. Parsons, T.; Stein, R.S.; Simpson, R.W. Stress sensitivity of fault seismicity: A comparison between limited-offset oblique and major strike-slip faults. *J. Geophys. Res. Solid Earth* **1999**, *104*, 20183–20202. [CrossRef]
33. Freed, A.M. Earthquake triggering by static, dynamic, and postseismic stress transfer. *Annu. Rev. Earth Planet. Sci.* **2005**, *33*, 335–367. [CrossRef]

34. Stein, R.S.; King, G.C.; Lin, J. Change in failure stress on the southern San Andreas fault system caused by the 1992 magnitude = 7.4 Landers earthquake. *Science* **1992**, *258*, 1328–1332. [CrossRef]
35. Wang, R.; Lorenzo-Martin, F.; Roth, F. PSGRN/PSCMP—A new code for calculating co-and post-seismic deformation, geoid and gravity changes based on the viscoelastic-gravitational dislocation theory. *Comput. Geosci.* **2006**, *32*, 527–541. [CrossRef]
36. Biasi, G.P.; Wesnousky, S.G. Steps and gaps in ground ruptures: Empirical bounds on rupture propagation. *Bull. Seismol. Soc. Am.* **2016**, *106*, 1110–1124. [CrossRef]
37. Zhang, P.; Slemmons, D.B.; Mao, F. Geometric pattern, rupture termination and fault segmentation of the Dixie Valley-Pleasant Valley active normal fault system, Nevada, USA. *J. Struct. Geol.* **1991**, *13*, 165–176. [CrossRef]
38. Wang, C.; Wang, X.; Xiu, W.; Zhang, B.; Zhang, G.; Liu, P. Characteristics of the seismogenic faults in the 2018 Lombok, Indonesia, earthquake sequence as revealed by inversion of InSAR measurements. *Seismol. Res. Lett.* **2020**, *91*, 733–744. [CrossRef]
39. Hubert, A.; King, G.; Armijo, R.; Meyer, B.; Papanastasiou, D. Fault re-activation, stress interaction and rupture propagation of the 1981 Corinth earthquake sequence. *Earth Planet. Sci. Lett.* **1996**, *142*, 573–585. [CrossRef]
40. King, G.C.P.; Cocco, M. Fault interaction by elastic stress changes: New clues from earthquake sequences. *Adv. Geophys.* **2001**, *44*, 1–38.
41. Kroll, K.A.; Richards-Dinger, K.B.; Dieterich, J.H.; Cochran, E.S. Delayed seismicity rate changes controlled by static stress transfer. *J. Geophys. Res. Solid Earth* **2017**, *122*, 7951–7965. [CrossRef]
42. Salman, R.; Lindsey, E.O.; Lythgoe, K.H.; Bradley, K.; Muzli, M.; Yun, S.H.; Chin, S.T.; Tay, C.J.; Costa, F.; Wei, S.J.; et al. Cascading partial rupture of the Flores thrust during the 2018 Lombok earthquake sequence, Indonesia. *Seismol. Res. Lett.* **2020**, *91*, 2141–2151. [CrossRef]
43. Ravilious, K. Data hint at quake forecasts Italian-earthquake analysis suggests possibility of predicting aftershocks of some quakes. *Nature* **2018**, *562*, 470–471. [CrossRef]
44. Ziv, A.; Rubin, A.M. Static stress transfer and earthquake triggering: No lower threshold in sight? *J. Geophys. Res. Solid Earth* **2000**, *105*, 13631–13642. [CrossRef]
45. Mildon, Z.K.; Toda, S.; Faure Walker, J.P.; Roberts, G.P. Evaluating models of Coulomb stress transfer: Is variable fault geometry important? *Geophys. Res. Lett.* **2016**, *43*, 12407–12414. [CrossRef]

remote sensing

MDPI

Article

A Modification to Phase Estimation for Distributed Scatterers in InSAR Data Stacks

Changjun Zhao [1,2], Yunyun Dong [2,*], Wenhao Wu [3], Bangsen Tian [4], Jianmin Zhou [4], Ping Zhang [4], Shuo Gao [4], Yuechi Yu [4] and Lei Huang [5]

1 School of Resources and Environment, University of Electronic Science and Technology of China, Chengdu 611731, China
2 Northwest Land and Resources Research Center, Shaanxi Normal University, Xi'an 710119, China
3 School of Earth Sciences and Spatial Information Engineering, Hunan University of Science and Technology, Xiangtan 411201, China
4 Aerospace Information Research Institute, Chinese Academy of Sciences, Beijing 100094, China
5 School of Civil Engineering and Geomatics, Southwest Petroleum University, Chengdu 610500, China
* Correspondence: dongyunyun@snnu.edu.cn

Abstract: To improve the spatial density and quality of measurement points in multitemporal interferometric synthetic aperture radar, distributed scatterers (DSs) should be processed. An essential procedure in DS interferometry is phase estimation, which reconstructs a consistent phase series from all available interferograms. Influenced by the well-known suboptimality of coherence estimation, the performance of the state-of-the-art phase estimation algorithms is severely degraded. Previous research has addressed this problem by introducing the coherence bias correction technique. However, the precision of phase estimation is still insufficient because of the limited correction capabilities. In this paper, a modified phase estimation approach is proposed. Particularly, by incorporating the information on both interferometric coherence and the number of looks, a significant bias correction to each element of the coherence magnitude matrix is achieved. The bias-corrected coherence matrix is combined with advanced statistically homogeneous pixel selection and time series phase optimization algorithms to obtain the optimal phase series. Both the simulated and Sentinel-1 real data sets are used to demonstrate the superiority of this proposed approach over the traditional phase estimation algorithms. Specifically, the coherence bias can be corrected with considerable accuracy by the proposed scheme. The mean bias of coherence magnitude is reduced by more than 29%, and the standard deviation is reduced by more than 18% over the existing bias correction method. The proposed approach achieves higher accuracy than the current methods over the reconstructed phase series, including smoother interferometric phases and fewer outliers.

Keywords: multitemporal interferometric synthetic aperture radar (MT-InSAR); coherence matrix; distributed scatterer (DS); phase estimation

1. Introduction

Multitemporal interferometric synthetic aperture radar (MT-InSAR) is a powerful technique in monitoring the displacement of Earth's surface [1–3], including a wide range of applications, such as land subsidence [4–6], underground mining [7,8], landslide [9–11], earthquake [12–14], volcanic dynamics [15–17] et al. Among various MT-InSAR techniques, the persistent scatterer InSAR (PSInSAR) is a high-precision geodetic approach [18,19]. The basic idea of this technique is to identify and analyze the phase-stable persistent scatterers (PSs) over the whole observation period. These scatterers do not undergo severe temporal decorrelation and usually correspond to man-made objectives. Despite the high precision of PSInSAR, the low spatial density of measurement points, especially over nonurban environments, limits its applications to some extent.

Distributed scatterers (DSs) are exploited to improve the measurement point density. Unlike PS, DS usually covers multiple small targets with the same backscattering behavior in a resolution cell. These targets suffer from geometrical and temporal decorrelation and are typically noisier than those of PSs. To reduce the decorrelation of DS, small baseline subset (SBAS) technique has been proposed by only exploiting interferograms with temporal intervals and spatial baselines smaller than the certain thresholds [20–22]. The decorrelation is further reduced by the spatial multi-looking processing. Since the PSs are also filtered with neighboring pixels, their backscattering properties may be contaminated.

To improve the measurement point density by jointly exploiting PSs and DSs, many efforts have been made [22–26], which can be broadly divided into two categories. One is to extend the SBAS technique by combining single-look and multi-look interferograms. PSs can be exploited to achieve fine-scale measurements [22,24]. The other is to extend the PSInSAR technique by adding DSs into the single-master model. The representative work is SqueeSAR [23], and some extended techniques include JSInSAR [27], CAESAR [28], PD-PSInSAR [29], GEOS-ATSA [30], CSI [9] et al. The decorrelation of DS can be significantly reduced by phase estimation.

Initially, the DS phase estimation was implemented based on a maximum likelihood estimator (MLE) [23,31,32], which reconstructs the consistent phase series by maximizing the joint probability density function (pdf) over all pixels in a statistically homogeneous pixel (SHP) set. Theoretically, MLE is the optimum approach for phase estimation. However, the assumptions are difficult to meet in practice, and the optimum performance is compromised. Then the variation is provided by the eigenvalue decomposition (EVD) algorithm [28,29]. Its advantage lies in separating multiple scattering mechanisms, and it has low power for a single scattering mechanism [33,34]. Recently, the eigen decomposition-based maximum-likelihood-estimator of interferometric phase (EMI) algorithm is provided [34]. It follows a similar estimation model as MLE, and has high computational efficiency. These estimators are mathematically compared, and the only difference is the weighting strategy [35]. Based on this, some estimators have been developed with different weights, such as the Fisher information index [36,37], equal weight [35], coherence weight [38,39], coherence power weight [40] et al.

Regardless of the model used by these phase estimation methods, the same data source is the covariance matrix, which is estimated by the maximum-likelihood estimation. As is well known, the estimation is suboptimal due to the heterogeneous samples and limited ensembles [41]. Recently, an alternative way is developed to mitigate the bias by jointly estimating the covariance matrix and the consistent phase series [42]. In general, these influencing factors are treated independently of the phase estimation. In terms of heterogeneous samples, advanced SHP selection algorithms have been developed to reduce the undesirable samples, such as probabilistic method [43], fast SHP selection (FaSHPS) [44], covariance matrix patch (CMP) [45] et al. Robust estimation has also been implemented to mitigate the impact of heterogeneous samples [46]. For limited ensembles, the corresponding covariance matrix usually does not satisfy the positive definiteness, which is required by some estimators for inverse matrix operation [23,34]. Regularization is exploited to solve this problem [47–50]. In addition, limited ensembles result in a biased covariance matrix, especially for low-coherence areas. The correction by inverting the analytical expression of the coherence magnitude can mitigate the bias [51]. Since the fixed rectangular window is used, the spatial resolution is reduced, and new bias may be introduced. The correction with the second kind of statistical characteristics is introduced to reduce the coherence magnitude bias [52] and shows promising performance [40,53,54]. However, compared with the true coherence, the improvement is inadequate due to the limited correction from a simple bias corrector [53]. Dedicated to accurate deformation monitoring, high-precision phase estimation is still lacking.

In this paper, a new approach is proposed to improve the accuracy of DS phase estimation for InSAR data stacks. Starting from the theoretical analysis of coherence magnitude matrix error, a systematic correction approach is developed by considering the information on both interferometric coherence and the number of looks. Besides, the CMP algorithm is adopted to select SHP set with a high detection rate, and the EMI is exploited to reconstruct the optimal phase series by combining the estimation and computational efficiency. The proposed approach is tested on both simulated and real Sentinel-1 data to demonstrate its effectiveness. The main contributions of this paper are as follows:

(1) A bias corrector is developed to reduce the error of the coherence magnitude matrix.
(2) The improvements in coherence bias correction for the state-of-the-art phase optimization algorithms are analyzed and evaluated.
(3) A processing chain is provided to achieve the high-precision DS phase estimation.

This paper is organized as follows. In Section 2, the related methods are briefly reviewed, and the existing limitation is introduced. We then propose and elaborate on our approach in Section 3. Section 4 is dedicated to the presentation of the experimental results on simulated and real InSAR data stacks. Section 5 presents some discussions. Finally, conclusions are drawn in Section 6.

2. Related Method

Given N co-registered single-look complex (SLC) SAR images, a complex vector $\mathbf{z}(x)$ at the position x can be formed as

$$\mathbf{z}(x) = [z_1(x), z_2(x), \ldots, z_N(x)]^T \tag{1}$$

where ^{T} denotes the transpose and $z_i(x)$ is the complex value of the ith acquisition at the position x.

Based on the central limit theorem, $\mathbf{z}$ follows a zero-mean N-variate complex circular normal distribution with a covariance matrix $\sum$ [55,56]. The pdf is

$$pdf(\mathbf{z}) = \frac{1}{\pi^N \det(\sum)} \exp(-\mathbf{z}^H \sum{}^{-1} \mathbf{z}) \tag{2}$$

where $\det(*)$ indicates the determinant and ^{H} stands for Hermitian transpose. When $\mathbf{z}$ is normalized such that $E\left(|z_i|^2\right) = 1$, the corresponding coherence matrix is equal to the covariance matrix [28] and can be estimated as

$$\hat{\mathbf{\Upsilon}} = \frac{1}{L} \sum\nolimits_{k \in \Omega} \mathbf{z}(k)\mathbf{z}(k)^H \tag{3}$$

where Ω is the SHP set with L adjacent pixels.

Although the phase of $\hat{\mathbf{\Upsilon}}$ can be used for unwrapping and deformation retrieval, it is corrupted by the spatiotemporal decorrelation [23]. Phase optimization is developed to minimize the effect of decorrelation by properly combining the information associated with all the interferograms [23,31]. It supposes that the true coherence matrix can be expressed as

$$\Sigma = \Xi \Upsilon \Xi^H \tag{4}$$

where

$$\Xi = \begin{bmatrix} e^{j\theta_1} & 0 & \cdots & 0 \\ 0 & e^{j\theta_2} & \cdots & 0 \\ \vdots & \vdots & \ddots & \vdots \\ 0 & 0 & \cdots & e^{j\theta_N} \end{bmatrix} \quad \Upsilon = \begin{bmatrix} 1 & \gamma_{1,2} & \cdots & \gamma_{1,N} \\ \gamma_{2,1} & 1 & \cdots & \gamma_{2,N} \\ \vdots & \vdots & \ddots & \vdots \\ \gamma_{N,1} & \gamma_{N,2} & \cdots & 1 \end{bmatrix}$$

where Ξ and Υ are the true phase and coherence magnitude matrix, respectively. Without loss of generality, θ_1 can be set to zero. Therefore, $\boldsymbol{\theta} = [0, \theta_2, \ldots, \theta_N]^T$ can be termed as the optimal phase series and needs to be estimated. The MLE obtains it by maximizing the joint pdf over all pixels in the SHP set Ω [23,31,32].

$$\begin{aligned}\hat{\theta}_{MLE} &= \underset{\theta}{\operatorname{argmax}}\left\{\prod_{k\in\Omega} pdf(\mathbf{z}_k)\right\} \\ &= \underset{\theta}{\operatorname{argmax}}\left\{\zeta^H\left(\Upsilon^{-1}\circ\hat{\mathbf{T}}\right)\zeta\right\}\end{aligned} \tag{5}$$

where $\zeta = \left[1, e^{j\theta_2}, \ldots, e^{j\theta_N}\right]^T$ and the symbol $\circ$ represents the Hadamard product. As the true coherence magnitude matrix Υ is unknown, it is substituted by the absolute of $\hat{\mathbf{T}}$.

$$\hat{\theta}_{MLE} = \underset{\theta}{\operatorname{argmax}}\left\{\zeta^H\left(\left|\hat{\mathbf{T}}\right|^{-1}\circ\hat{\mathbf{T}}\right)\zeta\right\} \tag{6}$$

Equation (6) is a nonlinear optimization problem. Although the Broyden–Fletcher–Glodfarb–Shanno (BFGS) algorithm can be considered as a possible solution, the process is highly time-consuming [23].

Following the MLE, EMI is developed by introducing an additional degree of freedom with the calibration dyadic [34]. Besides, it transforms the nonlinear optimization problem into a minimum eigenvector problem.

$$\hat{\theta}_{EMI} = \underset{\mathbf{u}}{\operatorname{argmin}}\left\{\mathbf{u}^H\left(\left|\hat{\mathbf{T}}\right|^{-1}\circ\hat{\mathbf{T}}\right)\mathbf{u}\right\} \tag{7}$$

where $\hat{\theta} = \angle\mathbf{u}$, $\mathbf{u}$ is the eigenvector of $\left|\hat{\mathbf{T}}\right|^{-1}\circ\hat{\mathbf{T}}$.

Compared with the MLE method, EMI is proven to be a more effective method, especially in terms of computational efficiency [34]. It is adopted in our proposed phase estimation algorithm, and the rationality can be found in Section 5.

As analyzed in [35], state-of-the-art phase estimation techniques adopt a similar mathematical model, such as MLE [23,31], EVD [28,29], EMI [34] and the nonlinear optimization estimation weighted with the Fisher information matrix (NLEFIM) [36]. The fundamental difference is the weight matrix, which assigns different weights to different interferograms. Furthermore, these weight strategies require the true coherence magnitude matrix Υ, which is replaced by $\left|\hat{\mathbf{T}}\right|$. As is well-known, Equation (3) is a suboptimal estimator, and the estimated coherence magnitude is biased [55]. The unsatisfactory factor makes the weight matrix inaccurate, resulting in severe damage to the accuracy of the estimated phase series $\hat{\theta} = \left[0, \hat{\theta}_2, \ldots, \hat{\theta}_N\right]^T$.

3. Methodology

In this section, the statistical characteristics of coherence magnitude bias are first analyzed. Then a systematic approach is developed to reduce the coherence bias. In the end, the bias-corrected coherence is combined with advanced SHP selection and phase optimization to obtain the consistent phase series.

3.1. Coherence Magnitude Bias Statistics

Let $\hat{\gamma}$ be an element of the coherence magnitude matrix $\left|\hat{\mathbf{T}}\right|$; its pdf can be expressed as a function of the true coherence magnitude γ; and the number of looks L as [57]

$$pdf\left(\hat{\gamma}\middle|\gamma, L\right) = 2(L-1)\left(1-\gamma^2\right)^L\hat{\gamma}\left(1-\hat{\gamma}^2\right)^{L-2}{}_2F_1\left(L, L; 1; \gamma^2\hat{\gamma}^2\right) \tag{8}$$

where F is the generalized hypergeometric function. Based on the pdf, the analytical expression of the expectation and standard deviation of $\hat{\gamma}$ can be derived as [58]

$$E(\hat{\gamma}) = \frac{\Gamma(L)\Gamma(3/2)}{\Gamma(L+1/2)}{}_3F_2\left(3/2, L, L; L+1/2, 1; \gamma^2\right)\left(1-\gamma^2\right)^L \tag{9}$$

$$D(\hat{\gamma}) = \left(\frac{\Gamma(L)\Gamma(2)}{\Gamma(L+1)} {}_3F_2(2, L, L; L+1, 1; \gamma^2)(1-\gamma^2)^L - (E(\hat{\gamma}))^2 \right)^{1/2} \tag{10}$$

where Γ is the gamma function.

Equations (9) and (10) are calculated numerically. The difference between the expectation of sample coherence magnitude $E(\hat{\gamma})$ and true coherence γ is displayed in Figure 1a. It can be seen that the $E(\hat{\gamma})$ is biased towards higher values, and the bias increases with the decrease of γ and L. Figure 1b shows the standard deviation of sample coherence magnitude $D(\hat{\gamma})$. It is clear that $D(\hat{\gamma})$ varies significantly with both γ and L. The lower the number of looks, the higher the standard deviation. Although the bias can be corrected by inverting Equation (9), the required condition with low $D(\hat{\gamma})$, corresponding to a sufficiently large L, is difficult to meet in practice.

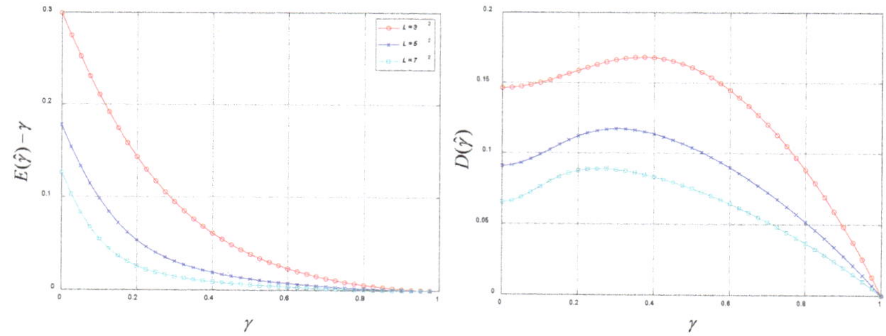

(a) (b)

Figure 1. (**a**) The difference between the expectation of sample coherence magnitude and true coherence γ for different numbers of looks L. (**b**) The standard deviation of sample coherence magnitude $D(\hat{\gamma})$ for different numbers of looks L.

Based on the above analysis, a bias corrector should be designed with consideration of the differences at different coherence magnitudes and numbers of looks.

3.2. Bias Mitigation for Coherence Magnitude

The Mellin transform is a valuable tool to analyze the pdf defined on the positive real number field. Based on the second kind second characteristic function, the Mellin transform allows the second kind moment M_s to follow the relation [52]

$$M_s = \int_0^1 (\ln(\hat{\gamma}))^s \, pdf(\hat{\gamma}|\gamma, L) d\hat{\gamma} \tag{11}$$

The above equation can also be termed as log moment $E\left((\ln(\hat{\gamma}))^s\right)$. Thus, by inverting Equation (11), an estimator with the corrected coherence magnitude $\tilde{\gamma}$ can be theoretically obtained as

$$\tilde{\gamma} = \exp\left((-1)^{s+1}(M_s)^{1/s}\right) \tag{12}$$

Section 3.1 shows that the bias of sample coherence magnitude $\hat{\gamma}$ is related to true coherence magnitude γ and the number of looks L. Here, the two factors are also considered. Based on the numerical calculation, the difference between the estimated coherence magnitude $\tilde{\gamma}$ and true coherence magnitude γ is plotted in Figure 2. It can be seen that the value of s has an important influence on the bias of the estimated $\tilde{\gamma}$. In general, to obtain a more accurate $\tilde{\gamma}$, s should be assigned a larger value when the true coherence γ is lower and the number of looks L is smaller. Thus, the value of s should be assigned carefully. Besides, when the parameter is set to the constant $s = 1$, the estimator (12) shares a simple form and is previously tested in [40,53,54]. In this paper, it is denoted by $\overline{\gamma}$ and is considered for comparison in the experimental section.

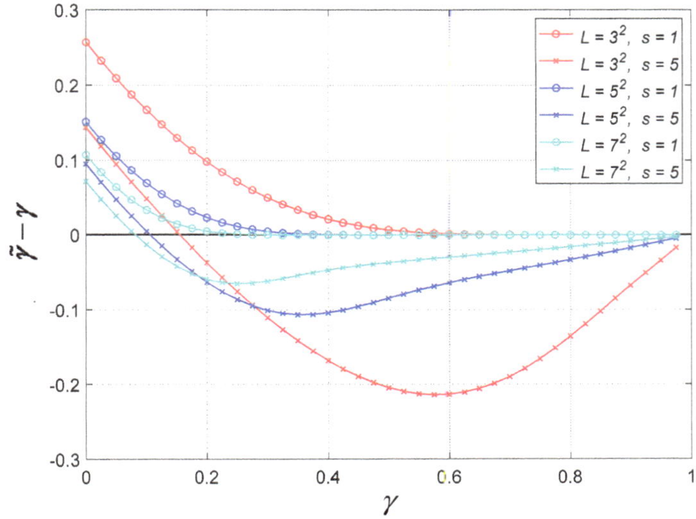

Figure 2. The difference between the estimated coherence magnitude $\widetilde{\gamma}$ and true coherence magnitude γ for different numbers of looks L and parameters s, using numerical calculation.

As the integral of Equation (11) is difficult to realize in practice, the log moment can be approximated by a statistical average over a large number of independent samples. Here, the SHP set Ω is used to ensure that the samples are independent and identically distributed. The log moment can be approximated as

$$M_s \approx \frac{1}{L}\sum_{k\in\Omega}(\ln(\hat{\gamma}(k)))^s \tag{13}$$

From the qualitative analysis in Figure 2, we know that s should be assigned a value that is inversely proportional to both the true coherence magnitude γ and the number of looks L. To obtain a quantified solution formula for s, the values of γ, L and s are differentiated over a large range into small intervals. The theoretical $\widetilde{\gamma}$ is numerically calculated using Equations (11) and (12). Aiming at the minimum difference between $\widetilde{\gamma}$ and γ, the optimal s can be determined as

$$s = \begin{cases} 1 & \gamma L > 5 \\ [7-\gamma L] & 1 < \gamma L \leq 5 \\ 6 & \gamma L \leq 1 \end{cases} \tag{14}$$

where $[*]$ rounds down to an integer. Although s should be assigned a larger value when $\gamma L \leq 1$, the upper limit is set to 6 with the consideration of the limited accuracy improvements from larger values. In general, the number of looks L is not equal to the sample number. As Equation (14) is an approximate relationship and is not strict, the number of SHP set is used. The true coherence magnitude γ is unknown and needs to be estimated. Considering the variance of sample coherence magnitude $\hat{\gamma}$ is relatively large, taking it as γ would result in an inaccurate s. Here, an empirical coherence magnitude is pre-estimated to replace γ.

$$\hat{\Gamma} = \hat{\Gamma}_{thermal}\hat{\Gamma}_{geom}\hat{\Gamma}_{temp} \tag{15}$$

where

$$\left.\begin{array}{l}\hat{\Gamma}_{thermal} = \left(1 + SNR^{-1}\right)^{-1} \\ \hat{\Gamma}_{geom} = \max(1 - |B_{\perp}|/B_{\perp\max}, 0) \\ \hat{\Gamma}_{temp} = \exp(-B_T/B_{T\max})\end{array}\right\}$$

where $\hat{\Gamma}_{thermal}$ is the thermal decorrelation, in which the signal-to-noise ratio (SNR) depends on system parameters and is usually assumed to be a constant value [58]. $\hat{\Gamma}_{geom}$ is the geometric decorrelation. $B_{\perp}$ is the perpendicular baseline, and $B_{\perp\max}$ is the spatial decorrelation baseline, which corresponds to zero correlation [58]. $\hat{\Gamma}_{temp}$ is the temporal decorrelation, and the B_T and $B_{T\max}$ are the temporal baseline and decorrelation rate [58]. The three parameters, including SNR, $B_{\perp\max}$ and $B_{T\max}$, are specified in Section 4.1.

As the empirical coherence magnitude $\hat{\Gamma}$ is a constant value for a single interferometric image, the sample coherence of each pixel can be appropriately corrected by different numbers of looks. The constant $\hat{\Gamma}$ also ensures that the computational cost is not too high. In addition, the empirical coherence magnitude $\hat{\Gamma}$ shares different values in different interferograms. For a single pixel, each element of $|\hat{\mathbf{T}}|$ can be corrected by the corresponding average coherence level. Therefore, the proposed algorithm can achieve effective correction for each element of all sample coherence magnitude matrices. In addition, compared to the sample coherence magnitude $\hat{\gamma}$ using only SHPs within the search window, the proposed approach actually exploits more pixels, including not only those inside the search window but also those outside the window, which also contributes to reducing the bias of estimated coherence magnitude $\tilde{\gamma}$.

3.3. Phase Estimation Algorithm

Since the SHP set is not only used in Eqation (1) to estimate the sample coherence but also used in Equations (13) and (14) to correct the coherence magnitude bias, it requires to be identified precisely. The CMP algorithm exploits complex information and maintains high accuracy in different sizes of data stacks [45]. It is adopted in this paper to select SHPs.

$$f_{CMP}(x_1, x_2) = \exp\left(-\frac{1}{M}\sum_{i=1}^{M}\frac{4}{\pi}\left(\frac{\hat{I}_1^2 + \hat{I}_2^2}{\hat{I}_1\hat{I}_2}\left(\frac{1 - \hat{T}_i^2\cos(\hat{\phi}_{1,i} - \hat{\phi}_{2,i})}{1 - \hat{T}_i^2}\right) - 2\right)\right) \tag{16}$$

where the subscripts 1 and 2 correspond to two pixels with a search window. M interferometric pairs are generated, and $\hat{\phi}_i$ is the ith original interferometric phase. $\hat{I}$ is the temporal mean intensity and can be estimated as $\hat{I} = \sum_{j=1}^{N} I_j/N$. $\hat{T} = h\hat{\Gamma}$ is an empirical coherence, where h acts as a factor to balance $\hat{\Gamma}$ and $\hat{\phi}_i$. Based on a pre-defined threshold, the homogeneity of two pixels can be judged by whether f_{CMP} is greater than the threshold.

The whole procedure of the proposed phase estimation algorithm can be described as follows (see Figure 3).

(1) Apply the CMP algorithm to select SHP set Ω for each image-pixel p.
(2) Estimate the coherence matrix $\hat{\mathbf{T}}$ using the selected SHP set Ω and Equation (3).
(3) Pre-estimate the empirical coherence magnitude $\hat{\Gamma}$ based on the InSAR stack information and Equation (15).
(4) Determine parameter s with empirical coherence magnitude $\hat{\Gamma}$, SHP set Ω and Equation (14).
(5) Estimate the log moment M_s using the sample coherence magnitude $\hat{\gamma}$, parameter s and Equation (13).
(6) Calculate the corrected coherence magnitude $\tilde{\gamma}$ with the log moment M_s and Equation (12).
(7) Reconstruct the consistent phase series using EMI and the bias-corrected coherence matrix.

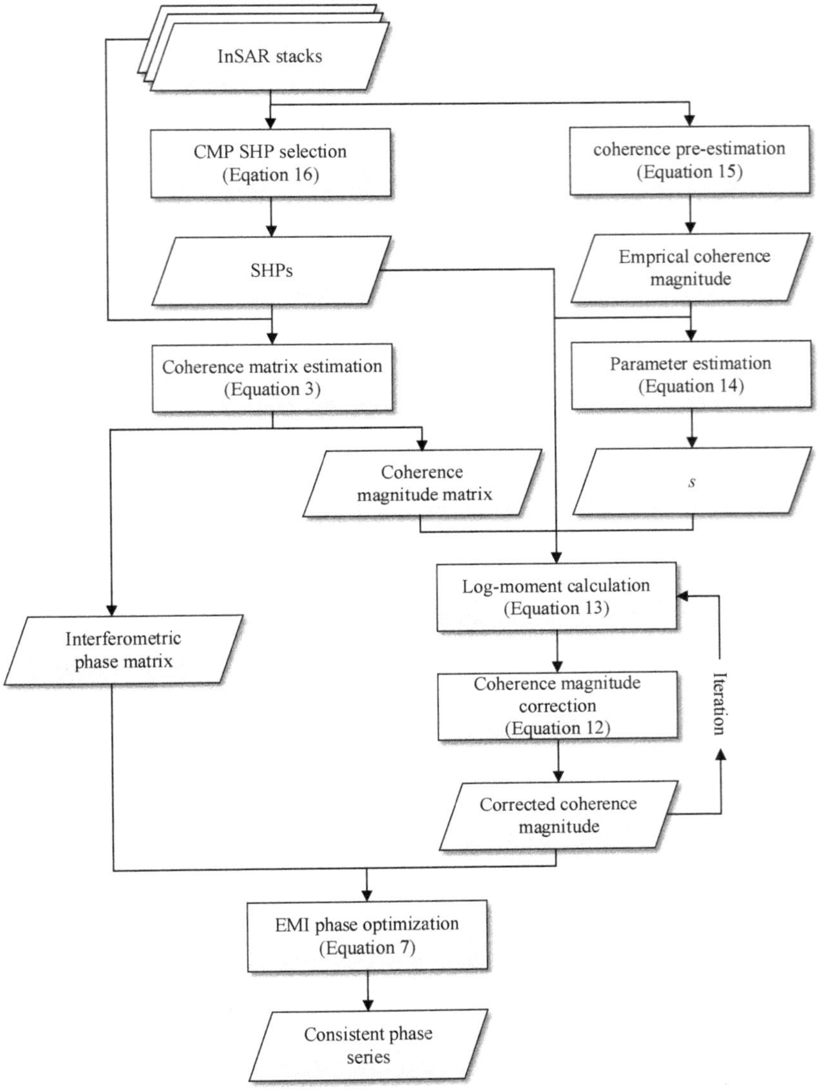

Figure 3. Flowchart of the proposed phase estimation algorithm.

Note that the proposed approach with coherence magnitude bias correction can be termed a general strategy and can be used in other DS phase estimators, such as MLE, EVD and NLEFIM. In practice, Equation (13) is calculated with a limited number of samples, which is generally difficult to meet the assumption of a large number of samples. Here, steps 5–6 are performed iteratively to mitigate this conflict. Considering a trade-off between accuracy improvement and computational cost increase, iteration is typically performed twice. When the computational cost is not considered, more iterations are recommended. In addition, the matrix inversion operation is required by EMI. For cases where the coherence matrix is not positive, definite regularization is committed to resolving the occasional problems via gradually adding a small negative eigenvalue of coherence [46].

4. Experimental Results

4.1. Test on Synthetic InSAR Data Stacks

The simulated data are synthesized based on the coherence matrix, in which the coherence magnitude can be derived as [59]

$$\gamma = (\gamma_0 - \gamma_\propto)\gamma_{thermal}\gamma_{geom}\gamma_{temp} + \gamma_\propto \tag{17}$$

where γ_0 and $\gamma_\propto$ are the short-term and long-term coherence, and are set to 0.7 and 0.03, respectively. $\gamma_{thermal}$, γ_{geom} and γ_{temp} are the thermal, geometric, and temporal decorrelation, and can be calculated using Equation (15). The SNR is set to 12 dB, resulting in $\gamma_{thermal} = 0.92$. The perpendicular baselines are normally distributed with a mean of zero and a standard deviation of 50 m, and the spatial decorrelation baseline is 1100 m. The revisiting time and radar wavelength, similar to Sentinel-1, are set to 12 days and 56 mm, respectively. The decorrelation rate is 200 days. The interferometric phases are only related to displacement with a velocity of 1 mm/year. The true data of interferometric phase matrix and coherence magnitude matrix are displayed in Figure 4a,b, respectively. Based on the complex coherence matrix, a stack of 40 images is simulated using a similar procedure to simulate polarimetric SAR images [60]. The size of the simulated image is 100×100 pixels. In addition, since the $\hat{\Gamma}$ in Equation (15) is an average coherence, the SNR, $B_{\perp\max}$, and $B_{T\max}$ are empirically set to 12 dB, 1100 m and 200 days, respectively.

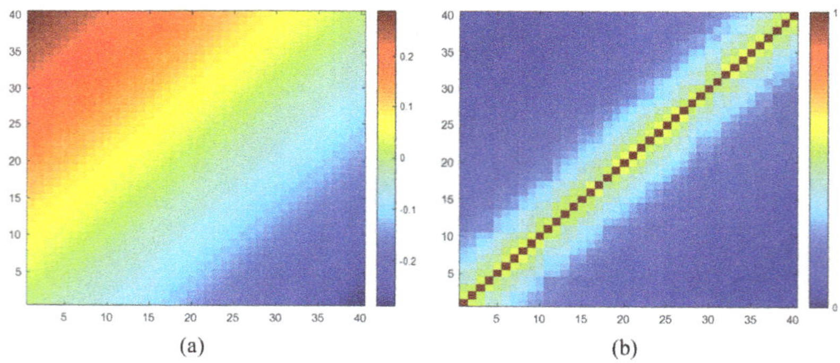

Figure 4. True data of (**a**) interferometric phase matrix and (**b**) coherence magnitude matrix.

The values of s with a window of 5×5 and 7×7 pixels are shown in Figure 5, corresponding to the coherence matrix. From Figure 5a, it can be seen that s increases as the coherence magnitude decreases. Comparing Figure 5a,b, it can be found that s is larger when the sample number is smaller. These results are consistent with the theoretical analysis in Section 3.2, indicating the effectiveness of calculating s.

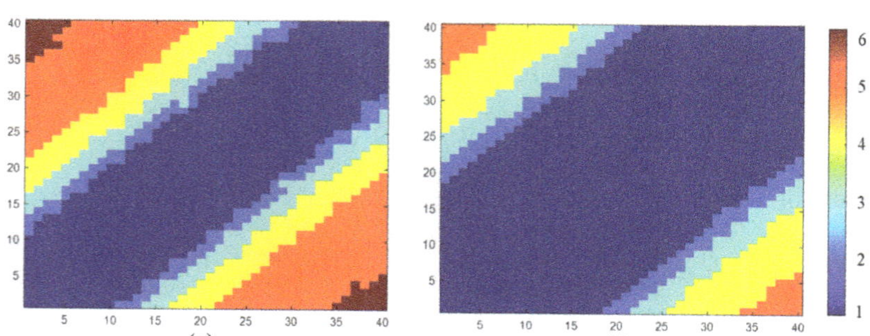

Figure 5. The value of s with a window of (**a**) 5×5 pixels and (**b**) 7×7 pixels.

Figure 6 shows the results of coherence matrix estimation with a window of 5×5 pixels. Comparing the true data in Figure 4b and the sample coherence magnitude $\hat{\gamma}$ in Figure 6a, overestimation can be clearly observed, and it is more severe over the low coherence interferogram. Correcting bias with the method proposed in [53], the coherence magnitude is improved to some extent. Nevertheless, overestimation can still be seen. By performing the correction method proposed in this paper, the coherence magnitude is significantly improved and asymptotically approaches the true data.

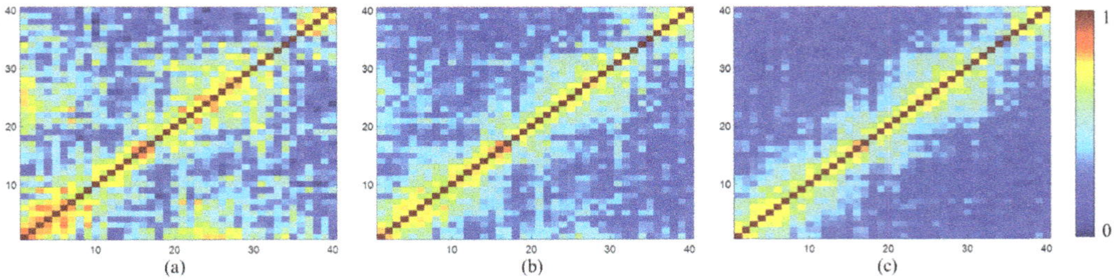

Figure 6. Coherence matrix estimation with a window of 5×5 pixels. (**a**) Sample coherence magnitude $\hat{\gamma}$. (**b**) Corrected coherence magnitude $\overline{\gamma}$. (**c**) Corrected coherence magnitude $\widetilde{\gamma}$ with the proposed method.

To further quantitative evaluation, the means and standard deviations of the estimated coherence magnitude are calculated from all $N(N-1)/2$ interferograms and all pixels, and shown in Figure 7. Considering that the pixel number of SHP set of a DS generally has a threshold [23], e.g., $L > 20$, two windows with size of 5×5 and 7×7 pixels are set. From the means in Figure 7a, the overestimation by the sample coherence $\hat{\gamma}$ can also be observed, and it is more severe when the number of looks is smaller. The mean bias is reduced by 64% by the correction coherence $\overline{\gamma}$ proposed in [53] over the sample coherence $\hat{\gamma}$. Compared with it, our proposed method achieves a significantly better correction with a bias reduction of more than 29% over the correction coherence $\overline{\gamma}$. This is mainly because that s is appropriately assigned by considering the information on both interferometric coherence and the number of looks. In addition, comparing the standard deviations in Figure 7b, an average reduction of 33% by the corrected coherence $\overline{\gamma}$ over the sample coherence $\hat{\gamma}$, and 45% by the proposed coherence $\widetilde{\gamma}$. The improvement of $\widetilde{\gamma}$ over $\overline{\gamma}$ is more than 18%. The lower biases and standard deviations indicate that the proposed method achieves more accurate coherence magnitude estimation. The qualitative and quantitative results jointly demonstrate the effectiveness of the proposed method in correcting the bias of coherence magnitude matrix, especially over the low coherence region.

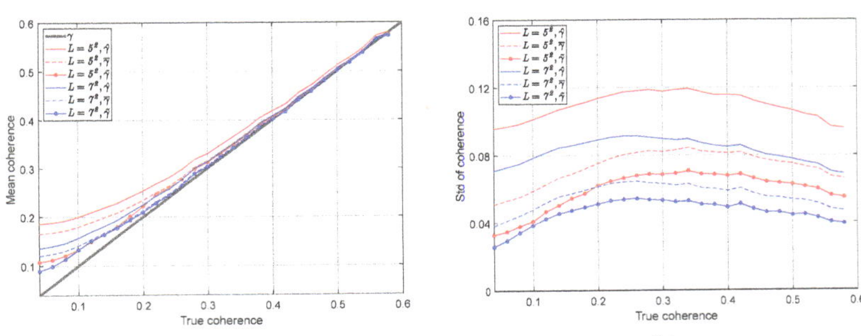

Figure 7. (**a**) Means and (**b**) standard deviations for different coherence magnitude estimators using different numbers of looks.

The empirical standard deviation of phase residuals is calculated to provide the quantitative evaluation of phase optimization results. For ith image ($i \neq 1$), it is defined as

$$std_i = \sqrt{\frac{1}{K}\sum_{j=1}^{K}\left(R_{i,j} - \overline{R}_i\right)^2} \tag{18}$$

$$R_{i,j} = \arg\left(\exp\left(j\left(\hat{\theta}_{i,j} - \theta_{i,j}\right)\right)\right) \tag{19}$$

where K is the total number of pixels of the simulated data. $R_{i,j}$ is the residual of the ith image and jth pixel. $\hat{\theta}_{i,j}$ and $\theta_{i,j}$ are the reconstructed phase and the truth value. $\arg(*)$ denotes the argument of a complex number. $\overline{R}_i$ is the mean residual of the ith image and can be estimated as $\frac{1}{K}\sum_{j=1}^{K} R_{i,j}$. The smaller std means that the reconstructed phase is closer to the truth data.

To evaluate the improvement of coherence magnitude bias correction on phase optimization, different coherence magnitude matrices are used based on the EMI algorithm, and the corresponding standard deviations of residuals are displayed in Figure 8. The theoretically highest achievable precision is provided by the Cramér–Rao lower bound (CRLB) [32]. In general, for different methods, the precision of the phase optimization is higher when the number of looks is larger. This is because more samples can obtain a more accurate complex coherence matrix, including more accurate coherence magnitudes and interferometric phases. Comparing the results with different coherence, it can be found that the coherence magnitude has a noticeable influence on the accuracy of phase optimization. The reconstructed phase with coherence magnitude $\tilde{\gamma}$ proposed in this paper has a higher precision than that with coherence magnitude $\overline{\gamma}$ and approaches the result with true coherence magnitude γ. The average phase residual with $\tilde{\gamma}$ is 0.11 rad lower than that with $\overline{\gamma}$. In addition, the reconstructed phases with $\tilde{\gamma}$ have a higher precision, an average residual reduction of 0.48 rad, than traditional sample coherence magnitude $\hat{\gamma}$. This is equivalent to 2.4 mm deviations for the C-band of Sentinel-1, which can lead to a noticeable difference in deformation results. The simulation results demonstrate the effectiveness of performing coherence magnitude bias correction for phase optimization and the superiority of the proposed coherence bias correction method over the existing correction method in phase optimization.

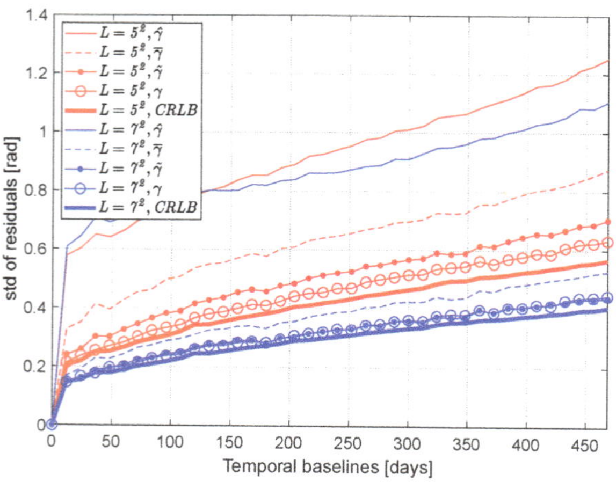

Figure 8. Standard deviation of the residuals for reconstructed phase series using different coherence magnitude estimators. The colors indicate the number of looks.

The reconstructed phase series can be further evaluated by the multi-looking results of a single point. Figure 9 shows the results at any point and the true data. It can also be seen that the reconstructed phases from more samples are closer to the true data. In addition, the reconstructed phases with $\widetilde{\gamma}$ have slightly higher precision than that with $\overline{\gamma}$ and are significantly more accurate than that with $\hat{\gamma}$. The results further demonstrate that the proposed approach can obtain more accurate reconstructed phase series.

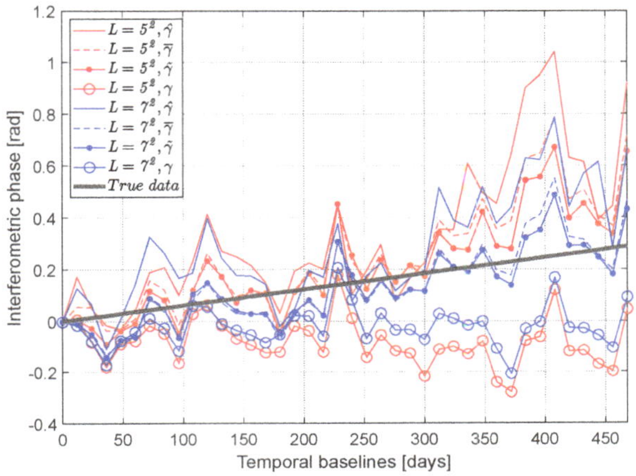

Figure 9. Reconstructed phase series of a single point using different coherence magnitude estimators. The colors indicate the number of looks.

4.2. Test on Real InSAR Data Stacks

A stack of 40 Sentinel-1 images over the Volcán Alcedo is used to test the performance of the proposed algorithm. Figure 10 shows the optical and averaged SAR intensity data, revealing the variety of land cover in the scene. Sentinel-1 images are obtained in wide-swath mode and VV polarization, and from January 2021 to May 2022 in a descending orbit. The test region is limited to an area of 650 × 2400 pixels. The CMP algorithm is exploited to select SHPs in a 7 × 13 path. Only pixels with more than 20 SHPs are selected as DS candidates for phase estimation.

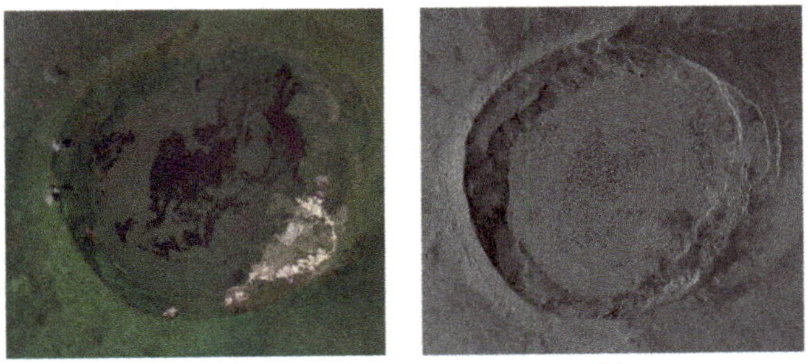

(**a**) (**b**)

Figure 10. Study area in Volcán Alcedo. (**a**) Optical image from Google Earth. (**b**) Averaged intensity map from 40 SLCs of the Sentinel-1 image stacks.

The performance of the proposed approach is visually assessed by inspecting the reconstructed interferograms with the longest temporal baseline of 288 days. The results are displayed in Figure 11. To better compare the details, a selected caldera indicated by the red rectangle is enlarged. A comparison of Figure 11a,b reveals a significant noise suppression of traditional EMI phase optimization. By adopting the corrected coherence magnitude $\overline{\gamma}$, the results are improved with smoother interferometric phases. However, some noise points can still be clearly observed in Figure 11c. The result using the corrected coherence magnitude $\widetilde{\gamma}$ proposed in this paper is displayed in Figure 11d, which yields better reconstructed phases with fewer noise points..

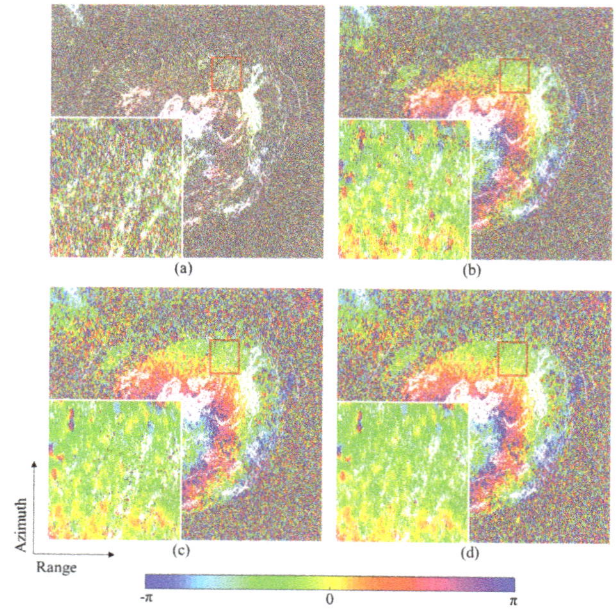

Figure 11. The original and reconstructed interferometric phases with the longest temporal baseline of 288 days. An area denoted by the red rectangle is enlarged. (**a**) Original single look interferogram. Reconstructed phases using: (**b**) the sample coherence magnitude $\hat{\gamma}$, (**c**) the corrected coherence magnitude $\overline{\gamma}$, (**d**) the corrected coherence magnitude $\widetilde{\gamma}$ proposed in this paper.

The reconstructed interferograms can be further visualized by profile analyses. Figure 12 presents the profiles of original and reconstructed interferograms along the horizontal and vertical black solid lines depicted in Figure 11a. We can see that the profile lines from the corrected coherence magnitude $\overline{\gamma}$ are smoother than those from the sample coherence magnitude $\hat{\gamma}$, but still contain some outliers. Evidently, the proposed approach with the corrected coherence magnitude $\widetilde{\gamma}$ generates smoother profiles with fewer outliers. The better performance indicates the effectiveness of the proposed approach, and can be attributed to the effective correction of coherence magnitude bias.

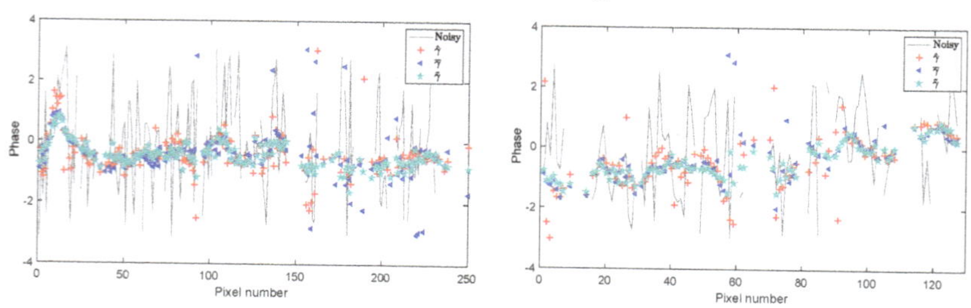

(a) (b)

Figure 12. (**a**) Horizontal and (**b**) vertical profiles of original and reconstructed interferometric phases along solid black lines depicted in Figure 11a.

Furthermore, a quantitative evaluation of the reconstructed phases is provided by the temporal coherence, which reads as [23]

$$\gamma_{PTA} = \frac{2}{N(N-1)} \sum_{i=1}^{N} \sum_{j=i+1}^{N} \cos(\hat{\varphi}_{i,j} - \hat{\theta}_i + \hat{\theta}_j) \tag{20}$$

where $\hat{\varphi}_{i,j}$ is the interferometric phase in the coherence matrix $\hat{\mathbf{T}}$. $\hat{\theta}_i$ and $\hat{\theta}_j$ are the reconstructed phase with the phase estimation algorithm. Figure 13 shows the histogram of temporal coherence for phase estimation using different coherence magnitude estimators. Improvements can be clearly found between the corrected coherence magnitude $\overline{\gamma}$ and the sample coherence magnitude $\hat{\gamma}$ over the low temporal coherence regions ($\gamma_{PTA} < 0.2$), where the frequency is reduced to near zero by $\overline{\gamma}$. The low temporal coherence regions ($0.2 < \gamma_{PTA} < 0.45$) are further improved by the corrected coherence magnitude $\widetilde{\gamma}$ proposed in this paper. Visual inspection reveals that these improvements are mainly located in densely vegetated areas with low coherence magnitude, which corresponds to high coherence magnitude bias. The experimental results over real SAR data indicate the proposed phase estimation approach can reconstruct better phase series, including smoother phases, fewer outliers and higher temporal coherence.

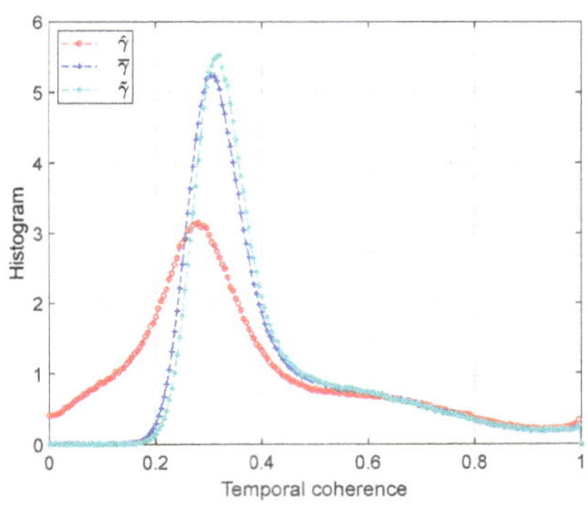

Figure 13. Histogram of temporal coherence for phase estimation using different coherence magnitude estimators.

5. Discussion

The current phase optimization algorithms, such as MLE [23,31], EVD [28,29], EMI [34] and NLEFIM [36], adopt the coherence matrix and its variant as the weight matrix [35]. Thus, the proposed coherence bias correction may be effective for all these phase optimization algorithms. The standard deviation of residuals with the sample coherence magnitude $\hat{\gamma}$ and bias-corrected coherence magnitude $\widetilde{\gamma}$ are displayed in Figure 14. The simulated data in Section 4.1 is adopted and the size of SHP set is 7×7 pixels. It is clear that the corrected coherence magnitude obtains higher accuracy than the traditional sample coherence magnitude. The mean phase residuals are reduced by 0.32 rad, indicating the effectiveness and necessity of performing coherence bias correction. The accuracy improvements of MLE and EVD are more evident than those of EVD and NLEFIM. This is because that the inversion of coherence matrix is executed by the MLE and EMI, which amplify the coherence magnitude bias. When the sample coherence magnitude $\hat{\gamma}$ is adopted, the NLEFIM is recommended to emphasize estimation accuracy. Since the power of EVD lies in separating scattering mechanisms from different heights, its accuracy is inferior to other methods. For MLE and EMI, the optimum performance can be achieved theoretically when their assumptions are valid. One of the violations of the assumptions is the coherence bias. Thus, the highest accuracy is obtained by MLE and EMI when the bias-corrected coherence magnitude is adopted. Considering that EMI has a computational efficiency advantage over MLE, our proposed phase estimation approach adopts the EMI algorithm.

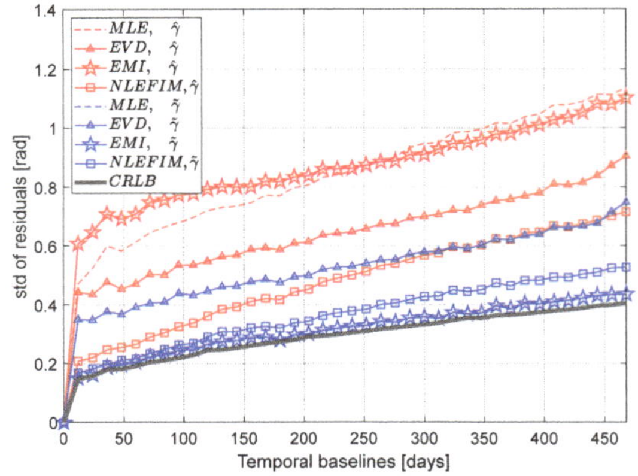

Figure 14. Standard deviation of the residuals for reconstructed phase series using different phase estimators. The colors indicate the coherence matrix estimator used.

To evaluate the computational efficiency, the processing time, including coherence matrix estimation and phase optimization, is provided in Figure 15 over the real data in Section 4.2. The image size is 650 × 2400 pixels and the search window size is 7 × 13 pixels. The calculation is in MATLAB R2019a software with an Intel Core I7 processor (3.0 GHz) and 32-GB RAM. In coherence matrix estimation procedure, Since the coherence bias correctors contain the processing of sample coherence estimation, the computational burden increases. The developed corrector is more complex due to the consideration of more information, and takes 2.5 times as long as the previous corrector. During the phase optimization procedure, computation with sample coherence estimation is time consuming. Compared with it, the processing time is improved by 42.2% by that with the previous correction, and by 43.1% by that with the proposed correction. This is because that the additional computation, regarding the coherence matrix regularization, is reduced. Fewer DSs with the non-positive definite coherence matrix are obtained by the developed correction. Considering the total processing time of the proposed approach is high, it is generally recommended for small-sized scenes. In addition, a possible strategy for large-sized images is to introduce high-performance parallel computing technology.

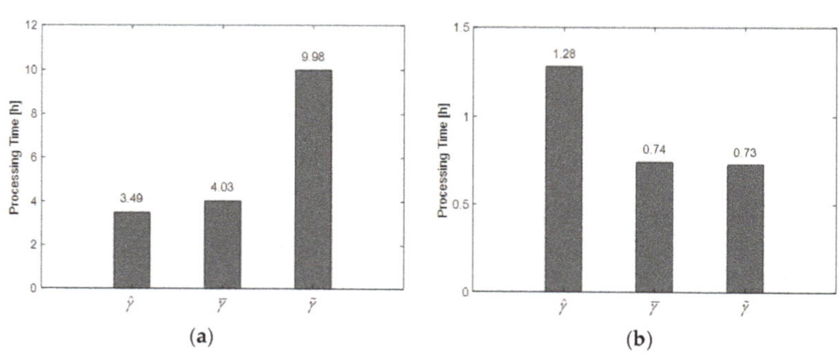

Figure 15. Processing time over: (**a**) the coherence matrix estimation; (**b**) the EMI phase optimization.

6. Conclusions

In this article, a modified DS phase estimation has been proposed for InSAR data stacks. The main contribution lies in effectively correcting the bias of coherence magnitude matrix.

The core idea is to incorporate the information on both interferometric coherence and the number of looks to adaptively correct each element of the coherence matrix. The proposed approach is established by combing the coherence magnitude bias corrector, the CMP SHP selection and the EMI phase optimization, achieving high-precision phase reconstruction.

The experimental results with the simulated data have shown that more accurate coherence magnitude can be obtained by the proposed correction method, including lower mean bias (reduced by more than 29%) and smaller standard deviation (reduced by more than 18%), than the existing bias correction method. The reconstructed phase series with the proposed approach is closest to the CRLB, demonstrating the effectiveness of the results. The experimental results with the Sentinel-1 images also verify the effectiveness of the proposed approach with smoother interferometric phases and fewer outliers.

Author Contributions: Conceptualization, C.Z.; methodology, C.Z. and B.T.; software, C.Z.; validation, C.Z., J.Z. and Y.D.; formal analysis, C.Z. and W.W.; data curation, S.G., Y.Y. and L.H.; writing-original draft preparation, C.Z.; writing-review and editing, B.T., P.Z. and C.Z.; visualizations, C.Z.; supervision, Y.D.; project administration, W.W. and C.Z; funding acquisition, C.Z. and W.W. All authors have contributed significantly and have participated sufficiently to take responsibility for this research. All authors have read and agreed to the published version of the manuscript.

Funding: This work was supported by the Natural Science Basic Research Plan in Shaanxi Province of China under Grant 2022JQ-239, the National Natural Science Foundation of China under Grant 42004006 and 42071084, and the Fundamental Research Funds for the Central Universities under Grant GK202103130.

Institutional Review Board Statement: Not applicable.

Informed Consent Statement: Not applicable.

Data Availability Statement: The data are contained within this article.

Acknowledgments: The author would like to thank the anonymous reviewers for the constructive as well as encouraging comments on this paper. The Sentinel-1 data were provided by the European Space Agency/Copernicus.

Conflicts of Interest: The authors declare no conflict of interest.

References

1. Zhu, X.X.; Wang, Y.Y.; Montazeri, S.; Ge, N. A Review of Ten-Year Advances of Multi-Baseline SAR Interferometry Using TerraSAR-X Data. *Remote Sens.* **2018**, *10*, 1374. [CrossRef]
2. Even, M.; Schulz, K. InSAR Deformation Analysis with Distributed Scatterers: A Review Complemented by New Advances. *Remote Sens.* **2018**, *10*, 744. [CrossRef]
3. Minh, D.H.T.; Hanssen, R.; Rocca, F. Radar Interferometry: 20 Years of Development in Time Series Techniques and Future Perspectives. *Remote Sens.* **2020**, *12*, 1374. [CrossRef]
4. Teatini, P.; Tosi, L.; Strozzi, T.; Carbognin, L.; Wegmüller, U.; Rizzetto, F. Mapping regional land displacements in the Venice coastland by an integrated monitoring system. *Remote Sens. Environ.* **2005**, *98*, 403–413. [CrossRef]
5. Hu, J.; Ding, X.L.; Li, Z.W.; Zhang, L.; Zhu, J.J.; Sun, Q.; Gao, G.J. Vertical and horizontal displacements of Los Angeles from InSAR and GPS time series analysis: Resolving tectonic and anthropogenic motions. *J. Geodyn.* **2016**, *99*, 27–38. [CrossRef]
6. Qu, F.; Lu, Z.; Kim, J.-W.; Zheng, W. Identify and Monitor Growth Faulting Using InSAR over Northern Greater Houston, Texas, USA. *Remote Sens.* **2019**, *11*, 1498. [CrossRef]
7. Jiang, L.; Lin, H.; Ma, J.; Kong, B.; Wang, Y. Potential of small-baseline SAR interferometry for monitoring land subsidence related to underground coal fires: Wuda (Northern China) case study. *Remote Sens. Environ.* **2011**, *115*, 257–268. [CrossRef]
8. Perski, Z.; Hanssen, R.; Wojcik, A.; Wojciechowski, T. InSAR analyses of terrain deformation near the Wieliczka Salt Mine, Poland. *Eng. Geol.* **2009**, *106*, 58–67. [CrossRef]
9. Dong, J.; Zhang, L.; Tang, M.; Liao, M.; Xu, Q.; Gong, J.; Ao, M. Mapping landslide surface displacements with time series SAR interferometry by combining persistent and distributed scatterers: A case study of Jiaju landslide in Danba, China. *Remote Sens. Environ.* **2018**, *205*, 180–198. [CrossRef]
10. Zhao, C.; Kang, Y.; Zhang, Q.; Lu, Z.; Li, B. Landslide Identification and Monitoring along the Jinsha River Catchment (Wudongde Reservoir Area), China, Using the InSAR Method. *Remote Sens.* **2018**, *10*, 993. [CrossRef]
11. Intrieri, E.; Raspini, F.; Fumagalli, A.; Lu, P.; Conte, S.D.; Farina, P.; Allievi, J.; Ferretti, A.; Casagli, N. The Maoxian landslide as seen from space: Detecting precursors of failure with Sentinel-1 data. *Landslides.* **2018**, *15*, 123–133. [CrossRef]

12. Wang, R.; Xia, Y.; Grosser, H.; Wetzel, H.U.; Kaufmann, H.; Zschau, J. The 2003 Bam (SE Iran) earthquake: Precise source parameters from satellite radar interferometry. *Geophys. J. Int.* **2004**, *159*, 917–922. [CrossRef]
13. Moreno, M.; Li, S.; Melnick, D.; Bedford, J.R.; Baez, J.C.; Motagh, M.; Metzger, S.; Vajedian, S.; Sippl, C.; Gutknecht, B.D.; et al. Chilean megathrust earthquake recurrence linked to frictional contrast at depth. *Nat. Geosci.* **2018**, *11*, 285–290. [CrossRef]
14. Motagh, M.; Klotz, J.; Tavakoli, F.; Djamour, Y.; Arabi, S.; Wetzel, H.U.; Zschau, J. Combination of Precise Leveling and InSAR Data to Constrain Source Parameters of the M w = 6.5, 26 December 2003 Bam Earthquake. *Pure Appl. Geophys.* **2006**, *163*, 1–18. [CrossRef]
15. Tomiyama, N.; Koike, K.; Omura, M. Detection of topographic changes associated with volcanic activities of Mt. Hossho using D-InSAR. *Adv. Space Res.* **2004**, *33*, 279–283. [CrossRef]
16. Vajedian, S.; Motagh, M.; Nilfouroushan, F. StaMPS Improvement for Deformation Analysis in Mountainous Regions: Implications for the Damavand Volcano and Mosha Fault in Alborz. *Remote Sens.* **2015**, *7*, 8323–8347. [CrossRef]
17. Schaefer, L.N.; Di Traglia, F.; Chaussard, E.; Lu, Z.; Nolesini, T.; Casagli, N. Monitoring volcano slope instability with Synthetic Aperture Radar: A review and new data from Pacaya (Guatemala) and Stromboli (Italy) volcanoes. *Earth-Sci. Rev.* **2019**, *192*, 236–257. [CrossRef]
18. Ferretti, A.; Prati, C.; Rocca, F. Nonlinear subsidence rate estimation using permanent scatterers in differential SAR interferometry. *IEEE Trans. Geosci. Remote Sens.* **2000**, *38*, 2202–2212. [CrossRef]
19. Ferretti, A.; Prati, C.; Rocca, F. Permanent scatterers in SAR interferometry. *IEEE Trans. Geosci. Remote Sens.* **2001**, *39*, 8–20. [CrossRef]
20. Berardino, P.; Fornaro, G.; Lanari, R.; Sansosti, E. A new algorithm for surface deformation monitoring based on small baseline differential SAR interferograms. *IEEE Trans. Geosci. Remote Sens.* **2002**, *40*, 2375–2383. [CrossRef]
21. Goel, K.; Adam, N. An advanced algorithm for deformation estimation in non-urban areas. *ISPRS J. Photogramm. Remote Sens.* **2012**, *73*, 100–110. [CrossRef]
22. Lanari, R.; Mora, O.; Manunta, M.; Mallorqui, J.J.; Berardino, P.; Sansosti, E. A small-baseline approach for investigating deformations on full-resolution differential SAR interferograms. *IEEE Trans. Geosci. Remote Sens.* **2004**, *42*, 1377–1386. [CrossRef]
23. Ferretti, A.; Fumagalli, A.; Novali, F.; Prati, C.; Rocca, F.; Rucci, A. A New Algorithm for Processing Interferometric Data-Stacks: SqueeSAR. *IEEE Trans. Geosci. Remote Sens.* **2011**, *49*, 3460–3470. [CrossRef]
24. Hooper, A. A multi-temporal InSAR method incorporating both persistent scatterer and small baseline approaches. *Geophys. Res. Lett.* **2008**, *35*, 96–106. [CrossRef]
25. Goel, K.; Adam, N. A Distributed Scatterer Interferometry Approach for Precision Monitoring of Known Surface Deformation Phenomena. *IEEE Trans. Geosci. Remote Sens.* **2014**, *52*, 5454–5468. [CrossRef]
26. Perissin, D.; Wang, T. Repeat-Pass SAR Interferometry With Partially Coherent Targets. *IEEE Trans. Geosci. Remote Sens.* **2012**, *50*, 271–280. [CrossRef]
27. Lv, X.; Yazıcı, B.; Zeghal, M.; Bennett, V.; Abdoun, T. Joint-Scatterer Processing for Time-Series InSAR. *IEEE Trans. Geosci. Remote Sens.* **2014**, *52*, 7205–7221. [CrossRef]
28. Fornaro, G.; Verde, S.; Reale, D.; Pauciullo, A. CAESAR: An Approach Based on Covariance Matrix Decomposition to Improve Multibaseline-Multitemporal Interferometric SAR Processing. *IEEE Trans. Geosci. Remote Sens.* **2015**, *53*, 2050–2065. [CrossRef]
29. Cao, N.; Lee, H.; Jung, H.C. A Phase-Decomposition-Based PSInSAR Processing Method. *IEEE Trans. Geosci. Remote Sens.* **2016**, *54*, 1074–1090. [CrossRef]
30. Ge, L.; Ng, A.H.-M.; Li, X.; Abidin, H.Z.; Gumilar, I. Land subsidence characteristics of Bandung Basin as revealed by ENVISAT ASAR and ALOS PALSAR interferometry. *Remote Sens. Environ.* **2014**, *154*, 46–60. [CrossRef]
31. Guarnieri, A.M.; Tebaldini, S. On the Exploitation of Target Statistics for SAR Interferometry Applications. *IEEE Trans. Geosci. Remote Sens.* **2008**, *46*, 3436–3443. [CrossRef]
32. Guarnieri, A.M.; Tebaldini, S. Hybrid Cramér–Rao bounds for crustal displacement field estimators in SAR interferometry. *IEEE Signal Process. Lett.* **2007**, *14*, 1012–1015. [CrossRef]
33. Ansari, H.; Zan, F.D.; Bamler, R. Sequential Estimator: Toward Efficient InSAR Time Series Analysis. *IEEE Trans. Geosci. Remote Sens.* **2017**, *55*, 5637–5652. [CrossRef]
34. Ansari, H.; Zan, F.D.; Bamler, R. Efficient Phase Estimation for Interferogram Stacks. *IEEE Trans. Geosci. Remote Sens.* **2018**, *56*, 4109–4125. [CrossRef]
35. Cao, N.; Lee, H.; Jung, H.C. Mathematical Framework for Phase-Triangulation Algorithms in Distributed-Scatterer Interferometry. *IEEE Geosci. Remote Sens. Lett.* **2015**, *12*, 1838–1842. [CrossRef]
36. Zhao, C.; Li, Z.; Tian, B.; Zhang, P.; Chen, Q. A Ground Surface Deformation Monitoring InSAR Method Using Improved Distributed Scatterers Phase Estimation. *IEEE J. Sel. Top. Appl. Earth Obs. Remote Sens.* **2019**, *12*, 4543–4553. [CrossRef]
37. Samiei-Esfahany, S.; Martins, J.E.; Leijen, F.v.; Hanssen, R.F. Phase Estimation for Distributed Scatterers in InSAR Stacks Using Integer Least Squares Estimation. *IEEE Trans. Geosci. Remote Sens.* **2016**, *54*, 5671–5687. [CrossRef]
38. Zhang, B.; Wang, R.; Deng, Y.; Ma, P.; Lin, H.; Wang, J. Mapping the Yellow River Delta land subsidence with multitemporal SAR interferometry by exploiting both persistent and distributed scatterers. *ISPRS J. Photogramm. Remote Sens.* **2019**, *148*, 157–173. [CrossRef]
39. Song, H.; Zhang, B.; Wang, M.; Xiao, Y.; Zhang, L.; Zhong, H. A Fast Phase Optimization Approach of Distributed Scatterer for Multitemporal SAR Data Based on Gauss–Seidel Method. *IEEE Geosci. Remote Sens. Lett.* **2022**, *19*, 1–5. [CrossRef]

40. Li, S.; Zhang, S.; Li, T.; Gao, Y.; Chen, Q.; Zhang, X. An Adaptive Phase Optimization Algorithm for Distributed Scatterer Phase History Retrieval. *IEEE J. Sel. Top. Appl. Earth Obs. Remote Sens.* **2021**, *14*, 3914–3926. [CrossRef]
41. Jiang, M.; Ding, X.; Li, Z. Hybrid Approach for Unbiased Coherence Estimation for Multitemporal InSAR. *IEEE Trans. Geosci. Remote Sens.* **2014**, *52*, 2459–2473. [CrossRef]
42. Vu, P.; Breloy, A.; Brigui, F.; Yan, Y.; Ginolhac, G. Robust Phase Linking in InSAR. *IEEE Trans. Geosci. Remote Sens.* **2022**. *in review*.
43. Schmitt, M.; Schönberger, J.L.; Stilla, U. Adaptive Covariance Matrix Estimation for Multi-Baseline InSAR Data Stacks. *IEEE Trans. Geosci. Remote Sens.* **2014**, *52*, 6807–6817. [CrossRef]
44. Jiang, M.; Ding, X.; Hanssen, R.F.; Malhotra, R.; Chang, L. Fast Statistically Homogeneous Pixel Selection for Covariance Matrix Estimation for Multitemporal InSAR. *IEEE Trans. Geosci. Remote Sens.* **2015**, *53*, 1213–1224. [CrossRef]
45. Zhao, C.; Li, Z.; Tian, B.; Zhang, P.; Wenhao, W.U.; Gao, S.; Yu, Y.; Dong, Y. A statistically homogeneous pixel selection approach for adaptive estimation of multitemporal InSAR covariance matrix. *Int. J. Appl. Earth Obs. Geoinf.* **2022**, *110*, 102792. [CrossRef]
46. Wang, Y.; Zhu, X.X. Robust Estimators for Multipass SAR Interferometry. *IEEE Trans. Geosci. Remote Sens.* **2016**, *54*, 968–980. [CrossRef]
47. Zwieback, S. Cheap, Valid Regularizers for Improved Interferometric Phase Linking. *IEEE Geosci. Remote Sens. Lett.* **2022**, *19*, 1–4. [CrossRef]
48. Zwieback, S.; Meyer, F.J. Reliable InSAR Phase History Uncertainty Estimates. *IEEE Trans. Geosci. Remote Sens.* **2022**, *60*, 1–9. [CrossRef]
49. Wang, C.; Wang, X.S.; Xu, Y.; Zhang, B.; Jiang, M.; Xiong, S.; Zhang, Q.; Li, W.; Li, Q. A New Likelihood Function for Consistent Phase Series Estimation in Distributed Scatterer Interferometry. *IEEE Trans. Geosci. Remote Sens.* **2022**, *60*, 1–14. [CrossRef]
50. Even, M. A Study on Algorithms and Parameter Settings for DS Preprocessing. *IEEE Geosci. Remote Sens. Symp.* **2021**, 3975–3978. [CrossRef]
51. Eppler, J.; Rabus, B.T. Adapting InSAR Phase Linking for Seasonally Snow-Covered Terrain. *IEEE Trans. Geosci. Remote Sens.* **2022**, *60*, 1–13. [CrossRef]
52. Abdelfattah, R.; Nicolas, J. Interferometric SAR coherence magnitude estimation using second kind statistics. *IEEE Trans. Geosci. Remote Sens.* **2006**, *44*, 1942–1953. [CrossRef]
53. Zhao, C.; Li, Z.; Zhang, P.; Tian, B.; Gao, S. Improved maximum likelihood estimation for optimal phase history retrieval of distributed scatterers in InSAR stacks. *IEEE Access.* **2019**, *7*, 186319–186327. [CrossRef]
54. Li, S.; Zhang, S.; Li, T.; Gao, Y.; Zhou, X.; Chen, Q.; Zhang, X.; Yang, C. An Adaptive Weighted Phase Optimization Algorithm Based on the Sigmoid Model for Distributed Scatterers. *Remote Sens.* **2021**, *13*, 3253. [CrossRef]
55. Bamler, R.; Hartl, P. Synthetic aperture radar interferometry. *Inv. Probl.* **1998**, *14*, R1–R54. [CrossRef]
56. Goodman, N.R. Statistical analysis based on a certain multivariate complex Gaussian distribution (an introduction). *Ann. Math. Stat.* **1963**, *3*, 152–177. [CrossRef]
57. Touzi, R.; Lopes, A.; Bruniquel, J.; Vachon, P.W. Coherence estimation for SAR imagery. *IEEE Trans. Geosci. Remote Sens.* **1999**, *37*, 135–149. [CrossRef]
58. Hanssen, R.F. *Radar Interferometry Data Interpretation and Error Analysis*; Kluwer: Dordrecht, The Netherlands, 2001.
59. Morishita, Y.; Hanssen, R.F. Temporal Decorrelation in L-, C-, and X-band Satellite Radar Interferometry for Pasture on Drained Peat Soils. *IEEE Trans. Geosci. Remote Sens.* **2015**, *53*, 1096–1104. [CrossRef]
60. Lee, J.S.; Grunes, M.R.; Kwok, R. Classification of multi-look polarimetric SAR imagery based on complex Wishart distribution. *Int. J. Remote Sens.* **1992**, *15*, 2299–2311. [CrossRef]

MDPI AG
Grosspeteranlage 5
4052 Basel
Switzerland
Tel.: +41 61 683 77 34

Remote Sensing Editorial Office
E-mail: remotesensing@mdpi.com
www.mdpi.com/journal/remotesensing

www.ingramcontent.com/pod-product-compliance
Lightning Source LLC
Chambersburg PA
CBHW040822250926
51850CB00007BA/1238
* 9 7 8 3 7 2 5 8 5 3 6 3 2 *